Common Core Progress®

English Language Arts

Sadlier School

Cover: *Series Design:* Studio Montage; *Title design:* Quarasan, Inc. **Photo Credits:** *Cover:* Alamy/Alexandra Morrison: *top left.* Corbis/Godong/Philippe Lissac: *bottom right.* Science Source/Laguna Design: *bottom left.* Used under license from Shutterstock.com/Jezper: *top right;* nikolarisim: *background.* *Interior:* Alamy/age Fotostock/Javier Larrea: 267; Blend Images: 165, 167; BSIP SA/AJ Photo: 193; IMANE: 192; Scott Camazine: 177; ClassicStock/Camerique: 83; DIZ Muenchen GmbH, Sueddeutsche Zeitung: 168; Everett Collection: 66, 70, 72, 73, 74, 80; CSU Archives: 75, 82; FDA: 270; Paul Fleet: 170; Image Asset Management Ltd./World History Archive: 290; ITAR-TASS Photo Agency: 284; Alexandra Morrison: 8 *center;* National Geographic Image Collection/Michael S. Yamashita: 281; Stock Connection Blue/Steve Gottlieb: 64; Stocktrek Images, Inc./John Parrot: 81, 89; The Print Collector: 266; UpperCut Images/Jerry Marks Productions: 47, 49; US Marines: 88; White House: 273; ZUMA Press, Inc.: 278. Corbis: 86, 99; Lucien Aigner: 78; All Canada Photos/Tom Nevesely: 151, 153; Bettmann: 76, 101; Blend Images/Jose Luis Pelaez, Inc.: 218; Kidstock: 100; Demotix/Ilya Varlamov: 274; Kevin Dodge: 62; epa: 282; Issei Kato: 284; Nippon News/Mainichi: 280; Ocean: 10, 48, 166; Onoky/Eric Audras: 114; Strauss/Curtis: 152; the food passionates: 268; Visuals Unlimited: 309 *top.* Dreamstime/Brickvision: 283; Leofrancini: 276; Onur Ersin: 65; Valentyne75: 8 *bottom right.* Fotolia/EastWest Imaging: 178; Dmitry Knorre: 180; Kondor83: 195; Mona Makela: 309 *bottom;* Oleksandr Moroz: 50; visdia: 275. Getty Images/AFP/Sam Panthaky: 188; DEA/A. Dagli-Orti: 176; Rebecca Ellis: 262; Justin Horrocks: 204; Mondadori: 102; SelectStock: 248; SuperStock/Kike Calvo: 186; Time & Life Pictures/Jay Leviton: 171; David Young-Wolff: 203, 205. HubbleSite: 172. Library of Congress: 61, 63, 67, 68. National Archives and Records Administration: 84. Used under license from Shutterstock.com/abutyrin: 185; Action Sports Photography: 169; Nate Allred: 194; Ammit Jack: 8 *top left;* Sam Chadwick: 250; Lim ChewHow: 265; Goodluz: 261; hxdyl: 184; Swill Klitch: 66, 68; Vladimir Koletic: 247, 249; Olivier Le Quenec: 190; Shane Wilson Link: 264; luchunyu: 206; nikolarisim: 1, 8 *background;* M. Uznal Ozmen: 265; Mahesh Patil: 265; raulbaenacasado: 187; Reddogs: 154; Shnycel: 8 *top right;* urfin: 8 *bottom left.* **Illustration Credits:** Timothy Banks: 228, 229, 230, 231, 232, 234. David Belmonte: 236, 237, 238, 239. David Harrington: 9, 11, 28, 29, 30, 31, 32, 34. Seitu Hayden: 220, 221, 222. Fabio Leone: 132, 133, 135, 136, 138. Wes Lowe: 124, 125, 126, 127, 128, 130. Tom McNeely: 20, 21, 22, 23, 24, 26. Peter Bull Art Studio: 90, 113, 115, 116, 117, 118, 119, 120, 122, 134, 174, 179, 286, 288, 289. Q2A Media: 217, 219, 223, 224, 226. Amy Ning: 12, 13, 14, 15, 16, 18. Rob Schuster: 140, 141, 142, 143. Lois Rosario Sprague: 36, 37, 38, 39.

For additional online resources, go to sadlierconnect.com.

William H. Sadlier, Inc.
9 Pine Street
New York, NY 10005-4700

Printed in the United States of America.
ISBN: 978-1-4217-3058-5
3 4 5 6 7 8 9 WEBC 19 18 17 16

CONTENTS

COMMON CORE STATE STANDARDS

continued next page

Unit 8 Research to Build and Present Knowledge: Write Research Reports

Unit 9 Reading Literature: Integration of Knowledge and Ideas

Unit 10 Text Type and Purposes: Write Argumentative Essays

continued next page

COMMON CORE STATE STANDARDS

Welcome

You have an exciting year ahead of you! You will be reading fascinating texts in a variety of genres, including adventure stories, traditional tales, myths, novel excerpts, speeches, historical fiction, science articles, and editorials. You'll read about topics as varied as the ancient Greeks and their gods, the Boston Tea Party, survival in nature, life at a space colony camp, radio wave technology, and near-Earth objects. Along the way you'll learn and practice reading skills and strategies that will help you better understand what you read.

Writing is important, too. This year you'll study how successful writers tell a story, explain ideas, analyze literature, argue convincingly, and present research. You'll have the opportunity to apply writers' skills and techniques when writing your own stories, essays, and reports about the power of ideas, confronting social problems, problem-solving science, and more.

This book, ***Common Core Progress***, will guide you on the path to improvement in reading and writing. That's why it's called *progress*.

Have a great year!

Introducing UNIT 1

In this unit, you will focus on looking for key ideas and details as you read a variety of literary texts. Such ideas and details can be found in every type, or genre, of literature, but the strategies you use to identify key ideas and details in a poem may be different from the ones you apply to your reading of a short story. In this unit you will look for key ideas and details in a myth, a traditional tale, a drama, and a piece of historical fiction. You will learn to use textual evidence to analyze different elements of each literary text, such as meaning, theme, and plot or character development.

The literary texts in this unit all have one thing in common: they deal with the theme of using good judgment or making good choices. You will be able to use the analytical skills you develop while working with these texts on other works of literature you read. The next time you check out a book from the library, you'll be able to analyze its key ideas and details to understand its meaning, determine its theme, and analyze its plot and character development.

Progress Check Can I?

Before Unit 1		After Unit 1
☐	Analyze explicit and implied meanings in a literary text.	☐
☐	Determine the theme or central idea of a literary text and analyze how it is developed through characters, setting, and plot.	☐
☐	Summarize a text objectively.	☐
☐	Analyze how dialogue and story events move a plot forward or reveal character.	☐
☐	Figure out the meanings of unfamiliar words by using context clues.	☐

HOME ✦ CONNECT...

One of the beauties of literature is that a literary text can contain a multitude of meanings and possibilities for interpretation. By studying literature, your child can learn to **evaluate specific ideas and details** in texts. You can help your child start to notice details in texts by making a list of important details in an "everyday" text such as a newspaper article.

In this unit, your child will also practice **analyzing literary texts in order to find their themes.** Help your child practice finding themes by listing the people, interactions, ideas, and statements he or she notices throughout a day. Find the common elements in the list to help your child determine the day's "theme."

You can assist your child in **evaluating plot** by discussing a favorite television show. Ask him or her to explain the events and details of a previous episode. Discuss how both events and dialogue move a story along. Practicing these techniques will lead your child to a deeper understanding of literary texts.

Activity: Discuss favorite books and stories with your child. Choose a story that interests him or her, and work together to list ways in which that story reflects real-life issues. Find a particular issue in the story to focus on, such as relationships between siblings or courage in the face of danger, and help your child make connections between the story and his or her personal experiences and knowledge.

IN THIS UNIT, YOUR CHILD WILL...

- Read four literary texts, including a myth, a traditional tale, a drama, and a piece of historical fiction.
- Find and use evidence from a literary text to determine the text's meaning.
- Analyze the theme of a literary text.
- Summarize the events of a literary text.
- Analyze the plot of a literary text.
- Assess how specific elements of a literary text advance its plot.
- Find the definitions of previously unknown words by examining how they are used in a literary text.
- Compare and contrast ideas on the theme of using good judgment across four selections.

NOTE: All of these learning goals for your child are based on the Grade 8 Common Core State Standards for English Language Arts.

WAYS TO HELP YOUR CHILD

At dinnertime, ask your child to tell you about three specific details (such as statements or events) he or she noticed during the school day. Talk over each event and find its significance. Ask how, when taken together, these ideas shape your child's understanding of the day as a whole.

ONLINE

For more Home Connect activities, continue online at sadlierconnect.com

Reading Literature: Key Ideas and Details

UNIT 1

Essential Question:
How can analyzing meaning, theme, plot, and character help readers understand literary texts?

Guided Instruction

RL.8.1

WORDS TO KNOW

calamity
discord
domesticity
engraved
interacted
omission

Finding meaning in a literary text is like looking for treasure: It might be buried beneath the surface. Look for obvious, or **explicit**, details and **implied meanings** when you **analyze meaning** in a text.

CITE EVIDENCE

A Descriptive words such as adjectives can create shades of meaning in a literary text. Underline all the adjectives you can find on this page. What general attitude toward the characters and the situation do these adjectives suggest?

B To find meaning in a text, you may have to **make inferences**, or educated guesses. Circle the paragraph that describes Eris. What information about her is **implied**, or suggested, and what information is **explicit**, or direct? What inferences can you make about her character based on textual evidence?

The Judgment of Paris

(Genre: Greek Myth)

1 Long ago, in the time of the ancient Greeks, men and gods walked the earth together; a mortal's encounter with a god or goddess could end in tremendous fortune or incredible terror. While some folk might wait all their lives in hope (or fear) of meeting an immortal, others routinely **interacted** with the gods when the the gods came down from Mount Olympus.

2 Such fateful interactions could sometimes result in marriages, as when Peleus, the Phthian King, wed the ocean nymph Thetis. Although Peleus was not kin to the gods, Thetis was; thus, the pair included all the immortals they knew in their wedding. They welcomed every god and goddess to the ceremony, from King Zeus and Queen Hera to nymphs and sprites.

3 However, they made one exception. Any wedding, but especially the wedding of an immortal like Thetis, should be a joyous occasion, one free of **calamity**. For that reason, Peleus and Thetis decided not to include Eris, the goddess of strife and **discord**, in their celebration, and that was a serious mistake.

4 As might have been expected, Eris did not take kindly to her **omission** from the festivities. The day of the wedding, she gazed down on the gods and goddesses from afar, sighing with misery and envy. The wedding guests ate, drank, and danced with abandon; the air was full of the sounds of laughter and gaiety. And Eris was not allowed to have any part of it. She thus became determined to make her presence felt at the celebration.

RL.8.1

5 Eris quickly thought up a plan to punish Peleus and Thetis for leaving her out. She conjured up an apple made of pure, sparkling gold and **engraved** on it the phrase "For the most beautiful of all." Then, she cast the apple of gold into the crowd of immortals.

6 The apple whipped through the throng, glittering as it moved, and bounced once or twice before it settled. Although they had the power of immortal beings, the assembled gods and goddesses watched the apple with riveted attention; they were a pride of lions tempted by the sight of nearby prey.

7 A demigod caught the apple and held it up, reading off the inscribed phrase. "To whom does this apple belong, then?" he asked.

8 The surrounding goddesses reacted quickly, and three of the most gorgeous and powerful stepped forward almost immediately.

9 "It belongs to me," claimed Hera, the goddess of **domesticity**. She was the queen of the gods, tremendously powerful in her own right, and she possessed a mature and full beauty.

10 "It must be for me," stated Athena, the goddess of wisdom. Famed for her knowledge and intelligence, she was as lovely as she was wise.

11 "It is clearly mine," declared Aphrodite, the goddess of love. While she had the ability to make any person fall in love with another, her own remarkable attractiveness ensured that she herself never wanted for suitors.

12 With that, the three goddesses turned to Zeus, imploring him to end the argument and declare who was the most beautiful among them.

Comprehension Check

Why does Eris create the apple of gold? Identify both the explicit and the implied details that support your response.

Guided Instruction

CITE EVIDENCE

C Look for something that seems important to one or more characters. Circle the paragraph that gives details about an important object. Consider why the characters might want it or what significance it has in order to understand its role in the plot.

D An author may use figurative language, such as a **metaphor**, to compare ideas or objects and **imply** a meaning. Double underline the metaphor that describes the gods and goddesses. What does this metaphor imply?

E A text may describe characters in a way that highlights both their similarities and differences. Put an asterisk by each description of the three main goddesses. How would you sum up the ways in which they are alike and different?

Guided Instruction

RL.8.1

WORDS TO KNOW

attribute
epiphany
fostered
justification

CITE EVIDENCE

A Evaluate characters' thoughts to infer the deeper meaning behind their actions and choices. Circle the paragraph that provides an explanation of why each goddess feels she is the one who should be selected.

B What reasons does Zeus give for being unable to decide who should get the apple of gold? Underline each reason he cites. Explain how his thought process reveals his inner conflict. What consequences of making a decision is he trying to avoid? How will any decision he makes affect the rest of the story?

The Judgment of Paris *continued*

13 While Hera thought it only natural that Zeus should select her, since he was her husband, Athena thought it only fitting that Zeus should select her, since she was his daughter. In the meantime, Aphrodite thought it only fair that Zeus should select *her*, since she had once been the object of his desire.

14 Yet after just a few moments, Zeus decided he had no wish to select one woman over the others. He found he could provide no **justification** for considering any one of the three goddesses as more beautiful than the others. Besides, any decision would be a foolish one, he thought. How could any god claim that his wife was not the most beautiful? And yet, how could he say that his own daughter was not the most beautiful? Finally, how could he say that the goddess of love, famed for her physical **attributes** among men and gods alike, was not the most beautiful?

15 "Dearest Hera, lovely Athena, and sweet Aphrodite, I can no more choose among you than I could select one star to elevate above the others in the sky. It is an impossible task." Zeus paused, and then he had an **epiphany**. He knew of a mortal, a young man from Troy named Paris, who had exhibited refined judgment when dealing with gods and goddesses. Zeus would send word to Paris, requesting that the young man be the one to make the decision. In that way, the harmony of Peleus and Thetis's wedding festivities would be restored.

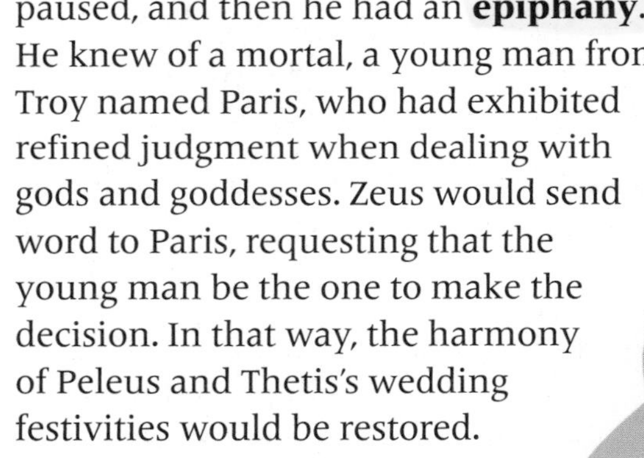

16 His mind made up, Zeus beckoned to Hermes, the god in charge of relaying information between the immortals. "Hermes, take Aphrodite, Athena, and Hera to meet young Paris."

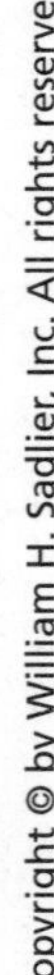

RL.8.1

Guided Instruction

17 Hermes, the speediest of all the gods, nodded. "Yes, my lord Zeus."

18 "Instruct him in the debate **fostered** by this apple of gold and require him to select the apple's recipient," Zeus demanded. "The rest of us will return to the celebration."

19 Hermes took hold of the apple of gold and beckoned to Athena, Hera, and Aphrodite. The goddesses followed him without a moment's hesitation. They cared not a bit that they would be missing the rest of the wedding. Deciding who was the most beautiful was a question of much more importance. As the goddesses leapt into the sky, each felt sure that this human, whoever he was, would see her as more beautiful than her immortal peers.

20 Meanwhile, many miles away, Paris reclined upon a forested mountaintop, lost in his thoughts. The soft-footed arrival of Hermes and the three beautiful goddesses took his breath away. One moment he was all alone, and the next, he was surrounded by divinity.

21 He wasn't sure what to do. At first, he was taken aback just to be in their presence. But after a few moments, Paris had relaxed enough to accept the honor of being visited by not just one, but three, goddesses (and Hermes, too).

22 "How may I serve you, gracious Olympians?" he asked.

Comprehension Check

What do the three goddesses think will happen as a result of following Hermes to allow Paris to choose between them? Use text evidence to explain whether their expectations are likely—or unlikely—to be met. They will think that Paris is indisicisive. They all expect Paris to pick one of them.

CITE EVIDENCE

C Double underline the words that indicate Zeus's commands to Hermes. What do these words imply about Zeus?

D Place a box around the sentence that explicitly states what is most important to the three goddesses. Based on this, what character trait do you infer they all have in common?

E Circle the paragraphs that give you information about Paris. What information about him is given explicitly? What inferences can you make about him? Based on text evidence, would you infer that Paris is a good candidate to make this important decision?

Paris is not a good candidate because he is indesisive.

Guided Practice

RL.8.1

WORDS TO KNOW

coveted
inscription
luminous
luxurious
symbol

CITE EVIDENCE

A What information does Paris have to guide him when choosing among the goddesses? Put an asterisk next to the paragraph that explicitly describes their physical traits.

B How does Paris react to each of the goddesses? Underline the sentences that explicitly express Paris's dilemma, or problem, in making a choice. Discuss with a partner what Paris's inability to make a decision implies about him, and predict how his problem will be resolved.

The Judgment of Paris *continued*

23 Hermes wasted no time in informing Paris of Zeus's request. Paris would need to make a choice. He would have to decide which of the three incredible goddesses should be granted the apple of gold and, thereby, its accompanying title.

24 When he properly understood what Zeus was asking of him, Paris felt deeply honored. He took the apple of gold, the **symbol** of such a difficult choice, in his hand. Then, he glanced at the **inscription**, and then he looked at each of the goddesses in turn.

25 Athena, Hera, and Aphrodite were all tall and elegant. They all had noble features, graceful limbs, and **luxurious**, wavy hair. Each had a special quality: for instance, Athena's eyes were a deep and **luminous** gray, Hera's hair shimmered like the shining feathers of the peacocks she loved, and Aphrodite's lips were the color of peaches.

26 The three goddesses, Paris marveled, were more magnificent than any mortal woman of his acquaintance. Paris gazed at Athena, then Hera, and after that, Aphrodite; then, he glanced from Aphrodite to Hera to Athena. Each time he looked at one goddess, he thought he should pick her, but then he would look at the next goddess and start to think he should pick *her* instead.

27 The more Paris thought the matter over, the more difficult his decision became. "How can I choose?" he asked eventually. "You are all so beautiful. In fact, you are incomparable, and it is impossible for me to select among you." He bowed his head. "How can I do better than the King of the Gods?"

28 The goddesses would not let the matter rest, however: each **coveted** the apple of gold, and each wanted to be named "the most beautiful of all."

29 Hera spoke first. "Choose me, and I will reward you beyond imagining. You will become a king of kings, the highest ruler of mortal lands, and your throne will be almighty." She showed a vision of thrones and scepters, armies and castles. Paris saw himself reflected in Hera's vision as a regal, dominating figure. If he picked her, he could become the most powerful ruler on Earth.

Comprehension Check

1. Why does each of the three goddesses want to be awarded the apple of gold?

- **a.** It would mean she is the kindest.
- **b.** It would mean she is the most powerful.
- **c.** It would mean she is the most loved.
- **d.** It would mean she is the most beautiful.

2. Why is Paris's decision so difficult?

- **a.** He is young and inexperienced.
- **b.** He worries that Zeus will disagree.
- **c.** He finds all the goddesses beautiful.
- **d.** He is afraid of angering Hera.

3. Hera promises Paris

- **a.** rulership of a mighty kingdom.
- **b.** a throne on Mount Olympus.
- **c.** wealth and immortality.
- **d.** eternal happiness.

4. After Hera offers her reward to Paris, you can infer that the other goddesses

- **a.** will become angry and turn on Hera.
- **b.** will also offer rewards to Paris.
- **c.** will give up trying to win.
- **d.** will claim the contest is unfair.

5. Select and analyze the meaning of specific words or phrases in the text that reveal the ways Paris responds to the challenge of the task Zeus gives him. How do these words and phrases help you infer Paris's feelings about his task?

Paris responds to the challenge by sceing what the other godesses have to offer.

Independent Practice

RL.8.1

WORDS TO KNOW
acolyte
enticed
exquisite
immensity

CITE EVIDENCE

A Underline the details and phrases that show the benefits Paris will gain if he chooses Aphrodite. What does she offer that Hera and Athena do not?

B How does the text reveal Paris's motivation? Circle the paragraph that explicitly reveals Paris's thought process as he considers the goddesses' offerings. What does the text help you infer about Paris's values?

A. Aphrodite says that Paris will marry the loviest mortal and Hera + Athena can't offer that

B. You infer that Paris is selfish because he will only marry the most beautiful one

The Judgment of Paris *continued*

30 Athena spoke next. "Pick me, and I will give you a prize beyond compare. You will become the greatest warrior alive, and you will remain unconquered and become rich beyond measure." She conjured a scene of triumphs and riches, with images of **acolytes** and flags. Now Paris saw himself projected as Athena described him, a brawny man who could defeat anyone. If he picked her, he knew, he could be rewarded with renown beyond his own comprehension.

31 Aphrodite spoke last. "Select me, and I will offer you a jewel beyond price. Choose me, and you will wed the loveliest woman mortal man has ever seen. Her name is Helen." She summoned the outline of an incomparably beautiful figure, a mortal with a face like that of a goddess. This time, Paris saw himself happy and fulfilled, more in love than he had ever been; if he picked Aphrodite, he reasoned, it would be like picking love itself.

32 Paris paused, finding himself stunned by the **immensity** of such a decision. How amazing, he thought, that with just a few words, he could decide whether to take his own crown, win every possible battle, or earn the love of this beautiful Helen. He examined his heart, considering each of the visions, and found that one promise **enticed** him more than the others.

33 "You offer me too much honor, but I must make a choice, and I choose Aphrodite. Aphrodite, I accept what you offer me, and I declare you the most beautiful of all." Paris dropped to one knee and offered her the apple of gold.

34 An **exquisite** smile broke across Aphrodite's face. "You have chosen well, and I will keep my promise. Soon, I will bring Helen, whose face and form are superior to those of any woman breathing, to you."

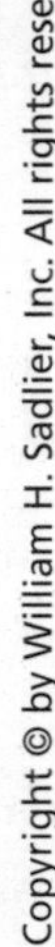

Little did Paris know that Helen was not Aphrodite's to give: he had no idea that Helen was already promised to another man. In making this choice, Paris was contributing to his own undoing, and to the undoing of his beloved city. However, that is another myth for another day.

Comprehension Check

MORE ONLINE **sadlierconnect.com**

1. What "prize beyond compare" does Athena offer Paris?
   - **a.** a place among the gods
   - **b.** renown as a warrior
   - **c.** the love of a beautiful woman
   - **d.** happiness and fulfillment

2. Paris's choice of the goddess Aphrodite as "the most beautiful of all" implies that
   - **a.** he is much wiser than Zeus and makes more careful decisions.
   - **b.** he really believes Aphrodite is the most beautiful goddess.
   - **c.** he makes decisions rashly, without much thought.
   - **d.** he is more motivated by a desire for love than by a desire for power or wealth.

3. Which textual evidence best supports the answer to question 2?
   - **a.** "Paris saw himself projected as...a brawny man who could defeat anyone."
   - **b.** "Paris saw himself reflected in Hera's vision as a regal, dominating figure."
   - **c.** "Paris saw himself happy and fulfilled, more in love than he had ever been."
   - **d.** "The three goddesses...were more magnificent than any mortal woman...."

4. The ending of the myth implies that
   - **a.** the three goddesses will never again engage in such a contest.
   - **b.** Paris's choice will have negative consequences later.
   - **c.** Aphrodite will never be trusted again.
   - **d.** Zeus will be happy with Paris's choice.

5. What textual clues help explain why Paris makes the choice that he does? Refer to specific evidence from the text in your answer.

It would be like picking love itself. Paris wants to be happy and fullfilled

Guided Instruction

RL.8.2

WORDS TO KNOW

detriment
distribution
entreated
temperate
tribulation

Theme is the message or **central idea** of a literary text. To **analyze the development of a theme**, look at the characters, setting, and plot to see what ideas or messages are being suggested through the interaction of these elements.

CITE EVIDENCE

A Most folk tales have simple themes that deal with the basic concerns of everyday life. Circle words in the first paragraph that connect to the idea of wisdom from the past. Why might this idea be important to understanding the story's theme?

B Our understanding of literature is enriched by reading works from different cultures. Put an asterisk next to the paragraph that identifies the culture this tale comes from. What is the value in knowing the cultural background of a story?

Charlie and the Advice

(Genre: Scottish Traditional Tale)

1 There is much wisdom to be found in the lessons of our ancestors. I heard this tale from my mother, who heard it from her mother. She in turn heard it from *her* mother, who had heard it from her great-grandmother. Thus, it has been passed down through the generations of my family. You may be assured of the truth of it.

2 There was a time long ago in our history when the Scots and the English spoke different tongues, when a speaker of one language could not understand a speaker of the other. In those days there lived in the wild Highlands of Scotland a young couple, Charlie and Fiona. Their life was difficult and their resources were few. Yet their love was a foundation strong enough to see them through whatever trials and **tribulations** would come their way.

3 To their **detriment**, during the first year of marriage their harvest was poor. However, with only two mouths to feed, Charlie and Fiona adapted and made ends meet. The next year of their marriage was not as easy. The winter was crueler, their bodies weaker and wearier, and their store of food that much more depleted. In that bad time, Fiona found herself with child.

RL.8.2 RL

4 She turned to Charlie in tears, asking how they could possibly ensure their survival. At first, Charlie had no words. He could only share in Fiona's grief and desperate wonder at how they might live, let alone thrive, once their baby came into the world.

5 Not knowing what to do, Charlie and Fiona consulted with the village's wise woman. She instructed Charlie to make his way south to England, where the weather was more **temperate** and the harvest more bountiful. The harvests were so bountiful, in fact, she assured them, that every landholder for miles around would be grateful for an extra pair of hands. The longer Charlie stayed away, the more he could put by a store of funds to support Fiona and the child. In the meantime, Fiona could help the wise woman and share in the latter's harvest.

6 Fiona and Charlie agreed with the wisdom of their elder, and they went their separate ways in early spring. Fiona watched with tears in her eyes as Charlie began walking away, heading south to England to seek his fortune.

7 After a lengthy but uneventful journey, Charlie arrived in England and began searching for work. Although he spoke no English, his broad shoulders and strong body told of his capability as a good and hard worker. Soon, Charlie was hired by a wealthy, kind landholder. The man had more crops than he could manage with his current employees.

8 Summer followed spring, and then the cycle began again. Charlie worked hard through it all. He found his employer to be wise and just. He missed Fiona deeply, but he was content to build up a store of funds and count the days until their reunion.

9 Each quarter, when it was time for the **distribution** of earnings, Charlie did not take the coins he had earned. Instead, he **entreated** the landowner to keep them safe for him. Otherwise, Charlie worried, he might be tempted to spend the money buying trinkets for Fiona or new shirtcloth for himself.

Comprehension Check

Based on details from the text, what theme is suggested in the tale so far? Is this a universal theme, common to many cultures, or one that is specific to the story's culture of origin? Be sure to include specific words and phrases from the text in your answer.

Guided Instruction

CITE EVIDENCE

C A story's title can sometimes give you clues to its theme. Underline actions Charlie and Fiona take together that connect to the idea expressed in the title.

D The actions characters take in a story advance the plot and help to develop the theme. Place a box around the paragraph that tells what Charlie does to save money. Why might this action be important to the story's theme?

Guided Instruction

RL.8.2

WORDS TO KNOW

exemplary
monotony
obliged
reflective

CITE EVIDENCE

A In folk tales from many cultures, a good character may be granted a wish or given a special gift by a wiser or more powerful character. Put an asterisk by the paragraph that describes something special being offered to Charlie. What is being offered? How does this offer relate to ideas you have already encountered in the story?

B A **summary** of a story includes key events but not unimportant details. Box the important decision Charlie makes. Why is this a key event? In a summary, what other key events on this page and the next would you include? What details would you leave out?

Charlie and the Advice *continued*

10 The longer he stayed with the landowner, the harder Charlie concentrated on putting away a goodly sum. He was saving for the time when he could return to Fiona and their young child. Finally, one day, he knew it was time. The sun set over the English fields where he had toiled for so long and with such effort, and all for the benefit of another man's fortune. Charlie determined it was time he returned to the beloved wife and child he had left behind in the Highlands.

11 The landowner recognized the moral qualities of the man in his employ. He **obliged** Charlie in accepting his resignation and made ready the funds that he had laid aside for his worker for so long. Yet, since Charlie had been such an **exemplary** employee, the landowner wanted to offer him something more than just payment. So, as Charlie prepared to depart, the landowner took him aside and made him a proposal. He could give Charlie his hard-earned funds, or, instead of money, he could give Charlie some important advice to use on the road and in life itself.

12 It may be shocking to learn that Charlie accepted the advice instead of the money. He had worked so hard and for so long to build up his fortune, and he had sacrificed much by spending years away from Fiona. Perhaps he remembered the importance of following advice. After all, it was the wise woman's advice that had encouraged him to travel to England, where he had indeed found employment.

13 "First," the landowner told Charlie, "of this make sure, that you do not take any shortcuts, but stay on the main pathway. You may be tempted by these other roads, but hold fast to your original map." Charlie nodded, promising never to vary from his chosen course. "Next," the landowner said, "beware of any home in which a couple, married but far apart in age, live together."

RL.8.2

14 Charlie thought this sounded odd, but he assured his employer he would watch for such a thing. "And finally," the landowner instructed, "think first, act second, in all that you encounter, no matter how strange or unsettling." That sounded easy, Charlie assured him, because he was by nature a **reflective** person and could keep his temper well controlled.

15 Before they parted ways for good, the landowner handed Charlie a large cake wrapped in cloth. "Take this to your Fiona, with regards from me," he remarked. Charlie thanked the landowner for the wisdom and the present. Carefully reviewing each of the three pieces of advice once more, he prepared to leave.

16 His goodbyes said, Charlie headed north, and home. His wish to return quickly to Fiona lent his legs speed, and he began making progress in what seemed like hardly any time at all. Not long into his journey, Charlie met and agreed to walk with another traveler, a hiker named Georgie. Georgie had a wealth of jokes and an easy way with language, and the two men journeyed together in comfort.

17 Georgie and Charlie's path eventually led to a crossroads. In one direction pointed the main road, flat and broad for several miles more, while slightly to the right pointed a smaller road, one less trodden and more overgrown with brush. Georgie, tiring of the **monotony** of the main road, became excited at the prospect of this new path and encouraged Charlie to take it, too. "Come on, man! Have a little adventure before going back to your wife."

18 It sounded like a pleasant venture, and Charlie was tempted. Yet he hesitated, thinking of his former employer, who had advised him to remain on his selected path and not turn from it.

Comprehension Check

How does Charlie's choice of payment from the landowner contribute to the story's theme? Use specific details from the text to support your answer.

Guided Instruction

CITE EVIDENCE

C Key ideas and details can aid your understanding of theme. In European folk tales, images and events often occur in threes. There may be three special objects or three attempts to accomplish something. On these two pages, circle the paragraphs that concern something presented in three parts. How might this information play out in the rest of the story?

D Causes and effects in a story are often clues to the theme. Underline the sentence on this page that describes a decision Charlie makes (effect) as a result of what the landowner told him (cause). Explain whether you expect to see this cause-and-effect pattern continue in the rest of the story.

Guided Practice

RL.8.2

WORDS TO KNOW

cordial

distraught

recoiled

tedious

CITE EVIDENCE

A Place an asterisk by the paragraph that explains why Charlie was right in following the advice to stay on the main road. How does this information help to develop the story's theme?

B Circle the paragraph that describes another cause-and-effect relationship between the advice Charlie received and his actions. What is likely to be revealed about the innkeepers?

Charlie and the Advice *continued*

19 With that resolution in mind, Charlie bid his new friend farewell and decided to continue on his journey alone. True, following the main road was somewhat **tedious**, especially without **cordial** company to help him pass the time. However, Charlie busied himself with imagining Fiona's face and the face of his child. He became caught up in considering what they might look like now. Thus, he was taken aback when, another few miles ahead, he discovered Georgie crumbled in dismay, and soaking wet, at the side of the road.

20 Charlie rushed to comfort Georgie, and quickly learned that he had been right to follow the landowner's advice and stay on the main road. Georgie had gone only a short way down the side path when two robbers had approached him. To escape them, he had hurled himself off the road, rolling down a steep and rocky hillside into a stream, where he was thoroughly soaked.

21 Georgie was **distraught**, but he still managed to congratulate Charlie for having the good sense to keep to the main road. The two determined to continue traveling together until nightfall approached. They found themselves near a pleasant, if somewhat unremarkable, village. There they decided to seek shelter. Charlie noticed a small inn that looked neat and clean. Weary, and with his clothes soaked in mud and grime, Georgie determined they should rest at this particular inn for the night.

22 Charlie, also tired, was about to agree when he saw the innkeepers come out to greet them. The owner of the inn was a white-haired man of at least seventy years, while the wife by his side appeared to be several decades younger. She might have been forty years old, yet she had a very youthful appearance.

23 At once, Charlie **recoiled**, thinking of what the landowner had told him. Here, remarkably, were the very people he had been warned against. Seeing them gave him an uneasy feeling, and he refused to cross their threshold. He bid Georgie good night and determined to seek shelter elsewhere. Charlie slept outside a local bakery and passed the night in safety, although he was rather cold from time to time.

Comprehension Check

1. When the two travelers come to a crossroads, what does Charlie do?

- **a.** He stays on the main path.
- **b.** He refuses to go any further.
- **c.** He takes the shortcut.
- **d.** He pauses to search for food.

2. What happens to Georgie when he takes the shortcut?

- **a.** He stumbles onto hidden treasure.
- **b.** He has a pleasant, leisurely walk.
- **c.** He is robbed and beaten.
- **d.** He escapes robbers and falls into a stream.

3. The sight of the innkeepers makes Charlie

- **a.** tremble in fear.
- **b.** remember the second piece of advice he received.
- **c.** realize that he does not have a place to stay.
- **d.** believe that staying at the inn will be safe and relaxing.

4. Based on what has happened in the story so far, Charlie is probably

- **a.** foolish to sleep outside the bakery.
- **b.** wise to not stay at the inn.
- **c.** sorry he stayed on the main path.
- **d.** worried that the landowner lied to him.

5. Work with a partner to identify the two actions Charlie has taken in the story thus far after hearing the landowner's advice. Explain how Charlie's actions contribute to the development of the theme. Refer to textual evidence in your answer.

____

____

____

____

____

____

Independent Practice

Charlie and the Advice *continued*

RL.8.2

24 The next morning, Charlie awoke to a great **commotion**. He saw the local constable outside the inn, pushing a handcuffed Georgie before him. Charlie ran over to his friend and soon learned that the innkeeper's wife had accused Georgie of stealing a prized ruby necklace from a guest's room. Georgie was being taken to jail.

25 "Believe me, Charlie, I didn't take anything from anyone!" Georgie cried.

26 Charlie happened to glance across the road and notice a flash of red coming from the neck of a woman who looked similar to the innkeeper's wife. He quickly surmised that the missing necklace was fastened safely around the woman's neck. Charlie let the constable know what he had seen. The innkeepers, it was later discovered, had stolen the valuable necklace from a wealthy guest and had attempted to keep suspicion off themselves by falsely accusing the **hapless** Georgie. The wife had given the necklace to her younger sister for safe-keeping. Georgie was freed once the true story came out.

27 Georgie, grateful to have escaped criminal **accusations**, hugged Charlie with **ferocity**, begging his friend to stay with him a while. Charlie, **undeterred**, continued on his journey. The closer he got to home, the faster he went. He raced across the paths and fields and threw open the door to his family's cottage.

28 Then he stopped, his face full of surprise and fear. A youth he had never seen before was sitting in his wife's chair, and Fiona was nowhere to be found. Charlie was filled with great anxiety. His imagination started to run wild with all the horrible things that could have happened to his wife, but he thought of the English landowner's final piece of advice and tried to stay calm.

29 Then he heard footsteps that were slow at first, and then faster and faster. He turned and saw Fiona, who flung her arms around his neck. Charlie and Fiona embraced, and then she introduced him to the unfamiliar boy. "Charlie, this is our son, James."

WORDS TO KNOW

accusation
commotion
ferocity
hapless
undeterred

CITE EVIDENCE

A Circle the paragraph in which Charlie remembers the third piece of advice from his former employer. What was that advice, and how does Charlie follow it?

B Put asterisks next to the paragraphs that show how Charlie is rewarded for following the landowner's advice. How do these story events serve as the final development of the theme? What other traditional tales does this ending remind you of?

30 Upon seeing his son for the first time, Charlie felt so lucky he could burst. "Here, my darling, is a present from my employer," he said to Fiona, and handed her the cake. At once she unwrapped it, handing each family member a piece. Charlie bit down eagerly, and could not believe his senses when he tasted silver instead of sugar. He felt even luckier than before. His employer had intended to pay him all along; the cake was baked full of money, all the wages Charlie had earned in England.

Comprehension Check

MORE ONLINE **sadlierconnect.com**

1. Who is the person in the chair?

a. a strange boy

b. the innkeepers' cousin

c. Charlie's own son

d. Fiona's new friend

2. If Charlie had not heeded the third piece of advice, he might have

a. decided not to return home.

b. made a fool of himself.

c. harmed his own son.

d. decided to return to England.

3. When Charlie bites into the cake at the end of the story, he finds that

a. it contains a ruby necklace.

b. it contains silver.

c. it has spoiled.

d. it contains crop seeds.

4. What is the best statement of this story's theme?

a. It is wise to heed good advice.

b. Honesty is the best policy.

c. A penny saved is a penny earned.

d. Don't believe everything you see.

5. Write a summary of this story. Include the key events and details, but leave out unimportant details. Your summary should be objective, or without opinions and judgments. At the end of your summary, include a statement of the story's theme.

Guided Instruction

RL.8.3

WORDS TO KNOW

congregated

flustered

logical

To **analyze plot and character** in a story or drama, pay attention to the way **dialogue** and **story incidents** propel the plot, reveal character, and lead logically to the conclusion.

CITE EVIDENCE

A You can analyze **dialogue** to find out more about what a character is really like. Underline each of the statements Alexa makes in Scene 1. What do her words reveal about her character?

B Characters' actions can reveal important plot points. Circle the action a character takes that leads to the discovery of missing equipment.

Good Sports

(Genre: Drama)

Scene 1

1 *A middle school. Three girls,* SYDNEY, MAYA, *and* ALEXA, *have* **congregated** *in the locker room, which also contains equipment for their soccer games. They are wearing their soccer uniforms.*

SYDNEY: We had such a fantastic practice yesterday! I think we're going to slam the other team this weekend.

MAYA: I agree! We're on a roll. And if we win the next one, that's five games in a row. We'll be undefeated!

ALEXA: Yeah, I hate losing. We've gotta win our next game.

5 JAMIE *jogs into the room, pulling her shoulder-length hair back into a ponytail.*

JAMIE: Hey, guys! Coach wants me to set out the cones and run some warm-ups. Will any of you help?

SYDNEY AND MAYA: Sure!

ALEXA: Why don't you guys get started without me? I… um… have to make a call on my cell phone. [*She exits quickly.*]

SYDNEY: That was odd! What do you think's going on with her?

10 **JAMIE:** Who knows? She's been acting sort of strange for at least a week, I think. Anyway, let's get going.

MAYA: [*Goes over and counts out the cones.*] Jamie? How many of these does Coach want? I only see six.

JAMIE: That's impossible! We should have at least sixteen. Are you missing some?

SYDNEY: It looks like Maya's right, Jamie. I don't see any others. We always keep them in the same place.

JAMIE: Maybe the girls who put them away last time put them with the spare net. I'll check. [*She does.*] That's gone too!

15 **SYDNEY:** Well, they can't have vanished into thin air. Alexa, didn't you help put them away last—"

RL.8.3

MAYA: She's not here, Syd, remember?

SYDNEY: Oh, right, she stepped out. Well, when she comes back, let's ask her.

JAMIE: I still think this is weird. Who would want to take our cones and the net? Well, at least we can get what we have ready and take it outside before practice.

[ALEXA *comes back in, looking a little* **flustered**.]

JAMIE: Hey, Alexa, the weirdest thing's happened. A bunch of our supplies look like they're missing. Do you want to go tell Coach about the problem? We'll finish setting up.

ALEXA: Um, no... that's okay. Why doesn't Maya go? I'll help you here.

MAYA: No problem. I'll go tell Coach. Alexa, you don't know if the missing equipment's anywhere else we haven't looked, do you?

ALEXA: No! Why would you think I'd know anything about it?

MAYA: Gee, chill out. I was just asking. You weren't here when we looked for it earlier. [*She leaves.*]

[ALEXA *looks distraught.*]

ALEXA: Sydney, I'm sorry. I just realized I left something in my locker. Can I catch you guys on the field? [*She leaves abruptly, without waiting for an answer.*]

SYDNEY: This is getting stranger by the second. What do you think her problem is?

JAMIE: Well, there's one **logical** way to explain all of this. Maybe *she* took the cones and the net!

SYDNEY: Why would she do something like that?

Comprehension Check

What things does Alexa do or say that make the others wonder about her? What do they suspect her of doing? Include specific words and details from the text to support your response.

CITE EVIDENCE

C Just as a character's words can reveal values, beliefs, and motivations, so can actions. Physical actions and gestures in a drama are described in stage directions. Look at the stage directions and box each of the actions Alexa takes in Scene 1. What do her actions suggest about her? What do they make you wonder?

D In most dramas, characters' dialogue is essential in moving the plot forward. Place an asterisk next to a statement suggesting who could have taken the equipment. Who makes this statement? How do the other characters react to it?

Guided Instruction

RL.8.3

WORDS TO KNOW

escalate
huddled
overreacting
signifying

CITE EVIDENCE

A Examine dialogue closely to figure out character relationships. Draw a box around the dialogue that makes it apparent that Sydney's views are different from Jamie and Maya's views. How do Jamie and Maya want to handle the situation? How are their ideas in conflict with Sydney's ideas?

B Look at word choices to determine characters' feelings. Underline the word that both Maya and Jamie use to question Sydney's ideas about Alexa. Why is this a "loaded" word, or a word with strong emotional connotations? How are Maya and Jamie trying to make Sydney feel by using this word?

Good Sports *continued*

Scene 2

SYDNEY, MAYA, *and* JAMIE *are* **huddled** *on the side of the field. It's midway through practice, and they're on their break.*

SYDNEY: Jamie thought that maybe Alexa has been stealing equipment from the team.

JAMIE: Wait a minute, ease up! I didn't say that. I just thought that Alexa might know where the equipment was.

MAYA: Lex has always had my back. If she does know something, I don't want to bother her. I don't think we should say anything. Let's just drop it. Coach will get us more cones.

JAMIE: [*laughs*] It's not as if we really need those silly cones, anyway. And it's not like they're worth anything either!

SYDNEY: Hold on, you guys. Don't you think we should talk to her? Maybe something's wrong. Why would she be taking the team's stuff? That is, if it is Alexa. And if it's not her, who else could it be?

MAYA: Just give it a rest, Syd. I'm not sure why you're making such a big deal out of it anyway. Who cares about the cones?

JAMIE: And why wouldn't you side with Alexa over Coach anyway?

SYDNEY: I didn't mean.... This isn't about Alexa versus Coach. Come on! It's like you're not even listening to me.

MAYA: Where's your loyalty, Syd? We've been friends with Lex since kindergarten.

JAMIE: Maybe you don't have as much loyalty. After all, by the time you moved here we were already in the third grade.

RL.8.3

SYDNEY: [*turns red*] That's harsh, Jamie. And this has nothing to do with that. I think you're **overreacting**.

MAYA: Fine, sorry. You're loyal. But let's leave Alexa out of this. It's bad enough we already had to tell Coach that the equipment is missing.

SYDNEY: [*annoyed*] She would have noticed anyway. [*pauses*] I'm just worried that something's going on with Alexa. She might need help. And if she did take anything from the team, shouldn't she confess right away, before the situation **escalates**?

JAMIE: You're making it sound like she committed a crime. And she didn't.

MAYA: Yeah, as far as we know her worst crime's making phone calls. We all do that.

[SYDNEY *looks frustrated. From offstage,* COACH *blows a whistle,* **signifying** *that the break is over.*]

COACH: [*still offstage*] That's it, ladies! Let's get back to work. Give me 10 laps each before we go back to running drills.

[MAYA, JAMIE, *and* SYDNEY *start jogging in place.*]

MAYA: I'm going to look for Lex and see if she's okay. Keep all this stuff to yourself, will you, Syd?

JAMIE: I'll come with you, Maya. And I agree, Syd. We've got to stand by Alexa.

SYDNEY: [*lost in her own thoughts*] Okay, sure. Of course. You're right. I won't say anything. [*She continues to jog in place, staring straight ahead.*]

[MAYA *and* JAMIE *exit, calling out their goodbyes.*]

[SYDNEY *jogs more slowly and starts talking to herself.*]

SYDNEY: I don't understand what's going on with Lex—and I don't agree with Jamie and Maya. I'll get to the bottom of this!

Comprehension Check

The three friends have different ideas about how to deal with Alexa. Using evidence from the text, explain who is being a better friend to Alexa: Jamie and Maya, or Sydney?

Guided Instruction

CITE EVIDENCE

C You may have to compare a character's words to her actions to determine her true intentions. Put an asterisk next to text evidence that suggests Sydney is saying and doing one thing but really thinking something else.

D Characters in drama may speak their thoughts aloud so that the audience is aware of plot developments. Circle the dialogue that reveals Sydney's intentions for the next scene. What is she likely to do?

Guided Practice

RL.8.3

WORDS TO KNOW

advocate
animatedly
confide
leisurely
solemn
trivial

CITE EVIDENCE

A Box an important point that Drew makes about why Sydney needs to take action not just for Alexa's good but for Sydney's own benefit. Discuss whether Drew's advice is sound or not. How does his advice to Sydney provoke a decision on her part?

B What does Sydney decide to do about Alexa? Underline the statement she makes about her intended actions. How does this decision propel the plot and reveal Sydney's character? Discuss with a partner what might happen next.

Good Sports *continued*

Scene 3

SYDNEY *is home. She's talking* **animatedly** *with her brother,* DREW, *who's 16. He's a soccer player, too.*

DREW: Wait, Sydney, slow down. I don't think I understood you. What did Alexa do?

SYDNEY: It sounds like it isn't a big deal. I know that. And Maya and Jamie were trying to convince me that it *wasn't* a big deal. And—

DREW: Just tell me what happened, again. In a **leisurely** way this time.

SYDNEY: Okay. [*She takes a deep breath.*] At practice today, we found that a bunch of equipment is missing. Like cones and nets. And right when we discovered it, Alexa started acting really strange and avoiding everyone.

DREW: Well, all your friends are strange. [*He laughs.*]

SYDNEY: Come on, you don't mean that. [*She looks* **solemn.**] That's the thing, they were all acting unusual today. 'Cause after Alexa ran out on us, Maya and Jamie stood up for her, almost too much. When I said that I thought she might be taking the equipment, they almost bit my head off.

DREW: You know that I'm no fan of tattletales. And being an **advocate** for your friends is important. Sometimes you have to stand up for other people without them knowing you're doing it. But, Sydney, you have to stand up for yourself, too—even if it's over something that sounds **trivial**, like orange soccer cones.

SYDNEY: I don't want to tell on Alexa. But maybe I could talk to her—even though Maya and Jamie don't think it's a good idea. See, I'm worried that something else is going on. Why else would Alexa act like this? It doesn't make sense.

DREW: It's probably nothing. But why don't you look for Alexa during homeroom tomorrow and ask her what's up? Maybe she just needs someone to **confide** in.

SYDNEY: Thanks, I will. That'll show Jamie and Maya.

Comprehension Check

1. What do you infer Drew and Sydney's sibling relationship is usually like?

- **a.** He is supportive, and she trusts him.
- **b.** He thinks she's silly, and she wishes he respected her more.
- **c.** He likes her, but she thinks he doesn't care about her.
- **d.** He puts up with her, but she adores him.

2. Drew asks Sydney to tell him what happened again because

- **a.** she was whispering.
- **b.** she was talking too quickly.
- **c.** he couldn't believe what she was saying.
- **d.** he wasn't listening.

3. Drew advises Sydney to talk to Alexa because

- **a.** he is tired of hearing Sydney talk about it.
- **b.** he is worried about what Alexa might do next.
- **c.** it's the only way to find out what's really going on.
- **d.** he wants Sydney to overcome her shyness.

4. In addition to worrying about what's going on with Alexa, Sydney is concerned that

- **a.** Maya and Jamie are pressuring her.
- **b.** Maya and Jamie really hate her.
- **c.** Maya and Jamie are right.
- **d.** Maya and Jamie practice too little.

5. How does Sydney's conversation with Drew reveal her thoughts about Alexa and her plans to act? Use evidence from the text to support your claims about Sydney's thoughts and intended actions.

____

____

____

____

Independent Practice

RL.8.3

WORDS TO KNOW
composure
fathom
immobilized
varsity

CITE EVIDENCE

A Put an asterisk next to the words Sydney says to reassure Alexa. Why do these words give Alexa the courage to finally confess what she has been doing?

B Why did Alexa take the soccer team's equipment? Circle the paragraph that provides the reason for her actions. Are her reasons valid? What else might she have done?

Good Sports *continued*

Scene 4

The following day, SYDNEY, MAYA, JAMIE, *and* ALEXA *are all in their homeroom. When the bell rings, announcing the end of class,* MAYA *and* JAMIE *file out with the other students.* SYDNEY *pulls* ALEXA *aside.*

SYDNEY: Alexa, can I talk to you for a second? I just want to make sure everything's all right.

ALEXA *looks like she's about to start crying.*

ALEXA: I just don't feel like I can tell anyone about this. You won't think of me the same way again. [*She loses her* **composure** *and starts to cry.*]

SYDNEY: I'm your friend, Lex. I wouldn't turn on you.

ALEXA: [*looking sad, but also relieved*] You guessed, didn't you?

SYDNEY: That you're taking our stuff from the soccer team? Yeah, but what I don't understand is why. It's just—

ALEXA: A bunch of cones and a net? I know. Stupid. I shouldn't have done it. [*She wipes her face.*]

SYDNEY: [*gently*] Well, why did you?

ALEXA: I can't stand the thought of losing. Winning soccer games is everything to me. If we don't win all our games, the high school coach won't notice me, and I won't get on the **varsity** team next year. I have to practice constantly to get as good as I need to be.

SYDNEY: [*laughs with relief*] Lex, you're the best player I know! Of course you're going to make the high school team! But why did you need the equipment? What were you doing with it?

ALEXA: My parents think I already spend too much time playing and practicing soccer at school, so they don't want me practicing at home all the time, too. I know they just want me to be well-rounded, but they really can't **fathom** how important playing on the varsity team is to me. I couldn't buy equipment, or my parents would have found out. So taking equipment from school and setting up a practice area in the field by the creek was the only thing I could think of. I was going to return everything I took. But I was **immobilized** with fear, worrying that I'd be discovered first.

SYDNEY: Do you still have the equipment? After school, let's go get it and take it to Coach. I'm sure she'll understand once you explain. She knows you're a good person. Maybe she'll let us schedule extra practices if we ask.

ALEXA: Thanks, Sydney, thank you so much. I'm so glad you understand. You're an amazing person—a real friend.

SYDNEY: [*grins*] And a good sport. Right?

Comprehension Check

MORE ONLINE **sadlierconnect.com**

1. Why was Alexa taking the equipment?

- **a.** so she could sell it for extra cash
- **b.** so she could practice more after school
- **c.** so the team couldn't practice
- **d.** so the team would worry about her

2. Sydney solves Alexa's problem by

- **a.** suggesting they propose extra practices.
- **b.** suggesting that they not tell anybody.
- **c.** deciding that she should turn Alexa in.
- **d.** saying that they should go to Alexa's parents.

3. What is most important to Alexa?

- **a.** winning
- **b.** practicing
- **c.** studying
- **d.** learning

4. Alexa never told anyone what was going on because

- **a.** she didn't want people to know that she couldn't practice at home.
- **b.** she didn't want people to know how competitive she was.
- **c.** she thought people would no longer think well of her.
- **d.** she thought she could get away with it.

5. How do Alexa's words and actions in this scene reveal her inner feelings and motivation? Use specific evidence in the text to support your answer.

One Step Closer to Freedom

(Genre: Historical Fiction)

1 When the knock at the door came, we were not expecting it. At least, I was not, since it was long after supper on a fall evening, and dark outside. We did not receive many visitors in our small corner of Philadelphia. Of course (though I had not known it at the time), that had been slowly changing for months, thanks to certain clandestine actions undertaken by my family—a secret known only to them and the people whom they had helped.

2 The knock was a strange one: three slow raps followed by three rapid ones. When we heard it, my older sister Mary's face flushed with color, and she hollered for our father. She was fifteen then, just three years older than I was at that time, but I thought her every bit as mature as our parents.

3 Papa came rushing in and answered the door, all the while ignoring my questions about what was amiss. Outside was a respectable-looking gentleman, a man who appeared to be about as old as Papa. But he, unlike my father, had a handlebar mustache and a travel-stained suit.

4 "Have you come a long way?" Papa asked the question and grasped the stranger's hand simultaneously, which I found odd. They were not engaging in any preliminaries, and there were no formal introductions, either. It seemed like Papa knew this man, but I had never seen him before.

5 "I have traveled a great distance, and I fear I cannot stay," the man replied quickly. "As you know, my accommodation is arranged another five miles from here. However, my horse is tired, and I wondered whether I might feed her before continuing my journey." I did not understand why the man would come all this way, only to move on without pausing for so much as a cup of tea.

6 Yet Papa seemed to have no issue with the man's words or actions. He nodded and then turned to me, telling me to stay at the door and keep watch. Before I could I ask him what I should watch for, Papa was already disappearing with the stranger into the dark night. I looked after them, puzzled.

7 Mary, who had stepped up behind me, answered my unspoken question. "Evil men might be coming, Jake, and it is we who have to protect this house now."

8 She waited with me until Papa came back, which was almost a quarter of an hour. The stranger had made good on his word; he was not with Papa and must have already taken off into the night.

RL.8.1, RL.8.2, RL.8.3, RL.8.6.a, RL.8.10

9 Papa, seeming distracted, patted me on the head and kissed Mary on the cheek, then quickly vanished into our parlor—to speak with our mother, I supposed.

10 I turned to Mary to express my frustration, still having no idea who we were supposed to be on guard against, or why.

11 Mary leaned over to me and whispered back an explanation. "We are watching for slave traders, Jacob. We are on guard against people who stand against free will and liberty for all."

12 I was speechless. I had no idea at first what she could possibly mean. I couldn't fathom the idea of my family fighting against the slave traders. My kind father wouldn't even hurt a fly, while my poor mother had been abed with sick headaches ever since our baby sister had been born. Of course, my lack of understanding did not stem from not wanting to help. We were a family of freeholders, and we believed in the liberty of every man. I had seen many black families walking around Philadelphia, their gait as free as mine. They did not belong to anybody, I knew, as they only belonged to themselves.

13 However, I knew that not all people with skin of different colors were so fortunate, particularly since we had heard tales, at church, of how black people were treated in Southern states. Each week, congregants who had traveled to Georgia or South Carolina would step forward to describe what they had seen and share what they had heard. Everyone in our community agreed that our brothers and sisters in the South were treated as lesser people than the rest of us, and we could not stand for it.

14 Slavery was the most awful thing I had ever heard of. However, I was only twelve years old, and I had no idea what I could possibly do to help, or what my family could do. I said as much to Mary that night, and I'll never forget what she said back.

15 "Oh, you are a fool sometimes, Jacob. There are many ways to help. We have been helping free men, and women, take back their liberty for nearly a twelvemonth now."

16 My jaw dropped so low at that it almost hit the floor. "I don't understand what you could mean. I haven't seen anyone."

17 "That 'horse' that has been brought to us is no horse. It's actually a woman. She will be staying in our stables tonight, hidden away, like others this past year." When I asked her how I could have missed any of that, she smirked. "Papa and Mama thought you might be too young to keep the secret."

One Step Closer to Freedom *continued*

18 This riled me to no end. I might not have been fifteen, like Mary, but I was honest, I tried my best to be good, and I knew what was right and what was wrong. "Mary, you know full well I can keep a secret. I haven't told anyone about seeing you eat a whole apple pie last year!"

19 At that Mary relented, and her smile became a little kinder. "Well, that was good of you, and they're letting you help now, aren't they? Papa had you keep watch, and he said I could tell you about what we were doing."

20 This only strengthened my resolve to pitch in, too. I was determined I wasn't going to be left out of this, and I asked what else I could do. Mary patted me on the shoulder, and we decided to ask our father, who confirmed I could take our visitor her supper. After he gave permission, Mary and I started to put together a meal on one of our stoneware plates, combining cornbread, some apples, and a quarter-wheel of cheese.

21 Before I left to take our visitor, whose name was Leah, her supper, Mary gave me some advice. "Make sure to stay quiet when you go over to the barn. You should try not to draw attention to yourself." She covered the plate with a woven napkin and handed it to me, warning me to stay in the shadows.

22 I promised to obey, faithfully, and I walked through the house and out the front door, which I closed behind me as quietly as I could. While remaining close to the wall, I scurried along the front porch and into the grass, and then from there, I tiptoed over to the barn. I went inside the barn, but I did not see anything at first, so I called out a soft greeting. When nobody answered, I decided to explain who I was and give assurance that I was trustworthy.

23 I heard rustling in the upstairs loft, so I hurried over to the ladder and started climbing. It was difficult to climb with just one hand and to hold the plate in the other, but I managed.

24 Leah was a young woman, simply dressed and wearing men's breeches. She thanked me and took the plate. As she ate, I couldn't help but wonder about the circumstances that had brought her to us. "Where have you come from, and where are you going?"

25 "I'm from Charleston, but I'm going to New York," she explained. "My brother was enslaved, too, but he ran away six months ago. He sent a message, telling me how he was and asking me to join him in New York."

26 When I asked how she had managed to run away, she explained that her brother had helped her make plans. "Many people are helping us, including good people like your family."

27 I smiled. My family had been making a difference, and now I was, too. "How do you know which people will help you, and how do you know where to go?"

28 "There are many kind people who wish to help," Leah explained. "They live in slave states and free states, and I've followed a path from one's home to the next. The man who brought me here tonight will be going back South to help rescue someone else. Your father will be taking me to the next stop, since he knows where it is, but I don't."

29 Then we heard footsteps outside, followed by my father's voice. "Jacob, it is too late for you to still be outside. Come in and go to bed, or you'll be no use to your mother on the morrow."

30 I said goodbye and turned to go, realizing that while I couldn't know the future, I certainly hoped I would see Leah again.

Comprehension Check

1A. What is Jacob's reaction when he makes the discovery about his family?

a. dismay

b. anxiety

c. surprise

d. joy

1B. Which quotation from the text supports the answer to Part A?

a. "Papa came rushing in. . . ignoring my questions about what was amiss."

b. "This riled me to no end. I might not have been fifteen..."

c. "'There are many kind people who wish to help.'"

d. "My jaw dropped so low... it almost hit the floor."

2A. Which is the BEST statement of the theme or central idea of this story?

a. Family always comes first.

b. Freedom is worth taking risks for.

c. Young people can be trusted.

d. We should try to understand people.

2B. Which textual evidence supports the answer to Part A?

a. "'. . .we are on guard against people who stand against. . . liberty for all.'"

b. "'Mary, you know I can keep a secret. . . .'"

c. ". . .I didn't know if I'd ever see her again. . ."

d. "'. . .they're letting you help now, aren't they?'"

3A. How does Jacob feel about what his family is doing to help Leah and others?

a. He thinks they are risking too much.

b. He is afraid and worried.

c. He fully supports it.

d. He is uncertain what to think.

3B. Which evidence from the text supports the answer to Part A?

a. ". . .I was only twelve years old. . ."

b. "I did not know who we were supposed to be on guard against. . . "

c. "This riled me to no end. . . ."

d. "I was determined I wasn't going to be left out of this."

4A. Leah is on her way to New York to be with her brother. We can infer that

a. she feels she cannot stand on her own.

b. her brother is free and living in better circumstances.

c. she misses having family around.

d. she thinks city life is better than country life.

4B. Which words from the text support the answer to Part A?

a. "'. . .he ran away six months ago.'"

b. "'Many people are helping us. . . .'"

c. "'He sent a message, telling me how he was and asking me to join him.'"

d. ". . .she explained that her brother had helped her make plans."

5A. How does Jacob feel about slavery?

a. He has never heard much about it.

b. He thinks it only concerns the South.

c. He hates it.

d. He has no opinions about it.

5B. Which text evidence best supports the answer to Part A?

a. "Slavery was the most awful thing I had ever heard of."

b. "I had no idea what I could possibly do to help."

c. "I knew what was right. . ."

d. ". . .I certainly hoped I would see Leah again."

6. What actions does Jacob take when he finds out what his family has been doing? Summarize two or three events from the text in your answer.

____

____

____

____

7. List the incidents that propel the plot of the story and lead up to Jacob's discovery of what his family has been doing.

8. How does Jacob's cultural background shape his approach to the topic of slavery? Explain, using textual references to support your answer.

9. What actions taken by Jacob's family enable them to protect their overnight visitor?

10. Basing your answer on specific details from the text, describe the kind of relationship Mary and Jacob have.

Support a Claim

RL.8, RL.9, SL.8.1.a, SL.8.1.c, SL.8.1.d, SL.8.3

In this unit, you have analyzed meaning, theme, plot, and characters by drawing inferences and finding explicit textual evidence. All four texts explore the theme of using good judgment to make choices. In the four boxes below, answer these questions about each selection: What was the problem? Who was the decision-maker? What was the result of the decision? Then, on a separate sheet of paper, write a brief essay in which you use the information in the boxes to support the claim in the center. Be prepared to discuss your ideas with the class.

"The Judgment of Paris"	**"Good Sports"**

CLAIM: Making a difficult decision requires thoughtfulness and the courage to follow one's values and beliefs.

"Charlie and the Advice"	**"One Step Closer to Freedom"**

Return to the Essential Question

How can analyzing meaning, theme, plot, and character help readers understand literary texts?

In small groups or as a class, discuss the Essential Question. Consider what you have learned about studying literary texts in order to analyze meaning, theme, plot, and character. Use key ideas and details from this unit's reading selections as the basis for your responses.

L.8.4, L.8.4.a

Context Clues

Guided Instruction The more you read, the more likely you are to see words you don't know. You can sometimes figure out the definitions of unfamiliar words by looking at the surrounding text for clues. This is known as using **context clues**.

Context Clue Strategy	Example	Explanation
• Look for other words in the same sentence that might have a similar meaning.	• "…**clandestine** actions under-taken by my family—a secret known only to them"	The word ***secret*** helps you understand the meaning of ***clandestine.***
• Examine the word against another word it describes or is connected to.	• "..give **assurance** that I was trustworthy."	The word ***assurance*** is connected to the meaning of ***trustworthy.***

Guided Practice Use context clues to fill in the blanks in the following sentences, using the words *clandestine* or *assurance* from the above chart.

1. No one else could know about the ______________ decision.

2. She needed ______________ that the used car salesperson could be trusted.

3. I love these ______________ meetings; they make me feel like a spy.

Independent Practice Return to the Close Reading selection and identify two words whose definitions you are unsure of. Use context clues to determine the meaning of each word and check your results against a dictionary. Then, on the lines below, write two sentences using each word, making sure to use the word correctly.

____

____

____

____

____

____

____

UNIT 1 COMMON CORE REVIEW

RL.8.1, RL.8.2, RL.8.3, L.8.4, L.8.4.a

Read the following texts in order to practice analyzing meaning, theme, plot, and character in literary texts. When you have finished reading, answer the questions on pages 45–46.

Searching for Treasure

1 Mike brushed the sand away from his watch and double-checked; he had about three minutes before the tide started coming in, and he still hadn't found the treasure his sister Lacey had said was hidden in the cove.

2 He reviewed his options. He was tempted by the idea that he could sweep the area and make one last calculation about where the treasure might be stowed. Alternatively, he could abandon the bounty and get back to his parents' yacht before they noticed where he'd run off to. Since he was fifteen now, they trusted him to leave the boat whenever they docked at shore, but he always had strict time limits, and his hour was almost up. If he waited until the tide started in, he could get stuck by the cove, and then he wouldn't be able to make it back.

3 *Mom and Dad will be furious if I'm not back on time*, he thought. He was so close to finding the treasure, though; he was sure of it. He and Lacey had ruled out four other hiding places, and this one was the last on their list. *If I come back empty-handed, Lacey might not let me help with the next search.*

4 Frowning, he reached into the sand and dragged his fingers around. *I'll give it one more minute, and then I'm out of here.* As soon as the last word formed in his mind, his fingers touched something cold, hard, and round. It was a gold piece! Mike turned on his heel and started running back to the yacht. *As soon as I show this to Lacey, she'll help me convince Mom and Dad we need to stay on the island overnight. There's treasure here for sure!*

Searching for Ghosts

1 As soon as our family arrived at the dank, mysterious manor home, Frankie, my twin, announced, "Well, this place is obviously haunted!" That first night, she told me her plan: "Okay, we'll wait until Mom and Dad are asleep, then sneak out of our room and into the great hall." She exlained that the great hall seemed like the most likely place for specters to hang out. She was quite excited by the idea.

2 I had my doubts about her plan, but Frankie could be persuasive, and so I found myself, a little after midnight, following her down the stairs. The great hall was a cold, grim place, made scarier by the fact that candles were all we had to light the way. I suddenly realized that I was scared, and I decided I wanted no part of any of this. "Let's go back," I whispered.

3 Frankie only laughed. "I'm not a bit scared," she said. "You can go back, if you want, but I'm going to stay until I meet a ghost!" she declared.

4 A loud clap of thunder suddenly shook the hall, and the little candle I was holding went out. My fingers were trembling; it took me a while to light the flame again. When I finally did, I couldn't believe my eyes: Frankie had disappeared!

RL.8.1, RL.8.3, L.8.4, L.8.4.a

Circle the letter next to the best answer choice.

1A. What is Mike's plan at the end of "Searching for Treasure"?

a. to stay and keep looking for treasure
b. to leave the cove and not come back
c. to convince his family to stay overnight
d. to stop looking for treasure and go home

1B. Which detail from the text is evidence to support the answer to Part A?

a. "he still hadn't found the treasure"
b. "she'll help me convince Mom and Dad"
c. "he was tempted by the idea"
d. "she might not let me help"

2A. How does the narrator of "Searching for Ghosts" feel about what she and her sister are doing?

a. She thinks it is scary.
b. She thinks it is all a joke.
c. She thinks it is a great adventure.
d. She thinks it is stupid.

2B. Which phrase from the text supports the answer to Part A?

a. "I told Frankie, but she only laughed."
b. "I suddenly realized that I was scared."
c. "'. . .I'm going to stay until I meet a ghost!'"
d. ". . .I couldn't believe my eyes. . ."

3A. Which character might have made a poor decision?

a. Mike in "Searching for Treasure"
b. Lacey in "Searching for Treasure"
c. the narrator of "Searching for Ghosts"
d. Frankie in "Searching for Ghosts"

3B. Which phrase from the text supports the answer to Part A?

a. "My fingers shook. . ."
b. "Frankie had disappeared!"
c. "Lacey had ruled out. . ."
d. "Mike brushed the sand. . ."

4A. Which of the following most closely matches the meaning of the word *bounty*?

a. prize
b. boat
c. person
d. watch

4B. Which word from the text is a context clue to the answer to Part A?

a. treasure
b. cove
c. parents
d. yacht

5A. Which event in "Searching for Treasure" leads Mike to make an important discovery?

a. He stays a minute longer and puts his hand in the sand.
b. He realizes that the tide is about to come in.
c. He thinks about how angry his parents will be if he is late.
d. He remembers something Lacey said.

5B. Which words from the text support the answer to Part A?

a. "He and Lacey had ruled out four other hiding places. . . ."
b. "It was a gold piece!"
c. "He was so close to finding the treasure. . ."
d. ". . .he wouldn't be able to make it back. . ."

RL.8.1, RL.8.2, RL.8.3, L.8.4, L.8.4.a

6A. Which of the following words most closely matches the meaning of the word *specter*?

a. spirit
b. house
c. twin
d. candle

6B. Which word from the text is a context clue to the answer to Part A?

a. ghost
b. shook
c. candle
d. midnight

7. How does Frankie's dialogue in "Searching for Ghosts" propel the action of the story and reveal her character?

8. Explain how the theme of making choices is developed through characters and plot in both "Searching for Treasure" and "Searching for Ghosts."

9. Explain what you learn about the different personalities of the twins in "Searching for Ghosts" from both explicit and implied details in the text.

10. How do the settings of "Searching for Treasure" and "Searching for Ghosts" contribute to the characters' experiences? Cite textual details in your response.

Introducing UNIT 2

In this unit about making decisions and using good judgment, you will learn how to write a fictional narrative. A fictional narrative is a story; it describes an imaginary event or experience. A fictional narrative can be realistic, so that it *seems* like something that could really happen, or it can be completely fantastic, with settings and characters that could not really exist. A fictional narrative includes literary elements, such as characters who develop or evolve throughout the story, realistic dialogue that helps to propel the plot, and descriptive details that bring the story to life for the reader.

As you write your fictional narrative, establish a narrator with a clear point of view. A sequence of events should unfold from a conflict in the story. Use effective pacing to engage readers, and use transition words to connect events, different time frames, or settings. Describe the action using precise words and sensory language. Finally, wrap up the story in a satisfying way with a strong conclusion that follows logically from the narrated events.

Progress Check Can I?

Before Unit 2		After Unit 2
☐	Write a narrative about an imaginary event.	☐
☐	Establish the context of a narrative, introduce a point of view, and organize a sequence of events.	☐
☐	Use dialogue and description to develop the narrative.	☐
☐	Use transition words to connect events.	☐
☐	Use precise words, descriptive details, and sensory language.	☐
☐	Provide a satisfying conclusion.	☐
☐	Explain the function of verbals in sentences.	☐

HOME ✦ CONNECT...

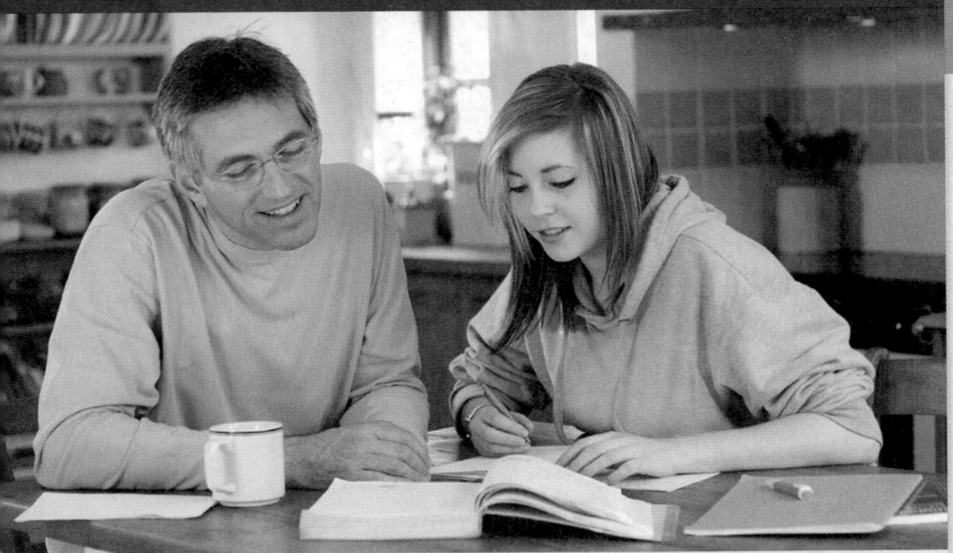

In this unit, your child will learn about writing a fictional narrative. Explain that this type of narrative describes an imaginary event or experience, such as in a novel or a short story. A fictional narrative includes a **plot**, **characters**, a **setting**, and **dialogue**. It also includes **descriptive details** and **vivid language** to make the story come to life for readers. Help your child develop these skills by sharing a piece of short fiction you have read or heard about. Discuss different elements in the story, including the characters, sequence of events, and descriptive details.

Tell a brief story to your child about an imaginary event or experience. Tell the story with the events in sequential order. You can make your narrative richer by including dialogue and description to make the story come to life. Ask your child to contribute details as well. Together, make sure the narrative has a **strong conclusion** that provides a final thought. You might also put your fictional narrative in writing for your child to study and explore.

Activity: Explore the unit theme, making decisions and using good judgment, with your child. Explore books or websites to find stories, such as fairy tales, fables, and myths, about characters who use good judgment. You and your child might choose one story from your research and create a flowchart that shows the step-by-step order of events in the story. Discuss how you and your child could use this chart to together write your own fairy tale, fable, or myth.

IN THIS UNIT, YOUR CHILD WILL...

- Learn how to write a narrative text about an imaginary event.
- Establish a narrator with a point of view and organize a sequence of events that unfolds naturally.
- Use dialogue, pacing, and description in a narrative text.
- Include transition words to convey a sequence of events or a shift in time or setting.
- Use precise words and phrases and sensory language.
- Provide a conclusion that reflects on the experiences or events.
- Explain the function of gerunds, participles, and infinitives.
- Use verb moods correctly.

NOTE: All of these learning goals for your child are based on the Grade 8 Common Core State Standards for English Language Arts.

WAYS TO HELP YOUR CHILD

Have your child describe a story he or she has read or heard about. Remind your child to focus on the order of events, the characters, the details, and the conclusion. Discuss how to structure the story in sequential order. Then ask your child to write a piece of short fiction about a similar event or experience. Encourage him or her to share the completed narrative with family members or friends.

ONLINE

For more Home Connect activities, continue online at sadlierconnect.com

Text Types and Purposes: Write Fictional Narratives

UNIT 2

Essential Question:
How can writers describe imaginary experiences?

W.8.3.a, W.8.3.d

Read a Student Model

Miles is a student in Mr. Jackson's eighth-grade Language Arts class. Mr. Jackson gave the class an assignment to write a fictional narrative about making decisions and using good judgment. Mr. Jackson expects the narratives to include a narrator with a point of view. The narratives should also have a clear sequence of events. Think about good judgment and an imaginary event to write about for your own fictional narrative.

CREATING AN ORGANIZATIONAL STRUCTURE

Miles used a graphic organizer like the one below to organize his narrative.

Title:

Characters:

Setting:

Point of View:

Sequence of Events:

Conclusion:

TITLE

Gives readers a clue about the imaginary event in the narrative

POINT OF VIEW

Tells the story from a particular perspective. The narrator is not one of the characters or part of the story, so the narrative has a third-person point of view.

DESCRIPTIVE DETAILS

- Help readers visualize the story's characters, events, and setting
- Appeal to the five senses

Put a box around an example of a vivid detail in the second paragraph.

An Unexpected Afternoon

As the bus pulled up to the corner, Hal dejectedly stepped down onto the curb. Slinging a backpack over his shoulder, the teenager turned and walked toward an apartment building. It was going to be a very long afternoon, he thought, and this was the absolute last place he wanted to be. Most of his friends were at the movie theater on Third Street, about to watch the latest blockbuster superhero movie.

Hal was a big comic book fan, and it was the first time his favorite superhero, the Golden Glimmer, was appearing on screen. Hal wondered if the special effects would truly capture the hero's signature power, the golden light that streamed from his fingertips like crackling electricity. He also wondered if the film would include the Golden Glimmer's catchphrase from the comics: "All that glitters is gold!"

W.8.3.b–d

Hal had purchased an opening-day ticket online a month ago. Now the opening day had arrived, and he was nowhere near the theater. Instead, he was riding an elevator up to his uncle's apartment. Uncle Teddy was his mother's older brother and had recently broken his hip. He was a widower, and his daughter lived across the country in California. Hal and his parents were the only family Uncle Teddy had in town.

Hal's mother had been looking in on his uncle all week, but that afternoon, she had an important meeting and couldn't get away. So the night before, she had told Hal, "Go to your uncle's place after school and check on him. If there's anything he needs, please take care of it for him." Hal frowned bitterly and thought about going to the movies anyway. But he knew that wasn't the right decision to make, so he did what he had been asked to do.

Using a spare key to enter the apartment, Hal called out, "Uncle Teddy, I'm here!"

His uncle croaked out a reply. "I'm in the living room!"

A home-care nurse had been by in the morning to help Uncle Teddy get up and get dressed, so Hal found him propped up on a sofa, reading a book. His uncle had always been so active and vital, even as he got older, but now he looked thin and frail. Uncle Teddy smiled wanly at his nephew. "It's good to see you, Hal," he said. For the next few hours, Hal did all sorts of chores and errands. He made the bed and washed dishes. He ran to the grocery store and picked up some dry cleaning.

TRANSITIONS

Use transition words and phrases to connect events or show a shift in the setting. In this paragraph, "Now the opening day had arrived" is a transition, shifting the time frame from the past back to the present.

Circle a transition phrase in the final paragraph on this page.

DIALOGUE

Include dialogue to make the story more realistic.

Underline the dialogue in the second paragraph.

PRECISE LANGUAGE

Use precise language that identifies exact details, such as *home-care nurse*. Also, use precise adjectives to describe people, places, and objects specifically, such as *active* and *vital*.

Put an asterisk next to two other precise adjectives in this paragraph.

W.8.3.b–e

SENSORY LANGUAGE

Include details that show what the characters saw, heard, or felt. Hal remembers "hearing the crack of the bat and smelling hot dogs and popcorn" during baseball games as a boy. Sensory language helps bring the characters' experience to life for readers.

Put a box around one other example of sensory language in this paragraph.

CONCLUSION

This fictional narrative ends with a conclusion that reflects on the imaginary event and wraps up the story.

Underline the text that wraps up this narrative. How else could Miles have concluded his story?

As the evening approached, Hal's final chore was to dig through a hall closet to find a small, knitted quilt his late aunt had made. Uncle Teddy was feeling sentimental, and the quilt would bring him some comfort. The closet was a jumbled mess, so finding the quilt was not an easy task. Hal shifted through old papers, extension cords, and tools. Then he found something surprising.

He found two worn baseball gloves. One was big enough for an adult, while the other was small enough for a child. Hal realized the smaller glove was his. His father had never been a big sports fan, so Uncle Teddy had been the one to teach Hal how to play baseball. Uncle Teddy had also been the one to take Hal to his first baseball games. The teenager thought back to those afternoons sitting in the stands, hearing the crack of the bat and smelling hot dogs and popcorn. Those were good times. Smiling warmly, he rubbed his hand over the smaller glove, which felt rough against his fingertips.

After finding the quilt, Hal carefully draped it over his uncle's legs.

"That's perfect, Hal, just perfect," his uncle said, "I don't need anything else today. You can get on home now, if you like. I really appreciate your help."

Checking his watch, Hal thought he might be able to catch a late showing of The Golden Glimmer, but then another idea popped into his head.

"Hey Uncle Teddy, isn't there a game on tonight? Want to watch?"

Uncle Teddy grinned, and so did Hal as he sat down beside him and turned on the TV.

W.8.3.a–e, W.8.4, W.8.5, W.8.10

Use this graphic organizer to create a fictional narrative for the Common Core Review on page 60. Write a fictional narrative that explores the theme of good judgment. Follow a logical sequence of events using transitional words. Include literary elements such as dialogue and description to keep your audience engaged, and use precise verbs and adjectives as well as sensory language to bring your details to life. Then write your first draft on a separate sheet of paper.

Title: ______________________________

Characters: ______________________________

Setting: ______________________________

Point of View: ______________________________

Sequence of Events:

Conclusion: ______________________________

____

Verbals

Guided Instruction A **verbal** is a verb that functions as a different part of speech. It can function as a noun, an adjective, or an adverb. There are three main types of verbals: **gerunds**, **participles**, and **infinitives**.

- **Gerunds**

  Gerunds function as nouns and can be the subject or object of a sentence. They end in *–ing.*

  Biking is my least favorite form of exercise.

  (This gerund functions as a noun and is the subject.)

  Clarice loved eating cereal for breakfast.

  (This gerund functions as a noun and is the object.)

- **Participles**

  Participles function as adjectives. There are two types of participles. **Present participles** end in *–ing*. **Past participles** often end in *–ed*. Participles usually precede a noun or pronoun.

  The hall closet is a big, jumbled mess.

  (This past participle functions as an adjective.)

  The woman wearing the green jacket is my mother.

  (This present participle functions as an adjective.)

- **Infinitives**

  Infinitives can function as nouns, adjectives, or adverbs. Infinitives include the word *to* plus a verb. Infinitives that function as nouns can be subjects or objects.

  Uncle Teddy had been the one to teach him baseball.

  (This infinitive functions as an adjective.)

  Students must get passing grades to graduate.

  (This infinitive functions as an adverb.)

  After a long flight, Carlos was eager to arrive.

  (This infinitive functions as a noun.)

L.8.1.a

Guided Practice Circle the verbal in each sentence. Then identify what type of verbal it is and which part of speech it forms.

1. Sharon liked ordering her salad separately. ______________________
2. Her only goal was to live a full life. ______________________
3. The actor did breathing exercises before the show. ______________________
4. Excited, I eagerly purchased a ticket for the film. ______________________
5. Standing patiently, Anna waited with the others. ______________________
6. To succeed was his primary goal. ______________________
7. The candidates must possess signed petitions. ______________________
8. Traveling is great if you can afford it. ______________________
9. Studying habits are important to school success. ______________________
10. The crippled airplane couldn't take off. ______________________

Independent Practice Write five original sentences using gerunds, participles, and infinitives. At least one sentence should include a gerund, one a present or past participle, and one an infinitive.

1. ____

____

2. ____

____

3. ____

____

4. ____

____

5. ____

____

L.8.1.c

Verb Moods

Guided Instruction Verbs can have different **moods**. Each mood has a different function. Three verb moods are **indicative, imperative**, and **interrogative**.

- **Indicative**

  The **indicative mood** expresses a fact or an opinion. It is used to make a declaration.

  The astronaut strapped into his seat and prepared for liftoff.

  I heard we're going to have nice weather all weekend.

  Soccer practice starts promptly at 3 o'clock.

  The parking garage closes at midnight.

  Danielle decided to take up swimming.

- **Imperative**

  The **imperative mood** provides a direction. It is used to give a command or make a request. The subject is usually not stated, but is typically understood to be *you: (You) Take the dog for a walk.*

  Buy your ticket before the concert sells out!

  Please take your shoes off the new sofa.

  Close the window before the rain starts.

  Pick up some cat food on your way home.

  Don't forget to take the books back to the library.

- **Interrogative**

  The **interrogative mood** expresses a query and so is used to ask a question. Often, the verb appears before the subject in the sentence.

  Can I check out my groceries in this line?

  How many presidents were from Virginia?

  Did you see the fireworks on the Fourth?

  Will you help me finish my chores?

  Where can I drop off the clothes I'm donating?

L.8.1.c

Guided Practice Identify the verb mood in each sentence.

1. Jeremy was afraid of his own shadow. ____________________
2. Go upstairs and clean your bedroom. ____________________
3. A Dalmatian dog became the team mascot. ____________________
4. I left your cookbook on the kitchen counter. ____________________
5. Did you take that salsa dance class? ____________________
6. Wipe your boots before coming inside. ____________________
7. We decided to help our neighbors move in. ____________________
8. Who is the new student? ____________________
9. Please play the piece again from the beginning. ____________________
10. How did you manage to accomplish so much? ____________________

Independent Practice Rewrite each sentence using a different mood.

1. May I borrow your blue shirt to wear out tonight?

____

____

2. I think Mr. Davidson said we're having a test tomorrow.

____

____

3. Pick up your little sister from school this afternoon.

____

____

4. Go see that new science fiction movie before it leaves the theaters.

____

____

5. Will you help me fix dinner for the family?

____

____

SL.8.1.a–d, SL.8.3, SL.8.4, SL.8.6

Discuss the Essential Question

How can writers describe imaginary experiences?

Prepare for a class discussion about the Essential Question by responding to the questions below. Support your point of view with reasons and examples.

1. What is the sequence of events in the narrative Miles wrote?

____

____

2. What literary elements did Miles include to bring the story to life?

____

____

3. How did Miles connect ideas and events in his narrative?

____

____

Use your notes above to discuss the Essential Question in small groups or as a class. Use the rules for being a good speaker and a good listener in the checklist below.

Did I?

- ☐ Build on ideas expressed by others and express my own ideas clearly?
- ☐ Come to the discussion prepared and stay on the topic?
- ☐ Help define individual roles during discussions?
- ☐ Revise my own views when presented with new evidence or information?
- ☐ Distinguish claims that are supported by reasons and evidence from claims that are not?
- ☐ Present relevant claims and other ideas in a logical manner?
- ☐ Speak in an appropriate volume, pronounce words clearly, and make eye contact?
- ☐ Use formal English when appropriate?

W.8.3. a–d

Read this draft introductory paragraph from a student narrative and answer the questions below.

(1) It was not Marisol's idea to spend a Saturday afternoon at the South Shore Hospital, but her grandmother had fallen sick, and the whole family was going for a visit. (2) "Be ready to leave at noon," her mother instructed her and her younger sister Carmen, and that was only the beginning of the night-mare. (3) First, the ride to the hospital was excruciating be-cause they got stuck in a big traffic jam. (4) Her father drove into the wrong parking lot by mistake. (5) It was the farthest lot from Building B, which was where they needed to go, so they had to walk a very long way.

1. This narrative is told from the point of view of

- **a.** a teenage girl.
- **b.** a hospital doctor.
- **c.** a sick grandmother.
- **d.** an outside narrator.

2. Which sentence would add effective sensory language to this paragraph?

- **a.** The hospital was on Oak Street.
- **b.** Her feet ached from the long walk.
- **c.** The two girls sat in the back seat.
- **d.** Her father pulled into a parking space.

3. Which is an example of a precise adjective from the text?

- **a.** *big*
- **b.** *whole*
- **c.** *younger*
- **d.** *excruciating*

4. Based on this introduction, which event would BEST fit in this narrative?

- **a.** the ride to the hospital
- **b.** breakfast with the family
- **c.** the grandmother's return home
- **d.** a visit from the grandmother's doctor

5. Based on this introduction, which detail would NOT fit in this narrative?

- **a.** a description of Marisol
- **b.** a description of the hospital
- **c.** a description of the traffic jam
- **d.** a description of a doctor's office

6. Which transition word or phrase would BEST fit at the beginning of sentence 4?

- **a.** Next,
- **b.** However,
- **c.** The following day,
- **d.** On the other hand,

W.8.3.a–e, W.8.4, W.8.5, W.8.10, L.8.1.a, L.8.1.c

Read these next two paragraphs from the student narrative and answer the questions below.

(1) As they entered the hospital, Marisol was hit by a strong, antiseptic smell that made her want to gag. (2) Then, her family stepped onto an elevator crowded with visitors; Marisol hated tight, cramped spaces. (3) As she muttered under her breath, her mother, unable to ignore her, threw Marisol a look. (4) Marisol stopped talking, pressing her lips together.

(5) Finally, they reached the patient's wing on the ninth floor. (6) As they stepped into a room at the end of the hall, Marisol saw her grandmother sitting up in bed, looking sad and alone as she stared out a window. (7) Hearing the family, she turned and burst into a big smile. (8) Marisol suddenly remembered the time her grandmother had taken care of her when she had the flu, wetting her forehead when she was hot and covering her with a blanket when she was cold. (9) With that memory in her head, Marisol let go of her bitter feelings. (10) "Abuelita!" she called, "How are you?" (11) She hugged her grandmother, careful not to hold her too tightly.

7. Circle a sentence with an interrogative mood.
8. Box the verbal infinitive in sentence 3, and above it write the part of speech it forms.
9. Underline the verbal present participle in sentence 6, and above it write the part of speech it forms.
10. Write a concluding paragraph for this fictional narrative.

____

____

____

Assignment: On a separate sheet of paper, provide a final draft of the fictional narrative you began on page 53. Use what you learned about verbals and verb moods in the Language section of this unit. Think about how you and your classmates answered the Essential Question. Check your graphic organizer to be sure you put events in the correct sequence. Be sure to use precise language and transitions. End with a conclusion that wraps up the story and provides a final thought.

Introducing UNIT 3

In this unit, you will use a variety of techniques to analyze ideas in informational texts. You will use textual evidence to identify the stated, or explicit, ideas in a text as well as the ideas that must be inferred. You will learn to determine the main idea of an informational text and trace its development through supporting details, then make an objective summary of the text. You will also analyze how an author uses analogies, comparisons, categorization, and other techniques to connect ideas, individuals, or events, as well as show distinctions between them.

The informational texts in the unit sometimes present information with objectivity and sometimes with an agenda, or hidden purpose. You will learn how to recognize and analyze both. The texts you will explore come from a variety of genres, but all are connected to topics in United States history and social studies, and all share the same theme: the idea of the importance of standing up for one's beliefs.

Progress Check Can I?

Before Unit 3		After Unit 3
☐	Use textual evidence to analyze the implicit and explicit ideas in an informational text.	☐
☐	Determine the central idea of a text and analyze how it is developed with supporting ideas over the course of a text.	☐
☐	Summarize an informational text objectively.	☐
☐	Analyze how a text uses comparisons, analogies, or categories to present connections among and distinctions between individuals, ideas, or events.	☐
☐	Find the definitions of words based on roots and affixes.	☐

HOME ✦ CONNECT...

This unit begins with an exploration of a fundamental skill used in reading informational texts: **using evidence to analyze explicit and implicit aspects of a text**. During dinner, ask your child to characterize his or her day in a word or phrase. Then, follow up by finding three pieces of evidence (encounters, events, statements) that support this assessment of the day.

Next, the unit teaches how to **analyze the main and supporting ideas of a text, and to summarize them** without including personal opinions. Help your child understand this skill by watching a news segment together. Ask your child to summarize the main ideas and key supporting details of the segment without including his or her opinion.

Finally, this unit provides instruction in assessing a text's use of devices such as **comparisons, analogies, and categories to make connections in a text**. Ask your child to create an analogy (extended comparison) that describes how he or she feels about outdoor activities at different times of the year.

Activity: Brainstorm with your child a short list of causes that really matter to him or her. After identifying at least three causes, discuss situations in which each cause might be at risk. Discuss strategies that could be used to fight for and protect each cause. If applicable, your child might even enjoy putting one of these strategies into action, such as volunteering for a charity or writing to an elected official about an important matter.

IN THIS UNIT, YOUR CHILD WILL...

- Read informational text selections, including an explanatory text, an online article, a magazine article, and a journal article paired with a presidential speech.
- Learn new academic and domain-specific vocabulary.
- Cite textual evidence to support a text's explicit meaning; draw inferences to find implied ideas.
- Determine a text's central ideas and trace their development, with reference to supporting ideas.
- Create an objective summary.
- Analyze connections among and distinctions between individuals, ideas, or events in a text.
- Use Latin and Greek affixes and roots to enrich vocabulary.
- Compare and contrast ideas across texts that share the theme of fighting for beliefs.

NOTE: All of these learning goals for your child are based on the Grade 8 Common Core State Standards for English Language Arts.

WAYS TO HELP YOUR CHILD

Help your child learn to summarize texts objectively. Choose a subject your child knows and has strong opinions about, and find an article that expresses an opposite opinion. Challenge your child to summarize the article without bias.

ONLINE

For more Home Connect activities, continue online at sadlierconnect.com

Reading Informational Text: Key Ideas and Details

UNIT 3

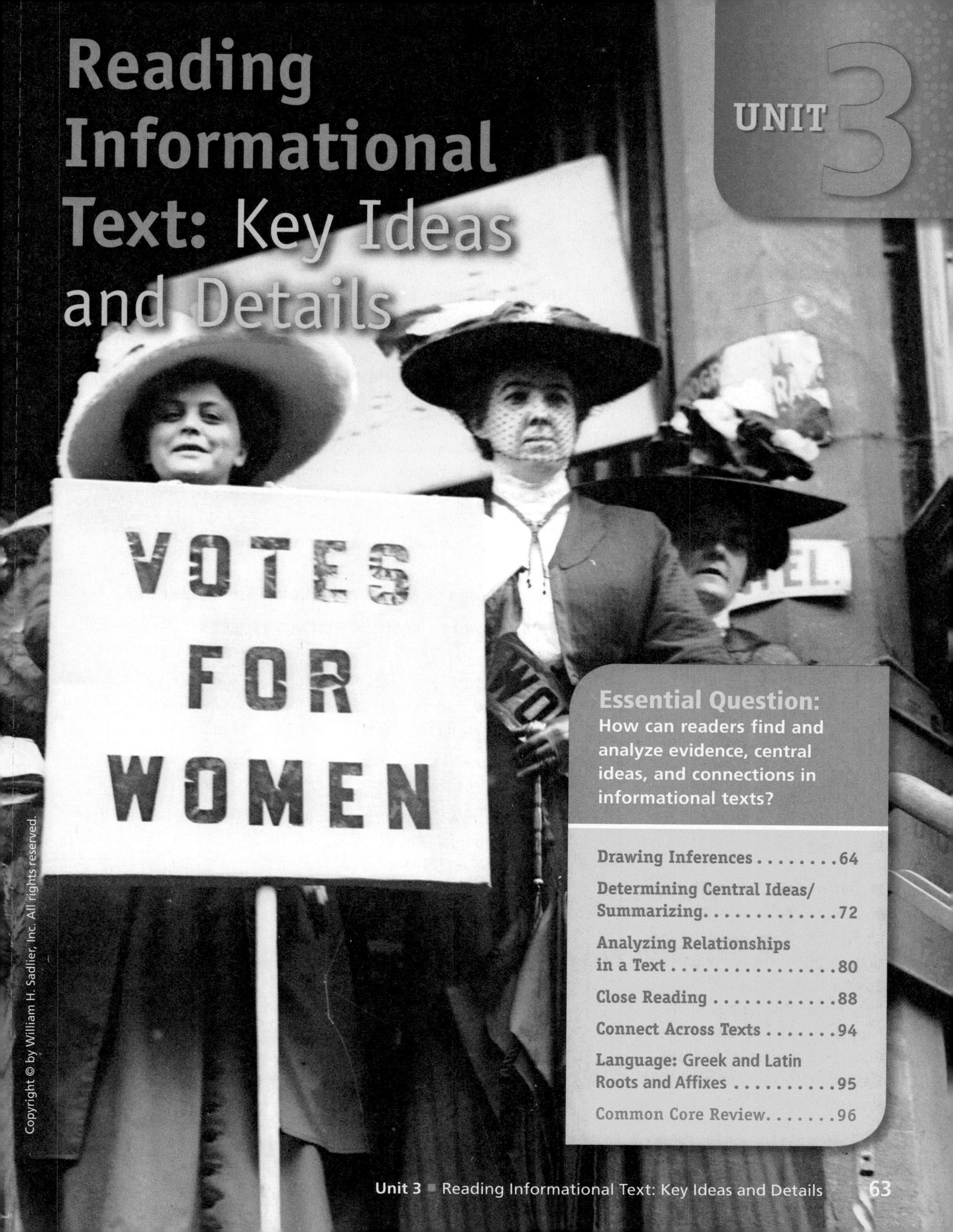

VOTES FOR WOMEN

Essential Question:
How can readers find and analyze evidence, central ideas, and connections in informational texts?

Guided Instruction

RI.8.1, RH.8.3, RH.8.5

WORDS TO KNOW

amendment
ensuring
ratification
suffrage
turmoil

Read closely to determine a text's **explicit meaning**—what the text says directly. After figuring out the explicit meanings of a text, use textual evidence to **draw inferences** and then **analyze** the more subtle meanings in the text.

CITE EVIDENCE

A To determine a text's **explicit meaning**, first identify the author's topic. Circle the paragraph that introduces the topic: the Constitution. What is the author's main idea here? Is it stated explicitly, or implied?

B Different text structures may be used to convey specific information. Numbered items may signal a time sequence or process. Box the numbered sentence on this page that describes what happens to an amendment after Congress approves it. What was the author's purpose in numbering this section?

American Women and the Right to Vote

(Genre: Explanatory Text)

1 The United States Constitution did not originally grant everyone the opportunities and rights enjoyed by American citizens today. As first written, it omitted some essential civil rights.

2 Fortunately, the Constitution is a living document that may be amended, or changed. Typically, an **amendment** must be proposed and ratified, or approved, by a majority of the Congressional houses and the states. Each amendment must pass through four main steps, starting with a senator's or representative's proposal and ending with **ratification** from a three-fourths majority of the states. As of 2013, there were twenty-seven Constitutional amendments.

The Four Steps of the Constitutional Amendment Process

1. **Initial Entrance:** A senator or representative puts forth the potential amendment in Congress.
2. **Congressional Proposal:** A two-thirds majority of Congress must agree in order to propose the amendment to the states. Two-thirds of the House and the Senate must each vote in favor of the amendment.
3. **State Evaluation:** Each state's legislature separately evaluates the proposed amendment.
4. **Ratification:** A three-fourths majority of the states must vote in favor of the new amendment. Currently there are fifty states in the union, so thirty-eight must agree on an amendment for it to become law. According to an alternative, although unused method, an amendment may be proposed and ratified in a different way.

RI.8.1, RH.8.5

3 A group of states' representatives may gather at a special meeting, the purpose of which is Constitutional amendment, and a majority must both propose and ratify the amendment in question.

4 The Founding Fathers put the amendment process into action rapidly. First, they quickly remedied some of their initial omissions, such as freedom of speech and freedom of religion, through the Bill of Rights, ratified in 1791. The Bill of Rights included the first ten amendments to the Constitution. Within a short time, two more were ratified. After passage of the Twelfth Amendment in 1804, sixty-one years would pass before the Constitution would be changed again.

5 While making these first twelve amendments, the early American government did not act to grant all Americans other important markers of equality, such as **suffrage**. This might be surprising, considering that the ability to vote was a key contributor to the rise of the American Revolution. It mattered as a means of **ensuring** the people's own representation in government. Yet, at this point in history, no country had granted the right to vote to all of its citizens.

6 Today, any free American citizen over eighteen can vote, no matter his or her economic status, gender, family background, or skin color. Initially, however, the voting pool in the United States included only men of a certain age and with certain characteristics. The essential characteristics were whiteness and wealth. These same privileged men were the ones who made the law determining who could vote. A long struggle by both women and people of color to gain the right to vote in the United States followed. Looking back at the **turmoil** endured by these Americans in this struggle reminds us that the right to vote is a hard-won civic privilege.

Comprehension Check

What can you infer about the status of women in American society at the time of the adoption of the Constitution? Use text evidence to support your answer.

Guided Instruction

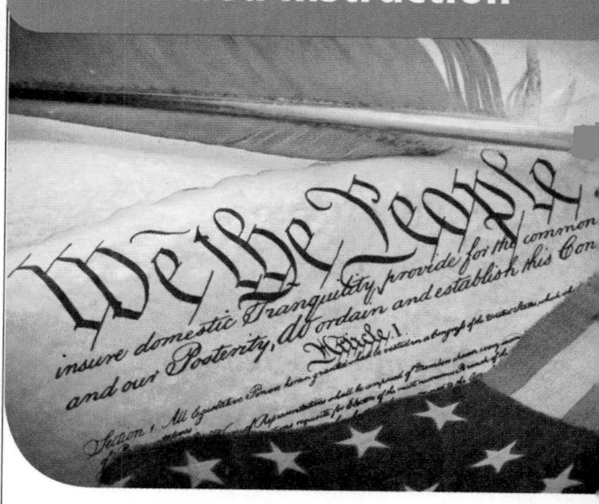

CITE EVIDENCE

C Authors may emphasize essential information by setting it off in a separate feature, such as a call-out box or sidebar. Put an asterisk next to the feature inserted into this part of the article. Why is the information presented this way?

D Authors of informational texts may use different text structures to express different ideas. Look for a paragraph that is primarily organized in a time order sequence. Underline the words that identify the sequence of time.

E Explanatory texts may include evidence of the author's opinions and assumptions. You can **infer** the author's viewpoint by looking for words and phrases with strong connotations. Double underline the sentence in paragraph 6 that reveals the author's position on those who were not allowed to vote. What expectation does this sentence set up?

RI.8.1, RH.8.5

WORDS TO KNOW

complicated
eradicating
involuntary servitude
obligation
prominence

CITE EVIDENCE

A One technique authors may use in an explanatory text is to introduce information by asking—and then proceeding to answer—a question. Put an asterisk by the paragraph that begins this question-and-answer process. Is the answer to this question given explicitly in a specific sentence or paragraph, or must you infer the answer by putting information together?

B When you read explanatory texts, look for specific facts from which you can infer ideas. Underline details on these two pages that support the inference that people from different races worked together to support suffrage.

First Steps Toward Women's Suffrage

7 Over half the citizens of this country (women) have been able to vote for fewer than a hundred years. Why did it take so long for women to receive the right to vote in America?

8 The answer is a **complicated** one. In the years following the initial Constitutional amendments, both women and men worked hard to achieve suffrage for women. This slow process picked up speed in the mid-1800s with an important event: a meeting to discuss the civic **obligations** the country owed to its female residents. This meeting was the Women's Rights Convention of 1848. With this official convention, the women's suffrage movement began to increase in visibility and significance.

Elizabeth Cady Stanton

9 Just three years later, in 1851, three of the most important initial suffragists were gaining **prominence**. Two eventual leaders of the movement, Elizabeth Cady Stanton and Susan B. Anthony, began to work together to achieve women's equality through gaining suffrage. Fourteen years later, they would bring women together to fight for suffrage through the American Equal Rights Association.

10 Another influential speaker, Sojourner Truth, also gained notice at this time, arguing for equality in her famous speech "Ain't I a Woman?" Truth's position in the women's suffrage movement underscored the importance of universal suffrage, the idea that the right to vote is every adult citizen's right. She was African American, and African Americans did not have the right to vote.

Suffrage and Slavery

11 By 1851, women's suffrage had become increasingly combined with many other civil rights issues. First and foremost among them was the issue of racial equality. Slavery was still

legal in the United States, and so black women like Sojourner Truth had the doubly difficult task of seeking equal personhood first, suffrage second.

12 As the 1850s drew to a close, tensions between the northern and southern states were increasing. Slavery was still permitted in southern states, but it was increasingly outlawed in northern ones. During this time, women and men, white and black, continued to work toward civil equality. They focused primarily on **eradicating** slavery and its corresponding racial inequality. The unrest over race led to the Civil War, which lasted from 1861 to 1865. The American government had to address a country that was splitting in half. In the concluding year of the war, the United States government ratified the Thirteenth Amendment. The Thirteenth Amendment outlawed slavery in the United States: "Neither slavery nor **involuntary servitude** [...] shall exist within the United States" (Thirteenth Amendment).

13 The Civil War and the Thirteenth Amendment did not address the issue of suffrage. Women and people of color still did not have the right to vote. They kept fighting for their rights, and Elizabeth Cady Stanton and Susan B. Anthony remained prominent in the women's suffrage movement. The two women's colorblind American Equal Rights Association, which they formed in 1866, encountered differences among members and separated three years later. Anthony and Stanton led one group, while well-regarded suffragist Julia Ward Howe led the other. (In 1890, the groups would come back together to form the National American Women's Suffrage Association).

Comprehension Check

Based on the text so far, what is the text suggesting about the speed with which women received the right to vote in the United States? Use textual evidence to support your answer.

I Sell the Shadow to Support the Substance.
SOJOURNER TRUTH.

CITE EVIDENCE

C Look for contrasts between ideas, sometimes identified by connecting words like *but*, *yet*, or *however*. Double underline two sentences on this page that create a contrast between two things.

D To draw an inference about a text, try to read between the lines. Look for missing or omitted information in the presentation of facts or ideas. Circle the paragraph that describes the passage of the Thirteenth Amendment. What can you infer from this paragraph?

Guided Practice

RI.8.1, RH.8.3

WORDS TO KNOW

abolished
abridged
assemblage
secular

Susan B. Anthony

CITE EVIDENCE

A Underline sentences that describe different goals in the women's suffrage movement at the time of the Fifteenth Amendment. How might women suffragists have felt after passage of the Fifteenth Amendment?

B Working with a partner, circle the paragraph that describes the first presentation of a women's suffrage amendment. At what step in the amendment process did this amendment fail?

American Women and the Right to Vote *continued*

The Fifteenth Amendment

14 In the meantime, the individual states were beginning to endorse women's suffrage. In 1869, women gained the ability to vote in Wyoming. More federal progress on the issue of universal suffrage came one year later, with the passage of the Fifteenth Amendment. In explicit terms, this amendment **abolished** racial discrimination in regard to suffrage: "The right of citizens of the United States to vote shall not be denied or **abridged** by the United States or by any State on account of race, color, or previous condition of servitude" (Fifteenth Amendment).

15 With the ratification of this amendment in 1870, African American men achieved suffrage. Women did not. In 1872, Susan B. Anthony went to the polls anyway and cast her vote. According to the United States government, this was illegal; she went to jail.

16 A victory in suffrage had been achieved with the Fifteenth Amendment, but it was only a partial one. Some female suffragists had wanted to concentrate on women's suffrage, rather than universal suffrage. Others had believed universal suffrage to be the only possible approach.

17 Eight years after the success of the Fifteenth Amendment, supporters of the women's suffrage movement gained new ground. They worked, successfully, to enter a women's suffrage amendment into the Congressional Houses in 1878. Despite tremendous efforts and support, the amendment did not leave Congress for states' approval. It was buried in Congress instead.

Disappointment and Perseverance

18 Women kept pursuing their right to vote. Several influential **assemblages** of women lent their voices to the cause: the Women's Christian Temperance Union, the National Council of Jewish Women, and the National Association of Colored Women. These assemblages represented religious and **secular** women. They included Caucasians and African Americans. They included people from various economic levels.

19 Despite the unity that came from women putting aside religious differences and working together to achieve suffrage, the women's suffrage movement began facing more pushback

than ever. The National Association Opposed to Woman Suffrage (NAOWS), its mission and actions clear from its name, formed in 1911. Two more amendments were legalized in 1913, but neither addressed women's suffrage.

Comprehension Check

1. Which of the following is an inference that may be made from the text's description of events between 1869 and 1878?

- **a.** Women suffragists were discouraged by the lack of support for their movement.
- **b.** Women suffragists were inspired to continue working for their cause.
- **c.** Women suffragists were divided about the best way to pursue their dream.
- **d.** Women suffragists were encouraged that their goals would soon be realized.

2. The text describes the arrest of which woman when she tried to vote?

- **a.** Julia Ward Howe
- **b.** Sojourner Truth
- **c.** Susan B. Anthony
- **d.** Elizabeth Cady Stanton

3. Based on events described in the text, what was the immediate reaction of women suffragists to the Fifteenth Amendment?

- **a.** They tried to pass a women's suffrage amendment.
- **b.** They tried to pass a universal suffrage amendment.
- **c.** They decided to appeal directly to the U.S. president.
- **d.** They decided to appeal directly to the U.S. Congress.

4. Which of the following BEST describes the kind of people who were involved in the suffragist movement by 1911?

- **a.** women who supported women's suffrage but not universal suffrage
- **b.** white and black women from poor backgrounds
- **c.** middle and upper-class Christian white women
- **d.** a religiously, racially, and economically diverse group of women

5. Using textual evidence, explain which of the historic amendments described so far had the biggest impact on the women's civil rights movement, and why.

____

____

____

____

Independent Practice

RI.8.1, RH.8.5

WORDS TO KNOW

distracting
encapsulated
proponent
sanctioning

CITE EVIDENCE

A Put an asterisk by the paragraph that connects the Fifteenth and Nineteenth Amendments. Is the author's conclusion explicitly or implicitly stated?

B Circle the paragraph that summarizes the time it took for women's right to vote to become law. Why might the author present the information by emphasizing the years between historic events?

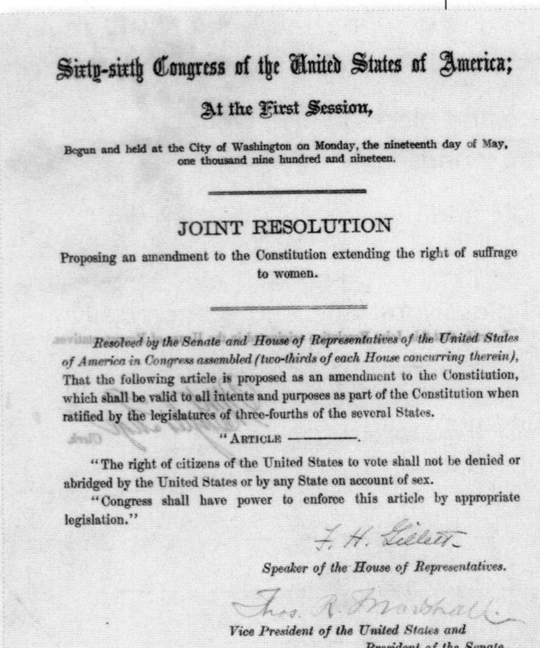

Sixty-sixth Congress of the United States of America;

At the First Session,

Begun and held at the City of Washington on Monday, the nineteenth day of May, one thousand nine hundred and nineteen.

JOINT RESOLUTION

Proposing an amendment to the Constitution extending the right of suffrage to women.

Resolved by the Senate and House of Representatives of the United States of America in Congress assembled (two-thirds of each House concurring therein), That the following article is proposed as an amendment to the Constitution, which shall be valid to all intents and purposes as part of the Constitution when ratified by the legislatures of three-fourths of the several States.

"ARTICLE ———.

"The right of citizens of the United States to vote shall not be denied or abridged by the United States or by any State on account of sex.

"Congress shall have power to enforce this article by appropriate legislation."

F. H. Gillett

Speaker of the House of Representatives.

Thos. R. Marshall

Vice President of the United States and President of the Senate.

American Women and the Right to Vote *continued*

20 The next year came a dangerous and **distracting** complication on the world stage: World War I. This war lasted four years. During the war, advocates for women's suffrage made some notable advances to their cause. In particular, they showed their value as citizens of the United States by participating in and supporting the American armed forces. Yet they did not gain official universal suffrage at this time. However, women in particular states enjoyed an expansion of their civil rights. At the midpoint of World War I, suffragists across America celebrated a victory for their cause as a woman, Jeannette Rankin of Montana, entered the Congressional Houses as a representative.

21 The goal of universal suffrage grew closer as each barrier was overcome. After World War I ended in 1918, supporters of the women's suffrage movement came close to achieving their dream at last. The next year, the amendment originally proposed in 1878 returned to the Congressional Houses. This time, it received a two-thirds majority vote and went out to the states for ratification. Thirty-six states would need to vote for the amendment, and the states did so rapidly, Tennessee coming in at number thirty-six.

The Nineteenth Amendment

22 In 1920, the Nineteenth Amendment was written into law. Its language is brief and direct: "The right of citizens of the United States to vote shall not be denied or abridged by the United States or by any State on account of sex" (Nineteenth Amendment). It uses similar language to that of the Fifteenth Amendment, as well it should—the **proponents** of the causes **encapsulated** in both amendments shared common goals and beliefs. People of different races, religions, and economic backgrounds worked together, sometimes at great personal cost, to win an essential civil right: the right to vote.

23 This achievement for women's rights and equality was a long time coming. It arrived one hundred thirty years after the **sanctioning** of the Constitution, seventy-two years after the initial Women's Rights Convention, and forty-two years after the issue first entered Congress as an amendment.

24 After 1920, no female citizen of the United States could be legally denied the right to vote. Yet, in practice that was only true for white women. Black women (and men) would struggle with injustices regarding their voting rights for decades to come. And there were still many gender inequalities for all women to overcome. The fight for gender and racial equality in America would continue.

Comprehension Check

MORE ONLINE sadlierconnect.com

1. Which textual evidence would support the text's description of events culminating in the passage of the Nineteenth Amendment?

   a. the number of women voting in the late 1930s

   b. the number of women voting in the early 1920s

   c. the number of women in the House in the late 1910s

   d. the number of women in the Senate in the early 1930s

2. Which of the following events was the last major occurrence prior to the passage of the women's suffrage amendment?

   a. the formation of NAOWS

   b. the passage of the Fifteenth Amendment

   c. the end of the Civil War

   d. the end of World War I

3. What step in the amendment process did women's suffrage achieve in 1919 that it had failed to achieve in 1878?

   a. proposal to Congress

   b. ratification by Congress

   c. proposal by the states

   d. none of the above

4. All of the following may be inferred from this text EXCEPT

   a. acceptance of women's rights occurred at the state level before the national level.

   b. the Fifteenth Amendment was important to the success of the suffrage movement.

   c. the Eleventh Amendment was very important to the suffrage movement.

   d. women's roles in World War I helped the women's rights movement.

5. Make an inference about the significance of the length of time and the degree of difficulty of the fight for women's rights. Use textual evidence to support your answer.

Guided Instruction

RI.8.2

WORDS TO KNOW
calamitous
dynamism
fiscal
judicial
ramification

Central ideas are the most important ideas an author develops over the course of a text. Look for ideas that are emphasized and **supported** with evidence.

CITE EVIDENCE

A An informational text's **central idea** is often presented in the introductory paragraph as a general statement about the topic. Double underline such a statement in paragraph 1. Note that there are several parts to this statement. What three aspects of the topic is this article going to cover?

B To **summarize** a text, disregard details and focus on the main ideas the author presents. Look at each paragraph to determine its topic. Underline the topic sentence in each paragraph, from 2 to 5. What are the topics?

American Labor and the Great Depression

(Genre: Online Article)

1 Welcome to the next section of our online series on the history of workers' rights in the United States. Here, we take a look at a defining event, the Great Depression. We'll examine the events of the Great Depression, along with the governmental and **judicial** responses to those events, and see how those responses contributed to the rules and regulations overseeing workers' rights in the United States.

History and Background

2 What was the world like when the Great Depression took place? What happened during the corresponding era? The Great Depression struck at the end of the 1920s, a decade of cultural **dynamism** and economic growth. It followed American achievements at home and abroad—the victory of the Allies (including the United States, Great Britain, France, and Russia) in World War I (1918), and the guarantee of women's right to vote, assured by the passage of the Nineteenth Amendment (1920). These events helped ensure that the beginning of the decade known as the "Roaring Twenties" would be characterized by general **fiscal** strength and a sense of social prosperity. Unfortunately, by the end of the decade, with the positive aftereffects of World War I receding, economies around the world became increasingly shaky.

3 Most people agree that the Great Depression began on Tuesday, October 29, 1929, known as "Black Tuesday," a day that marked a **calamitous** drop in the stock market and led to the

RI.8.2, RH.8.1, RH.8.2

worst economic disaster Americans had experienced. People went from rich to bankrupt in a single day. And that was just the beginning. As 1930 rolled around, the American economy grew worse and worse. Staggering numbers of American workers lost their jobs. By 1932, the number of jobless peaked at almost 25 percent of the workforce. As a result, other seemingly guaranteed elements of American life began to quickly slip away. People could no longer take gainful employment, a place to live, or food on the table for granted.

4 Although the Great Depression's negative **ramifications** could be seen and felt in all aspects of life, its effects on American labor were especially profound—ultimately, in a positive way. To demonstrate why, this article will examine how this disastrous event gave rise to reforms in the American workplace. Click Great Depression Facts and Figures to get to more information about the Great Depression on this site.

First Years of the Great Depression: 1929–1933

5 The first year of the Great Depression was also the first year of Herbert Hoover's short-lived presidency. During Hoover's single term in the White House, American workers benefited from the passage of a few important acts specifically related to unionization of laborers and workers' rights. Workers needed these laws so they could group together and protect their rights as workers. For example, in 1932, Hoover passed the Norris-LaGuardia Act, which stated, "the individual unorganized worker is commonly helpless to exercise actual liberty of contract and to protect his freedom of labor" (Section 2, Norris-LaGuardia Act). A year later, shortly after his inauguration in 1933, President Franklin D. Roosevelt passed the Emergency Banking Relief Act. By doing so the government was trying to support the banking systems, which were suffering tremendously in the severe economy.

Guided Instruction

CITE EVIDENCE

C The author **supports the central idea** about workers' rights by connecting it to events of the Great Depression. Circle statements that provide facts about the effect of the Great Depression on workers. Why does the author provide this information?

D Look for an author's citations, or references, to additional sources. These references provide information an author uses to make his or her points. Put an asterisk by the hyperlink cited in this section.

E Authors may use material from primary sources (quoted, summarized, or paraphrased) to support their points. Put a box around the quotation from a primary source used in this section. What effect does the use of the quotation have?

Comprehension Check

What is the author's central idea about the relationship between the Great Depression and workers' rights?

Guided Instruction

RI.8.2

WORDS TO KNOW

collective bargaining

espoused

regulate

reverberate

CITE EVIDENCE

A The author supports his central idea by describing parts of FDR's New Deal legislation. Underline information on page 74 that connects New Deal legislation to workers' rights.

B In order to determine how a text's central idea is developed, look at its key supporting ideas. Put an asterisk before four important supporting ideas on these two pages. Then, on a separate piece of paper, objectively summarize the central idea of the text up to this point.

American Labor and the Great Depression *continued*

6 Overall, however, Hoover was not able to fix the economic and other problems stemming from the Great Depression. At the next presidential election, Franklin D. Roosevelt took over, taking office in 1933. Roosevelt would be president through the remainder of the Great Depression and beyond. Click The American Presidents to get to more information about Hoover and Roosevelt and the challenges of their terms on this Web site.

Roosevelt and the New Deal: 1933–1935

7 Roosevelt remains America's longest-serving president. He rose to power in large part because of his promises to help the United States overcome the Great Depression. These promises were encased in a set of policies generally referred to as the New Deal. With the New Deal, Roosevelt **espoused** his faith that the United States could not only see its way through the Great Depression, but emerge a stronger country. Roosevelt promised that the New Deal policies and actions would pull the economy together and help jobless Americans rejoin the workforce.

8 Two landmark pieces of legislation from the New Deal era—the National Industrial Recovery Act of 1933 and the Wagner Act of 1935—shared common ground, both of them serving to further **regulate** the processes of **collective bargaining**. Collective bargaining is a significant means by which unionized employees negotiate with employers. Both acts are worth examining on an individual basis.

RI.8.2, RH.8.1, RH.8.2

9 The purposes of the National Industrial Recovery Act were primarily "[t]o encourage national industrial recovery, to foster fair competition, and to provide for the construction of certain useful public works" (National Industrial Recovery Act).

10 The Wagner Act is also referred to as the National Labor Relations Act. It too had several purposes, including: "To diminish the causes of labor disputes burdening or obstructing interstate and foreign commerce, [and] to create a National Labor Relations Board" (National Labor Relations Act). This act contributed greatly to the labor union movement. Significantly, it made legally possible the existence of a workplace with only unionized employees. Moreover, through the foundation of the National Labor Relations Board, or the NLRB, it enabled a regulating body to keep the work of labor unions, employees, and employers alike both lawful and fair.

Life-Changing Laws: 1935–1938

11 During his tenure, President Roosevelt approached economic improvement from several angles. Primarily, he focused on stabilizing American finance. In addition, he increased the number of available jobs. Ultimately, he went so far as to found government programs, like the Works Progress Administration, or WPA, to oversee these processes.

12 Roosevelt continued to enact and develop many important, wide-ranging pieces of legislation, including two acts related in particular to workers' rights. The changes of these acts would **reverberate** throughout American society. They are still felt today.

Comprehension Check

Explain how descriptions of the actions of Presidents Hoover and Roosevelt help you understand and give support to this text's central idea of how the Great Depression affected labor laws.

Guided Instruction

CITE EVIDENCE

C Authors will present essential supporting information from outside sources in quotations. Box the quotation that supports the author's claim that the Wagner Act made it legally possible to have a workplace consisting of only employees who were union members.

D To find important pieces of information that support an author's central idea, look for transitional words and phrases such as *furthermore* and *additionally* that are used to introduce a significant idea or concept. Double underline such transitions on this page. Why are the ideas that these transitions introduce important?

Guided Practice

RI.8.2

WORDS TO KNOW

compensation
generated
implemented
inability
provision

CITE EVIDENCE

A Working with a partner, identify and place an asterisk by the paragraph that describes the limits and benefits of the Social Security Act as it applies to workers' rights.

B Circle the sentence describing the main concepts of the Fair Labor Standards Act. How does this act support the author's central idea about the Great Depression and workers' rights?

American Labor and the Great Depression *continued*

13 One of Roosevelt's most important changes to American labor legislation came through the Social Security Act, or SSA. The government developed this act in 1935 in order to "provide for the general welfare by establishing a system of Federal old-age benefits [... and] unemployment compensation laws" (Social Security Act). It had other considerations, too. With this legislation, the government became responsible for providing money to individuals who had spent time in the workforce, but no longer could work. Their **inability** to work was usually because of age, disability, or joblessness.

14 In other words, the government provided certain funds to workers who had retired (similar to the pension system). It also regulated insurance funding for workers. Specifically, workers who either had become injured on the job or who had lost their job were insured. All these **provisions**, however, relied upon the idea of Americans contributing portions of their salaries to the government through taxes. This tax money would then be returned to them through Social Security. This act, slightly revised, still applies to Americans today.

15 The Social Security Act accomplished a great deal in terms of comfort and security for those no longer in the workforce. Yet it did not address conditions within the workplace. Instead, Roosevelt's government **generated** another act in 1938 to meet these needs for the first time.

16 The Fair Labor Standards Act of 1938 set up requirements about how people could reasonably be expected to work in terms of hours, payment, and age-appropriateness. The act regulated the number of hours people could legally be required to work in a week. The government set this limit at forty hours, and established a policy of **compensation** for those working overtime. The Fair Labor Standards Act also established a national minimum wage, or salary. Finally, this act made the important distinction between adult and child workers, explaining that children could not be laborers except according to strict, additional regulation.

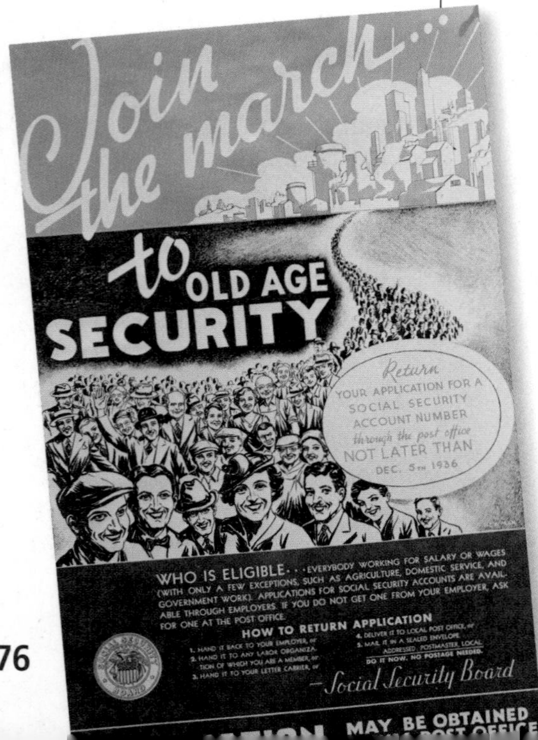

17 By the end of 1938, Roosevelt's administration had successfully **implemented** its New Deal policies. These policies enforced legal, financial, and job-creation changes. They bettered the lives of millions of American citizens.

Comprehension Check

1. Which of the following did the Social Security Act achieve for American laborers?

a. It enforced laws governing child labor.

b. It enforced benefits for the jobless.

c. It enforced an overtime policy.

d. It enforced the 40-hour work week.

2. Which central idea is discussed in "American Labor and the Great Depression"?

a. the effects of Roosevelt's labor legislation ending the Depression

b. the effects of most labor legislation enforced by Roosevelt

c. the effects of two labor laws passed during the Roosevelt administration

d. the effects of Roosevelt's New Deal in general on labor law

3. The author's central idea makes a connection between

a. current events and historic events.

b. historic events and laborers' rights.

c. laborers' rights and women's rights.

d. women's rights and current events.

4. Which of the following types of supporting sources for the article's central idea does the author include?

a. quotations and interviews

b. interviews and a summary

c. graphics and interviews

d. hyperlinks and quotations

5. What evidence in this section supports the central idea that workers benefited from New Deal legislation during the Great Depression?

Independent Practice

RI.8.2

WORDS TO KNOW

ameliorated
definitive
dramatically
encroaching
integrated
unionization

CITE EVIDENCE

A Circle the sentences that explain the cause-and-effect relationship between World War II and the strengthening of the American economy.

B Underline specific details that describe benefits gained by American workers during the Great Depression. Explain whether or not these details would appear in a summary of the article.

End of the Great Depression

18 Historians do not agree on a **definitive** end point of the Great Depression. Some consider the era over in 1939, others sometime later in the following decade. Certainly, improving the economy took much longer than witnessing its collapse. Yet the economic horrors of the Great Depression would soon be eclipsed by horrors of a different kind.

19 In the years leading up to 1938, slowly but surely, the difficulties caused by the Great Depression were **ameliorated**. Americans **integrated** themselves back into the workforce. Soon, it became time to reengage with the rest of the world.

20 Between 1933 and 1939, Roosevelt led the United States back to financial security. Simultaneously, the dangerous dictator Adolf Hitler was coming to power in Germany. His armies were **encroaching** on other European countries. In 1939, World War II began. Just as with other wars, World War II created jobs in the countries involved in the battle, such as Great Britain. It also created jobs for other countries supporting the war effort, such as the United States. Throughout World War II, the American economy strengthened, most **dramatically** after Roosevelt directed American soldiers to officially join the fight in 1941.

21 Before the end of World War II, strong labor laws were in place in the United States. Many of those working in America could expect to benefit from **unionization**, and even more workers could expect to benefit from federal legislation designed to protect them in the work-place and after they retired from that workplace.

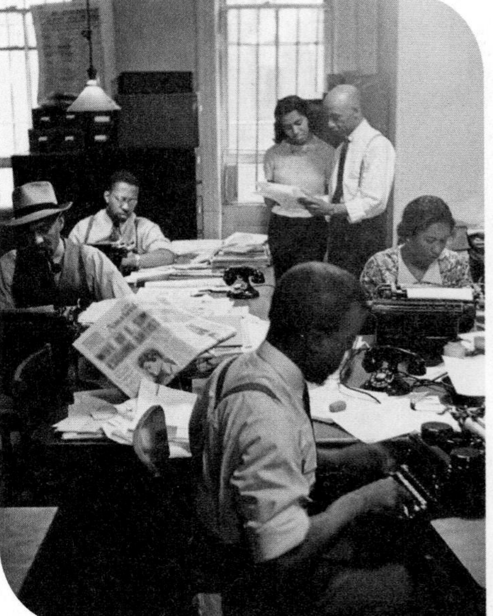

Journalists working in newsroom at the *Amsterdam News*, a prominent African American newspaper in Harlem (1936)

22 A teenager entering the American workforce in 1945 would encounter a far different environment from that of a worker twenty years earlier. This new worker could expect to work forty hours a week, make at least a minimum wage, receive overtime payments and insurance benefits, and collect Social Security after retirement. All of these reforms enabled the achievement of the American Dream.

Comprehension Check

MORE ONLINE **sadlierconnect.com**

1. To support a description of the end of the Great Depression, the author uses

a. historic events.

b. quotations.

c. Web links.

d. citations.

2. How does the author's description of a young worker in 1945 connect to the article's central idea?

a. It suggests that a teenager in 1945 worked much harder than one in 1925.

b. It suggests that workers had no rights in 1925.

c. It suggests that work was more secure and stable in 1945 than previously.

d. It suggests that a teenager in 1945 made much more money than one in 1925.

3. The author concludes with the idea that the workplace changed greatly

a. between 1900 and 1920.

b. between 1900 and 1930.

c. between 1920 and 1940.

d. between 1925 and 1945.

4. Which pieces of evidence would NOT be good support for this article?

a. quotes about pre-Great Depression workplaces

b. summaries of labor laws made later than the Great Depression

c. quotes about Great Depression workplaces

d. summaries of labor laws made before the Great Depression

5. Write an objective summary of this article. Use specific textual details in your answer.

Guided Instruction

RI.8.3

WORDS TO KNOW

begrudges
industrial
rationing
reserves
unfaltering

Analyzing relationships in a text means understanding how **people, events, and ideas in a text connect** to and influence one another.

CITE EVIDENCE

A Authors may **link their ideas** to direct quotations or references to historical figures. Put an asterisk before the sentences that introduce both of these techniques.

B The author uses a quotation from Roosevelt to link the idea of civilians and soldiers fighting together in the war effort. Underline sentences in the quotation that explicitly, or directly, refer to the unity of effort among soldiers and civilians.

The Home Front of the War

by Agatha Eustace Randall

(Genre: Magazine Editorial)

A Nation of Heroes

1 It is November of 1942. We have been at war for a year. Our Allies have been at war for three years. So much has changed since 1939.

2 The Axis Powers continue to draw on a seemingly endless supply of **reserves**. Our brave men and women who fill the ranks of the Army, the Navy, and the Air Force have been fighting hard this last year. Many have fallen. They have lost their limbs; they have lost their friends; they have lost their lives. No one **begrudges** any of them the title of hero. We know them all to be heroes, the named and the unnamed alike.

3 Yet not all American heroes are beyond our shores, as President Roosevelt reminded us in his recent Fireside Chat, "On the Home Front":

This whole nation of one hundred and thirty million free men, women, and children is becoming one great fighting force. Some of us are soldiers or sailors, some of us are civilians. Some of us are

fighting the war in airplanes five miles above the continent of Europe or the islands of the Pacific—and some of us are fighting it in mines deep down in the earth of Pennsylvania or Montana. A few of us are decorated with medals for heroic achievement, but all of us can have that deep and permanent inner satisfaction that comes from doing the best we know how—each of us playing an honorable part in the great struggle to save our democratic civilization.

4 There are heroes elsewhere in the United States, too; heroes on the "Home Front," just as there are heroes on the war fronts of Europe and Asia. Like our fighting men and women, these home-front heroes have also experienced loss and sacrifice. And this fact has been made clear to me by recent tragedies experienced by people in my town of Farmingdale, New York. Several families have already lost sons. One man of my acquaintance experienced an **industrial** accident at the Republic plant, where airplane parts are made; he will never again have use of his right arm. Families are stretched to the breaking point when a husband is away at sea, children spend their free time looking for discarded rubber and metal and glass that can be used in the war effort, and mothers take jobs outside the home. And doesn't everyone go without in this time of **rationing**?

5 Certainly, those who serve in the military know the courage of the men and women fighting alongside them. And they also recognize the courage and grace of the folks at home who support them and make their fight possible. President Roosevelt says that those of us on the home front should be content with the "deep and permanent inner satisfaction that comes from doing the best we know how." It is true that anything we here at home can do for the war effort is done with **unfaltering** good will toward our armed forces. We neither want nor need awards and honors for doing so. And yet, I ask: May the nation not find some way to acknowledge the ongoing sacrifices of those struggling so valiantly on the home front? They too are fighting hard, but in a different place, under different circumstances.

Comprehension Check

Which two major groups of people is the author comparing in this text? On what basis are they being compared?

I'm proud of YOU FOLKS too!

CITE EVIDENCE

C Look for connecting words and phrases to see how authors link elements of a text. Box the words and phrases in paragraph 4 that compare two ideas or groups of people.

D The way text is phrased can offer evidence of an author's opinion or purpose. Double underline a question that suggests civilians in the war effort should be more recognized. What does the question reveal about the author's opinion?

Guided Instruction

RI.8.3, RH.8.4, RH.8.6

WORDS TO KNOW

insidious
invidious
regularity
till

CITE EVIDENCE

A Readers can use context clues to figure out the significance of individuals, events, or ideas that are referenced in a text. Underline the proper nouns in paragraph 6. Explain the meaning of each based on context clues.

B **Comparison** is a way to connect elements in a text. Box two sentences on this page that directly compare two groups of people. What is the author's purpose in making these connections?

The Home Front of the War *continued*

Heroes at the Home Front

6 The brave members of our armed forces ably display their courage in battle, on the streets of an occupied country, in a prisoner-of-war camp, or in a military hospital. They are called upon to enact such courage at every moment. While it may seem small in comparison, being at home, too, takes courage. It takes courage for a mother to explain rationing to her young children. It takes courage for the elderly to **till** the Victory Gardens that help to keep down demands on the public food supply. It takes courage for women to step up, like Rosie the Riveter, and take factory jobs previously reserved for men.

7 It takes courage to send spouses, siblings, or parents to don the proud uniform of the Red, White, and Blue. It takes courage to stay behind as loved ones leave for a fight: to say all the goodbyes before parting. Most of all, it takes courage to wait at home for a reunion that is never to be. There is greatness of character displayed in all of this, just as there is greatness of character displayed by those who enlist, who put on the uniform, and who follow our generals and leaders willingly into the dark fight to prevent a fate that is darker still.

8 Our country will not, and cannot, grind to a halt while this war rages on. We civilians at home are as dedicated to the war effort as our soldiers on the firing lines are. And this is just as it should be. All of us are working together for our common goal of victory. Ultimately, we all make up one tremendous team.

If Wishes Were Horses

9 The men and the women on the front lines face danger with **regularity**. This danger seems far more present and immediate than the danger facing those at home. Consider, though, that fear and danger are **insidious**, **invidious** things in wartime. And these things are contagious, like the influenza; they can spread and grow from a small germ to a large illness. They must be faced as much by those at home as those abroad.

10 Think of the war effort as a thoroughbred horse. Our country has bred this horse to be a champion. Its coat is brushed and glossy, its mane braided. It is given the best food and the purest water to drink. Its vitality is supported by many: the farmers who grow the food it eats, the owners of the stalls where it rests and the land on which it runs, the groomers who maintain its appearance. Then there are the trainers who prepare the horse for the race, the blacksmiths who fit the horse for shoes, the veterinarians who care for its ailments. Further efforts of others, both direct and indirect, assure that the thoroughbred can live up to the potential of its breeding.

11 During a race, the horse displays strength and skill as it speeds to the finish line. After the horse wins, it is admired and praised. Perhaps the jockey who rode the steed to victory is recognized, but no one bestows honors on the stable workers, the groomers, the veterinarians, the food growers, or the little girl who visits the horse every day in its stall with a treat in hand. And yet their work is essential to the final victory.

Comprehension Check

How does the second analogy on this page link to the author's purpose? Explain how analyzing relationships in a text helps you to recognize all the connections the author is making in this analogy. Is the analogy appropriate for the subject matter?

CITE EVIDENCE

C Authors may use an **analogy** to explain an idea. Circle the analogy in paragraph 9. What is being compared to what? How does the analogy connect ideas and events? Explain how the connection helps reveal the author's point of view.

D Put an asterisk next to the paragraph that introduces the second analogy in this section. What is the analogy, and why is it effective—or not effective?

Guided Practice

RI.8.3, RH.8.6

WORDS TO KNOW

compatriot

harmonious

laurels

monies

regulation

CITE EVIDENCE

A Working with a partner, underline the sentence in paragraph 12 that explicitly connects to the analogy of the thoroughbred. Based on this sentence, what is the author's point of view in this paragraph?

B The author, writing in 1942, wants every American, regardless of age, race, or gender, to feel connected to the war effort and capable of making a contribution. Circle a sentence in paragraph 14 that relates this idea to the greater goal of the war.

The Home Front of the War *continued*

12 In this war effort, those at the home front are like the farmers, groomers, caretakers, veterinarians, and other invisible supporters who make it possible for the horse to win the race. Without these unseen helpers, that horse cannot win its race; in fact, it cannot race at all. All of us, both at the home front and abroad, must work together to cross the finish line in victory.

13 The men and women at the front and center of the war effort should indeed receive whatever lauds and **laurels** are bestowed upon them for their sacrifices and hard work. Yet we must not forget that the war effort would not be possible without the work of all who support it, just as a horse could not win a race without the contributions of dozens of unseen and unsung workers. Work done on the home front contributes to our nation's **harmonious** effort to achieve victory in something far more important than any race.

Laurels for All

14 Each American citizen is crucial to the war effort. How wonderful it would be if all of us could honor this effort in our **compatriots**, both at home and on the front lines. I humbly suggest that local governments increase their recognition of those supporting the war effort from the home front, by commending the bravery of all who fight for its goals and the strength of all who enable that fight. This recognition should be based on honor, not any material reward; all our country's spare **monies** must be saved and put toward the war effort. What an effort it will be, though, if everyone at all times feels an equal part in it. People in communities across the country should know how crucial their role in the war is. Then we can assure our continued great effort to defeat the terrible aggression of our enemies.

15 To bring recognition to those on the home front may be met with resistance from the very folks whom it intends to honor. "Save your ceremonies and medals for the boys at the front," they may insist. And the boys at the front should have those medals and ceremonies: they should be celebrated first and foremost. It cannot hurt, however, to honor the efforts of those at home who, by following **regulation**, by rationing, and by believing, keep the flame burning for those on the front lines.

Comprehension Check

1. Which of the following is a distinction the text makes between those who stay on the home front and those who go away to fight the war?

   a. The people on the home front are doing more for the war effort.

   b. The people fighting the war are doing more for the war effort.

   c. Both groups are aiding the war effort, but in different ways.

   d. Both groups are aiding the war effort in very similar ways.

2. This editorial compares all of the following EXCEPT

   a. winning a war to winning a race.

   b. horse groomers to people on the home front.

   c. a horse's beauty to the courage of people on the home front.

   d. a horse to the United States' war effort.

3. Which of these additional analogies would work BEST to describe the relationship between people at the home front and those on the front lines?

   a. comparing the home front to flower petals and the front lines to the flower's stem

   b. comparing the home front to a house's foundation and the front lines to the actual house

   c. comparing the home front to a single fish and the front lines to a school of fish

   d. comparing the home front to a horse and the front lines to a group of horses

4. Which of the following best matches the definition of *lauds* (paragraph 13)?

   a. apologies

   b. compliments

   c. garlands

   d. disparagement

5. In addition to including analogies, how does the text make connections between the people fighting the war at the front lines and those tending the home front?

____

____

____

____

____

____

____

____

Independent Practice

RI.8.3, RH.8.4

WORDS TO KNOW

cumulative
emulate
feted
mobilized
replicate

CITE EVIDENCE

A Underline the sentence that implicitly connects the groups of people described earlier in the piece. How does the author bring the two groups together?

B Circle the phrase that provides clues to the meaning of the word *cumulative* in paragraph 16. Why is this word central to the meaning of this paragraph?

C Double underline the recommendation the author makes near the end of her editorial. What is she suggesting? What does she think will be achieved if her idea is put into action? Explain how she has used all of the points and examples made in her editorial up to this point to lead up to and provide support for this suggestion.

American citizens donating household metals to be melted down to help supply industry in the war effort.

The Home Front of the War *continued*

16 Every action an American citizen takes on behalf of the war effort, no matter how slight that action may be, counts. For when small actions combine and build on each other, their **cumulative** strength is powerful indeed. Let every citizen, young and old, be **mobilized** for the war effort. The more we at home can nourish ourselves from our Victory Gardens, the more food there will be to sustain our armed forces. The braver our families can be, the more inspirational we can become to loved ones fighting far away. Every action we take has the potential, directly or by example, to support the war effort.

17 Seeing the efforts our neighbors make to support our nation, no matter how large or small those efforts may be, will encourage the rest of us to **replicate** such efforts in our own endeavors. Thus, I suggest that once a week, every community should recognize one or two individuals who have contributed in some way, large or small, to our war effort. Perhaps your neighbor is giving extra vegetables from his garden to neighbors in need; perhaps your sister is working in a factory while raising a family. Let these people's names run in the newspaper; let these members of our community be **feted** at the town hall.

18 Acknowledging the hard work of our neighbors and the strength behind their actions will have the positive effect of increasing our desire and commitment to defeat the enemy and to win this war. As more people are recognized for their efforts, more of their neighbors will **emulate** them and double their willingness to share in this important work on the home front.

19 Community acknowledgment will not consist of empty words or promises, nor of grand gestures, but simply of heartfelt appreciation for the important work those at the home front do. This recognition will remind everyone of the value all citizens have toward the war effort. It will remind us of how much stronger we become when we work together. Let us celebrate the wonderful qualities of each man, woman, and child who is fighting the war from home.

Comprehension Check

MORE ONLINE **sadlierconnect.com**

1. Which of the following would NOT support the point of view being presented?

a. reports of how people on the home front support those fighting the war

b. lists of war-effort achievements people on the home front have made

c. interviews showing how people on the home front feel about helping

d. battle reports from various locations where the war is being waged

2. Which piece of evidence would BEST support the author's point of view?

a. details of soldiers' heroism

b. details of civilians' sacrifices

c. details of politicians' patriotism

d. details of the enemy's weaknesses

3. Based on how it is used in the text, what does the word *replicate* mean?

a. copy

b. avoid

c. invent

d. finish

4. Ultimately, the author uses the topic of the differences between the home front and the front lines to show that

a. American soldiers must be supported no matter what.

b. all Americans are indispensable to the war effort.

c. Americans on the home front must not be discouraged.

d. Americans on the home front should honor soldiers.

5. Describe the claim made in the last paragraph about acknowledging those who work on the home front. How will this recognition plan influence the war effort?

Fireside Chat 19

On the War with Japan (Dec. 9, 1941)

Franklin Delano Roosevelt (abridged)

(Genre: Speech)

President Roosevelt gave this talk by radio two days after the Japanese attack on Pearl Harbor, which sparked the U.S. entry into World War II against Japan, Germany, and Italy.

1 My fellow Americans:

2 The sudden criminal attacks perpetrated by the Japanese in the Pacific provide the climax of a decade of international immorality.

3 Powerful and resourceful gangsters have banded together to make war upon the whole human race. Their challenge has now been flung at the United States of America. The Japanese have treacherously violated the longstanding peace between us. Many American soldiers and sailors have been killed by enemy action. American ships have been sunk; American airplanes have been destroyed.

4 The Congress and the people of the United States have accepted that challenge.

5 Together with other free peoples, we are now fighting to maintain our right to live among our world neighbors in freedom, in common decency, without fear of assault. . . .

6 We are now in this war. We are all in it—all the way. Every single man, woman, and child is a partner in the most tremendous undertaking of our American history. We must share together the bad news and the good news, the defeats and the victories—the changing fortunes of war. . . .

7 . . . We must be set to face a long war against crafty and powerful bandits. The attack at Pearl Harbor can be repeated at any one of many points, points in both oceans and along both our coastlines and against all the rest of the Hemisphere.

8 It will not only be a long war, it will be a hard war. That is the basis on which we now lay all our plans. That is the yardstick by which we measure what we shall need and demand; money, materials, doubled and quadrupled production—ever increasing. The production must be not only for our own army and navy and air forces. It must reinforce the other armies and navies and air forces fighting the Nazis and the war lords of Japan throughout the Americas and throughout the world.

9 I have been working today on the subject of production. Your government has decided on two broad policies.

10 The first is to speed up all existing production by working on a seven day week basis in every war industry, including the production of essential raw materials.

11 The second policy, now being put into form, is to rush additions to the capacity of production by building more new plants,

by adding to old plants, and by using the many smaller plants for war needs.

12 Over the hard road of the past months, we have at times met obstacles and difficulties, divisions and disputes, indifference and callousness. That is now all past. . . .

13 The fact is that the country now has an organization in Washington built around men and women who are recognized experts in their own fields. I think the country knows that the people who are actually responsible in each and every one of these many fields are pulling together with a teamwork that has never before been excelled.

14 On the road ahead there lies hard work—grueling work—day and night, every hour, and every minute.

15 I was about to add that ahead there lies sacrifice for all of us.

16 But it is not correct to use that word. The United States does not consider it a sacrifice to do all one can, to give one's best to our nation, when the nation is fighting for its existence and its future life.

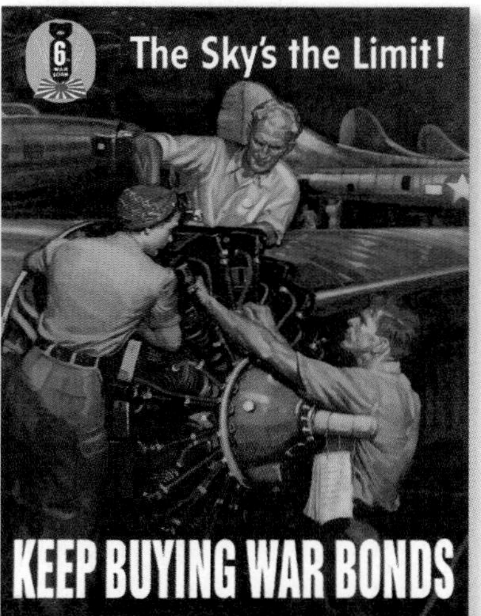

17 It is not a sacrifice for any man, old or young, to be in the army or the navy of the United States. Rather it is a privilege.

18 It is not a sacrifice for the industrialist or the wage earner, the farmer or the shopkeeper, the trainmen or the doctor, to pay more taxes, to buy more bonds, to forego extra profits, to work longer or harder at the task for which he is best fitted. Rather it is a privilege.

19 It is not a sacrifice to do without many things to which we are accustomed if the national defense calls for doing without it.

20 And I am sure that the people in every part of the nation are prepared . . . to win this war. I am sure that they will cheerfully help to pay a large part of its financial cost while it goes on. I am sure they will cheerfully give up those material things that they are asked to give up. . . .

21 I repeat that the United States can accept no result save victory, final and complete. Not only must the shame of Japanese treachery be wiped out, but the sources of international brutality, wherever they exist, must be absolutely and finally broken.

22 In my Message to the Congress yesterday I said that we "will make very certain that this form of treachery shall never endanger us again." In order to achieve that certainty, we must begin the great task that is before us by abandoning once and for all the illusion that we can ever again isolate ourselves from the rest of humanity. In these past few years—and, most violently, in the past three days—we have learned a terrible lesson.

23 It is our obligation to our dead—it is our sacred obligation to their children and to our children—that we must never forget what we have learned.

24 And what we have learned is this:

25 There is no such thing as security for any nation—or any individual—in a world ruled by the principles of gangsterism.

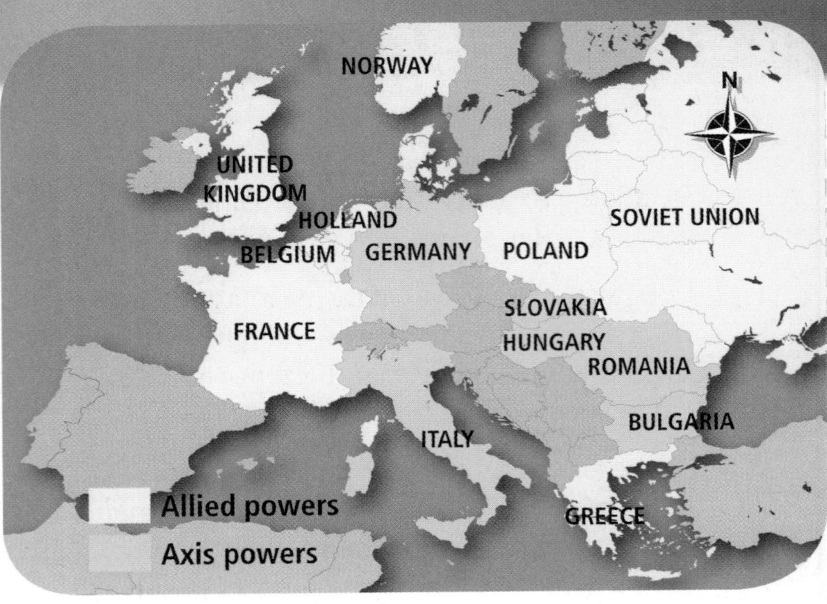

26 There is no such thing as impregnable defense against powerful aggressors who sneak up in the dark and strike without warning.

27 We have learned that our ocean-girt hemisphere is not immune from severe attack—that we cannot measure our safety in terms of miles on any map any more.

28 We may acknowledge that our enemies have performed a brilliant feat of deception, perfectly timed and executed with great skill. It was a thoroughly dishonorable deed, but we must face the fact that modern warfare as conducted in the Nazi manner is a dirty business. We don't like it—we didn't want to get in it—but we are in it and we're going to fight it with everything we've got.

29 I do not think any American has any doubt of our ability to administer proper punishment to the perpetrators of these crimes.

30 Your Government knows that for weeks Germany has been telling Japan that if Japan did not attack the United States, Japan would not share in dividing the spoils with Germany when peace came. She was promised by Germany that if she came in she would receive the complete and perpetual control of the whole of the Pacific area—and that means not only the Far East, but also all of the Islands in the Pacific, and also a stranglehold on the west coast of North, Central, and South America.

31 We know also that Germany and Japan are conducting their military and naval operations in accordance with a joint plan. That plan considers all peoples and nations which are not helping the Axis powers as common enemies of each and every one of the Axis powers.

32 That is their simple and obvious grand strategy. And that is why the American people must realize that it can be matched only with similar grand strategy. We must realize, for example, that Japanese successes against the United States in the Pacific are helpful to German operations in Libya; that any German success against the Caucasus is inevitably an assistance to Japan in her operations against the Dutch East Indies; that a German attack against Algiers or Morocco opens the way to a German attack against South America and the Canal.

33 On the other side of the picture, we must learn also to know that guerilla warfare against the Germans in, let us say Serbia or Norway, helps us; that a successful Russian offensive against the Germans helps us; and that British successes on land or sea in any part of the world strengthen our hands.

34 Remember always that Germany and Italy, regardless of any formal declaration of war, consider themselves at war with the United States at this moment just as much as they consider themselves at war with Britain or Russia. And Germany puts all the other Republics of the Americas into the same category of enemies. The people of our sister Republics of this Hemisphere can be honored by that fact.

35 The true goal we seek is far above and beyond the ugly field of battle. When we resort to force, as now we must, we are determined that this force shall be directed toward ultimate good as well as against immediate evil. We Americans are not destroyers—we are builders.

36 We are now in the midst of a war, not for conquest, not for vengeance, but for a world in which this nation, and all that this nation represents, will be safe for our children. We expect to eliminate the danger from Japan, but it would serve us ill if we accomplished that and found that the rest of the world was dominated by Hitler and Mussolini.

37 So we are going to win the war, and we are going to win the peace that follows.

38 And in the difficult hours of this day—through dark days that may be yet to come—we will know that the vast majority of the members of the human race are on our side. Many of them are fighting with us. All of them are praying for us. But, in representing our cause, we represent theirs as well—our hope and their hope for liberty under God.

Comprehension Check

1A. On page 88, what is the first action Roosevelt's government takes to address the problem of "production"?

- **a.** Start war immediately and increase production slowly.
- **b.** Speed up production by working seven days a week.
- **c.** Hold off on production.
- **d.** Stay focused on winning.

1B. Which piece of textual evidence supports the answer to Part A?

- **a.** "Your government has decided on two broad policies . . ."
- **b.** "It is not a sacrifice for the industrialist or the wage earner . . ."
- **c.** "So we are going to win the war, and we are going to win the peace . . ."
- **d.** ". . . it is our sacred obligation to their children and to our children . . ."

2A. Which of the following BEST summarizes Roosevelt's central idea?

- **a.** a rationale for fighting Italy
- **b.** a rationale for fighting Germany
- **c.** a rationale for fighting Japan
- **d.** all of the above

2B. All of the following textual details support the answer to Part A EXCEPT

- **a.** ". . . Japanese successes against the United States in the Pacific are helpful to German operations in Libya."
- **b.** ". . . the vast majority of the members of the human race are on our side."
- **c.** "The Japanese have treacherously violated the longstanding peace between us."
- **d.** ". . . the sources of international brutality . . . must be absolutely and finally broken."

3A. What would you NOT infer from Roosevelt's reference to privilege rather than sacrifice in the war effort?

a. He believes the American soldiers will be proud to defend themselves.

b. He believes that fighting treachery and brutality is an honorable cause.

c. He believes that American soldiers will be proud to defend the nation.

d. He believes that no one is willing to make sacrifices in the war effort.

3B. Which of the following supports the answer to Part A?

a. "The United States does not consider it a sacrifice to do all one can . . . when the nation is fighting for its existence."

b. ". . . the United States can accept no result save victory, final and complete."

c. "There is no such thing as security for any nation . . . in a world ruled by the principles of gangsterism."

d. On the road ahead there lies hard work . . . day and night, every hour, and every minute."

4A. How does Roosevelt characterize the actions of the Axis powers?

a. They are acting like heroes.

b. They are acting like warriors.

c. They are acting like gentlemen.

d. They are acting like criminals.

4B. Which of the following words from the text supports the answer to Part A?

a. declaration

b. gangsterism

c. dishonorable

d. treachery

5A. Which is the BEST summary of a central idea stated at the end of Roosevelt's speech?

a. The ultimate goal is helping allies like Britain and France.

b. The ultimate goal is shutting down the Axis powers.

c. The ultimate goal is winning the war definitively.

d. The ultimate goal is what happens after the war's end.

5B. Which phrase from the text supports the answer to Part A?

a. "expect to eliminate the danger"

b. "not for conquest, not for vengeance"

c. "administer proper punishment"

d. "everything we've got"

6. Describe two types of evidence Roosevelt presents to support his assertions.

7. Explain one way in which Roosevelt supports the speech's central idea that justifies U.S entry into the war. Use specific words and/or phrases from the text to support your response.

8. Explain in what sequence Roosevelt describes the dangers that lie beyond fighting only Japan in the war. How does he connect important world powers in his discussion? Include details from the text in your response.

9. What language does Roosevelt use to contrast the Americans with their opponents? Be specific.

10. Explain how the last sentence of the speech supports Roosevelt's central idea and point of view.

RI.9, SL.8.1.a, SL.8.1.c, SL.8.1.d

Compare and Contrast Texts

In this unit, you have learned about four historic twentieth-century movements or events through various informational texts: the women's suffrage movement, changes in workers' rights during the Great Depression, efforts on the home front in World War II, and the United States's decision to go to war in 1941. Each of these events involved people fighting for what they thought was right. Fill in the chart below to identify the similarities and differences among these battles. Then use a separate sheet of paper to write two paragraphs in which you contrast two of the movements or events. Be prepared to discuss your ideas.

"American Women and the Right to Vote"	**"The Home Front of the War"**
"American Labor and the Great Depression"	**"Fireside Chat 19"**

Return to the Essential Question

How can readers find and analyze evidence, central ideas, and connections in informational texts?

In small groups or as a class, discuss the Essential Question. Think about what you have learned about inferring the implied ideas of a text, finding the central ideas of a text, and analyzing the connections within a text. Use evidence from the four texts in this unit to answer the question.

L.8.4, L.8.4.b

Greek and Latin Roots and Affixes

Guided Instruction When you come across a word you do not know, see if you recognize the **root** and/or its **affix** (suffix or prefix connected to the root). Often, the root and affix will be derived from the ancient Greek and Latin languages. Knowing some common Greek and Latin roots and affixes can help you determine word meanings.

Root or Affix	Meaning	Combined	New Word
cracy (Greek) *mono-* (Greek)	rule one	mono + cracy (prefix + root)	*monocracy* (rule by one)
psych (Greek) *-logy* (Greek)	mind field of study	psych + logy (root + suffix)	*psychology* (study of the mind)
port (Latin) *-able* (Latin)	carry capable of	port + able (root + suffix)	*portable* (able to be carried)
act (Latin) *-ion* (Latin)	to do act; process	act + ion (root + suffix)	*action* (carrying out an act)
form (Latin) *uni-* (Latin) *trans-* (Latin)	form one; single across	uni + form trans + form (prefix + root)	*uniform* (single form) *transform* (change)

Guided Practice Fill in the blank with a word that combines the root or affix provided with one of the roots or affixes from the chart.

1. The ball flew so fast that I didn't have a chance to ______________ to it. (*re-*)

2. The actor spoke in a dull ______________ that soon put me to sleep. (*mono-*)

3. Hector buys teas and spices at the ______________ store in the mall. (*im-*)

4. Emily was reprimanded because her behavior in the game did not ______________ to the standards set by her coach. (*con-*)

Independent Practice For each of the five roots you studied in this lesson, find another word that is built on the root. On a separate sheet of paper, write five sentences, one per new word, that use the words correctly. After you have written the sentences, circle the affix(es) in each word.

RI.8.1, RI.8.2, RI.8.3, L.8.4, L.8.4.b

Read the following journal article and speech that include implied claims, central and supporting ideas, and connections to people and events. Then answer the questions on pages 97–98.

The Beginnings of World War I

1 World War I, also known as the Great War, began in 1914 with the assassination of Austrian Archduke Franz Ferdinand, a member of the aristocracy. After this event, the great empires of Europe toppled into a battle that raged fiercely for several years. At first, seeing no direct threat to its democracy, the United States did not follow its allies into war against Germany, Austria-Hungary, and the other enemy nations. Between 1914 and 1916, under President Woodrow Wilson's leadership, the United States lent support to its allies Britain and France by sending supplies, including food and medical equipment.

2 Although Britain and France had already deployed soldiers for battle, the United States had not. With each passing month, however, the United States' entrance into the war seemed more inevitable. Citizens grew impatient with President Wilson's plan for peace. In early 1917, innocent Americans abroad lost their lives in a submarine battle between the Germans and the British. Then, in April of 1917, Congress declared war. The deployment of American soldiers in massive numbers drastically affected the following year of the war and reshaped its eventual outcome.

Address to Congress

(April 2, 1917)

1 . . . It is a distressing and oppressive duty, gentlemen of the Congress, which I have performed in thus addressing you. There are, it may be, many months of fiery trial and sacrifice ahead of us. It is a fearful thing to lead this great peaceful people into war, into the most terrible and disastrous of all wars, civilization itself seeming to be in the balance. But the right is more precious than peace, and we shall fight for the things which we have always carried nearest our hearts—for democracy, for the right of those who submit to authority to have a voice in their own governments, for the rights and liberties of small nations, for a universal dominion of right by such a concert of free peoples as shall bring peace and safety to all nations and make the world itself at last free.

2 To such a task we can dedicate our lives and our fortunes, everything that we are and everything that we have, with the pride of those who know that the day has come when America is privileged to spend her blood and her might for the principles that gave her birth and happiness and the peace which she has treasured. . . .

—Woodrow Wilson, from "Address to Congress Requesting a Declaration of War Against Germany"

RI.8.1, RI.8.2, RI.8.3, L.8.4, L.8.4.b

Circle the letter of the correct answer choice.

1A. Which of the following BEST describes a central idea in the Address to Congress?

a. The country will win the war easily.
b. The battle will be tough but necessary.
c. The country will almost certainly lose.
d. The battle will be short but brutal.

1B. Which of the following phrases from the text supports the answer to Part A?

a. "many months of fiery trial and sacrifice"
b. "a universal dominion of right"
c. "it is a fearful thing to lead"
d. "dedicate our lives and our fortunes"

2A. Which of the following makes a connection between events in "The Beginnings of World War I"?

a. how World War I differed from World War II
b. how Germany's actions led to the war
c. how Britain's actions led to the war
d. how the United States entered World War I

2B. Which of the following supports the correct answer to Part A?

a. "an official declaration of war"
b. "referred to as the Great War"
c. "allies such as Britain and France"
d. "great empires of Europe toppled"

3A. Which of the following BEST describes the explicit ideas presented in "The Beginnings of World War I"?

a. an argument about the single most defining cause of WWI
b. a defense of President Wilson's approach to WWI
c. an explanation of why the United States delayed entry into WWI
d. an account of the global events leading up to WWI

3B. Which of the following does NOT support the answer to Part A?

a. "World War I, also known as the Great War..."
b. ...began ... with the assassination of Austrian Archduke Franz Ferdinand..."
c. "Citizens grew impatient with President WIlson's plan for peace."
d. "...innocent Americans abroad lost their lives..."

4A. How does "The Beginnings of World War I" structure its information?

a. by using facts
b. by using descriptions
c. through time sequence
d. through comparison and contrast

4B. Which evidence supports the answer to Part A?

a. "also known as the Great War"
b. "a battle that raged fiercely"
c. "Although Britain and France . . ."
d. "Then, in April of 1917 . . ."

5A. Which word used in both texts contains a Greek or Latin root?

a. *referred*
b. *democracy*
c. *official*
d. *deploy*

5B. Which of the following words from "The Beginnings of World War I" uses the same Greek or Latin root as the correct answer to Part A?

a. *aristocracy*
b. *dedicate*
c. *reshaped*
d. *peaceful*

RI.8.1, RI.8.2, RI.8.3

6A. Which of the following does Wilson compare in his Address to Congress?

a. war and peace

b. right and peace

c. peace and duty

d. duty and war

6B. Which phrase from the text supports the answer to Part A?

a. "To such a task we can dedicate our lives and our fortunes . . ."

b. "It is a fearful thing to lead this great peaceful people into war . . . "

c. "It is a distressing and oppressive duty . . . I have performed in thus addressing you."

d. "But the right is more precious than peace . . ."

7. In the Address to Congress, what is President Wilson's point of view toward America's entry into World War I? Explain, using textual evidence.

____

____

____

8. Which of the two selections presents a persuasive idea in a way that forces the reader to make inferences? Support your answer with details from the text.

____

____

____

9. Without including your own opinion, or references to the author's opinion, write a summary of the events described in Selection 1.

____

____

____

____

10. Compare the ways in which the two selections present the decision for the United States to enter World War I. Use text evidence to support your answer.

____

____

____

____

____

____

Introducing UNIT 4

In this unit about fighting for one's beliefs, you will learn how to write a kind of expository essay called an informative or explanatory essay. When you write this type of essay, you examine and develop a topic in order to provide your reader with information and deeper understanding.

The information in your essay should be thoroughly researched and clearly structured. Information should be presented logically, with each new idea or point leading naturally to the next. Explain each important point clearly, and include supporting facts, details, and examples that will help your reader understand the information. If necessary, use strategies such as defining, comparing, and cause-effect analysis to help explain the topic.

Progress Check Can I?

Before Unit 4		After Unit 4
☐	Introduce a topic clearly.	☐
☐	Organize information logically, using text features such as headings and graphics to make ideas and organization clear.	☐
☐	Develop a topic with facts, details, and examples.	☐
☐	Include transitions to link ideas and create coherence.	☐
☐	Choose precise language and maintain a formal style.	☐
☐	Provide a strong conclusion.	☐
☐	Correct inappropriate shifts in verb voice and mood.	☐
☐	Use ellipses to indicate that text has been omitted.	☐
☐	Use commas, dashes, and other punctuation to suggest a pause or break.	☐

HOME ◆ CONNECT...

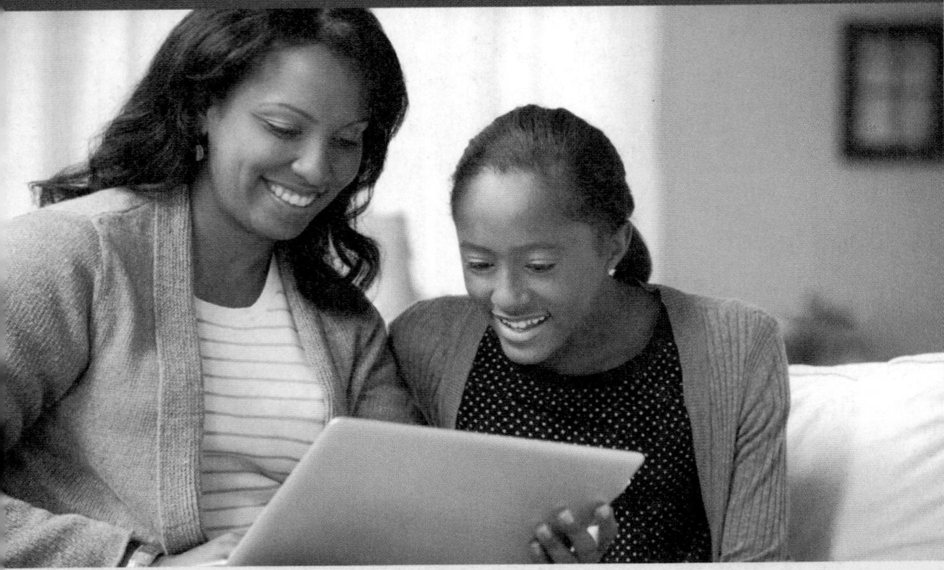

In this unit your child will learn to convey ideas and information more effectively in writing. Your child will use **key facts and details to develop an expository essay**. His or her essay will **organize information in a logical structure**. To assist your child, begin by working together to locate strong examples of informational or explanatory writing. Options could include online articles from reliable websites as well as technical manuals, newspapers, books of nonfiction essays, or other nonfiction sources.

Help your child research topics that stimulate his or her interest. A quick way to start would be to scan authentic websites related to the topic, such as those sponsored by a known media organization, a museum, or a university. You may also find a list of relevant books on the Internet or by consulting your local librarian. Urge your child to explain what he or she has learned from these resources by asking questions that prompt a more detailed explanation. Encourage your child to use **precise language** and to connect ideas with **transition words and phrases**.

Activity: Explore with your child the unit theme, "fighting for beliefs." Together, research and discuss men and women throughout history who have stood up to established structures in order to defend their beliefs or urge social reform. You and your child might choose a biography of one famous figure and create a timeline that shows major milestones and events in the life of that person. Include key details that illustrate the person's contributions.

IN THIS UNIT, YOUR CHILD WILL...

- Learn to write an informative or explanatory text that introduces a topic, organizes information logically, and ends with a conclusion.
- Use facts, details, and examples to develop the topic.
- Include text features such as subheadings and graphics to help communicate information.
- Use transitions such as *because* (to signal a cause or reason) or *consequently* (to signal a result).
- Choose precise language over vague or general terms.
- Avoid inappropriate shifts in verb voice and mood.
- Use punctuation, such as the ellipsis, to indicate an omission or a pause or break.

NOTE: All of these learning goals for your child are based on the Grade 8 Common Core State Standards for English Language Arts.

WAYS TO HELP YOUR CHILD

Have your child practice communicating information about the life of someone he or she already knows well. For example, you might ask your child for a short biography of his or her own life (or the life story of a friend or sibling). Talk about the information that your child shared and where you need more information to answer your remaining questions.

ONLINE

For more Home Connect activities, continue online at sadlierconnect.com

Text Types and Purposes: Write Informative/ Explanatory Texts

UNIT 4

Essential Question:
How can writers present information effectively?

W.8.2.a, WHST.8.2.a

CREATING AN ORGANIZATIONAL STRUCTURE

Emilio used an outline like the one below to organize his essay.

Title ______

I. Introduction
   a. Topic: ______
   b. Preview information: ______

II. Supporting Resources
   a. First paragraph: information about ______
      1. Fact or detail ______
      2. Fact or detail ______
   b. Second paragraph: information about ______
      1. Fact or detail ______
      2. Fact or detail ______
   c. Third paragraph: information about ______
      1. Fact or detail ______
      2. Fact or detail ______

III. Conclusion

______

TITLE

- Helps the reader make predictions about the information that will be presented

INTRODUCTION

- Clearly introduces the topic
- Provides a preview of the information that will follow

ORGANIZATION OF INFORMATION

In a biographical essay, information is usually presented chronologically, or in time order, reflecting a timeline of the subject's life from birth to death, or to the current day.

Read a Student Model

Emilio is a student in Mrs. Pulley's eighth-grade Language Arts class. Mrs. Pulley gave Emilio's class an assignment to write an explanatory text about a famous person who had fought for his or her beliefs. Mrs. Pulley expects the essays to be written clearly and to be logically organized. Think about a famous person you might choose when you write your own explanatory essay.

The Legacy of Gandhi

Many consider Mohandas Gandhi to be the single most influential figure in the history of India. His unending fight for the rights of the oppressed, coupled with his personal dedication to peaceful resistance, created a legacy that endures to this day. Gandhi's beliefs and methods continue to influence people the world over. When speaking of Gandhi, Albert Einstein once said, "I believe that Gandhi's views were the most enlightened of all the political men in our time. We should strive to do things in his spirit. . . ."

His Early Life

Mohandas Gandhi was born on October 2, 1869, in Porbandar, India. Because he came from an upper-class family, Gandhi was able to attend school as a child. The education he received would help him later in life, when he would travel to Great Britain to attend university. At the age of thirteen, Mohandas Gandhi married Kasturba Kapadia, a young woman of the same

W.8.2.a–d, WHST.8.2.a–d

age, in an arranged marriage. They would remain married until her death in 1944.

At the age of 19, Gandhi travelled to Great Britain to study law at University College London. In England, Gandhi became increasingly aware of the social and political issues that surrounded him. Specifically, he was most disturbed by the plight of the oppressed in modern society.

Political Activist

Once his education in Great Britain was complete, Gandhi returned to India, intending to begin his own law practice. His practice never took hold. Subsequently, after joining an established firm, Gandhi was relocated to South Africa. There, he found himself inundated with the racial prejudices and injustices that would forever shape his personal beliefs.

It was during his time in South Africa that Gandhi first encountered prevalent prejudices against people of Indian descent. He was thrown out of trains because he was Indian. He was barred from entering hotels displaying the sign "for Europeans only." In court, he was asked to change his Indian clothing.

The turning point in Gandhi's life came right before he was to leave South Africa and return to India. Gandhi read a newspaper article detailing the Indian Franchise Bill that was being put forth by the Natal Legislature, a body of the British colonial government in South Africa. The bill sought to deny Indians in South Africa the right to vote. Consequently, the article spurred Gandhi to action, and he became a vocal opponent of the bill and of discrimination against Indians in general.

FORMATTING

Subheads aid comprehension by making the organization of ideas clear.

TRANSITIONS

Link your ideas so that the reader can follow your logic from one thought to the next. Emilio uses the transition word "subsequently," meaning "next," to show a cause-and-effect link in this paragraph.

Circle another transition word or phrase in the last paragraph on this page.

FACTS AND DETAILS

Emilio includes key facts and details about Gandhi's life.

Underline key facts and details in the "Political Activist" section.

PRECISE LANGUAGE

Use precise language that names exact things and ideas.

Put an asterisk next to examples of this kind of precise language in this paragraph.

W.8.2.a, W.8.2.b, W.8.2.f, WHST.8.2.a, WHST.8.2.b, WHST.8.2.f

QUOTATIONS

Direct quotations can help develop a topic. Citing the actual words of an historical figure or a subject expert can provide powerful support for points the writer makes.

Circle sentences that weave in direct quotations. Whose words are being quoted?

GRAPHICS

Information in the form of a chart, graphic organizer, table, diagram, or timeline helps make ideas clearer and easier to understand.

Place an asterisk beside an entry on the timeline that provides information the essay does not include.

CONCLUSION

Emilio's conclusion summarizes the central idea and refers to earlier parts of his essay.

Underline the statement that summarizes the essay's central idea.

Protest Through Peaceful Resistance

In India, Mohandas Gandhi became a leader in the fight for Indian independence from the British Empire. His methods were revolutionary in that he believed the oppressed could best fight their oppressors through peaceful resistance. Rather than a battle for independence, he advocated peaceful civil disobedience, in protest of the actions of the established law. In speaking of his belief in nonviolent protest, Gandhi once said, "Nonviolence is not a garment to be put on and off at will . . . it must be an inseparable part of our being."

The Life of Mohandas Gandhi

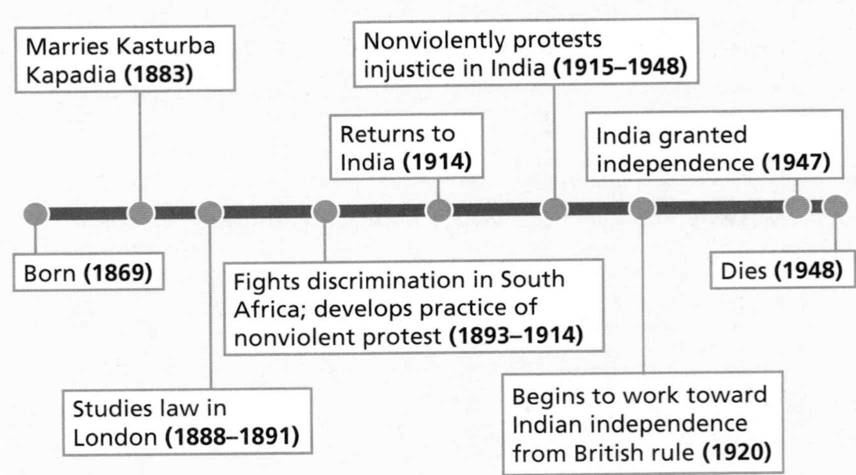
Born (1869)
Marries Kasturba Kapadia (1883)
Studies law in London (1888–1891)
Fights discrimination in South Africa; develops practice of nonviolent protest (1893–1914)
Returns to India (1914)
Nonviolently protests injustice in India (1915–1948)
Begins to work toward Indian independence from British rule (1920)
India granted independence (1947)
Dies (1948)

Mohandas Gandhi became the most important political and social leader in India in the 1930s and 1940s. He spoke out against injustices, participated in political actions and protests, and was even jailed for his beliefs. However, he never wavered from his commitment to nonviolence. As he stated, "I am prepared to die, but there is no cause for which I am prepared to kill." Mohandas Gandhi died on January 30, 1948. His legacy, however, lives on.

W.8.2.a–f, W.8.4, W.8.5, W.8.7, W.8.8, W.8.10, WHST.8.2.a–f

Use this outline to organize your informative/explanatory essay for the Common Core Review on page 111. Write an informative/explanatory essay about a famous person who fought—or is fighting—for his or her beliefs. Begin by researching this figure in both print and reliable online sources. Remember to introduce your topic clearly and give the reader some idea of the information that will follow. Develop the topic with well-chosen facts and concrete details. Use a formal style and precise words to explain your topic and appropriate transitions to connect ideas. Write your first draft on another sheet of paper.

Title ______________________________

I. Introduction

a. Topic: ______________________________

b. Preview information: ______________________________

II. Supporting Resources

a. First paragraph: information about ______________________________

1. Fact or detail ______________________________

2. Fact or detail ______________________________

b. Second paragraph: information about ______________________________

1. Fact or detail ______________________________

2. Fact or detail ______________________________

c. Third paragraph: information about ______________________________

1. Fact or detail ______________________________

2. Fact or detail ______________________________

III. Conclusion

____

____

____

____

L.8.1.d

Shifts in Verb Voice

Guided Instruction: A verb in the **active voice** indicates a subject that performs an action. A verb in the **passive voice** indicates a subject that is acted upon. It is important to avoid shifting between active and passive voice in the same sentence.

Active: *The students respect the teacher.*

Passive: *The teacher is respected by the students.*

Shifting verb voice (incorrect): *Expensive cars were seen as he entered the auto show.*

Corrected: *He saw expensive cars as he entered the auto show.*

Guided Practice For each sentence, indicate whether the verb voice is *Correct* or *Incorrect*.

1. When the man turned on the computer, a screeching sound was heard.

   ____

2. He tried to avoid being seen, but he was still noticed by the other students.

   ____

3. Many visitors at the park enjoyed the hiking path, and they visited it frequently.

   ____

Independent Practice For each sentence, identify the incorrect shift in verb voice and write the corrected version.

1. Jaime enjoyed skating, but swimming was also enjoyed by him.

   ____

2. Lisa worked two jobs, but her leisure time was devoted to soccer.

   ____

3. He cleaned the kitchen and the living room was vacuumed by him.

   ____

4. The problem was solved by Lenora because she was great at math.

   ____

5. The cat fled when her tail was accidentally stepped on by my brother.

   ____

L.8.1.d

Shifts in Verb Mood

Guided Instruction It is also important to avoid shifts in the **mood** of verbs. Verbs in the **indicative mood** state facts or beliefs: *I will pass the test.* Verbs in the **imperative mood** give commands: *Wash the dishes.* Verbs in the **conditional mood** indicate a state, or condition, that will cause something else to happen: *If you practice, you will improve.* Verbs in the **subjunctive mood** indicate something hypothetical, or imagined: *If I were an artist, I'd paint your portrait.*

Indicative: *Emily will fly to Atlanta tomorrow.*

Imperative: *Go get the clothing.*

Conditional: *If I jiggle the switch, the light will come on.*

Subjunctive: *If I were a bird, then I would fly above the ground.*

Shift from imperative to indicative (incorrect): *First, start the water; then you should wash the dishes.*

Corrected (all in the imperative): *First, start the water; then wash the dishes.*

Guided Practice One of the sentences in each pair below contains a shift in mood; the other does not. Underline the sentence that contains a shift.

1. a. All students should assemble in the gym, then go to first period.
   b. All students should assemble in the gym before first period.
2. a. If you were to trust your instincts, you would listen to your heart.
   b. If you were to trust your instincts, you will listen to your heart.
3. a. Stand up, and then you should begin your speech.
   b. Stand up and begin your speech.

Independent Practice Correct the sentences below to eliminate the shifts in mood.

1. Take out the jelly, and then you should make your sandwich.

   ____

2. I would buy more sunflower seeds if the birds eat what they have now.

   ____

3. If you were to do your homework, you will get a good grade.

   ____

L.8.2.b

Ellipses to Indicate Omitted Text

Guided Instruction An **ellipsis** (. . .) is a series of three evenly spaced dots that take the place of omitted text. An ellipsis is a particularly helpful device when you are quoting someone and need to leave out some of the speaker's words.

"I applaud the students in our grade who have volunteered for the camp counselor training."

Now, leave out the phrase "in our grade":

"I applaud the students . . . who have volunteered for the camp counselor training."

If the omitted text is at the end of a quote, the ellipsis is placed before the period, for a total of four dots.

The First Amendment prohibits laws "respecting an establishment of religion. . . ."

Guided Practice The first sentence below is a complete quotation, while words are omitted from the second. Indicate whether the use of the ellipsis in the omission is *Correct* or *Incorrect*.

1. "I look only to the good qualities of men. Not being faultless myself, I won't presume to probe into the faults of others." — Mohandas Gandhi

   Omission: "I look only to the good qualities of men . . . to probe into the faults of others." ________________

2. "Nonviolence, which is the quality of the heart, cannot come by an appeal to the brain." — Mohandas Gandhi

   Omission: "Nonviolence . . . cannot come by an appeal to the brain." ________________

Independent Practice Use an ellipsis to replace words that could logically be omitted in each Gandhi quote below.

1. "Increase of material comforts, it may be generally laid down, does not in any way whatsoever conduce to moral growth."

   ____

   ____

2. "It passes my comprehension how human beings, be they ever so experienced and able, can delight in depriving other human beings of that precious right."

   ____

   ____

   ____

L.8.2.a

Punctuation for Pauses or Breaks

Guided Instruction Three common types of **punctuation** can be used to indicate a **pause or break** in a sentence. The **comma**, the **ellipsis**, and the **dash** all force the reader to pause. However, they are used for different purposes and effects.

- A comma (,) indicates a short pause in the sentence.

  My band teacher, Mrs. McGregor, reminded us to practice our instruments tonight.

- An ellipsis (. . .) indicates a pause or break in the speaker's or writer's thinking.

  "What . . . What just happened?" she asked.

- A dash (—) indicates a sudden pause, as if a thought has been interrupted. It can also be used to insert parenthetical information that makes a sentence more precise.

  Look at all the constellations out tonight—whoa, a shooting star!

  My brothers—the two who live on the East Coast—are going to Europe.

Guided Practice Add ellipses, commas, or dashes to punctuate each sentence correctly.

1. My next-door neighbor Mr. Jacobs has a really nice car.
2. "I'm here! Are you? I can't see you!" I yelled.
3. Two of my cats the big fluffy one and the little gray one have an appointment with the groomer today.

Independent Practice Write three sentences with a pause or a break. Use each type of punctuation—ellipsis, dash, and comma—once in each sentence.

1. ____

   ____

2. ____

   ____

3. ____

   ____

SL.8.1.a–d, SL.8.3, SL.8.4, SL.8.6

Discuss the Essential Question

How can writers present information effectively?

Prepare for a class discussion about the Essential Question by responding to the questions below. Support your point of view with reasons and examples.

1. How did Emilio organize information about his topic?

____

____

____

2. What facts and details did Emilio use to develop the essay?

____

____

____

3. What kind of language did Emilio use to discuss concepts and connect ideas?

____

____

____

____

Use your notes above as you discuss the Essential Question with your class or in small groups. Follow the discussion rules on the "Did I?" checklist (page 58). Use the organizer below to record your ideas and what you hear in the discussion.

Ideas I Agree or Disagree With		Questions I Asked
Agree		
Disagree		
New Ideas I Had During Discussion		**Questions I Answered**

W.8.2.a, W.8.2.b, W.8.2.d, L.8.1.d, L.8.2.a

Read this draft introductory paragraph from a student essay and answer the questions below.

(1) In the United States today, all citizens can vote as soon as they are 18 years old. (2) However, this was not always the case. (3) Women were not granted the right to vote until 1920. (4) At that time, the 19th Amendment to the Constitution was ratified, so women attained the same rights of citizenry that men had long enjoyed. (5) This landmark shift occurred thanks to the work of many dedicated men and women, who believed that denying any citizen the right to vote was against the very principles of the Constitution. (6) Elizabeth Cady Stanton was one of the influential people who helped give women in the United States equal voting rights.

1. Which of these does sentence 5 contain?
   a. a shift in mood
   b. punctuation to show a pause or break
   c. punctuation to show omitted text
   d. a shift in verb voice

2. Which contains a shift in verb voice?
   a. sentence 4
   b. sentence 5
   c. sentence 6
   d. none of the above

3. Which is an example of precise language from the text?
   a. "influential people"
   b. "19th Amendment to the Constitution"
   c. "voting rights"
   d. "not always the case"

4. Which of the following details supports the development of this topic?
   a. Women were not granted the right to vote until 1920.
   b. Elizabeth Cady Stanton was influential in gaining the vote for women.
   c. The 19th Amendment to the Constitution was ratified.
   d. all of the above

5. Based on this introduction, which of the following is NOT a subhead you might expect to see in this essay?
   a. The Life of Elizabeth Cady Stanton
   b. The 1848 Women's Rights Convention
   c. Speaking Up for Women
   d. Women's Voting Rights in England

W.8.2.a–f, W.8.4, W.8.5, W.8.7, W.8.8, W.8.10, L.8.1.d, L.8.2.a, L.8.2.b

Read the next paragraph from the student essay and answer the questions below.

(1) Cady Stanton, a well-educated, outspoken woman from New York, was instrumental in organizing a popular movement for women's voting rights. (2) Stanton—along with her close colleague Lucretia Mott—was responsible for organizing the 1848 Women's Rights Convention. (3) Cady Stanton believed that if she were to speak out on women's rights, then she will have her voice heard. (4) It was during the Convention that Cady Stanton wrote a modified version of the Declaration of Independence called the Declaration of Sentiments. (5) In it, Cady Stanton wrote, "We hold these truths to be self-evident: that all men and women are created equal. . . ." (6) This convention, and the Declaration of Sentiments, were turning points in the women's rights movement. (7) Eventually, both led to the ratification of the 19th Amendment.

6. Circle the transition word in this paragraph.

7. For what reason does the writer use an ellipsis in sentence 5?

____

8. Why does the writer use dashes in sentence 2?

____

9. Box the sentence in this paragraph that contains a shift in mood.

10. Write a conclusion for this essay:

____

____

Assignment: On a separate piece of paper, provide a final draft of the essay you began on page 105. Use what you learned about avoiding shifts in verb tense and mood, using ellipses, and indicating pauses and breaks. Think about how you and your classmates answered the Essential Question. Be sure you organized your ideas well and used information from reliable sources. Use precise language and transitions, and end with a concluding statement.

Introducing UNIT 5

Have you ever traveled to different parts of North America? In this unit, you will read stories and poems that center around the theme of American places. In these selections, you'll appreciate how authors use craft and structure to create meaning and specific effects in their work. For example, an author's use of figurative language can help you better understand and visualize characters, settings, or other elements of a story. Authors also make use of the connotations of words—the various emotional associations we make to specific terms—to create tone and meaning in their work. Structure, or the way a text is organized, also helps to convey meaning. By comparing and contrasting the organization of different texts, you can see how structure shapes a story. Finally, you will analyze how the point of view of a character or narrator differs from your own point of view about story events, creating such effects as humor and suspense. Learning about these elements of craft and structure will help you get the most out of the stories and poems about American places in this unit.

Before Unit 5

Progress Check Can I?

After Unit 5

- ☐ Analyze how specific word choices, such as connotative meanings and figurative language, affect meaning and tone. ☐
- ☐ Compare and contrast text structures, determining how the differing structures contribute to meaning and style. ☐
- ☐ Identify differences in the points of view of the reader and the characters in a story and how these differing points of view affect meaning. ☐
- ☐ Interpret various figures of speech, such as verbal irony and puns. ☐

HOME ✦ CONNECT...

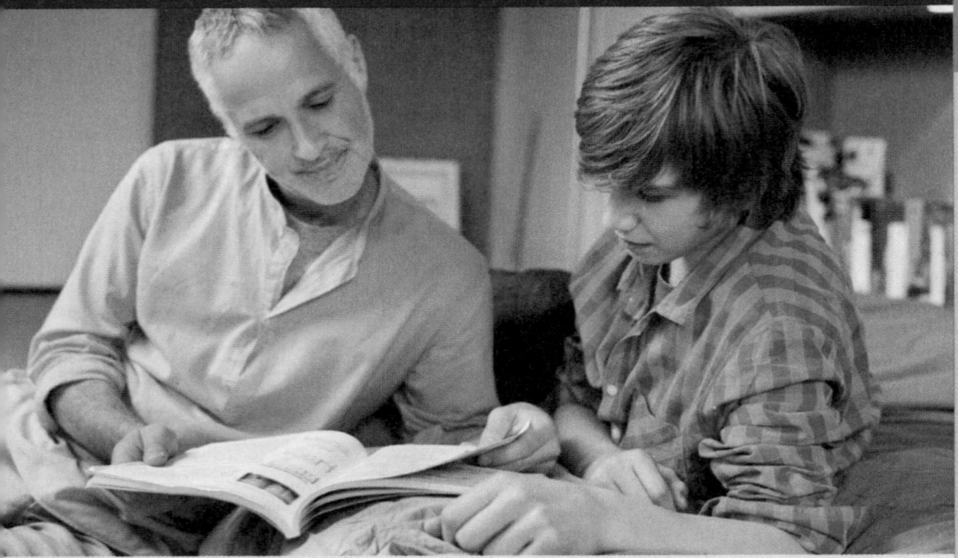

Short stories, poems, and other forms of literature use **figurative language** and **connotative meanings of words** to convey meaning and tone in a text. Read a favorite work of fiction with your child. Work together to identify examples of figurative language. Then talk about the connotations of specific word choices.

Students are already familiar with **text structures** in literature, such as stanzas in a poem or chapters in a novel. As they read more complex texts, they will encounter more sophisticated structures, such as a short story in the form of letters or diary entries. Find an example of a nonconventional narrative structure in a piece of literature. Discuss why the author might have used this structure.

In fiction, different characters have different **points of view**, or perspectives. Readers also bring their own points of view. These different perspectives help shape a story and add new elements, such as humor or suspense. Find a piece of fiction and, with your child, identify the point of view of the narrator or a character in the story.

Activity: Work with your child to conduct an Internet search on different places in the United States that he or she would like to visit, such as the nation's capital, the Atlantic or Pacific coast, or the Rocky Mountains. Talk about why some Web sites are more helpful than others. Make a list of new information you discover that interests you both.

IN THIS UNIT, YOUR CHILD WILL...

- Read four literary selections, including a poem and stories.
- Learn new academic and content-area vocabulary.
- Identify and interpret figurative language, such as metaphors, similes, analogies, and allusions.
- Learn about connotations, or the emotional associations of words.
- Compare and contrast the text structures of different kinds of literature.
- Identify a character's point of view, or perspective, in a text and contrast it with that of the reader.
- Interpret figurative language, such as verbal irony and puns.
- Compare and contrast ideas about the theme "American Places."

NOTE: All of these learning goals for your child are based on the Grade 8 Common Core State Standards for English Language Arts.

WAYS TO HELP YOUR CHILD

Ask your child to tell a story about something that he or she has recently experienced. Listen closely to see if your child uses figurative language. If not, challenge your child to come up with metaphors, similes, and analogies to enliven the account. Discuss how using figurative language can enrich the storytelling experience and enhance self-expression.

ONLINE

For more Home Connect activities, continue online at sadlierconnect.com

UNIT 5

Reading Literature: Craft and Structure

Essential Question:

How do authors use language, structure, and point of view to create meaning?

Guided Instruction

RL.8.4

WORDS TO KNOW

avail
dauntless
intent
noble
yore

Authors make **specific word choices** to create meaning and tone in their works. Look for both the **figurative** and **connotative meanings** of words, as well as the use of **analogies** and **allusions** to other texts.

CITE EVIDENCE

A Authors may describe a subject by using words and phrases that suggest certain "shades of meaning," also known as **connotative** meanings. Underline the words on this page that suggest what the poet thinks "the men of yore" in Boston were like. What "portrait" of these men emerges?

B **Personification** is a type of **figurative language** that gives human qualities to objects, animals, or parts of the natural world. Put an asterisk next to each line on page 117 that uses personification to describe ocean waves or the wind. What is the effect of the personification?

Boston

by Ralph Waldo Emerson

(Genre: Poem)

This poem was read in Boston's Faneuil Hall on the 100th Anniversary of the Boston Tea-Party, during which American colonists disguised as Native Americans raided British ships in Boston Harbor and dumped their stores of tea, which had been subjected to a new tax.

The rocky nook with hill-tops three
  Looked eastward from the farms,
And twice each day the flowing sea
  Took Boston in its arms;
  The men of **yore** were stout and poor,
  And sailed for bread to every shore.

And where they went on trade **intent**
  They did what freemen can,
Their **dauntless** ways did all men praise,
  The merchant was a man.
  The world was made for honest trade,—
  To plant and eat be none afraid.

RL.8.4

Guided Instruction

The waves that rocked them on the deep
 To them their secret told;
Said the winds that sung the lads to sleep,
 "Like us be free and bold!"
 The honest waves refused to slaves
 The empire of the ocean caves.

Old Europe groans with palaces,
 Has lords enough and more;—
We plant and build by foaming seas
 A city of the poor;—
 For day by day could Boston Bay
 Their honest labor overpay.

We grant no dukedoms to the few,
 We hold like rights and shall;—
Equal on Sunday in the pew,
 On Monday in the mall.
 For what **avail** the plough or sail,
 Or land or life, if freedom fail?

The **noble** craftsmen we promote,
 Disown the knave and fool;
Each honest man shall have his vote,
 Each child shall have his school.
 A union then of honest men,
 Or union nevermore again.

Comprehension Check

Based on the author's word choice and connotative meanings, what were the values of the people who lived in Boston during the time described in the poem?

CITE EVIDENCE

C An author may add meaning to a text by repeating, and thus emphasizing, certain words. Find and circle an adjective that is used three times on this page. Do you also see this word on page 116? Why is this word repeated? What is the effect of this repetition?

D Authors may use several words that are related to a particular subject or category. These related words may refer to ideas that are central to a text's message. Box each word on this page that refers to aristocracy or nobility. How do these terms fit into the poem's message?

E Look for words or phrases that present ideas in a negative way (*no, not, never,* and words beginning with prefixes such as *non-* or *dis-*) in order to find what does *not* apply to the subject of a text. Underline each of the negative phrases on this page. What effect does the use of negative phrases have?

Guided Instruction

RL.8.4

WORDS TO KNOW

moat

rival

sluggard

thriving

CITE EVIDENCE

A Underline each example of the personification of nature on this page. What is the author suggesting about the relationship between Boston and the natural world?

B Circle the description of Boston and its setting on this page. What connotations are suggested by the poet's choice of words? Does the poet have a positive or negative view of the city?

Boston *continued*

The wild rose and the barberry thorn
  Hung out their summer pride
Where now on heated pavements worn
  The feet of millions stride.

Fair rose the planted hills behind
  The good town on the bay,
And where the western hills declined
  The prairie stretched away.

What care though **rival** cities soar
  Along the stormy coast:
Penn's town, New York, and Baltimore,
  If Boston knew the most!

They laughed to know the world so wide;
  The mountains said: "Good-day!
We greet you well, you Saxon men,
  Up with your towns and stay!"
  The world was made for honest trade,—
  To plant and eat be none afraid.

RL.8.4

"For you," they said, "no barriers be,
For you no **sluggard** rest;
Each street leads downward to the sea,
Or landward to the West."

O happy town beside the sea,
Whose roads lead everywhere to all;
Than thine no deeper **moat** can be,
No stouter fence, no steeper wall!

Bad news from George on the English throne:
"You are **thriving** well," said he;
"Now by these presents be it known,
You shall pay us a tax on tea;
'Tis very small,—no load at all,—
Honor enough that we send the call."

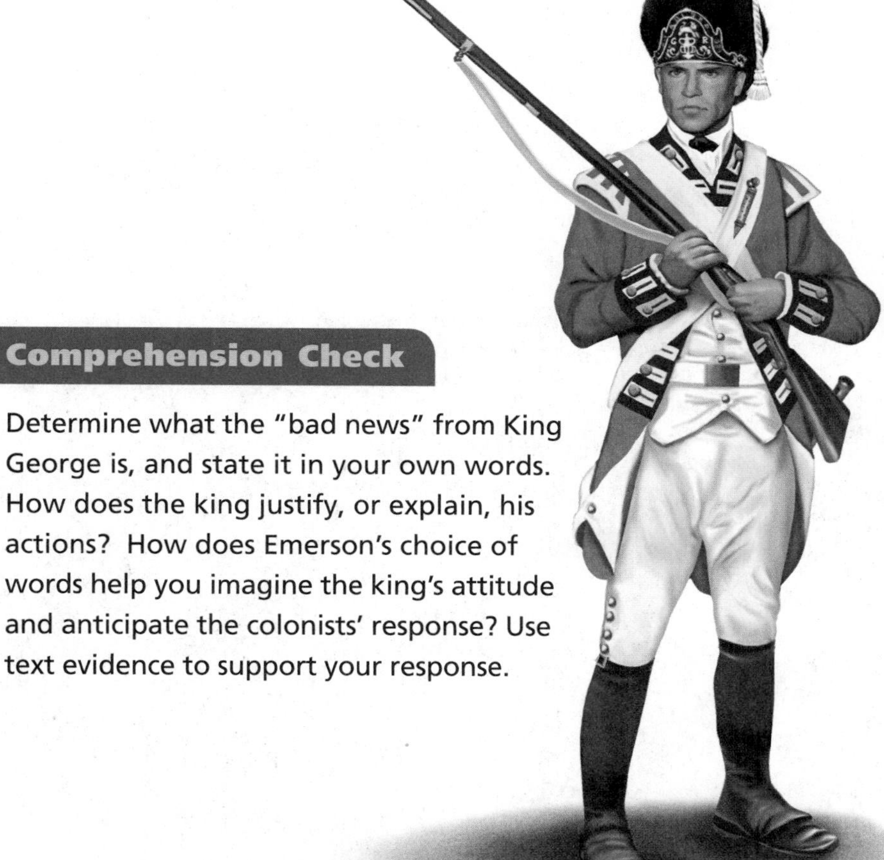

Comprehension Check

Determine what the "bad news" from King George is, and state it in your own words. How does the king justify, or explain, his actions? How does Emerson's choice of words help you imagine the king's attitude and anticipate the colonists' response? Use text evidence to support your response.

Guided Instruction

CITE EVIDENCE

C An **allusion** is a reference to a well-known person, event, or thing—or even to another text. Put an asterisk next to the line that makes a claim about Boston's roads. How is this line similar to the famous saying, "All roads lead to Rome"? What does this allusion add to the poem's meaning?

D Emerson wrote this poem in 1873, but some of the words and sentence structures he uses are archaic, or old-fashioned, even for his time. Double underline words and phrases on this page that seem archaic, suggesting a much earlier era. What time period do these words suggest? How do these words affect the **tone** and **meaning** of the poem?

E Circle the descriptive phrases that connote, or suggest, that Boston is a safe and secure city. What do these descriptions compare Boston to?

Guided Practice

RL.8.4

WORDS TO KNOW

abundant
bounteous
faltered
homely
wafted

CITE EVIDENCE

A Working with a partner, circle the lines on these two pages that personify Boston. How does the author's use of personification give the city of Boston its own character?

B Lafayette was a French military officer who became a general under George Washington in the Revolutionary War and fought for American freedom. Underline the lines that make an analogy, or comparison, to Lafayette. Work with a partner to determine the meaning of this analogy.

Boston *continued*

"Not so," said Boston, "good my lord,
We pay your governors here
Abundant for their bed and board,
Six thousand pounds a year.
(Your highness knows our **homely** word,)
Millions for self-government,
But for tribute never a cent."

The cargo came! and who could blame
If *Indians* seized the tea,
And, chest by chest, let down the same
Into the laughing sea?
For what avail the plough or sail
Or land or life, if freedom fail?

The townsmen braved the English king,
Found friendship in the French,
And Honor joined the patriot ring
Low on their wooden bench.

O **bounteous** seas that never fail!
  O day remembered yet!
O happy port that spied the sail
  Which **wafted** Lafayette!
  Pole-star of light in Europe's night,
  That never **faltered** from the right.

Kings shook with fear, old empires crave
  The secret force to find
Which fired the little State to save
  The rights of all mankind.

Comprehension Check

1. What does *tribute* mean in line 75?

a. goods exchanged in trade

b. wages for work

c. gift to a subject

d. payment to a ruler

2. Who are the "Indians" in the poem?

a. Englishmen in disguise

b. Bostonians in disguise

c. Frenchmen in disguise

d. American Indians in disguise

3. Which clues in the text support the correct answer to question 2?

a. the mention of the English king

b. the use of italics on the word *Indians*

c. the reference to a French general

d. the personification of Boston

4. Why does the poet say the townsmen "braved" the British king?

a. to make an allusion

b. to employ personification

c. because they were in disguise

d. to show their courage

5. How does understanding the connotations of words in this section of the poem help you understand the attitude of the Bostonians?

Independent Practice

RL.8.4

WORDS TO KNOW

clung
dweller
hurled
province

CITE EVIDENCE

A What ideas or places are personified in this section of the poem? Put an asterisk by each example of personification. Who is "her" in lines 106 and 108–109?

B Underline descriptive words that have a joyous or happy connotation. How do these words help you understand how the Bostonians feel after resisting King George?

Boston *continued*

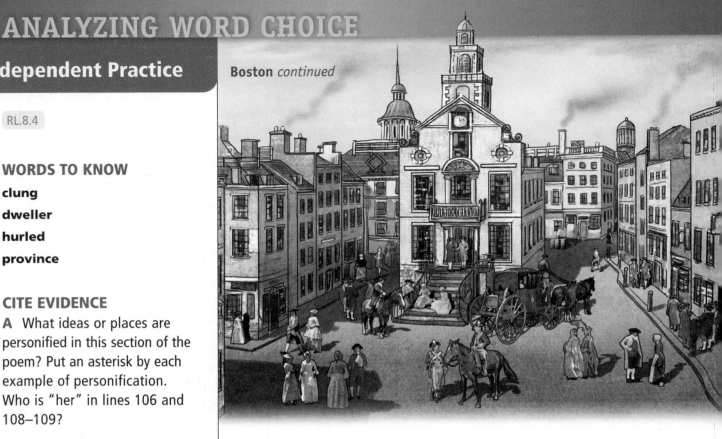

But right is might through all the world
  Province to province faithful **clung**,
Through good and ill the war-bolt **hurled**,
  Till Freedom cheered and the joy-bells rung.

The sea returning day by day
  Restores the world-wide mart;
So let each **dweller** on the Bay
  Fold Boston in his heart,
Till these echoes be choked with snows,
  Or over the town blue ocean flows.

Let the blood of her hundred thousands
  Throb in each manly vein;
And the wit of all her wisest
  Make sunshine in her brain.
  For you can teach the lightning speech,
  And round the globe your voices reach.

And each shall care for other,
  And each to each shall bend,
To the poor a noble brother,
  To the good an equal friend.

A blessing through the ages thus
Shield all thy roofs and towers!
God with the fathers, so with us,
Thou darling town of ours!

Comprehension Check

MORE ONLINE **sadlierconnect.com**

1. What personification does Emerson use to convey the joy of Boston's triumph?

a. "Freedom cheered. . ."

b. "The sea returning day by day. . ."

c. "Let the blood. . . /Throb in each manly vein."

d. "Till these echoes be choked with snows. . ."

2. Words and phrases such as "each to each" and "equal" in lines 112–115 suggest

a. a sense of duty.

b. a sense of victory.

c. a sense of equality.

d. a sense of history.

3. According to this section of the poem, why do the Bostonians win?

a. The king's army wasn't strong enough.

b. No one would have bought tea anyway.

c. They have right on their side.

d. They have much more military training.

4. The last four lines of the poem include all of the following except

a. repetition

b. personification

c. allusion

d. analogy

5. Think about the Bostonians' attitude as described in this final section of the poem. Describe the tone of this section. Use details from the text to support your answer.

Guided Instruction

RL.8.5, RH.8.5

WORDS TO KNOW

acclimate
boardinghouse
contraption
resonant
woe

Text structure is the way a text is organized. Text structure can refer to text format, such as chapters in a book or scenes in a play. It can also refer to the way ideas are presented, such as through description, cause/effect, or comparison/contrast. Text structure contributes to the **meaning** and **style** of a work.

CITE EVIDENCE

A A big decision authors make when they set out to tell a story is how to **structure the text** to convey information in the most effective way. Underline the setting in this text. How does the author present this information?

B Circle the name of the main character in this text. How does the author reveal this information? Why might the author have chosen this **text structure** to present a narrative with the title "A Mill Girl's Story"?

A Mill Girl's Story

(Genre: Realistic Fiction)

February 10, 1843
Dear Papa and Mama,

1 Today I finally reached my destination of the city of Lowell, Massachusetts; it is so different here, nothing at all like our farm in Vermont. The ticket taker on the coach told me that about 20,000 residents live in this growing city, so it is no wonder the streets bustle with activity; all of the people and noise make me so anxious!

2 It is so strange to think that I am miles away from everything I have ever known; it is hard to believe that only a few short weeks ago I answered an advertisement calling for girls and women aged 15 to 35 to work in the textile mills of northern Massachusetts.

3 At the time, it seemed like the answer to our money **woes**; however, I now worry that I have made a perilous mistake. I have never held a job before; how will I manage? How will I thrive, or even survive, in a city when all I have ever known is the country life? I am only sixteen years old; I do not think I am strong enough to handle this—please keep me in your thoughts!

Love, Sarah

March 5, 1843
Dear Papa and Mama,

4 Slowly, I have begun to **acclimate** to city life; I stay in a **boardinghouse** not far from the factory where I work, and all of the tenants are girls who work at the textile mill. There are about thirty residents, and I share a room with three others; there is very little privacy, and it feels odd to be so close to strangers all the time. Also, our room is small, only big enough for the beds, a chair, and a desk; so it is very cramped and crowded.

5 However, there are some good things about life in a boardinghouse; there is a full kitchen with a well-stocked pantry and an iron stove with an oven. I have never seen such a **contraption** before because I have only ever cooked food in a fireplace; I thought the food might taste unusual, but on the contrary, the meals are delicious. We eat in a large dining room with several tables, and there is a parlor where the tenants can sit together after work.

6 Mama will be pleased to learn that a house matron lives in the boardinghouse, too. She is very stern and strict and makes sure we all obey the rules; there are also curfews, so no staying out past nine o'clock at night!

Love, Sarah

April 1, 1843
Dear Papa and Mama,

7 The work at the mill is so different from our chores on the farm; we do not plant or pick crops here, nor do we cook or clean. Instead, we run industrial machines to spin threads from cotton fibers and weave them into cloth. One of the workers left an amusing note for me on my first day that said, "Our work at the cloth factory is sew much fun, it leaves us in stitches!"

8 My day begins at 4:30 in the morning. A clanging bell in a tower wakes everyone in the boardinghouse; the **resonant** sound is very different from a rooster's crow!

9 Some of the girls grumble as they stir in their beds, but I am used to rising in the early morning hours from living on a farm. After getting dressed, we report to the dining hall, where a heavy breakfast is served to all the tenants.

Comprehension Check

How is this text structured? How does the author use the structure to present information? What are the advantages and disadvantages of telling Sarah's story in this way? Cite evidence from the text in your response.

CITE EVIDENCE

C Authors can create different formats, or organizational structures, within literary forms like poems and stories. A long poem might be written in groups of stanzas that are organized like book chapters. Draw a box around three elements on this page that help you identify the text structure of this story. How does this format add to the realism of the story?

D Text structure may also refer to how ideas are presented, such as through description, cause/effect, or comparison. Place an asterisk next to each paragraph on this page in which Sarah comments on an aspect of her new life that is not the same as her old life. What text structure does the author use to present this information?

Guided Instruction

RL.8.5, RH.8.5

WORDS TO KNOW

anew
friction
periodical
repast
tuition

CITE EVIDENCE

A Underline the sentence that identifies where Sarah works. Then circle the description of the power that operates this place. What kind of text structure is used in this passage?

B Place an asterisk next to the paragraph in which Sarah directly addresses her family. What do you learn about her here? If this narrative were told in a conventional short story format, how might the author have conveyed this information?

A Mill Girl's Story *continued*

10 Then it is off to work for the Merrimack Manufacturing Company at a two-story textile mill constructed beside the Merrimack River. Rushing river water pours into a water wheel in the basement; it turns gears that rotate a shaft on the factory floor above. The shaft connects to a series of belts and pulleys that hang over our heads from the ceiling, and together they provide the power for every machine in the textile mill.

11 By five o'clock in the morning, the mill's spinning machines begin to run. I am one of three dozen workers who operate the machines. Most of the employees are young women in their mid-twenties; nevertheless, a number of workers are my age, or very close to it.

12 I stand at my station from early in the morning until seven o'clock at night; as night begins to fall, the bell in the tower clangs again, and I walk back to the boardinghouse for the evening **repast**. After dinner there is time to read or sew in the parlor before I shuffle off to bed, bone-tired and ready for sleep. Then, at 4:30 the next morning, the bell tower clangs and my daily routine begins **anew**.

13 At the end of the day, my feet are swollen and sore from standing for so long, my hands and fingers ache from operating the machine, and the temples in my head throb from all the dust, commotion, and noise in the factory. My heart aches too because I miss you all so much, but I know now that I am doing the right thing. I have enclosed money to help with Robert's **tuition**, and I hope he is faring well at college; please send love to my brother from me.

Love, Sarah

May 22, 1843
Dear Papa and Mama,

14 I have made several friends here in Lowell, and my companions all live in my boardinghouse and work at the textile mill as well. I also see Cousin Eliza frequently; she lives in another boardinghouse several streets away, and we visit each other from time to time.

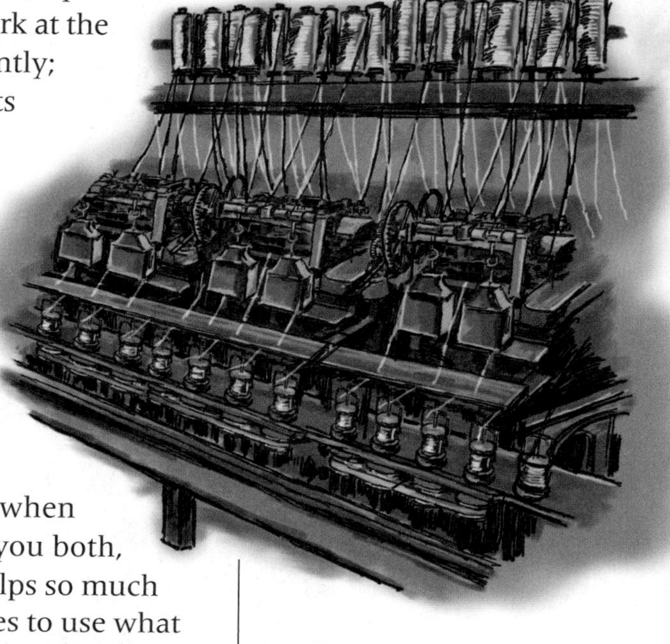

15 My friends and I gather on Saturday afternoons to share poetry, stories, or songs that we have written. I have composed several poems about my life here in Lowell; it helps to express my thoughts and feelings about being a "mill girl." I have sent one of my poems to a local literary **periodical** called *The Lowell Offering*, and the editor has promised to publish it; I will send you a clipping in the mail when I receive the issue. Although I continue to miss you both, and also Robert and Joseph, and little Anna, it helps so much to have good companions, as well as opportunities to use what small talent I have with words to convey the details of my experiences here.

Love, Sarah

June 10, 1843
Dear Papa and Mama,

16 You will never believe what happened today; a fire broke out in the factory! **Friction** from the moving belts that run the machines caused a spark, and a leather belt burst into flames. The workers all stopped and stared mutely, unsure what to do; I, however, knew exactly how to respond. With the memory of the barn fire from last spring whirling around my head, I quickly gathered everyone together and told them to go to the basement with buckets.

Comprehension Check

How does the structure of this story help you understand the main character's thoughts, feelings, and personality?

CITE EVIDENCE

C Box a sentence in which Sarah directly expresses an important change in how she feels about her new life. If this narrative had followed a more conventional short-story structure, how might the author have revealed this information?

D Double underline an incident that occurs in the factory. How would the style and tone of the text that follows be different if this were a newspaper article?

Guided Practice

RL.8.5, RH.8.5

WORDS TO KNOW

burgeoning
contagion
extinguish
grueling
lauded
workforce

A Mill Girl's Story *continued*

17 We hurriedly dipped the buckets into the water wheel and carried them back to the factory floor, using the river water to fully **extinguish** the fire. Everyone **lauded** me as a hero, and for a time I rather felt like one! I only wish I could be a true hero and do something to improve the working conditions in the textile mill; it has become a struggle to labor there day after day.

Love, Sarah

July 18, 1843
Dear Papa and Mama,

18 The long, **grueling** hours have begun to take a toll; it is back-breaking to stay on my feet for 12 to 13 hours a day. Also, the factory owners refuse to open the windows to let in fresh air; in fact, they have gone so far as to nail the windows shut! So, the air we breathe is filled with fumes and **contagions**. I worry about staying well in such unhealthy, uncomfortable conditions.

19 Several of the women have begun to talk about forming a labor union, and I have decided to join them because I believe I can help make a difference. My experiences here have taught me that I am as strong and as powerful as the rushing water that runs the mill.

Love, Sarah

* * * *

20 Although the story you have just read is fictional, it represents the experiences of many young women who lived and worked in Lowell in the 1800s. The Boston Associates, a group of investors, began operating textile mills in the **burgeoning** city starting in 1822. Over the years the mills hired thousands of young women as factory workers. At one time, women made up three-quarters of the **workforce**, and many of these workers came from family farms all over New England.

CITE EVIDENCE

A Circle the words that reveal Sarah's first-person point of view in paragraph 19. In a conventional short story structure, how would the author likely present Sarah's thoughts and beliefs here?

B Draw a box around the paragraph that begins a shift in the text structure. What is the purpose of this paragraph? Why is it presented in this text structure?

21 The Lowell Mill Girls, as they came to be known, worked in very difficult conditions. In 1845 they organized a labor union and successfully fought for a reduced workday; their efforts helped improve working conditions for workers across New England.

Comprehension Check

1. The text structure of paragraph 18 is

a. flashback.

b. cause and effect.

c. comparison/contrast.

d. problem and solution.

2. Paragraph 19 suggests that the solution to the problems in the textile mill that Sarah has identified in her letters is

a. opening the factory windows to let in fresh air.

b. getting the women together to form a labor union.

c. getting the workers together to talk to the factory's owners.

d. working to clean up the unhealthy conditions in the factory.

3. How do paragraphs 20 and 21 differ from the rest of the selection?

a. The paragraphs are narrative text.

b. The paragraphs are dramatic text.

c. The paragraphs are informational text.

d. The paragraphs are persuasive text.

4. The last two paragraphs of the selection are included mainly to let the reader know that

a. Sarah's story is based on historical fact.

b. the letters are real and Sarah was an actual person.

c. labor unions in the United States have been around since 1845.

d. conditions in textile mills today are much better than in the 1800s.

5. Work with a partner to describe how a reader's understanding of "A Mill Girl's Story" might change if the author presented it as a conventional narrative told from a third-person point of view.

____

____

____

____

____

Independent Practice

RL.8.5, RH.8.5

WORDS TO KNOW

oppressive
sentinel
stifling
throng

CITE EVIDENCE

A Underline the poem's similes—comparisons made using the words *like* or *as*. How does the way the poem's speaker describes the factory differ from the way Sarah describes it? What accounts for these differences?

B Circle the lines that describe the mill machinery as a living thing. How does the description of machinery in the poem differ in language, tone, and text structure from the descriptions you read in "A Mill Girl's Story"?

Human or Machine?

(Genre: Poetry)

As dawn breaks, the water rushes in.
The wheel grinds;
The machines pump;
The work begins.

The **throng** pours through the factory gate,
Like oil through a funnel;
Each to a station to stand **sentinel**.

Running belts, cranking pulleys;
Spinning thread, shifting looms;
The steady thrum of the machines;
The steady throb of my temples.

The air, hot and **oppressive**,
Smothers me like a blanket—
Stifling each breath!

The machine beside me feels alive.
It moves in jerks and jolts;
It speaks in bangs and clangs.

As dusk descends, the flow of water ends.
The wheel slows;
The machines stop;
The work ends.

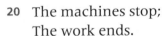

The **throng** drifts out of the factory gate,
Like smoke from a chimney,
Into the cool air of a lonely night.

Comprehension Check

MORE ONLINE **sadlierconnect.com**

1. The text structure of "Human or Machine?" can best be described as

a. a narrative written in lines.

b. a poem written as a letter.

c. a poem written in stanzas.

d. a drama written in scenes.

2. How does the structure of "Human or Machine?" contribute to its meaning?

a. Its poetic structure allows it to focus on sensory details.

b. Its poetic structure allows it to present character development over time.

c. Its poetic structure allows it to explore intricate cause-and-effect relationships.

d. Its poetic structure allows it to explain the technological workings of a textile mill.

3. Which of the following could a poem convey more effectively than narrative fiction?

a. powerful images of a particular person, place, or thing

b. changes in a person's viewpoint over a period of time

c. explanations of a technological process

d. a recollection of a particular moment in time

4. How are "Human or Machine?" and "A Mill Girl's Story" most alike?

a. Both present a bit of the history of a specific textile mill that actually existed.

b. Both convey how difficult and unpleasant it was to work in a textile mill.

c. Both describe the loneliness of being away from family.

d. Both explain why some people sought work at the mills.

5. How might the reader's understanding of "Human or Machine?" change if the author presented it as a series of letters from the worker to family members?

Guided Instruction

RL.8.6

WORDS TO KNOW

apprehension
frailty
instinct
intangible
subtle
temperamental

Each character in a story has a **point of view,** or a perspective, about the story's events. An author can create such effects as **suspense** or **humor** through the use of point of view. A reader brings a point of view as well, which contributes to a story's effect. For example, **dramatic irony** is created when a reader knows more about what is happening than a character does.

CITE EVIDENCE

A Authors may choose to tell a story from one of several different points of view. In the **third-person omniscient point of view,** a narrator knows what each character is thinking. Underline the main character and an example of his thoughts.

B The omniscient point of view can also reveal the narrator's thoughts. Circle a sentence that tells what the narrator thinks is the man's basic flaw.

To Build a Fire

by Jack London (abridged)

(Genre: Adventure)

1 Day had broken cold and grey, exceedingly cold and grey, when the man turned aside from the main Yukon trail and climbed the high earth-bank, where a dim and little-travelled trail led eastward through the fat spruce timberland. It was a steep bank, and he paused for breath at the top, excusing the act to himself by looking at his watch. It was nine o'clock. There was no sun nor hint of sun, though there was not a cloud in the sky. It was a clear day, and yet there seemed an **intangible** pall over the face of things, a **subtle** gloom that made the day dark, and that was due to the absence of sun. This fact did not worry the man. He was used to the lack of sun. . . .

2 The man flung a look back along the way he had come. The Yukon lay a mile wide and hidden under three feet of ice. On top of this ice were as many feet of snow . . . . North and south, as far as his eye could see, it was unbroken white . . . . save for a dark hairline that curved and twisted from around the spruce-covered island to the south, and that curved and twisted away into the north, where it disappeared behind another spruce-covered island . . . .

3 But all this—the mysterious, far-reaching hairline trail, the absence of sun from the sky, the tremendous cold, and the strangeness and weirdness of it all—made no impression on the man. It was not because he was long used to it. He was a newcomer in the land, a *chechaquo*, and this was his first winter. The trouble with him was that he was without imagination. He was quick and alert in the things of life, but only in the things, and not in the significances. Fifty degrees below zero meant eighty odd degrees of frost. Such fact impressed him as being cold and uncomfortable, and that was all. It did not lead him to meditate upon his **frailty** as a creature of temperature, and upon man's frailty in general, able only to live within certain narrow limits of heat and cold . . . .

RL.8.6

4 ... Undoubtedly it was colder than fifty below—how much colder he did not know. But the temperature did not matter. He was bound for the old claim on the left fork of Henderson Creek ... He would be in to camp by six o'clock; a bit after dark, it was true, but the boys would be there, a fire would be going, and a hot supper would be ready....

5 At the man's heels trotted a dog, a big native husky, the proper wolf-dog, grey-coated and without any visible or **temperamental** difference from its brother, the wild wolf. The animal was depressed by the tremendous cold. It knew that it was no time for travelling. Its **instinct** told it a truer tale than was told to the man by the man's judgment. In reality, it was not merely colder than fifty below zero; it was colder than sixty below, than seventy below. It was seventy-five below zero. Since the freezing point is thirty-two above zero, it meant that one hundred and seven degrees of frost obtained. The dog did not know anything about thermometers. Possibly in its brain there was no sharp consciousness of a condition of very cold such as was in the man's brain. But the brute had its instinct. It experienced a vague but menacing **apprehension** that subdued it and made it slink along at the man's heels, and that made it question eagerly every unwonted movement of the man as if expecting him to go into camp or to seek shelter somewhere and build a fire. The dog had learned fire, and it wanted fire, or else to burrow under the snow and cuddle its warmth away from the air.

The man and dog walk for several miles until they reach the frozen Henderson Creek, about ten miles from the first stopping point. Though the man's cheeks and nose are numb by this point, he does not think this is serious. He makes his way carefully around the creek area, wary of "traps": unfrozen pools of water from springs under the ice and snow. He sends the dog ahead of him, and the dog falls through the ice, wetting its legs. The dog instinctively bites the ice out of its toes.

Comprehension Check

A narrator who is not a character in a story may still have a point of view about events and characters. What is the narrator's point of view regarding the main character? Cite evidence from the text in your response.

Guided Instruction

CITE EVIDENCE

C Box the text that describes what the man thinks the outcome of his trek will be. What does this text tell you about his perspective on his situation?

D The omniscient point of view can reveal every character's thoughts. What does the man's dog know that the man does not? Circle the evidence.

E Dramatic irony describes a situation in which the reader has information or knowledge that a character in the story does not have. Dramatic irony can create suspense—a feeling of anxiety or anticipation about what will happen next in a story. Double underline a detail in paragraph 5 that the reader knows but the man does not know. Why does the author include this information? How does it add to the suspense you feel?

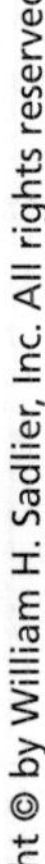

Guided Instruction

RL.8.6

WORDS TO KNOW

agitation

ancestry

avalanche

capsized

conflagration

CITE EVIDENCE

A Circle the sentences that introduce dramatic irony by describing what the dog knows that the man does not know.

B Underline the sentences that reveal the man's point of view toward the advice the old-timer at Sulphur Creek had given him about the weather in Yukon Territory. What do these thoughts tell you about the man?

To Build a Fire *continued*

At half past noon the man reaches the forks and stops to eat lunch, successfully building a fire. Intent on reaching the camp by six o'clock, he quickly moves on, though the dog instinctively knows that it is dangerous to forge ahead in such conditions.

6 The dog was disappointed and yearned back toward the fire. This man did not know cold. Possibly all the generations of his **ancestry** had been ignorant of cold, of real cold, of cold one hundred and seven degrees below freezing point. But the dog knew; all its ancestry knew, and it had inherited the knowledge. And it knew that it was not good to walk abroad in such fearful cold. It was the time to lie snug in a hole in the snow and wait for a curtain of cloud to be drawn across the face of outer space whence this cold came.

The man, thinking there are fewer noticeable "traps" in this part of the creek area, suddenly breaks through snow and ends up in water up to his knees. Angrily, he stops to build another fire to dry out his footgear. He finds some dry firewood among the spruce trees and works to build a fire.

7 . . . The fire was a success. He was safe. He remembered the advice of the old-timer on Sulphur Creek, and smiled. The old-timer had been very serious in laying down the law that no man must travel alone in the Klondike after fifty below. Well, here he was; he had had the accident; he was alone; and he had saved himself. . . . All a man had to do was to keep his head, and he was all right. Any man who was a man could travel alone. But it was surprising, the rapidity with which his cheeks and nose were freezing. And he had not thought his fingers could go lifeless in so short a time. Lifeless they were, for he could scarcely make them move together to grip a twig, and they seemed remote from his body and from him . . . .

8 There was the fire, snapping and crackling and promising life with every dancing flame. He started to untie his moccasins. They were coated with ice; the thick German socks were like sheaths of iron halfway to the knees; and the mocassin strings were like rods of steel all twisted and knotted as by some **conflagration**. For a moment he tugged with his numbed fingers, then, realizing the folly of it, he drew his sheath knife.

RL.8.6

Guided Instruction

9 But before he could cut the strings, it happened. It was his own fault, or, rather, his mistake. He should not have built the fire under the spruce tree. . . . Each time he had pulled a twig he had communicated a slight **agitation** to the tree. . . . High up in the tree one bough **capsized** its load of snow. This fell on the boughs beneath, capsizing them. This process continued, spreading out and involving the whole tree. It grew like an **avalanche**, and it descended without warning upon the man and the fire, and the fire was blotted out! Where it had burned was a mantle of fresh and disordered snow.

10 The man was shocked. It was as though he had just heard his own sentence of death. For a moment he sat and stared at the spot where the fire had been. Then he grew very calm. Perhaps the old-timer on Sulphur Creek was right. If he had only had a trail-mate he would have been in no danger now. The trail-mate could have built the fire. Well, it was up to him to build the fire over again, and this second time there must be no failure. Even if he succeeded, he would most likely lose some toes. His feet must be badly frozen by now, and there would be some time before the second fire was ready.

The man starts to build a second fire, out in the open, but he cannot use his fingers. His large bunch of matches falls to the ground. He struggles to pick them up and has to use his teeth to take hold of one match. It takes him twenty tries to light the match by holding it in his teeth and scratching it against his leg. Just as he gets it to light, he coughs and the match falls into the snow.

The man tries again, using the heel of his palms to pick up and hold the entire bunch of seventy matches, which he accidentally lights up all at once. As he holds the burning mass, his hands catch on fire, but he holds on. He starts a fire, adding twigs and grasses to make it burn more, but he is shivering so much that he scatters the twigs, and the little fire sputters out.

Comprehension Check

Explain the sequences of events that lead to the second and third fires going out. What details make the situation particularly suspenseful? In your answer, consider the man's point of view and the mood of the story.

CITE EVIDENCE

C Double underline the sentence that tells you what mistake the man realizes he has made. Is this the first mistake he has made? Explain.

D Underline the description of what happens to the first fire. How does this description build suspense? Explain what the incident reveals about the man.

E Place an asterisk next to the paragraph that shows a sharp change in the man's thoughts and attitude toward his situation. What is the effect of this change on the story?

Guided Practice

RL.8.6

WORDS TO KNOW

apathetically
carcass
floundered
poignant
wistful

CITE EVIDENCE

A Underline the sentence that describes how the dog's point of view toward the man changes at this point in the story. What is the dog reacting to? What effect does this change create for the reader?

B Double underline the statement in paragraph 13 that describes how the man's perspective changes. How does recognizing this shift in point of view add to the suspense?

To Build a Fire *continued*

11 The fire-provider had failed. As he looked **apathetically** about him, his eyes chanced on the dog, sitting across the ruins of the fire from him, in the snow, making restless, hunching movements, slightly lifting one forefoot and then the other, shifting its weight back and forth on them with **wistful** eagerness.

12 The sight of the dog put a wild idea into his head. He remembered the tale of the man, caught in a blizzard, who killed a steer and crawled inside the **carcass**, and so was saved. He would kill the dog and bury his hands in the warm body until the numbness went out of them. Then he could build another fire. He spoke to the dog, calling it to him; but in his voice was a strange note of fear that frightened the animal, who had never known the man to speak in such a way before. Something was the matter, and its suspicious nature sensed danger,—it knew not what danger but somewhere, somehow, in its brain arose an apprehension of the man. . . .

The man calls to the dog, and the dog comes to him. Using his arms, the man grabs the dog, who struggles against him. But the man realizes that his frozen hands are useless. He releases the dog and notes that his hands are like dead weights at the ends of his arms.

13 A certain fear of death, dull and oppressive, came to him. This fear quickly became **poignant** as he realized that it was no longer a mere matter of freezing his fingers and toes, or of losing his hands and feet, but that it was a matter of life and death with the chances against him. This threw him into a panic, and he turned and ran up the creek-bed along the old, dim trail. The dog joined in behind and kept up with him. He ran blindly, without intention, in fear such as he had never known in his life.

14 Slowly, as he ploughed and **floundered** through the snow, he began to see things again—the banks of the creek, the old timber-jams, the leafless aspens, and the sky. The running made him feel better. He did not shiver. Maybe, if he ran on, his feet would thaw out; and, anyway, if he ran far enough, he would reach camp and the boys. Without doubt he would lose some fingers and toes and some of his face; but the boys would take care of him, and save the rest of him when he got there. . . .

Comprehension Check

1. Which of the following is an example of dramatic irony that increases suspense in this part of the story?

a. We know that the man plans to kill the dog, but the dog does not know.

b. We and the dog both know that the man plans to kill the dog.

c. The narrator knows that the man plans to kill the dog, but we only suspect it.

d. The man does not know that he plans to kill the dog, but we and the dog know it.

2. What causes the man to start running in paragraph 13?

a. He panics as he realizes he could die.

b. He fears he might lose his hands and feet.

c. He feels guilty about the dog.

d. He thinks he can thaw out his feet.

3. What would the man have done differently if he knew everything the reader knew?

a. He would have traveled earlier in the day and brought more matches with him.

b. He would not have traveled alone and would have built a fire in a safer place.

c. He would have checked the weather report and not brought the dog along.

d. He would have brought more food and a map to the location of the camp.

4. How might the story differ if the main character knew as much as the reader?

a. It would be less realistic.

b. It would be more realistic.

c. It would be less suspenseful.

d. It would be more suspenseful.

5. How is your perspective as a reader similar to or different from the main character's perspective in this part of the story?

Independent Practice

RL.8.6

WORDS TO KNOW

anesthetic
bristle
conception
yearning

CITE EVIDENCE

A Place an asterisk next to the paragraph that shows how the main character's point of view changes in this part of the story. Describe the process that has brought the main character to this perspective on his situation.

B Underline the main character's changed opinion of the old man at Sulphur Creek. How does this change in the main character's perspective affect your own views of the story?

To Build a Fire *continued*

The man keeps running, but stumbles and falls. Sitting, he realizes that he is no longer shivering but feels "warm and comfortable." A vision of his body totally frozen frightens him enough that he tries running again. Then he falls one last time.

15 When he had recovered his breath and control, he sat up and entertained in his mind the **conception** of meeting death with dignity. . . . [H]e was bound to freeze anyway, and he might as well take it decently. With this new-found peace of mind came the first glimmerings of drowsiness. A good idea, he thought, to sleep off to death. It was like taking an **anesthetic**. Freezing was not so bad as people thought. There were lots worse ways to die.

16 He pictured the boys finding his body the next day. Suddenly he found himself with them, coming along the trail and looking for himself. And, still with them, he came around a turn in the trail and found himself lying in the snow. . . . He drifted on from this to a vision of the old-timer on Sulphur Creek. He could see him quite clearly, warm and comfortable, and smoking a pipe.

17 "You were right, old hoss; you were right," the man mumbled to the old-timer of Sulphur Creek.

18 Then the man drowsed off into what seemed to him the most comfortable and satisfying sleep he had ever known. The dog sat facing him and waiting. The brief day drew to a close in a long, slow twilight. There were no signs of a fire to be made, and, besides, never in the dog's experience had it known a man to sit like that in the snow and make no fire. As the twilight drew on, its eager **yearning** for the fire mastered it, and with a great

lifting and shifting of forefeet, it whined softly, then flattened its ears down in anticipation of being chidden by the man. But the man remained silent.

19 Later, the dog whined loudly. And still later it crept close to the man and caught the scent of death. This made the animal **bristle** and back away. A little longer it delayed, howling under the stars that leaped and danced and shone brightly in the cold sky. Then it turned and trotted up the trail in the direction of the camp it knew, where were the other food-providers and fire-providers.

Comprehension Check

MORE ONLINE **sadlierconnect.com**

1. What perspective does the man adopt after he falls for the last time?

a. He accepts the idea of death.

b. He learns to respect the dog.

c. He curses the foul weather.

d. He rages against his fate.

2. Which of the following is the central dramatic irony of this story?

a. The reader knows more than the dog and the man know.

b. The man knows more than the reader and the narrator know.

c. The narrator, the reader, and the dog know more than the man knows.

d. The dog knows more than the narrator and the man know.

3. What does the reader know that the dog does not when the man falls asleep?

a. The man is ill.

b. The man is cold.

c. The man is dying.

d. The man is dreaming.

4. In this story, the use of dramatic irony

a. creates humor.

b. highlights contrasts.

c. is more important than theme.

d. builds suspense.

5. How has analyzing different perspectives—the narrator's, the main character's, the dog's, and your own as a reader—helped you gain meaning from this story?

____

____

____

____

Life at Colony Camp: A Blog

(Genre: Science Fiction)

About Me
Name: Soledad Suarez
Age: Thirteen
Hometown: Chicago
Hobbies: Star-mapping, playing soccer, four-dimensional strategy games

April 1, 2073

Here We Go!

1 It is nighttime, and I sit at a computer nervously creating my first blog post. Everyone here is expected to share the good, the bad, and the freaky at Colony Camp. I'm with my parents and my younger brother Ramon; we are in training to move to Mars.

2 We arrived from Chicago last week. It was very difficult to say goodbye to my friends and my old life. I feel as if I'm about to become part of a Swiss Family Robinson, making a home in a faraway place using whatever resources we have at hand. But there's one big difference: we aren't going to be lost castaways trying to survive in the wilderness. We're part of a well-trained group of explorers who freely and knowingly signed up for the experience—no matter how challenging it turns out to be.

3 For the next two months, we will reside at the camp in Pensacola, Florida, and get intensive training on how to live on Mars. I have been into space before, of course; I mean, who hasn't taken a vacation on the moon? But it's an enormous responsibility, and I'm anxious; I hope I have what it takes to make it as a colonist on Mars. On the other hand, my little brother is enthusiastic and charged up about everything and can't wait to start training. We begin tomorrow.

April 2, 2073

All About Mars

4 This morning we attended a lecture by Counselor Kapoor, and I made certain I took copious and accurate notes. We learned a lot about the burgeoning colony and the planet we will soon call home. Naturally, I already knew that Mars is one of the closest planets to Earth, but this morning, I was also reminded that it will take us about eight months to travel through space to reach the colony. I keep forgetting that it takes that long. I still can't imagine being stuck in a spaceship for that length of time, and I hope we won't feel like sardines stuffed inside a tin can. I must remember to stock up on books, games, and movies before takeoff to help pass the time.

5 It was interesting to learn something new: that Mars has one of the biggest volcanoes in the known universe. Let's hope it doesn't erupt while we're there! The planet also has two moons; one is called Phobos, and the other is called Deimos. I wonder if they are ever both full at the same time. I try imagining what that might look like, and I envision two headlights in the sky that beam out into the unending darkness of space.

RL.8.4, RL.8.5, RL.8.6, RL.8.10

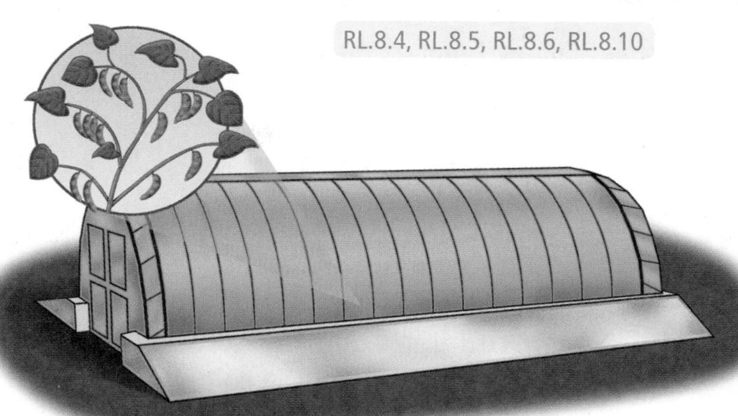

6 Mars is called the Red Planet, which makes a lot of sense since red rocks cover the surface. As a result, nothing can grow on the Martian surface. However, our scientists have set up greenhouses for farming. My family will be working in one of these greenhouses, and we will soon take classes to learn about greenhouse agriculture.

7 Typically, each greenhouse comes equipped with solar panels to provide sunlight for the growing plants and a water system to provide irrigation. We will need to know how it all works and how to cultivate the finest crops.

April 11, 2073

Our Daily Routine

8 Every day at Colony Camp, we wake at six in the morning, get dressed, and head to the dining hall to eat breakfast with the other new colonists. There are a dozen families in all, and we will travel together in the shuttle and all live in the same facility on Mars. Since we'll be spending a lot of time together, we have been trying to get to know our future neighbors and become friends.

9 After breakfast, we have lessons on greenhouse farming. Each family will be responsible for a different crop. The Suarezes—that's me and my family—are on soybean duty. Soybeans are very important for the colony; they're used to manufacture lots of different products, including vegetable oil, soy milk, and even tofu. Since it's one of the most valuable crops in the entire colony, there's a lot of pressure on us to make sure we know exactly what to do!

10 Following a lunch break, we have lessons to prepare us for colony life. We have a map of the planetary surface and the layout of the colony and are memorizing how to get around. We're also discovering how to use the vehicles and other equipment at the colony. Then we take a dinner break and have free time for the rest of the day.

April 23, 2073

Look Ma, No Gravity!

11 Today we spent our first day in the zero-gravity chamber. There's minimal gravity out in space, so anything that isn't nailed down floats. While traveling from Earth to Mars, we will have to know how to maneuver around the space shuttle. Therefore, Counselor Roberts taught us how to somersault through the air. Everyone got the hang of it really quickly. Even my little brother Ramon was somersaulting well enough to join The Celestial Circus. However, it took me a long time to become acclimated to zero gravity and to do the technique properly. I was so embarrassed, I wanted to crawl into the nearest closet!

12 When we finally arrive on Mars, there will be gravity, but it's only 40 percent of the gravity we experience on Earth. Consequently, we will have to wear special boots that will allow us to move around the planet's surface. The counselors gave us each a pair to try on, and when I looked at them, I immediately thought, "Oh great, they're exactly what I need—the world's ugliest boots!"

Life at Colony Camp *continued*

May 2, 2073

A Scary Day

13 Today we spent the entire day in a model of our future home on Mars to learn about the life-support system, which will provide oxygen, running water, and a source of power for our home on the colony. Oxygen is critical because the air on Mars is mostly carbon dioxide, and human beings can't survive on that.

14 Overly excited about everything, Ramon started pressing buttons, and he somehow pushed one connected to the air filters. Rapidly, we began to lose fresh air. Working frantically, we tried to fix the problem, but apparently there was a glitch in the system. As the room began to lose oxygen, an alarm sounded throughout the model home, loud and shrill. Struggling to take breaths, my brother and my parents became dizzy and lightheaded; they staggered, stumbled, and fell to the floor.

15 Fortunately, I was able to keep my head; I remembered the emergency oxygen tanks in the storage room and ran to get the portable ones. My heart was beating hard and fast; blood pounded in my veins like the steady beat of a drum. Hurriedly, I put on my oxygen mask, then helped everyone else with their masks; after a moment, we were all breathing easily again.

16 Greatly relieved, my parents sent for Colony Camp engineers to restore the system; Counselors Davidson and Fujimoto also showed us how to repair the glitch if the problem ever occurred again. Fortuitously, this happened while we were safely on Earth instead of on Mars. Mom said we should thank our lucky stars; however, I responded that we should thank our lucky emergency oxygen tanks instead!

May 12, 2073

Say Hello to Silas

17 This afternoon we met Silas X-73, who will be our robot companion on the colony. Silas is an android, which means he resembles a human being, sort of, if you can overlook the fact that his skin is shiny silver and he has a blinking control panel on his chest. Additionally, his eyes change color with the light. In bright light they look black, but in the dark they glow green with night vision like two shining emeralds.

18 Silas will help us run our greenhouse farm, operate our home, and record our experiences on Mars. One of Silas's eyeballs is also a camera, and each day we must make a short video to record our thoughts and describe our experiences at the colony. Silas will upload the videos and send them back to Earth to help train future colonists and provide the knowledge they will need before they set out for Mars.

19 Silas is very efficient, but not a lot of fun, so Ramon has been teaching him various jokes. Typically, they involve horrible puns. Ramon will ask, "How do you organize a birthday party in outer space?" Then there's a significant pause. "You planet, of course!" And he laughs, every time. If Silas is going to be programmed with stuff like this, I think I'll need to learn how to *de*-program him.

May 19, 2073

A New Suit

20 This afternoon we tried on our spacesuits for the first time; we will wear them anytime we step outside of the Mars colony. Modern in every way, the lightweight spacesuits provide breathable air, are weighted with gravity boots, and also have a mini computer and a handheld communicator.

May 30, 2073

Out of This World

21 This is our last night in Pensacola. Tomorrow we climb aboard the spaceship with the other new colonists and begin the voyage to Mars. As I reflect on our time here at Colony Camp, I experience a swirl of emotions and realize I am now much more excited than nervous. It's no wonder, because I learned a lot during our training, everything from greenhouse agriculture to zero-gravity maneuvers. Consequently, I feel strong and ready for almost anything. I can't wait to see our new home and experience life on Mars!

Comprehension Check

1A. What kind of figurative language does the narrator, Soledad, use in paragraph 2?

a. an analogy

b. an allusion

c. a metaphor

d. a simile

1B. What term from the text supports the answer to Part A?

a. "Chicago"

b. "I feel like"

c. "survive in the wilderness"

d. "Swiss Family Robinson"

2A. What kind of figurative language does the narrator use in paragraph 4?

a. an analogy

b. an allusion

c. a metaphor

d. a simile

2B. Which phrase from the text supports the answer to Part A?

a. "to help pass the time"

b. "the closest planet to our own"

c. "stuck in a space shuttle for so long"

d. "like sardines stuffed inside a tin can"

3A. What text structure does the author use to present this science-fiction story?

a. a series of newspaper articles

b. a series of blog posts

c. a series of stanzas

d. a series of chapters

3B. What detail from the text best supports the answer to Part A?

a. The selection has dated entries and begins with an "About Me" section.

b. The selection is written from the first-person point of view.

c. The selection's narrator is a teenage girl.

d. The selection focuses on personal observations.

4A. One advantage of using a blog structure to tell a story is that

a. there's no need to construct a plot.

b. you can use figurative language.

c. you can organize the story chronologically.

d. you can emphasize the main character's thoughts and feelings.

4B. Which phrase from the text supports the answer to Part A?

a. "like two shining emeralds"

b. "I am now much more excited than nervous."

c. "We arrived from Chicago last week."

d. "Rapidly, we began to lose fresh air."

5A. How has the narrator's point of view changed by the end of the story?

a. She is confident and ready for Mars.

b. She is sad to leave her friends behind.

c. She worries she will not do well.

d. She is scared about traveling into outer space.

5B. Which detail from the text best supports the answer to Part A?

a. Soledad describes the incident with the life-support system.

b. Soledad describes the spacesuit she will wear on Mars.

c. Soledad explains the role of Silas X-73, the robot companion.

d. Soledad feels excited as she recalls the things she learned in training.

6. At the beginning of the story, how does Soledad's point of view differ from her brother Ramon's?

___

___

___

___

7. Imagine this selection written as a short story told from the omniscient point of view. If the reader was given information that the life-support system was faulty, but the Suarez family did not have this information, how would the effect of the events in "A Scary Day" be different?

8. Explain what might have been the author's purpose in presenting this science fiction story using the text structure of a blog.

9. How would a reader's understanding of story events change if the author presented this text as a short story told from multiple points of view?

10. If this blog were written by Ramon instead of by Soledad, what major differences would you see in the blog's content? Which information would likely be presented differently in his blog?

RL.9, SL.8.1.a, SL.8.1.c, SL.8.1.d

Compare and Contrast Texts

In this unit, you've read a poem about colonial Boston, historical fiction and a poem about textile mill workers in New England, an adventure story set in the Yukon Territory, and a science-fiction blog about a Florida training camp for Mars colonists. In each selection, characters struggle to adapt to a new environment or new circumstances. Fill in the chart below to explain how all of these texts support the theme of living in and adapting to American places. List key details and important points from each selection as evidence. Use a separate sheet of paper if you need more room to write. Be prepared to discuss your ideas with the class.

"Boston"	"A Mill Girl's Story"

Theme: Living in American Places

"To Build a Fire"	"Life at Colony Camp"

Return to the Essential Question

How do authors use language, structure, and point of view to create meaning?

In small groups or as a class, discuss the Essential Question. Think about what you have learned about figurative language and connotation, how to compare and contrast text structures, and how to analyze point of view in a text. Use evidence from the four selections in this unit to answer the question.

L.8.5.a

Figurative Language

Guided Instruction **Figurative language** is language that is not meant to be taken literally. One kind of figurative language is **verbal irony,** which occurs when a speaker, author, or character says one thing while meaning the opposite. **Sarcasm** is a form of verbal irony. Verbal irony can also be expressed as **overstatement**, or exaggeration. Look at these examples.

- *"Oh great, they're exactly what I need—the world's ugliest boots!"*
  This is an example of sarcasm. The character means the opposite of what she says; she does not believe she needs (and she certainly doesn't want) a pair of ugly boots.
- *I was so embarrassed, I wanted to crawl into the nearest closet!*
  This is an example of an overstatement. The character does not actually want to crawl into a closet as a result of feeling embarrassed.

A **pun** is a humorous play on words that suggests two or more meanings. It substitutes one word for another word that sounds the same or is spelled the same way. A pun may also be based on a word with multiple meanings. Here are examples from the selections.

- *Our work at the cloth factory is sew much fun, it leaves us in stitches!*
  The word *sew* appears in place of the similar-sounding *so*. *Stitches* has a dual meaning, referring to both sewing stitches and to a slang word for laughter.
- *"How do you organize a birthday party in outer space? You planet, of course!"*
  The word *planet* is substituted for the phrase *plan it*, which sounds very similar.

Guided Practice Identify the type of figure of speech (sarcasm, overstatement, or pun), and explain its meaning in each example.

1. I'm so glad I lost! It's been a lifelong dream to come in last place in a race.

   ____

2. If this laptop freezes one more time, I'm going to kick it across the room.

   ____

3. The grammar expert was very smart because she had a lot of comma sense.

   ____

Independent Practice Write one sentence that includes verbal irony (sarcasm) and one sentence that includes a pun.

____

____

RL.8.4, RL.8.5, RL.8.6, L.8.5.a

Read the following texts, a short historical narrative and an e-mail message, that include figurative language, differing text structures, and differing points of view. Then answer the questions on pages 149 and 150.

On the Trail

1 As the wagons rumbled, Asa Middleton watched with distaste as the convoy passed tree after tree. Pondering the explorations of Lewis and Clark, he wondered why anyone would embark on such a journey. His family was traveling west to the wilds of Oregon. Leaving Indianapolis was arduous, but Asa had little say; his father intended to buy a piece of property and start a farm.

2 Slowly, the caravan of horses, oxen, and covered wagons traveled down the 2,000-mile-long trail from Missouri to Oregon; it was much safer for families to travel together like a pack of wolves than to do so alone. If someone became ill, others could help tend the sick; if a wagon broke down, others could help repair it. By day the families rode in wagons, and at night they made camp.

3 Along the way, Asa had waded through a rushing river that was as powerful as a steam locomotive and had knocked him off his feet; he had trekked miles up a mountain that reached into the sky.

4 A scout approached on horseback. Asa overheard the man tell the captain the trail was clear and there were only twenty miles to go. It would not be long now. This difficult trip would soon end.

On the Road

To: Claire Radcliffe
From: Aaron Radcliffe
Date: June 12
Hey Grandma,

1 Here's another missive from our massive cross-country trip; New York is long behind us, and San Diego is straight ahead. We've made great progress. I can tell Dad hates his new navigational system; he really misses the old days of getting lost every few miles. As for me, I can't wait to arrive. I don't think I can take one more motel; each one looks identical to the last. I feel like I'm trapped in the movie "Groundhog Day"!

2 It's been an exceptional trip, and we've all been enjoying our travels through so many states. As our car motors along the curving Pacific coastline, I can't help but reflect on all the wonderful things we've experienced, from the gargantuan Grand Canyon to bone-dry Death Valley. Death Valley was so hot, it felt like the inside of a dragon's stomach!

3 There are only 120 miles to go. Both Dad and Mom are excited to start their new jobs, Jenna can't wait to go to the beach, and I'm just looking forward to seeing our new home.

Love, Aaron

RL.8.4, RL.8.5, RL.8.6, L.8.5.a

Circle the letter of the correct answer choice.

1A. What kind of figurative language does the author use in paragraph 1 of "On the Trail"?

a. allusion
b. analogy
c. metaphor
d. simile

1B. What phrase from the text supports the answer to Part A?

a. "Pondering the explorations of Lewis and Clark..."
b. "...Asa Middleton watched with distaste as the convoy passed tree after tree."
c. "...he wondered why anyone would embark on such a journey."
d. "...his father intended to buy a piece of property and start a farm."

2A. What kind of figurative language does the author use in paragraph 1 of "On the Road"?

a. allusion
b. analogy
c. metaphor
d. simile

2B. What phrase from the text supports the answer to Part A?

a. "missive from our massive cross-country trip"
b. "trapped in the movie 'Groundhog Day'"
c. "each one looks identical to the last"
d. "I don't think I can take one more motel"

3A. What kind of figurative language does the author use in paragraph 2 of "On the Trail"?

a. allusion
b. analogy
c. metaphor
d. simile

3B. Which phrase from the text supports the answer to Part A?

a. "By day the families rode in wagons..."
b. "...it was much safer for families to travel together"
c. "...others could help tend the sick"
d. "travel together like a pack of wolves"

4A. What kind of figure of speech does the author use in paragraph 1 of "On the Road"?

a. pun
b. analogy
c. simile
d. sarcasm

4B. What phrase from the text supports the answer to Part A?

a. "New York is long behind us, and San Diego is straight ahead."
b. "I don't think I can take one more motel; each one looks identical to the last."
c. "I feel like I'm trapped in the movie 'Groundhog Day'!"
d. "I can tell Dad hates his new navigational system; he really misses the old days of getting lost every few miles."

5A. What kind of text structure is used in "On the Road"?

a. It takes the form of an e-mail.
b. It takes the form of a diary entry.
c. It takes the form of a magazine article.
d. It takes the form of a newspaper editorial.

5B. Which details from the text support the answer to Part A?

a. The story identifies the writer, the date, and the intended recipient of the text.
b. The story is written in a first-person perspective and includes the pronoun "I."
c. The story takes place in the present at an undetermined location.
d. The story describes the experiences of a teenage boy.

RL.8.4, RL.8.5, RL.8.6

6A. How does the text structure of "On the Trail" compare to that of "On the Road"?

a. "On the Trail" has a traditional narrative structure compared to "On the Road."

b. "On the Trail" has a more complicated structure compared to "On the Road."

c. "On the Trail" presents the story out of sequence, like "On the Road."

d. "On the Trail" presents the story out of sequence, unlike "On the Road."

6B. What details from the text support the answer to Part A?

a. "On the Road" includes unusual elements such as a greeting at the beginning of the text, while "On the Trail" does not.

b. Both "On the Road" and "On the Trail" include unusual elements, such as a closing at the end of each story.

c. "On the Road" describes events out of order, while "On the Trail" does not.

d. Both "On the Road" and "On the Trail" describe events out of order.

7. If a third-person omniscient narrator revealed that an earthquake was due to strike San Diego in the near future, while Aaron remained unaware of the danger, how would "On the Road" change?

8. Write a brief paragraph to compare and contrast the points of view in "On the Trail" and "On the Road." Include key details from each text.

9. What emotion or idea do you associate with the word *convoy*? How does this connotation affect your understanding of the situation in "On the Trail"?

10. How might a reader's understanding of "On the Road" be different if the author had written it as a short story told from the third-person point of view?

Introducing UNIT 6

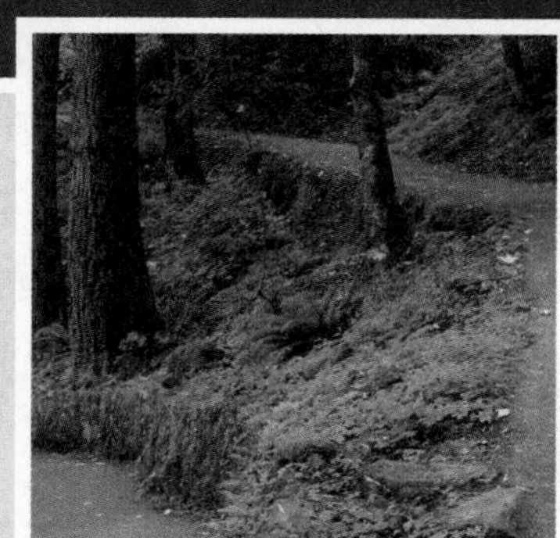

Have you ever enjoyed a story or poem and then explained to another person why you liked it? You may have talked about the exciting plot, or the funny language the author used, or the interesting characters. If so, you were engaging in a kind of literary analysis. In this unit about American places, you will learn how to write an evidence-based literary essay. A literary essay examines some aspect of a literary text, such as its language, themes, pattern of events, or characters.

As you write your literary essay, introduce the topic clearly and then develop your ideas with well-chosen quotations, facts, and details from the text. Include transition words or phrases to create cohesion and to connect your ideas. Incorporate precise language to explain the topic and clarify your meaning. Remember to establish and maintain a formal style. In addition, your literary essay must feature a strong conclusion that supports your interpretation or explanation of the text.

Progress Check Can I?

Before Unit 6 | After Unit 6

- ☐ Write an evidence-based essay about a literary text. ☐
- ☐ Introduce a topic clearly, previewing what is to follow. ☐
- ☐ Develop a topic with quotations and details from a literary text. ☐
- ☐ Include transition words or phrases to connect ideas. ☐
- ☐ Use precise language and a formal style. ☐
- ☐ Provide a conclusion that supports your interpretation. ☐
- ☐ Recognize the difference between active voice and passive voice. ☐
- ☐ Understand how to use the active or passive voice to achieve certain effects. ☐

HOME ✦ CONNECT...

In this unit, your child will learn about writing an evidence-based literary essay. Explain that this type of essay **analyzes a literary text**, such as a novel, short story, or poem. A literary essay might examine elements such as the plot, setting, or characters in a story, or the author's use of language in a poem. Such an essay may also explore the themes presented in a text to determine what the author is trying to communicate. A strong analysis develops an interpretation or explanation **using evidence from the text, including quotations and details,** to support the ideas presented in the essay. A literary essay also includes **precise language, transitions,** and a **formal style**. It ends with a **conclusion** that sums up the topic and supports the interpretation or explanation.

Help your child develop these skills by reading a short story or poem together and discussing it. Talk about different elements in the short story or poem, and explain what the text means to you. Work with your child to develop an interpretation or explanation of the literary text. Make notes as you develop the analysis together and give them to your child to examine and explore.

Activity: Explore the unit theme, "American places," with your child. Work together to make a list of American places he or she has visited. These places could be local or places your child has visited on school trips or vacations. Together, create a scrapbook that describes these different places. Include descriptive details. If possible, include photos or images from the Internet or other sources.

IN THIS UNIT, YOUR CHILD WILL...

- Learn how to write an analysis of a literary text.
- Develop an interpretation or explanation of a literary text with well-chosen evidence.
- Use a variety of transition words or phrases to connect ideas.
- Use precise language to help explain the topic of a literary essay.
- Establish and maintain a formal style throughout a literary essay.
- Provide a conclusion that supports the interpretation or explanation presented in a literary essay.
- Recognize the difference between the active and passive voices.
- Understand how to use the active voice or the passive voice to achieve certain effects.

NOTE: All of these learning goals for your child are based on the Grade 8 Common Core State Standards for English Language Arts.

WAYS TO HELP YOUR CHILD

Have your child interpret a short story he or she has read. Have him or her consider what the author wants the reader to know or think about after reading the text. Have your child write down notes as you discuss the text. Then have him or her consider how these notes could help a writer draft a literary essay about the story.

ONLINE

For more Home Connect activities, continue online at sadlierconnect.com

Research to Build and Present Knowledge: Write Evidence-Based Essays

UNIT 6

Essential Question:
How can writers support an analysis of a literary text?

W.8.2.a, W.8.2.e, W.8.9.a

Read a Student Model

Nadira is a student in Mr. Wood's eighth-grade Language Arts class. Mr. Wood gave the class an assignment to write a literary essay analyzing a poem by an American poet. Mr. Wood expects the essay to analyze the text and include quotations and strong supporting evidence. Think about a poem you have read that is by an American poet. Then analyze the poem in your own literary essay.

CREATING AN ORGANIZATIONAL STRUCTURE

Nadira used an outline like the one below to organize her essay.

Title: ____________

I. **Introduction**
   a. Topic of Essay: ____________

II. **Body Paragraphs**
   a. Main idea of first paragraph: ____________
      1. Supporting Evidence: ____________
      2. Supporting Evidence: ____________
   b. Main idea of second paragraph: ____________
      1. Supporting Evidence: ____________
      2. Supporting Evidence: ____________
   c. Main idea of third paragraph: ____________
      1. Supporting Evidence: ____________
      2. Supporting Evidence: ____________
   d. Main idea of fourth paragraph: ____________
      1. Supporting Evidence: ____________
      2. Supporting Evidence: ____________

III. **Conclusion**
   a. Concluding Statement: ____________

A Walk Down "The Road Not Taken"

In life, some of the choices we make lead to satisfaction and fulfillment while others lead to regret. Author Robert Frost deals with these ideas in his classic poem, "The Road Not Taken," exploring the theme of choices and consequences. The poem has a regretful tone and suggests that people often set themselves up to regret a choice, even without knowing its final outcome.

Using a first-person narrator, the poem describes a road that splits in two. In the first stanza, Frost writes, "Two roads diverged in a yellow wood, / And sorry I could not travel both / And be one traveler, long I stood" (lines 1–3). The two roads are a metaphor that represents a choice between two opportunities. The narrator says that he stood for a long time, weighing the decision of which path to take. As a result, the reader expects the opportunities represented by the roads to be very different, since the choice requires so much consideration.

TITLE

- Gives readers a clue about the poem that will be analyzed or the essay's topic

INTRODUCTION

- Introduces the topic
- Previews the content of the essay, in particular Nadira's interpretation of the literary text

FORMAL STYLE

- Includes academic language
- Avoids slang, contractions, and personal statements
- Uses complete sentences and clear explanations

W.8.2.b–d, W.8.9.a

However, as the narrator weighs both options, he sees that the roads have striking similarities. The second road is "just as fair" (6) as the first, and the two are "really about the same" (10). The narrator describes the second road as "having perhaps the better claim, / Because it was grassy and wanted wear" (7–8). It seems more attractive because fewer travelers have taken it. Yet the narrator also states that "both that morning equally lay / In leaves no step had trodden black" (11–12). Looking back on his choice, the traveler realizes that there was no strong reason to choose one road over the other, nothing pointing to the second road as definitely being better than the other.

This idea of similarity between two options reflects choices people face every day. For example, imagine a student choosing between two dance classes after school. One is ballet and the other is contemporary dance, but the student is interested in both styles. The contemporary dance class has a few more students signed up, but otherwise these two "roads" are not very different. How is one to choose?

In the poem, the narrator chooses the road "less traveled by," or the slightly less popular choice. The reader might think he would be pleased, having given the choice so much consideration. Yet, reflecting on his decision, the narrator states, "I shall be telling this with a sigh" (16). The word <u>sigh</u> implies that the narrator already regrets his choice or believes he will regret it later. The title of the poem also implies regret. It is called "The Road Not Taken," not "The Road Taken," which suggests the narrator is fixated on the choice he did not make.

EVIDENCE

Include evidence to support the essay's interpretation or explanation. Evidence can be quotations or details from the literary text, and it should include reference information. In this case, Nadira indicates the poem's line numbers in parentheses after each quotation.

Underline evidence in the first paragraph on this page.

TRANSITIONS

Use transitions to connect ideas within paragraphs, such as the phrase "For example" in this paragraph. Transitions can also connect one paragraph with another.

Circle two transition phrases in the third paragraph on this page.

PRECISE LANGUAGE

Use precise verbs to describe actions, such as how Nadira uses the word *states* rather than the word *said*.

Put an asterisk before five other precise verbs in this paragraph.

W.8.2.b, W.8.2.f, W.8.9.a

INTERPRETATION

Nadira's essay examines the poem to find a deeper meaning. In this paragraph, she provides a real-life example to help explain her interpretation of the text.

Draw a box around the sentence in this paragraph that explains how her example relates to the poem.

CONCLUSION

This literary essay ends with a conclusion that sums up and supports Nadira's interpretation of "The Road Not Taken."

Underline the text that sums up Nadira's interpretation. Which evidence does she use in the conclusion to support this interpretation?

However, the narrator does not yet know the final consequences of his choice and perhaps puts more significance into the choice than is warranted. After all, the roads seem nearly identical, based on the narrator's description. Could their outcomes really be so different? Consider again the example of the student. She has chosen the less popular ballet class, the "one less traveled by." But after making the choice, she imagines how much more she would have enjoyed the contemporary dance class. She constantly imagines what might have happened if she had chosen the other class. Perhaps she would have discovered a love of dance that would lead to a career on stage. Though she cannot know what would have come from the other choice, it looks more appealing in retrospect. This unwarranted feeling of regret is expressed by Frost's poem.

In the end, the poem's regretful tone suggests that people often put too much weight on the choices they make and their possible consequences. The narrator states, "Two roads diverged in a wood, and I— / I took the one less traveled by, / And that has made all the difference" (18–20). Has it, though? How can the narrator really know that the choice was that momentous? More likely is that the outcome of the choice not made would have been no better or worse than the outcome of the choice that was made. The option he did not choose only looks so appealing because it represents what might have been.

W.8.2.a–f, W.8.4, W.8.5, W.8.9.a, W.8.10

Use this outline to organize your evidence-based literary essay on a poem by an American writer for the Common Core Review on page 163. Be sure to follow a strong organization and support your analysis with relevant evidence from the text. Write your essay in a formal style, using precise language and transitions. Write your first draft on a separate sheet of paper.

Title: ______________________________

I. Introduction

a. Topic of Essay: ______________________________

II. Body Paragraphs

a. Main idea of first paragraph: ______________________________

1. Supporting Evidence: ______________________________

2. Supporting Evidence: ______________________________

b. Main idea of second paragraph: ______________________________

1. Supporting Evidence: ______________________________

2. Supporting Evidence: ______________________________

c. Main idea of third paragraph: ______________________________

1. Supporting Evidence: ______________________________

2. Supporting Evidence: ______________________________

d. Main idea of fourth paragraph: ______________________________

1. Supporting Evidence: ______________________________

2. Supporting Evidence: ______________________________

III. Conclusion

a. Concluding Statement: ______________________________

____

L.8.1.b

Active Voice and Passive Voice

Guided Instruction Verbs are either active or passive. The type of verb a writer chooses determines if a sentence is in the **active voice** or the **passive voice**.

- **Active Voice**

  In the active voice, the subject of the sentence performs the action expressed by the verb. Here is an example:

  Kirsten made pancakes for breakfast.

  Kirsten is the subject that performs the action. The active voice can be in any verb tense, including present, past, and future. Here are two more examples:

  Every day, Jonah rides his bicycle to work and back.

  Watching the news program will remind me about the upcoming election.

- **Passive Voice**

  In the passive voice, the action expressed by the verb is performed upon the subject of the sentence. So, the noun that would typically be the object becomes the subject. Here is an example:

  The pancakes were made by Kirsten for breakfast.

  The pancakes is the subject that is acted upon. Sometimes the noun that performs the action is included in the sentence, and sometimes it is not. Here is an example of a sentence that describes an action performed by an unnamed noun:

  The pancakes were placed on the kitchen table.

  In this case, it is not clear who or what placed the pancakes on the table. Like the active voice, the passive voice can be in any verb tense, including present, past, and future. The passive voice usually includes a form of the verb *to be*, such as *am*, *are*, *was*, *were*, *is*, *be*, or *been*.

  The laundry is being rinsed by the washing machine right now.

  Next week, the new video games will be shipped to stores all over the country.

  However, the presence of the verb *to be* does not always indicate the passive voice. Another way to recognize the passive voice is if the sentence includes a "by . . . " phrase after the verb. This phrase indicates that the subject of the sentence is being acted on instead of performing an action. Here is an example:

  For misbehaving, the boy was scolded by his mother.

L.8.1.b

Guided Practice Circle the verb in each sentence. Then identify whether the sentence is in the active voice or the passive voice.

1. Surprisingly, Mrs. Clark was the winner of the hot dog eating contest.

   ____

2. Mrs. Clark was entered into the contest by her husband.

   ____

3. Did you know the contest was sponsored by a local restaurant?

   ____

4. The restaurant posted flyers all around the neighborhood.

   ____

5. Unfortunately, some of the flyers were removed by mistake.

   ____

6. Still, most people in town had heard of the hot dog eating contest.

   ____

Independent Practice Write six original sentences. Three sentences should be in the active voice and three sentences should be in the passive voice.

1. ____
2. ____
3. ____
4. ____
5. ____
6. ____

L.8.3.a

Using Active Voice and Passive Voice

Guided Instruction Writers can choose the **active voice** or the **passive voice** for different reasons and to achieve certain effects.

- **Using the Active Voice**

Using the active voice makes your meaning very clear. Typically, sentences in the active voice are shorter and clearer. As a result, the active voice keeps a sentence from becoming too wordy or complicated.

- **Using the Passive Voice**

The passive voice can be unclear. It often creates awkward sentences. However, there are reasons that writers choose to use it. For example, using the passive voice focuses more attention on what would typically be the sentence's object. In some cases, writers might want to leave out the noun that performs an action to keep readers guessing, such as in a mystery novel. The passive voice can also be used to deflect responsibility, as in the statement, "Mistakes were made."

- **Changing the Passive Voice to the Active Voice**

To change the passive voice to the active voice, identify the noun that performs the action. Make that noun the subject and rewrite the sentence, changing the verb accordingly. If the subject was not part of the original sentence, you will need to include it (as in the fourth sentence below).

The table was set for dinner by Marla. (passive voice)

Marla set the table for dinner. (active voice)

The new attendance policy has been approved. (passive voice)

The school board has approved the new attendance policy. (active voice)

- **Changing the Active Voice to the Passive Voice**

To change the active voice to the passive voice, identify the noun of the subject. Rewrite the sentence. Change the verb accordingly.

Certain members of the Cabinet are advising the president. (active voice)

The president is being advised by certain members of the Cabinet. (passive voice)

L.8.3.a

Guided Practice Circle the verb in each sentence. If the verb is in the passive voice, change it to the active voice and write it on the line below the sentence. Change verbs in the active voice to the passive voice and write the verbs on the lines.

1. This week, Maria was featured in a story in our community newspaper.

   ____

2. The story's reporter described Maria's food pantry program.

   ____

3. Maria took the reporter on a tour of the facilities.

   ____

4. In addition, Maria introduced him to all of her volunteers.

   ____

5. The food pantry program was presented in a very favorable light.

   ____

Independent Practice Rewrite each sentence, changing the passive voice to the active voice.

1. Next month, several new channels will be offered by the cable company.

   ____

2. The missing phone was dropped into the lost-and-found box.

   ____

3. Will Hannah be picked up from school by her father?

   ____

4. In the restaurant kitchen, the oven was turned on to broil the salmon.

   ____

5. A penny was dropped in the fountain when they made their wish.

   ____

SL.8.1.a–d, SL.8.3, SL.8.4, SL.8.6

Discuss the Essential Question

How can writers support an analysis of a literary text?

Prepare for a class discussion about the Essential Question by responding to the questions below. Support your point of view with reasons and examples.

1. Describe Nadira's interpretation of the poem, "The Road Not Taken."

2. What evidence does Nadira include to support her interpretation?

3. How does Nadira establish and maintain a formal style in her essay?

Use your notes above to discuss the Essential Question with your class or in small groups. Follow the discussion rules on the "Did I?" checklist (page 58). Use the organizer below to record your ideas and what you hear in the discussion.

	Ideas I Agree or Disagree With	Questions I Asked
Agree		
Disagree		
	New Ideas I Had During Discussion	**Questions I Answered**

W.8.2.a–e, W.8.9.a, L.8.1.b

Read this draft introductory paragraph from a student literary essay and answer the questions below.

(1) Automobiles, airplanes, boats, and trains are not just modes of transportation to travel from one place to another. (2) Many people develop a personal attachment to their vehicles and almost see them as living things. (3) Boats are given names, like pets, by their owners. (4) In "The Railway Train," poet Emily Dickinson uses imagery and personification to compare a railroad to a living thing.

1. Which of the following is NOT true about this introductory paragraph?
   - **a.** It introduces the essay's topic clearly.
   - **b.** It makes a real-world connection to the topic.
   - **c.** It previews what will follow in the essay.
   - **d.** It cites specific evidence from the poem.

2. Which sentence could be added to the paragraph to contribute to the formal style?
   - **a.** I think boats are the best mode of transportation.
   - **b.** Many people select pet names for their cars, as well.
   - **c.** It would be super cool to ride on a high-speed train.
   - **d.** Emily Dickinson is the best poet ever!

3. Which is an example of the use of a precise verb in this paragraph?
   - **a.** *are*
   - **b.** *see*
   - **c.** *uses*
   - **d.** *compare*

4. Based on this introduction, which evidence would best fit in this essay?
   - **a.** facts about railway trains
   - **b.** lines from Frost's poem
   - **c.** lines from Dickinson's poem
   - **d.** information from the poet's biography

5. Which transition would best fit at the beginning of sentence 3?
   - **a.** However,
   - **b.** Therefore,
   - **c.** For instance,
   - **d.** On the other hand,

6. Which sentence is an example of the use of the passive voice?
   - **a.** sentence 1
   - **b.** sentence 2
   - **c.** sentence 3
   - **d.** sentence 4

W.8.2.a–f, W.8.4, W.8.5, W.8.9.a, W.8.10, L.8.1.b, L.8.3.a

Read these next two paragraphs from the student essay and answer the questions below.

(1) Throughout the poem, Dickinson creates an extended metaphor to describe a railway train. (2) She compares the train to a horse. (3) She writes, "I like to see it lap the miles, / And lick the valleys up" (lines 1–2). (4) The poet implies the train moved like a horse as it rolled through a valley, with the words "lap" and "lick" suggesting the movements of an animal. (5) Also, the reader's attention is drawn to these words by the use of alliteration in "like," "lap," and "lick." (6) At the end of the poem, the train stops at a terminal the poet compares to a "stable" (line 16), like the kind used to hold horses.

(7) Dickinson not only compares a railway train to an animal, she also compares it to a person. (8) She writes that the train would "neigh like Boanerges" (line 13). (9) "Boanerges" is a Biblical term that means "Sons of Thunder" and is often used to describe a preacher or speaker. (10) This allusion suggests that the train sounded like a thunderous speaker.

7. Circle the sentence that is in the passive voice.

8. Rewrite sentence 2, changing the active voice to the passive voice. Explain how this changes the effect of the sentence. ____________________

____

9. Underline the sentence in which the writer defines a difficult word for the reader.

10. Write a concluding paragraph for this literary essay. ____________________

____

____

____

Assignment: On a separate piece of paper, provide a final draft of the essay you began on page 157. Draw on what you learned about verb voices and how to use them from the Language section of this unit. Think about how you and your classmates answered the Essential Question. Check your graphic organizer to be sure you included enough supporting evidence for your ideas. Use precise language and transitions. End with a conclusion that supports your analysis.

Introducing UNIT 7

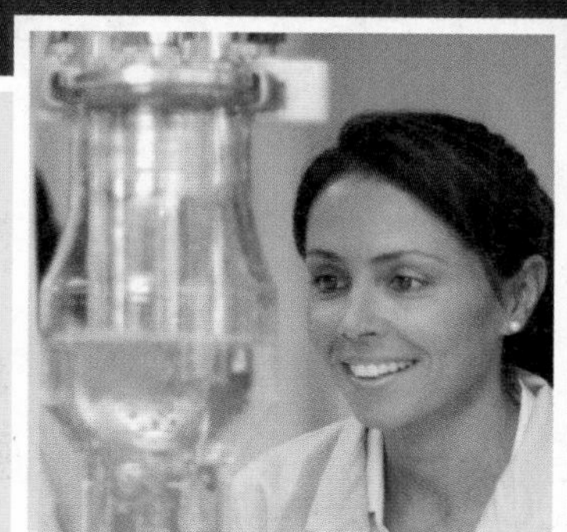

In this unit about scientific solutions to problems, you will learn about the craft and structure of informational texts. Authors of informational texts communicate their purposes and points of view through their word choices and the ways they structure their texts. You will often have to infer an author's point of view and purpose, and you will need to be aware of how the author acknowledges and responds to other viewpoints as well as to evidence that might seem to contradict his or her point of view.

In this unit, you'll find various informational texts, including magazine articles, a scientific journal article, and a persuasive essay. Informational texts about scientific topics usually include technical language, but they may also use language in figurative and connotative ways to build meaning and create a particular tone. Looking for context clues can help you determine the meaning of unfamiliar words and phrases, which you can then verify in reference works, such as print and online dictionaries.

Before Unit 7 — Progress Check — Can I? — After Unit 7

- ☐ Determine the meaning of figurative, connotative, and technical language in informational texts. ☐
- ☐ Analyze how specific word choices, including analogies and allusions, can affect meaning and tone. ☐
- ☐ Analyze the structure of a paragraph, noting how particular sentences help to develop or refine a concept. ☐
- ☐ Determine an author's point of view and purpose, and analyze how an author acknowledges and responds to conflicting evidence or viewpoints. ☐
- ☐ Use reference materials to find the pronunciation of a word and clarify or verify its meaning. ☐

HOME ✦ CONNECT...

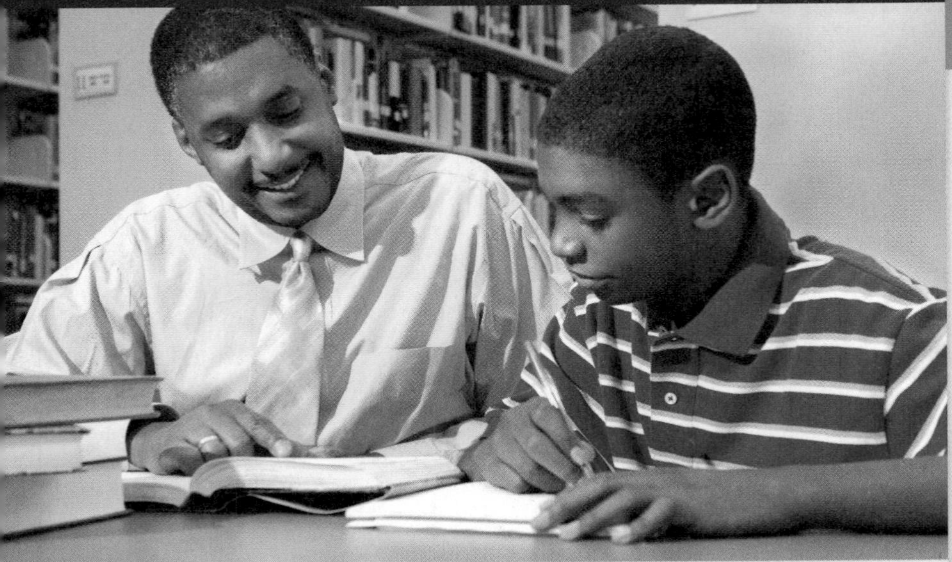

The purpose of an informational text is to inform readers about a topic. Authors of informational texts make specific word choices, using figurative, connotative, and technical terms to communicate information. Readers can often **determine the meaning of technical terms** using context clues in nearby text. To help with this skill, encourage your child to identify context clues for unfamiliar words in everyday conversations.

Students will also **analyze text structure,** learning how authors structure paragraphs to effectively develop their key concepts. Help your child by having him or her think about how the meaning of a paragraph in a news article changes if one or two sentences are not included.

Determining an author's point of view and purpose requires that students learn to infer how an author thinks and feels about a topic by looking for textual clues. Help your child by having him or her identify a word or phrase in a news article that gives strong clues to the author's point of view about the topic.

Activity: With your child, brainstorm problems in the world that could be solved through scientific solutions, such as removing garbage from the ocean. Then search the Internet for solutions that scientists have already invented or theorized about. Discuss which solution you think is the most feasible. Then try coming up with your own hypothetical solution for the problem.

IN THIS UNIT, YOUR CHILD WILL...

- Read four informational selections, including two magazine articles, a scientific journal publication, and a persuasive essay.
- Learn new academic and content-area vocabulary.
- Determine the meaning of technical language as well as figurative and connotative language.
- Analyze text structure.
- Determine an author's point of view and purpose for writing.
- Use reference materials to find the pronunciation of a word and determine its precise meaning and part of speech.
- Compare and contrast ideas across four selections on the theme of scientific solutions.

NOTE: All of these learning goals for your child are based on the Grade 8 Common Core State Standards for English Language Arts.

WAYS TO HELP YOUR CHILD

In conversations, ask your child to identify your point of view about a current event. Have your child identify which of the words that you used helped him or her identify your point of view. If your child cannot identify your point of view, ask questions that will help him or her recognize how you feel and think about the topic.

ONLINE

For more Home Connect activities, continue online at sadlierconnect.com

Reading Informational Text: Craft and Structure

UNIT 7

Essential Question:

How do authors use language and text structure to express their points of view?

Guided Instruction

RI.8.4, RST.8.4

WORDS TO KNOW
biosphere
catastrophe
estimate
seismologist

To **determine the meaning of technical language**, look at the author's specific word choices and analyze their impact on meaning and tone.

CITE EVIDENCE

A Informational texts, like literary texts, may include **figurative language** to help readers visualize and understand concepts. An **allusion** is a kind of figurative language that makes a reference to a person, event, or idea from history, the arts, or mythology. Circle an allusion on this page. Look up the reference and explain how it affects the meaning and tone of the text.

B Authors of scientific texts meant for the general public often provide context clues for the **technical terms** they include in their texts. Underline the details in paragraphs 1 and 2 that help you **determine the meaning** of the term *seismic waves*.

Near-Earth Objects

(Genre: Science Magazine Article)

1 Imagine that you are standing outside your home looking up at the morning sky. Suddenly, the sky fills with an exploding ball of fire. Rapid waves of thunderous noise batter your ears. The ground shakes violently beneath you. When you finally regain your composure, you see that miles of trees and grass in the distance have been burnt away. It is as though Phaeton's doomed fiery chariot from ancient Greek myth has passed by.

2 The people living near the Podkamennaya Tunguska River in Russia in 1908 did not have to imagine this scenario. They experienced it themselves. On June 20, at 7:17 a.m., an enormous fiery object from outer space burst through Earth's atmosphere and exploded. The energy released by the explosion was so great that **seismologists** as far away as England recorded seismic waves as powerful as those produced by a strong earthquake. Survivors later recalled a fire that was as intensely bright as the sun. As burning trees splintered and fell from the heat and flames, smoke as thick as fog started to cover everything.

3 Scientists thought the ball of fire may have been an asteroid or a comet. However, they have recently found evidence that suggests it may have been a meteorite. The Tunguska Event, as it was labeled, remains one of the most famous of all "impact events." But it was not the last. Today, scientists around the world study the potential for future impact events, trying to figure out ways to prevent such **catastrophes**.

Impact Events

4 It can seem like planet Earth, our sun, our moon, and the stars are the only objects in space. But there are hundreds of millions of astronomical objects. Sometimes these objects collide with

Damage from the Tunguska Event

each other. In fact, every day, microscopically tiny objects from outer space gently "collide" with Earth.

5 These tiny objects are called cosmic dust. Cosmic dust is not the kind of dust that gathers on furniture in your home; in fact, you cannot see cosmic dust at all. But scientists **estimate** that anywhere from 11,000 to 661,000 pounds of cosmic dust land on Earth every day! Of course, this gentle "dusting" has no serious or even noticeable effects on Earth. However, if the effects of a collision are measurable—such as the ground-shaking Tunguska Event—then the collision is considered to be an impact event.

6 An impact event involving Earth could result in physical changes to our planet, such as a miles-wide crater being blasted into its surface. It can also have consequences for our **biosphere**, such as causing animals to die and filling our atmosphere with gases and dirt.

7 A planet-sized body colliding with Earth would be like a gigantic wrecking ball smashing into a building; it would destroy the planet. But scientists have calculated that the probability of a planet or similar large body crashing into Earth is incredibly slim. They also say that it could not possibly happen until billions of years into the future.

Near-Earth Objects

8 Some asteroids and comets, however, do present a more immediate threat to Earth. The potential danger is so great that the National Aeronautics and Space Administration (NASA) has a program to identify and track these possible threats. The program is called the Near-Earth Objects Program. The scientists working in the program look for and track asteroids and comets that travel in an orbit that gives them a "perihelion distance *q* less than 1.3 AU," according to the program's Web site. AU means "astronomical unit," and 1 AU is Earth's distance from the sun. Scientists are looking for objects that, at their closest point to Earth during their orbit, are less than 1.3 astronomical units (194.5 million kilometers, or 120 million miles) away from the sun.

Comprehension Check

What is an "impact event"? Identify one detail that helped you determine the meaning of this scientific term.

Guided Instruction

CITE EVIDENCE

C An author may include a nonexample, or an example of what something is *not*, in order to help readers understand a technical term. Underline the nonexample on this page. Double underline the term it explains.

D An author may explain a technical term by providing an example. Box the effect of an impact event on our biosphere.

E To help readers understand a concept, an author may use an **analogy**, a comparison pointing out similarities between two different things. Place an asterisk next to an analogy on this page. What two things are being compared? How does the analogy help you understand what the author is describing?

Meteor Crater, Arizona

Guided Instruction

RI.8.4, RST.8.1, RST.8.4

WORDS TO KNOW

designation
diameter
elongated
interchangeably
spherical

CITE EVIDENCE

A You can sometimes determine the meaning of a technical term by looking for information that explains the term's effect on something. Double underline the effect that helps you understand the meaning of *gravitational force*.

B Technical terms may be defined over several sentences or even an entire paragraph. A series of facts and examples, taken together, may define the term in detail. Place an asterisk next to each paragraph on this page that provides an extended definition of a technical term.

C Look at nearby context clues to determine the meaning of an unfamiliar technical word or phrase. What is an *elongated elliptical orbit*? Underline the clue on this page that helps you understand what the term means.

Near-Earth Objects *continued*

9 That may seem like a long distance, but in terms of space, it is not. NASA scientists are particularly concerned about objects with an orbit that will eventually place them within 45 million kilometers (28 million miles) of Earth. If an asteroid or comet came that close to Earth, then Earth's gravitational force could pull it toward us—creating an impact event. These asteroids and comets are labeled "near-Earth objects." (Asteroids and comets that are not traveling on a path that could bring them close to Earth are not given this **designation**.)

10 Near-Earth objects are the focus of much scientific observation and study. On June 18, 2013, NASA detected the 10,000th near-Earth object: an asteroid that has been named "Asteroid 2013 MZ5." By late summer of 2013, NASA had identified close to 70 near-Earth objects.

Asteroids

11 What exactly is an asteroid? Asteroids, like all objects in our solar system, orbit the sun. Some asteroids are made of metal, such as iron and nickel. But most asteroids consist of rock and minerals. Some asteroids are **spherical**, like planets, but most are irregularly shaped. Asteroids can range in **diameter** from a few feet to several hundred miles. The largest asteroids are sometimes called *planetoids*.

Comets

12 A comet is made up of ice, pieces of rock, and dust. The ice holds the pieces of rock and dust together. Comets follow an **elongated** elliptical orbit. This orbit takes them far away from the sun and even far past the orbits of the outermost planets in our solar system. The orbit also brings comets close to the sun; when it does, the heat from the sun can melt the ice. This causes

RI.8.4, RST.8.4

dust and gases to trail behind the comet like a tail. An astronomer invented a popular term for comets: "dirty snowballs." The average comet has a diameter of 10 kilometers (6 miles) or less.

Meteoroids, Meteors, and Meteorites

13 People often use the terms *meteoroid, meteor*, and *meteorite* **interchangeably**. However, the terms do not have precisely the same meanings.

14 A meteoroid is a space rock much smaller than an asteroid or comet. Most meteoroids have a diameter of no more than 10 meters (33 feet). Some are chunks of rock that have fallen loose from a comet heated by the sun. Other meteoroids are bits of an asteroid that broke off when two or more asteroids collided into each other. Some meteoroids are even leftover material from the formation of our solar system billions of years ago.

15 Meteoroids often crash through Earth's atmosphere. Most of them burn up from the friction of passing through our atmosphere before they hit the ground. The light from their burning creates a bright streak in the sky. That streak is what we call a meteor, or, more poetically, a "shooting star." (Since a star is an enormous plasma sphere, such as our own sun, you can see that the popular term is not scientifically accurate.) If you carefully watch the nighttime sky, you might see several single meteors in just a single hour. Sometimes, a group of meteors flashes across the sky. That is called a meteor shower.

16 If a meteoroid does not completely burn up as it passes through our atmosphere, it will fall to the ground. Once it lands, it is called a meteorite. Though most meteorites are no bigger than a pebble, some weigh tons. The largest meteorite found so far weighs 66 metric tons (about 145,504 pounds).

17 There is no known modern-day instance of a meteorite killing anyone. But in 1954, Elizabeth Hodges got the surprise of her life. An 8.5-pound meteorite crashed through her roof, bounced off her radio, and hit her on her hip! Miraculously, the space rock did not break her hip bone—or do worse damage.

Comprehension Check

How does understanding the meaning of the word *orbit* help you understand how near-Earth objects can be a threat to Earth?

Guided Instruction

CITE EVIDENCE

D "Layperson's terms" are nontechnical words and phrases that average people— nonexperts— use to refer to technical or scientific concepts. *Heart attack*, for example, is the layperson's term for *myocardial infarction*. Layperson's terms are often **figurative**, based on imaginative comparisons. They may also be **connotative**, suggesting certain ideas and emotions. Circle two layperson's terms on this page and double underline the technical terms to which they refer.

E The "everyday" meaning of a word can help you determine its technical meaning. Think about the everyday meaning of *friction*. Then box two details on this page that help explain the technical meaning of *friction*. How does thinking about the everyday meaning of *friction* help you determine its technical meaning?

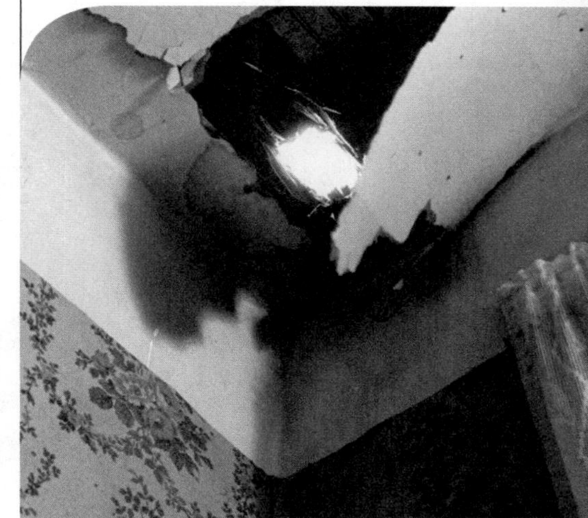

Guided Practice

RST.8.1

WORDS TO KNOW

monitors

peer

plausibly

radiates

verify

CITE EVIDENCE

A Circle the sentences that describe the steps NASA takes when tracking threats. How does reading the steps in sequence help you determine the meaning of the word *verify*?

B Working with a partner, underline details that help you understand what the word *radiates* means. Explain the type of context clue you are given. Is it an extended definition, an explanation of an effect, a nonexample, or an example?

Near-Earth Objects *continued*

Greater Threats

18 NASA analyzes meteor showers and meteorites, but NASA's Near-Earth Object program does not track meteoroids. The program **monitors** only near-Earth asteroids and comets—which pose a greater threat to humanity than damaged rooftops and bruised hips.

19 NASA has been particularly focused on objects with a diameter of 1 kilometer (.62 miles) or larger. "An asteroid of that size could **plausibly** end civilization," according to John Holdren, a White House science advisor. But now NASA is turning its attention to smaller asteroids as well. That's because the impact caused by an asteroid with a diameter of just 50 meters (165 feet) could destroy a city.

Tracking Threats

20 To identify and track threats, NASA uses powerful telescopes that can **peer** deep into space. If an object appears to be a threat, NASA will observe the object and collect data to determine its orbit. NASA determines an object's orbit by:

- identifying its location in space at the moment of discovery
- observing where it is located after a period of time has passed
- using data related to the change in location to make a prediction about where the object will be after additional time has passed
- checking to **verify** whether the prediction was correct

21 Once a potentially dangerous object is identified, NASA continues to observe it and refine its predictions based on each new set of verified data about the object's orbit. NASA checks some asteroids and comets on a daily basis. Others are checked on a weekly basis.

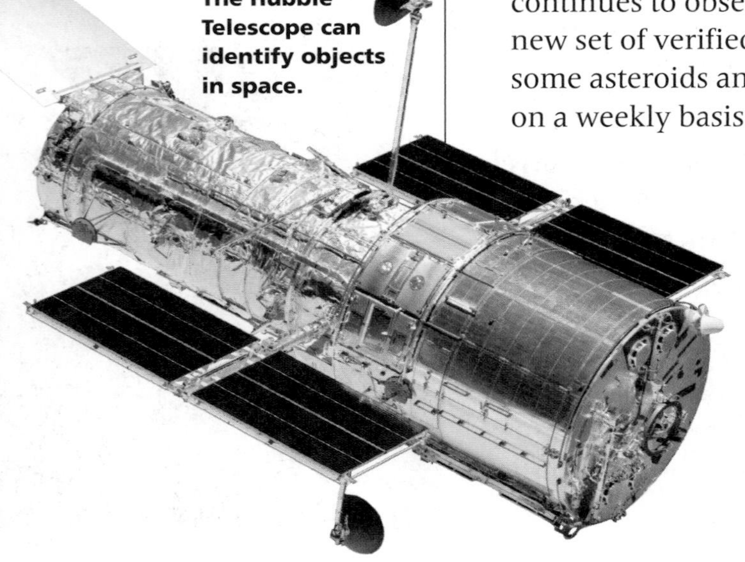

The Hubble Telescope can identify objects in space.

22 When refining its predictions, NASA considers the effects of the gravitational forces of the sun, the planets—including Earth—and our moon on the object. NASA also considers the likelihood that another object may collide with the object being tracked, which would affect its orbit.

23 In addition, NASA considers the effect of sunlight. Sunlight heats up the side of the object it hits. As the object rotates, it **radiates** heat back into the atmosphere on the side not facing the sun. The closer the object comes to the sun, the more sunlight it receives and radiates. This can affect the object's orbit. This effect is named the Yarkovsky effect, after Ivan Yarkovsky, a civil engineer who came up with the theory in 1888.

Comprehension Check

1. Which aspect of an asteroid does the term *diameter* describe?

a. its temperature

b. its speed

c. its size

d. its force

2. What do words like *refining* and *considers* in paragraph 22 suggest?

a. how impossible it is to make predictions

b. how thorough NASA is

c. how dangerous near-Earth objects are

d. how likely collisions are

3. Which of the following is NOT a factor that NASA studies when refining its predictions, according to the text?

a. gravitational force

b. possibility of collision

c. effect of sunlight

d. cost of measurement

4. Which words in paragraph 20 serve as context clues for the word *peer*?

a. *identify*; *threats*

b. *appears*; *observe*

c. *powerful*; *deep*

d. *determine*; *orbit*

5. Review the language the author uses in the paragraphs on pages 172 and 173 to describe NASA's work. What impact does the use of language have on the meaning and tone of what is being described?

____

____

____

____

____

Independent Practice

RI.8.4, RST.8.1, RST.8.4

Near-Earth Objects *continued*

Here Comes Apophis!

24 In 2004, NASA discovered an asteroid heading toward Earth. The asteroid has a diameter of 210–330 meters (690–1080 feet), so it is as large as two to three football fields. NASA named the asteroid 99942 Apophis, after an evil ancient Egyptian god of **chaos** and darkness. The name seemed highly **appropriate**, since NASA had calculated that the asteroid had a 2.7 percent chance of colliding with Earth in the year 2029! This is a very low **probability**, but was still of great concern.

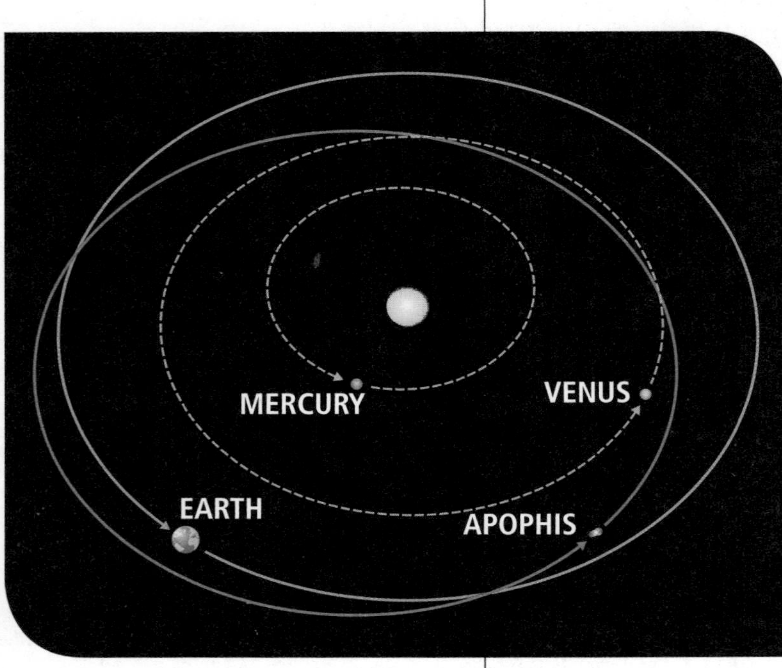

25 Recently, though, scientists revised their prediction. They now believe that Apophis will glide by Earth at a safe distance of 29,470 kilometers (18,300 miles) in 2029.

26 But what if another asteroid were to knock into Apophis? What if this collision changed the asteroid's orbit, putting Apophis on a collision course with Earth? It's possible that such an event could happen, though really not probable. Though Earth would likely not blow up, the effects would not be **minor**. Cities would be destroyed, landscapes would be drastically altered, and our climate would change for at least several years.

Protecting Against Threats

27 To protect Earth, NASA does not merely track near-Earth objects; it also investigates ways to avoid collisions with them. One idea NASA is looking into involves setting off an explosion near a threatening object in order to alter its orbit and put it on a path that takes it away from Earth. Another idea is to simply blow up the object. Some scientists suggest that aiming a laser at the object could add to the heat it absorbs from the sun and help to change its orbit. NASA is also assessing whether the gravitational force of a large spacecraft positioned next to the object could pull the object into a new orbit.

WORDS TO KNOW

accurate
appropriate
chaos
minor
probability

CITE EVIDENCE

A Circle the explanation of the name given to asteroid 99942. What does this name suggest? Why is the connotation fitting?

B Box the detail that helps you understand what a *laser* is. Which idea for avoiding impact events do you think is the best? Cite evidence from the text in support of your answer.

28 So just how concerned should we be about near-Earth objects? Donald Yeomans of NASA has said that there is very little likelihood that an asteroid or comet large enough to cause catastrophic damage will collide with Earth for at least "the next 100 years." That's good news for us! But, for the sake of future generations, NASA will keep working to develop **accurate** impact-avoidance mechanisms before a century has passed.

Comprehension Check

MORE ONLINE **sadlierconnect.com**

1. What does the author explain by using an analogy to football fields?

a. how 99942 Apophis was named

b. how much 2.7 percent is

c. what will happen in the year 2029

d. how large 99942 Apophis is

2. Which phrase in paragraph 25 helps the reader determine the meaning of the word *revised*?

a. "recently, though"

b. "now believe"

c. "will glide"

d. "a distance"

3. Which phrase in paragraph 27 helps the reader determine the meaning of the word *investigate*?

a. "to protect"

b. "avoid impacts"

c. "looking into"

d. "just track"

4. Which phrase in paragraph 27 does the figurative phrase "put it on a path" help define?

a. "alter its orbit"

b. "blow up the object"

c. "setting off an explosion"

d. "near a threatening object"

5. How does analyzing the effect of the technical terms *calculated* and *probability* help you better understand the meaning and tone of paragraph 24?

____

____

____

____

____

Guided Instruction

RI.8.5, RST.8.5

WORDS TO KNOW

bacterium
boil
contagious
epidemic
infectious
microorganism
parasite

Analyzing **text structure**—the way information is presented in sections and organized and developed within paragraphs—can help you understand the key concepts the author wants to communicate.

CITE EVIDENCE

A In **introductory paragraphs**, authors use various techniques to grab readers' interest. They may ask a question, tell a story from history or current events, or ask readers to imagine themselves in a particular situation. What device is this author using? Underline a detail that helps you identify this device.

B An author may present the topic of a text by asking and answering a question. Place an asterisk by the question the author asks on page 177. Box the answer the author gives. What is the topic of this text?

Controlling Disease Outbreaks

(Genre: Science Journal Article)

1 In 1347 a ship docked at the port of Messina on the island of Sicily, now a part of Italy. The people of Messina soon discovered that most of the sailors on the ship were dead. City leaders quickly figured out that the dead sailors must have been infected with some terrible disease. The city leaders ordered the ship to leave Messina, but the illness had already infected at least a few people in the trading town.

2 Within a short time, many people in Messina had died from the mysterious disease. Traders who had been in Messina on business returned to their own towns, bringing the illness with them. In turn, people who left those towns for other destinations also carried the disease. The illness spread like wildfire throughout Europe, reaching England in less than a year.

3 Over the next few years, the disease killed more than 20 million people in Europe. It also killed millions of people in the Middle East and Asia. People who became infected suffered from chills and fever. Their lymph nodes swelled, creating hideous black **boils** on their necks and armpits. Then most of them died. People called the disease "the Black Death." Centuries later, scientists identified the cause of the disease: a **bacterium** called *Yersinia pestis*, a highly **contagious** organism. It is the cause of three different kinds of plague known today as *bubonic plague*, *septicemic plague*, and *pneumonic plague*. Bubonic plague has a 50 to 60 percent fatality rate if left untreated. The other two forms

of the disease are almost always fatal if left untreated. Yet, an outbreak of a plague in Peru in 2010 infected only 17 people, did not travel far, and resulted in just one death.

4 Why were there such drastically different results from the fourteenth-century **epidemic** and the one in 2010? Outbreak control methods are a big part of the answer.

What Is an Outbreak?

5 In the scientific community, the word *outbreak* means the same thing as *epidemic*—the rapid spread of an **infectious** disease within a population. An infectious disease is a disease caused by a bacterium, virus, **parasite**, or another type of **microorganism**. Examples of infectious diseases include the common cold and influenza, or the flu. Examples of diseases that are not infectious—in other words, that are not caused by a microorganism that has entered the body—include skin cancer and diabetes.

6 For a situation to be considered an outbreak, the number of people who become infected—and the rate at which they become infected—must be much higher than what is typically expected in a particular area at a particular time. In other words, let's say that in Community A, the typical number of people who become sick with influenza, the flu, every March is 12. If 14 people come down with the flu one year, health experts would not consider the situation to be an outbreak. However, if 50 people were to become sick with the flu, the situation would be considered an outbreak.

Contagious or Noncontagious?

7 Outbreaks can involve contagious and noncontagious infectious diseases. A noncontagious infectious disease is one that cannot be spread from person to person. Lyme disease is a noncontagious infectious disease. A person can become infected with Lyme disease if he or she is bitten by a tick that carries a certain parasite. But a person infected with Lyme disease cannot pass on the disease to other people.

Comprehension Check

How does the author develop the idea that the bacterium *Yersinia pestis* is highly contagious?

Guided Instruction

CITE EVIDENCE

C Authors can use subheadings to divide a text into sections. Circle the sentence that answers the question posed in the subheading "What Is an Outbreak?" Why does the author include this section?

D To refine a concept or idea, an author may provide examples not only of what it *is* but also of what it is *not*. An example of what something is *not* is called a non-example. Underline the sentence that provides nonexamples of the term *infectious disease*.

E To **develop a concept** fully for readers, an author may state information and then follow it up with a specific, well-developed example. Double underline the phrase in paragraph 6 signalling that such an example is coming. How does this example develop the concept of an outbreak?

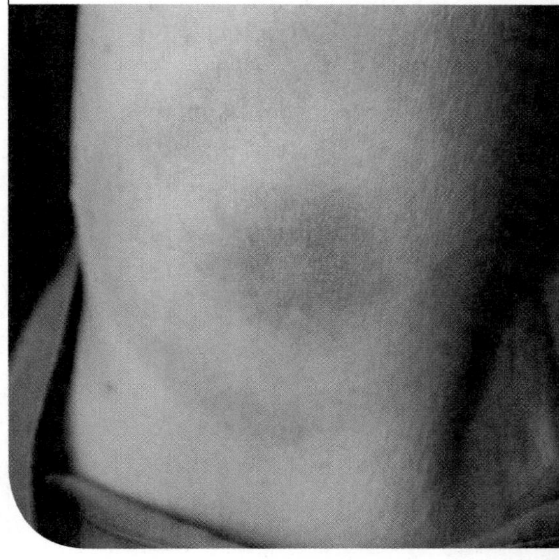

Guided Instruction

RI.8.5, RST.8.3, RST.8.5

WORDS TO KNOW

contract
exponentially
initially
intensify
linear

CITE EVIDENCE

A Authors may develop or refine a concept by giving readers a hypothetical, or imagined, situation as an example. Underline the sentence that puts the reader in a hypothetical situation. Double underline the concept that this example develops and refines.

B Scientific texts often describe multistep procedures. Box the multistep procedure the author includes in this section. Circle the sentence that gives the reason for following this procedure.

Controlling Disease Outbreaks *continued*

8 A contagious disease is one that can spread from person to person. Many contagious diseases in humans also **initially** begin, like Lyme disease, with an insect or animal bite. But, unlike Lyme disease, a contagious disease can spread from an infected person to others.

9 Some contagious diseases are airborne, which means you can **contract** the disease by breathing the same air as someone who has the disease. To contract nonairborne types of contagious diseases, you must come in direct or indirect contact with someone who has the disease. Direct contact means actually touching the person. Indirect contact means touching something that the person has touched. If you drink from the same cup as an infected person, you have had indirect contact with that person and could become infected with the disease.

10 The Black Death was a highly contagious infectious disease. It was airborne and could be contracted through both direct and indirect contact—all qualities that allowed it to spread quickly.

Identifying Outbreaks

11 When local health officials suspect that an outbreak of a disease has occurred or may occur, they typically follow a set of steps recommended by the World Health Organization:

1. Alert governmental health authorities.
2. Investigate the situation by identifying as many potentially infected people as possible and finding out how they may have been infected and whom they may have infected.
3. Confirm that those suspected of infection have actually been infected.
4. Treat those infected.
5. **Intensify** observations to identify whether the disease is spreading at a faster rate than expected.
6. Prepare for controlling an outbreak.

RI.8.5, RST.8.5

Why Must Outbreaks Be Controlled?

12 Controlling an outbreak of a disease means limiting the number of people who become infected. This reduces the number of people who could potentially die from the disease. It also reduces the number of people who could potentially simply suffer through symptoms or be left disfigured or disabled by the disease.

13 Infectious diseases do not spread in a **linear** pattern, from one person to just the next person and then to just the next person. Instead, they spread **exponentially**: one person may spread the disease to three or four people, who in turn spread it to three or four others, and on and on.

The Worst Infectious Diseases

14 It costs a lot of money to identify and control an outbreak. But if you consider the terrible effects of some of the worst infectious diseases, it is difficult to deny that controlling outbreaks is worth the cost.

15 **Influenza** Most people call this highly contagious disease "the flu," and it is caused by a virus, but not just one virus. A strain, or type, of influenza begins in birds and animals, such as pigs. Some form of the virus strikes every year. Symptoms include fatigue, chills, fever, muscle pains, and nausea. Healthy people usually recover from the flu with no treatment. Children and the elderly are at most risk from the flu. Worldwide, the flu kills between 250,000 to 500,000 people every year. However, in 1918, a particularly deadly form of the flu virus killed 50 million people all over the world.

Guided Instruction

CITE EVIDENCE

C An author can refine a concept by explaining its effects. Box the sentences that explain the effects of controlling an outbreak.

D Place an asterisk next to the sentence that explains the pattern in which infectious diseases spread. Circle the term that is explained in this sentence.

E An author may develop an idea or a claim by providing detailed information that demonstrates why the idea or claim is true. In the section on "The Worst Infectious Diseases," underline the claim that the information about influenza in paragraph 15 supports. Based on what you have read, do you agree with the author's claim?

Comprehension Check

How does the structure of this text so far help you understand that it costs a lot of money to identify and control outbreaks?

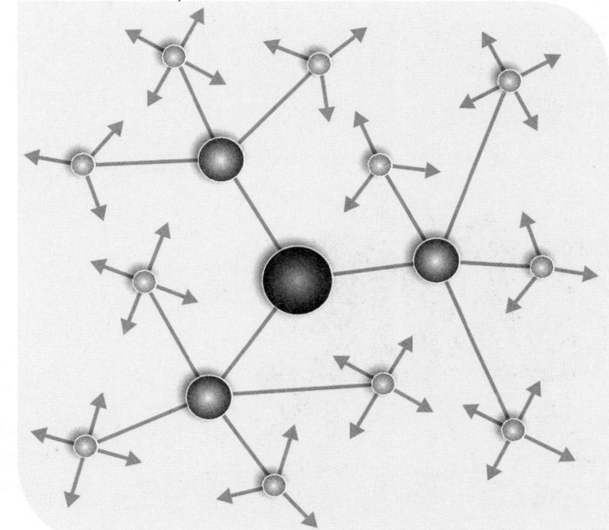

This diagram provides a visual representation of how an infectious disease may spread. The black dot represents the first person infected with the disease. During an outbreak, the disease spreads very quickly from person to person.

Guided Practice

RI.8.5, RST.8.3, RST.8.5

WORDS TO KNOW

confirmation
convulsion
diagnosis
jaundice
sanitary
surveillance

CITE EVIDENCE

A Underline the two sentences that most help to develop the idea that malaria is one of the six most deadly infectious diseases. What details in the sentences that follow most help to make the dangers of malaria clear?

B Double underline the sentence that explains the reason for providing the multistep procedure on this page. Asterisk the sentence that explains what doctors should do when they first suspect that an outbreak may be occurring. How does the author's inclusion of a numbered list of steps aid your understanding?

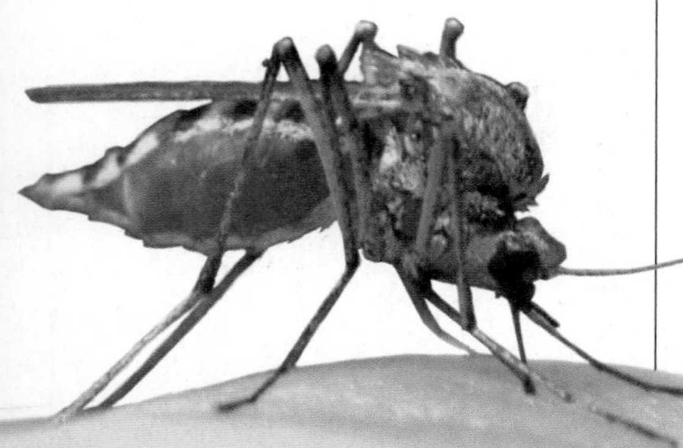

Controlling Disease Outbreaks *continued*

16 **Malaria** The World Health Organization has designated malaria as one of the six most deadly infectious diseases. Malaria kills 3,000 people every day. That adds up to over one million people each year. Of these victims of the disease, 75 percent are children. Symptoms of malaria include difficulty with breathing, **convulsions**, and fever. Some people infected with malaria also may suffer from **jaundice**. Malaria is caused by a parasite and is spread by mosquitoes. A mosquito sucks in a small amount of blood when it bites a person. If the person has malaria, the virus will be in the person's blood. When the mosquito bites the next person, it injects the blood—and the virus—from the first person into the new victim. Malaria is not contagious. You cannot contract it from someone who has malaria. You can only contract it from a mosquito that is carrying the virus.

17 **Tuberculosis** Every year, this disease kills 1.5 million people. It is caused by an airborne bacterium. If you are standing near someone with tuberculosis who is coughing, talking, sneezing, or even laughing, you could contract the disease. Symptoms include coughing, weight loss, fatigue, fever, and night sweats.

Laboratory Confirmation

18 Doctors familiar with infectious diseases will often recognize the symptoms of a particular disease and quickly be able to make a **diagnosis**. However, to make a **confirmation** of the diagnosis, samples from the sick patients must be analyzed at a laboratory. The following steps must be followed in order to ensure accurate testing of the sample and appropriate outbreak response:

1. Collect samples from patients using **sanitary** specimen containers and following sampling techniques appropriate for the disease and sample to be collected.
2. Transport samples in leakproof containers to a laboratory.
3. Test samples at the laboratory, following quality assurance procedures.
4. Report results to health officials.
5. Analyze the results in terms of what control measures are needed.

19 Accurately testing samples and confirming that the samples contain evidence of a disease is crucial to the early detection of an outbreak. And early detection is a primary goal of outbreak **surveillance**. According to the World Health Organization, "early detection can have a major impact in reducing the numbers of cases and deaths during an outbreak."

Comprehension Check

1. Which details about tuberculosis most help to develop the concept of an "airborne" disease?

   a. fatigue and fever
   b. coughing and sneezing
   c. mosquito bites
   d. the number of fatalities

2. Why does the author include the sections on malaria and tuberculosis?

   a. to explain how to test samples
   b. to explain the Black Death
   c. to explain how diseases spread
   d. to explain the cost of outbreak control

3. According to the text, what is the final step in laboratory confirmation of a disease outbreak?

   a. analyzing results to determine control measures
   b. collecting samples from patients
   c. reporting results to health officials
   d. accurately testing samples in the lab

4. How does the author develop the concept that tuberculosis is caused by an airborne bacterium?

   a. by explaining what it is and what it is not
   b. by putting the reader in a hypothetical, or imaginary, situation
   c. by recounting an historical event
   d. by restating the concept

5. What could happen if doctors and other healthcare workers did not handle samples from a sick patient properly? How does the text structure help to make it clear that this aspect of identifying outbreaks is critically important?

Independent Practice

RI.8.5, RST.8.3, RST.8.5

Controlling Disease Outbreaks *continued*

Controlling an Outbreak

20 Once an outbreak has been confirmed, it is important to effectively control it. To do this, outbreak control teams implement three control measures simultaneously. The three measures are:

Transmission	Contagiousness	Protective Measure
Direct or indirect contact	Moderate	Wash hands
Direct contact (non-respiratory diseases)	High	Avoid physical contact
Direct contact (respiratory diseases)	High	Wear mask, avoid physical contact, keep patient in a separate room
Airborne and direct contact	Very High	Keep patient in a separate room, wear biohazard gear

- **Prevent exposure** Patients who have been diagnosed with the disease are **isolated** to prevent them from infecting others.
- **Prevent infection** The public is alerted to the outbreak and educated on ways to protect themselves from infection and to recognize symptoms of infection and disease. Uninfected people are **vaccinated** against the disease.
- **Prevent disease/death** Treat infected patients to help prevent the infection from causing the disease. Care for disease patients to prevent them from dying.

Patient Zero

21 While some teams are working to control the outbreak, another team will conduct the **epidemiological** investigation. The goals of this investigation include determining how quickly the outbreak is likely to spread, how the outbreak is spreading, and who was the first person to become infected with the disease. This original human source of the infection is known as "Patient Zero."

22 To make these determinations, the team in charge of the investigation will collect data on all the patients infected or suspected of having been infected by the disease. They will ask questions about where the patient lives, when the patient first showed symptoms of infection, what the symptoms were, where the patient has recently traveled, and what he or she recently ate.

23 The team will use the data it collects to create a map of the outbreak. The map will show the location of all cases of infection and those that resulted in death. The map can help the team work backwards to find Patient Zero. Finding Patient Zero can

WORDS TO KNOW

epidemiological

isolated

stockpile

vaccinated

CITE EVIDENCE

A Circle the word in paragraph 20 that tells the order in which the three control measures should be implemented. How does this word clarify the information that follows?

B Box the sentence that describes the relevant data the epidemiological investigation team must collect from infected patients or those suspected of having been infected.

help the outbreak control team determine the source of the outbreak, such as infected animals at a certain farm or contaminated water at a certain well.

The Most Important Step

24 Controlling an outbreak is very important, of course. But control outbreak teams cannot work effectively if a community is not prepared for an outbreak. Being prepared includes keeping **stockpiles** of medications and vaccines as well as supplies like thermometers and even tents. If a community does not have the materials it needs to house and treat patients, it cannot control the outbreak.

Comprehension Check

MORE ONLINE **sadlierconnect.com**

1. What concept does the text detail "isolated to prevent them from infecting others" develop?

a. identifying an outbreak

b. preventing an outbreak

c. controlling an outbreak

d. confirming an outbreak

2. Which detail develops the idea that being prepared for an outbreak is necessary for controlling an outbreak?

a. "controlling an outbreak is very important . . ."

b. ". . . not prepared for an outbreak."

c. ". . . it cannot control the outbreak."

d. ". . . materials . . . to house and treat patients . . ."

3. The need to determine the source of an outbreak is a key concept developed by

a. the chart on page 182.

b. the section about Patient Zero.

c. the description of the three measures for controlling an outbreak.

d. the description of what a community needs in order to be prepared.

4. How does the author develop the concept of an epidemiological investigation?

a. by including information on a chart

b. by asking and answering a question

c. by including data and figures

d. by describing the steps involved

5. Why does the author make the section about being prepared for an outbreak the final section? What would have been the effect if it had appeared earlier?

____

____

____

____

Guided Instruction

RI.8.6, RST.8.6

WORDS TO KNOW

alternative
consumption
fossil fuel
turbine

Determining the author's point of view and purpose means figuring out how an author thinks and feels about a topic and why the author wrote the text.

CITE EVIDENCE

A Authors of persuasive essays typically state their **point of view** about the topic early in their text. Circle the topic of this essay. Then underline the statement that presents the author's point of view on the topic.

B Authors always have a **purpose** for including certain information in their texts. Box the statement in the section "Fossil Fuels" that helps the reader understand why the author thinks that readers must first be led to understand what fossil fuels are.

The Power of Solar Energy

(Genre: Persuasive Essay)

1 Every day, people around the world turn on lights and use computers. They heat and cool their homes and offices with heating and air conditioning devices. They use refrigerators to keep their food fresh and stoves to cook it. They drive to work in cars and fly to vacation spots in airplanes. They play video games and watch TV. Almost all of the machines people use on a daily basis are powered by energy from **fossil fuels**. In fact, fossil fuels are the source of more than 80 percent of all energy **consumption** around the world. That's because fossil fuels are relatively inexpensive to mine and to turn into electricity.

2 However, the use of fossil fuels is also the source of many environmental problems. Furthermore, some scientists claim that we will run out of fossil fuels in the near future. For these reasons, we should be developing **alternative** energy sources, particularly the use of solar energy.

Fossil Fuels

3 It is important to know what fossil fuels are and the problems related to their use before you can fully appreciate the need for developing alternative fuel sources. The main types of fossil fuels are coal, oil, and natural gas. Coal is a black or brown shiny rock. Oil is a black gooey liquid. Natural gas, of course, is a gas (other kinds of gases include oxygen and helium).

4 Natural gas is colorless and odorless. Gas companies add a scent to natural gas before delivering it to your house. That way, you can smell a gas leak and call the gas company to fix it before the situation becomes dangerous, since natural gas can explode. (Natural gas is not the gas people use to power a car. That is actually gasoline, and it is made from oil.)

5 Creating electricity from coal, oil, and natural gas at an energy plant is a fairly simple process. First, the fossil fuel is burned. The heat generated is used to boil water to create steam. The steam pushes against the blades of a **turbine**, making the turbine spin. This movement creates electricity.

A Limited Supply

6 The fossil fuels we use today were created more than 300 million years ago. They formed from the decaying remains of plants and animals. Layers of earth piled up on these remains, pressing them together until they turned into coal, oil, or gas. Today, power and mining companies dig or drill into the ground to collect coal and tap into pools of oil and pockets of natural gas.

7 However, there is not an unlimited supply of fossil fuels, and the process to create a fossil fuel takes millions of years. Some scientists say that we should not worry about this. They say that there are many undiscovered reserves of fossil fuels deep in the ground. They say that these undiscovered reserves will cover our energy needs well into the future.

8 But if these reserves are undiscovered, how do we know that they exist? There is little doubt that, if we keep using fossil fuels at our current rate, we could run out of them. Some scientists predict that we will use up all our known supplies of fossil fuels within the next 100 years or so. Even the World Coal Association has stated that "there is enough coal to last us around 112 years at current rates of production."

Comprehension Check

What does the author believe about the possibility that we will run out of fossil fuels? What text details help you determine this point of view?

Guided Instruction

CITE EVIDENCE

C Authors use headings to signal the central idea of a text section. Circle the heading on this page. Then underline one sentence in each paragraph that helps the reader determine the central idea of the section.

D To build their credibility, authors of persuasive texts will acknowledge and respond to conflicting evidence or viewpoints. Box the sentences in which the author presents a viewpoint that contradicts the idea that we may one day run out of fossil fuels.

E Authors sometimes present their point of view on a topic not by directly stating their own viewpoint but by choosing to include certain information that reflects their viewpoint. Double underline the two sentences that include expert opinions in support of the idea that we will run out of fossil fuels. What kind of information might the author have left out because it did *not* support his or her own point of view?

Guided Instruction

RI.8.6, RST.8.6

WORDS TO KNOW

infinite

prematurely

thermal

vastly

CITE EVIDENCE

A To emphasize their ideas, authors of persuasive essays sometimes present hypothetical or "What if?" scenarios. Asterisk the section that presents a hypothetical scenario. Why does the author include this information? How does the author "personalize" the information so that readers will think about how the scenario applies to their lives?

B To make a strong argument, an author usually needs to present more than one reason to support his or her viewpoint on a topic. In this essay, the author first discusses that we should develop alternative energy sources because we might run out of fossil fuels. Underline the sentence that states the author's second reason for being against fossil fuels.

The Power of Solar Energy *continued*

A Bleak Future

9 If we do run out of fossil fuels—and have not developed alternative sources of energy—humans will have to adapt to a **vastly** different and much less enjoyable, and perhaps even dangerous, way of life. People will have to suffer through cold winters and hot summers without any relief. Car and airplane travel will become a thing of the past, and people will have to get around on bicycles or walk. Food safety will become a major issue. There will be very few ways to preserve food or cook it properly. Many people will become sick and even die from harsh weather conditions and food-borne illnesses. And those are just a few of the problems people will suffer from. Imagine that you had to get through every day without using any electricity. It is almost unimaginable, isn't it?

Dirty Energy

10 Even if there was an unlimited supply of fossil fuels, we should still be actively working to develop alternative supplies of energy. That is because the use of fossil fuels has an incredibly damaging effect on our environment.

11 One of the biggest environmental concerns with the use of fossil fuels is the pollution it creates. Fossil fuels give off carbon dioxide when they are burned. Carbon dioxide is a type of greenhouse gas. Greenhouse gases rise up and form a blanket that traps heat in our atmosphere. For the most part, this is a good thing. Without that blanket to keep our air warm, we would all freeze to death. But when that blanket gets too thick with greenhouse gases, it traps in more heat than is healthy for our ecosystem. Polar ice caps melt, causing a rise in sea levels and flooding, and lush inland areas can turn into deserts.

RI.8.6, RST.8.2, RST.8.6

12 Furthermore, the pollution spewed into the air by energy plants, cars, trucks, and airplanes from the burning of fossil fuels dirties our air. This makes it harder for us to breathe. According to the National Oceanic and Atmospheric Administration (NOAA), 50,000 people die **prematurely** every year in the United States because of poor air quality.

Renewable Energy

13 We have two types of energy—nonrenewable energy and renewable energy. Fossil fuels are nonrenewable energy. They will run out one day and cannot be easily replaced. Renewable energy, however, is virtually **infinite**—it can never run out—and can be replaced. The wind, rivers and oceans, and the sun are all sources of renewable energy. Renewable energy is our best hope for the future.

Solar Energy

14 Our sun is one of our greatest underused sources of renewable energy. The sun produces enough energy in one second to provide more energy than humans have used since the beginning of time! Yet, in the United States, we rely on solar energy for less than one percent of our energy needs.

15 There are two ways to turn the sun's energy into electricity. Solar-**thermal** facilities create electricity in a way that is very similar to how electricity is generated from fossil fuels—by boiling water to create steam to spin a turbine. However, these power plants convert water into steam from the heat collected by solar collectors. Then the process is the same as at coal, oil, and natural gas power plants.

Guided Instruction

CITE EVIDENCE

C Word choice can reveal an author's point of view on a topic. Circle the words and phrases in paragraph 12 that help you understand the author's point of view about how fossil fuels pollute the air.

D Each text section has its own central idea. Underline the sentences that state the central idea of "Renewable Energy."

E To persuade a reader to agree with a certain viewpoint, an author may include dramatic or shocking facts that the reader likely did not know before reading the text. Box the two sentences that contain shocking facts. How would the effect of the text differ if the author had not included these facts?

Comprehension Check

Why does the author include information about how burning fossil fuels pollutes our air? How does understanding why the author includes this information help you determine the author's viewpoint?

Solar collectors capture energy from the sun at a solar-thermal power station.

Guided Practice

RI.8.6, RST.8.2, RST.8.6

WORDS TO KNOW

emitted

installed

photovoltaic

stark

CITE EVIDENCE

A Underline the sentences that make the information about photovoltaic cells "personal" for the reader. Why does the author personalize this information?

B Box the sentence that states the central idea of the section "Great Advantages!" Double underline the two sentences that develop this central idea by explaining the advantages of solar power.

The Power of Solar Energy *continued*

16 The other way to turn the sun's energy into electricity is through the use of solar panels lined with **photovoltaic** cells. These cells absorb sunlight and immediately convert it into electricity. This is how photovoltaic solar power plants create electricity. Have you ever used a calculator that had a glass strip divided into four cells above the display screen? Then you have used this type of solar power.

Great Advantages!

17 There are many advantages to using solar energy instead of fossil fuels. One of the main advantages is that converting solar energy into electricity does not produce carbon dioxide (a type of greenhouse gas). Therefore, it does not contribute to global warming.

18 Gujarat Solar Park is a group of solar power facilities in India. According to local government officials, the solar park will save 8 million tons of carbon dioxide from being **emitted** into the atmosphere. This is the amount of carbon dioxide that would have been emitted if the power created by the solar park were instead created by burning fossil fuels.

19 Solar plates, tubes, and panels create a great amount of power for solar power plants. But they can also be **installed** atop an individual home or office. This allows people and businesses to have power without any connection to a power company.

20 Another advantage to using solar energy is that our natural environment does not need to be destroyed to collect sunlight. This is in **stark** contrast to how mining and drilling for fossil fuels can devastate an area. For example, coal mining companies have bulldozed more than 300,000 acres of forests in West Virginia in order to access coal close to Earth's surface.

Gujarat Solar Park

21 One of the worst environmental disasters related to oil drilling took place in 2010. An offshore oil rig in the Gulf of Mexico exploded. The damaged well spewed up to 184 million gallons of oil into the water over the next 100 days. According to a report issued in April 2011 by the Center for Biological Diversity, more than 100,000 birds and animals may have been killed or harmed by the oil spill.

Comprehension Check

1. Based on information in the text, the author is in favor of using solar energy because (1) there is a limited supply of fossil fuels, and (2)

a. increasing greenhouse gases is important.

b. making photovoltaic cells is very expensive.

c. digging up coal is difficult and expensive.

d. burning fossil fuels is harmful to the environment.

2. The author explains the use of photovoltaic cells to show:

a. another way to turn solar energy into electricity.

b. the high cost of fossil fuels.

c. how inexpensive solar energy can be.

d. a negative aspect of solar energy.

3. Why does the author cite the detail about the number of acres bulldozed in West Virginia?

a. to state a central idea

b. to acknowledge a counterargument

c. to provide a contrast

d. to describe a procedure

4. Which word or phrase best conveys the author's viewpoint about the 2010 oil spill in the Gulf of Mexico?

a. "oil drilling"

b. "environmental disaster"

c. "oil rig"

d. "damaged"

5. How does determining the author's viewpoint toward solar energy help you understand why the author includes the information about Gujarat Solar Park? Work with a partner to identify what information about the park the author might have left out if it did not support his or her point of view.

Independent Practice

RI.8.6, RST.8.6

WORDS TO KNOW

cost effective

efficiency

innovator

trajectory

CITE EVIDENCE

A Underline the three sentences on this page that provide a conflicting viewpoint to the idea that solar energy has many advantages. Box the sentences the author includes to respond to each of these conflicting viewpoints.

B Double underline the sentence that restates the author's main point of view. Has the author convinced you that developing solar energy is a good idea? Why or why not?

The Power of Solar Energy *continued*

Any Disadvantages?

22 Critics of solar energy typically point out that the sun does not shine 24 hours a day. Usually, their goal in bringing up this point is to suggest that solar energy can provide only a patchy supply of power. It is true that solar energy can only be captured during the day. However, this does not mean that we cannot create a continuous supply of solar energy. That is because solar energy can be stored. We can use this stored energy later, at night or on cloudy days.

23 Another supposed disadvantage to solar power is the low **efficiency** of solar panels. Currently, a solar panel can only convert about 15–16 percent of the sun's energy that it collects into electrical energy. But this is a higher rate of efficiency than when solar panels were first developed. As solar companies continue to explore solar energy and invent new technologies, the efficiency rate will surely continue to improve.

Counting the Cost

24 Finally, critics of solar energy often mention the high cost of installing a home or office solar system or of building a solar power plant. But throughout history, new technologies have typically been very expensive at their introduction. They then decrease in price over the years. This is because **innovators** come up with more efficient ways of producing them. These more efficient ways prove to be more **cost effective**, as well.

25 We've already seen this price **trajectory** with solar energy. In early 2013, the Solar Energy Industries Association announced that, "the average price of a solar panel has declined by 60 percent since the beginning of 2011."

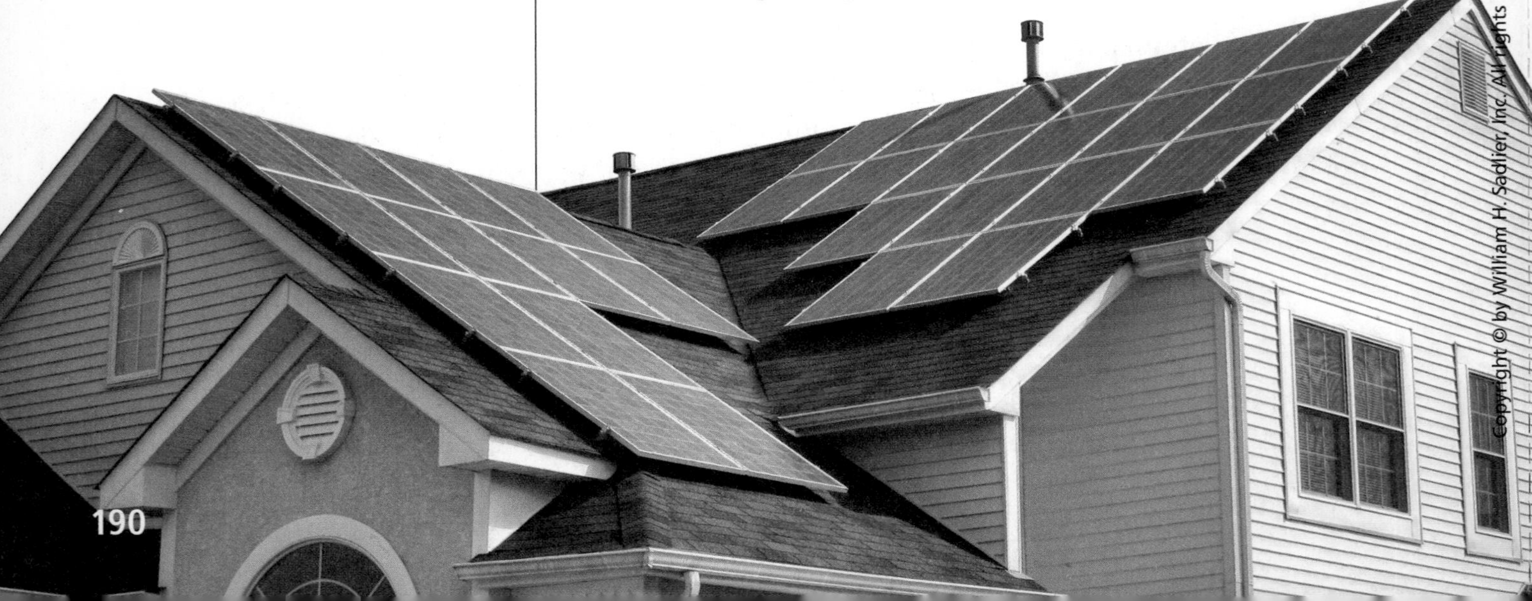

26 The only costs we should be considering in regard to solar energy are the costs of *not* using it. This includes the cost to our environment from digging and drilling for fossil fuels. This also includes the costs to human health and our atmosphere from the pollution generated by the burning of fossil fuels. To avoid these costs, we must begin developing and installing technologies to harness the energy from our greatest renewable source—the sun!

Comprehension Check

MORE ONLINE **sadlierconnect.com**

1. What is the central idea of the section "Any Disadvantages?"

- **a.** There are many disadvantages to using solar energy.
- **b.** There are many disadvantages to burning fossil fuels.
- **c.** There are no great disadvantages to developing solar energy.
- **d.** There are no great disadvantages to continuing to burn fossil fuels.

2. The author is most concerned about

- **a.** the high cost of solar energy.
- **b.** the efficiency of solar energy.
- **c.** the effects of burning fossil fuels.
- **d.** the ability to replace solar energy.

3. Which fact that supports a conflicting viewpoint does the author acknowledge?

- **a.** Solar panels have only a 15–16 percent efficiency rate.
- **b.** Fossil fuels are the source of 80 percent of all energy consumption.
- **c.** All fossil fuels were created more than 300 million years ago.
- **d.** We have enough coal for 112 years.

4. The author explains the price trajectory of new technologies to convince readers that

- **a.** all fossil fuels will be used up soon.
- **b.** solar energy will become cheaper.
- **c.** solar panels are efficient.
- **d.** innovators do not care about profit.

5. How does determining the author's point of view help you understand the author's purpose for writing the text? What does the author want readers to do? How does this affect the type of information the author includes in the text?

____

____

____

____

____

The Wonders of Medical Imaging

(Genre: Magazine Article)

1 Just over one hundred years ago, if you had a severe pain in your abdomen, your doctor had just two ways to diagnose your condition. Your doctor could ask you a few questions to see if your symptoms indicated an obvious and familiar illness, such as the stomach flu. Or, your doctor could do a surgical investigation by cutting open your abdomen.

2 If you had a huge tumor growing in your abdomen, it might have been your good fortune that your doctor had cut you open and could surgically remove the growth. But if all that was ailing you was a stomach virus, the procedure would have been a drastic measure, at best—and, at worst, could have been life-threatening!

3 Today, fortunately, doctors have a much easier—and safer—way of seeing inside our bodies to diagnose our ailments. They can use medical imaging technologies. These modern technologies create images of our bones, organs, and tissues without requiring even the smallest cut into our skin.

Radiography

4 It all started with the X-ray.

5 An X-ray is a type of electromagnetic radiation, or energy wave. (The energy wave produced by a microwave oven is another type of electromagnetic radiation.) In 1895, German physicist Wilhelm Conrad Röntgen discovered X-rays while conducting an experiment related to electrical discharges and gases. Soon after, the X-ray machine (or the technology of radiography) was invented.

6 Creating an image of the interior of a body part with an X-ray machine is fairly simple. Imagine that a patient comes in with an arm that may be broken. The patient positions his or her arm between the X-ray machine and a piece of special film. The X-ray machine emits X-rays toward the arm and the film. The bones—the densest parts of the arm—absorb all or most of the X-rays that hit them. The less dense parts of the arm, such as skin and muscle—as well as the open space that is the break in a broken arm—allow some or most of the X-rays to pass through them. The X-rays that pass through the arm hit the film. These X-rays create black or gray images on the film. The white areas that remain on the film form images of the dense parts of the arm that absorbed the X-rays.

7 Maybe a dentist has placed a small card behind your teeth and aimed a large camera hanging from a mechanical arm at your mouth. If so, then you have been X-rayed!

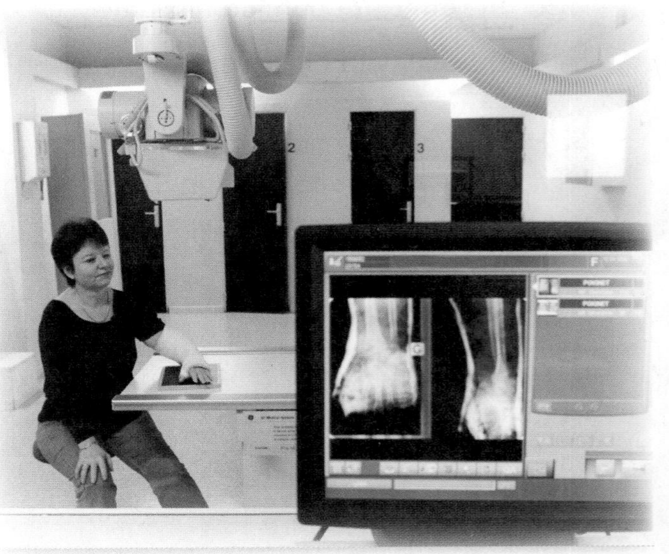

8 If a young child accidentally swallows a coin, button, or small piece of jewelry, guess how a doctor would figure out where it is in the child's body? That's right! The doctor would take an X-ray image of the child's digestive tract.

9 X-ray machines are most often used to identify problems with hard structures: bones and teeth. That is because it is easy to see the break in the bone on an X-ray image. An X-ray image, however, does not give a very detailed picture of the body part. One reason for this is that X-rays cannot distinguish among tissues, or cellular material, of the same density. So a tumor that happens to have the same density as the tissue that surrounds it will not be identifiable on an X-ray image. However, an X-ray image can reveal if a patient has a tumor if it is of a different density than the surrounding tissue.

Ultrasound Scanning

10 Ultrasound scanning was developed in the 1940s and is based on sonar technology. Sonar uses sound waves to detect objects underwater. Sonar was developed and refined between World War I and World War II as a means of identifying enemy submarines.

11 Today, ultrasound scanning uses sound waves to create images of the insides of a patient's body. To create an ultrasound scan, a doctor presses a small device back and forth over the area that needs to be examined. The device is called a transducer, and it emits sound waves. The sound waves are not audible to humans. The sound waves travel into the body and bounce back when they hit a bone, body fluid, or soft tissue, such as a muscle or organ. The transducer receives these signals and transmits them to a computer.

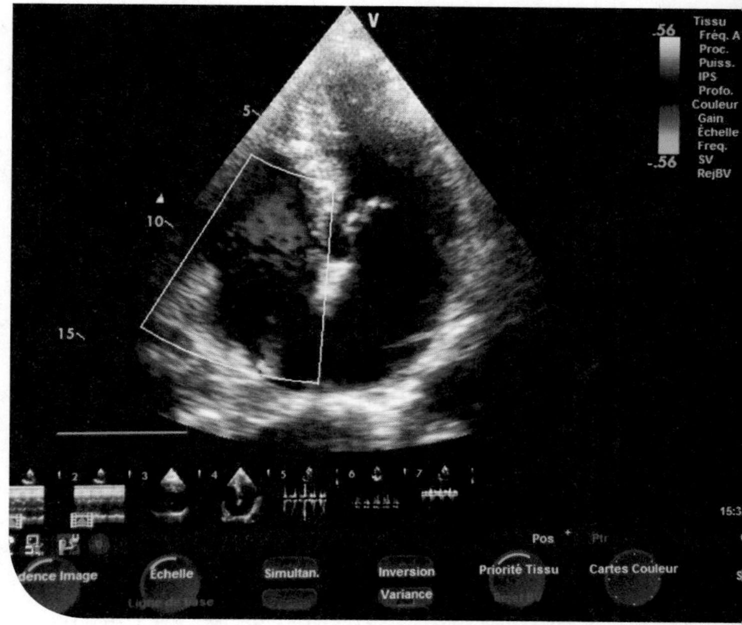

12 As the doctor moves the transducer back and forth, images of different angles of the organ or internal area are depicted on the computer screen. The doctor can also see movement within the body in real time, such as how blood flows through a valve in the heart. This is a very different way of seeing inside the body from other forms of medical imaging, which typically capture a static image.

13 Doctors use ultrasound scanning to diagnose diseases related to internal organs, as well as problems with blood flow. Ultrasound scans can also help doctors detect deterioration or damage to muscles and tendons.

Computed Axial Tomography

14 Computed axial tomography uses X-rays to create an image, but at a much lower dose than the traditional radiography machine. The image created by this type of technology is called a CAT scan. Sometimes it is called a CT (computed tomography) scan. CAT scan technology was invented in the 1970s.

15 The word *computed* in the name of this technology is a big clue to how it works. First, the patient lies down on a table. The table slides into a large, round device. An X-ray machine mounted inside the device then emits X-rays as it rotates around the patient. The X-rays that pass through the body are received on the other side of the device. The machine creates thousands of images in a matter of seconds. The images are called "slices." A computer then merges—or "computes"—these slices into a single, highly detailed image of the area scanned. And unlike a traditional X-ray image, the image created from a CAT scan does differentiate among tissues of similar density.

16 Doctors use CAT scans to diagnose many different types of conditions, including brain and spinal cord injuries, many different types of cancer, and circulatory and heart problems.

Magnetic Resonance Imaging

17 Magnetic resonance imaging works in much the same way as CAT scans. The patient lies on a bed and a machine rotates around the patient, taking pictures. However, an MRI machine does not use X-rays to create the images. Instead, an MRI machine uses a powerful magnet to move atoms in the patient's body. This movement is not visible to the human eye, and is so slight that the patient does not feel anything during the procedure. But when the atoms move, they give off radio waves. The radio waves are measured, and a computer translates the measurements into an image.

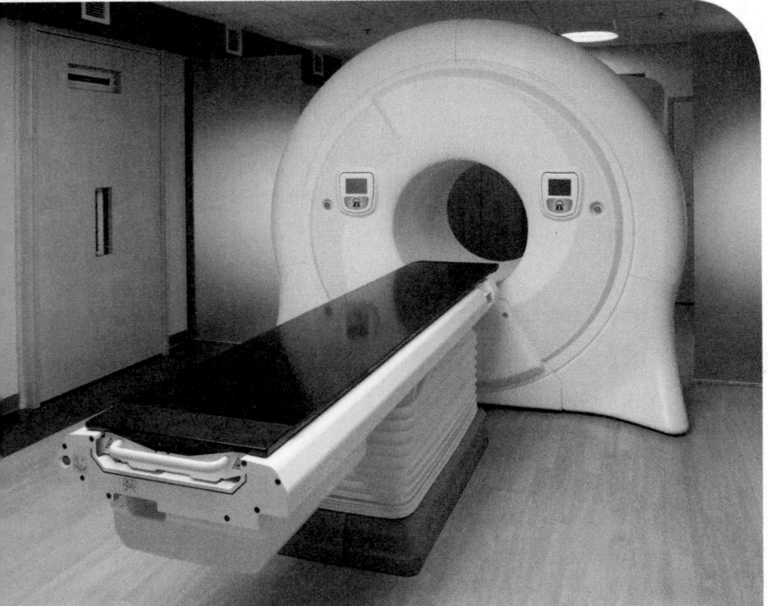

18 MRIs show an even higher level of contrast than CAT scans among tissues that are only slightly different in density. Some people think an MRI is always the better choice over a CAT scan. However, CAT scans are much quicker to administer. So if a doctor has only minutes to evaluate a brain injury in the emergency room, he or she will likely order a CAT scan.

Molecular Imaging

19 Molecular imaging, developed in the 1990s, is an amazing advancement in the field of medical imaging. This type of imaging allows a doctor to see a part of a patient's body at the cellular and even the molecular level.

20 The first step in creating a molecular image is to have the patient swallow a radioactive material. The material can also be injected into the patient. (But don't worry! The material has a very low level of radioactivity.) The material used is different depending on what condition the patient may have. For example, a patient with a thyroid problem would be given one type of radioactive material. A patient with heart disease would be given another type.

21 The material attaches to the organ or cellular area that is to be examined. Then the patient lies down on a table for 30 minutes to an hour while a scanner moves over the patient. The scanner detects emissions from the radioactive material. A computer uses this data to create a highly detailed image of the body part.

22 Molecular imaging is especially useful for detecting tumors and other abnormal cellular growth. This type of image can also reveal whether an organ is diseased or not functioning properly. That is because the radioactive material will adhere to and emit radiation from an unhealthy organ differently than it would from a healthy organ.

Future Images

23 It is hard to imagine how medical imaging will advance over the next 100 years. But it is likely that scientists will invent technology that allows us to create even clearer pictures that focus on even smaller areas and provide even greater information. And just as we do, the people of the future will have the X-ray to thank for these advancements.

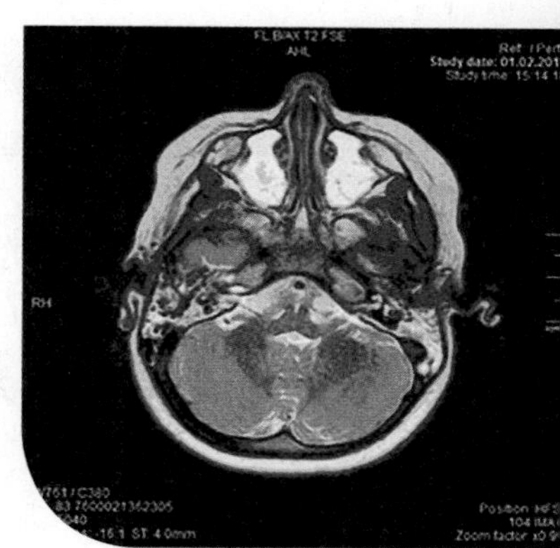

Researchers often use molecular images—such as this one of the brain—to assess how an organ is functioning.

Comprehension Check

1A. What is the meaning of the word *tissue*, as used in paragraph 9?

a. a soft, thin piece of paper

b. a group of cells made up of the same material

c. an image created from electromagnetic radiation

d. a type of disease

1B. What phrase from the text supports the answer to Part A?

a. "very detailed picture"

b. "bone is broken"

c. "cellular material"

d. "certain diagnoses"

2A. What is the purpose of paragraph 9?

a. to provide an expert opinion

b. to explain why X-Rays are frequently used

c. to explain a limitation of X-rays

d. to contrast X-rays with CAT scans

2B. What phrase from the text supports the answer to Part A?

a. ". . . does not give a very detailed picture of the body part."

b. ". . . it is easy to see the break in the bone . . ."

c. ". . . can reveal if a patient has a tumor . . ."

d. ". . . same density as the tissue that surrounds it . . ."

Comprehension Check

3A. When does the patient swallow radioactive material in the process of creating a molecular image?

a. after the scanner detects emissions

b. when the computer creates the image

c. before being scanned

d. while the doctor reviews the images

3B. What phrase from the text supports the answer to Part A?

a. "then the patient"

b. "to an hour"

c. "can also"

d. "the first step"

4A. What is the author's point of view toward medical imaging?

a. It is dangerous.

b. It is a great technology.

c. It is too expensive.

d. It is boring.

4B. What phrase from the text supports the answer to Part A?

a. "amazing advancement"

b. "electrical discharges"

c. "cannot distinguish"

d. "are called 'slices'"

5A. What is the author's purpose in writing this text?

a. to inform readers about the dangers of medical imaging

b. to entertain readers with wacky stories about medical imaging discoveries

c. to inform readers about the benefits of medical imaging

d. to persuade readers to avoid medical imaging

5B. What phrase from the text supports the answer to Part A?

a. "radioactive material"

b. "Today, fortunately"

c. "accidentally swallowed a coin"

d. "cut you open"

6. Which sentences in paragraph 12 help develop the idea that ultrasound scanning gives doctors a different way of seeing body parts from other imaging technologies? How do these sentences develop this idea?

____

____

____

____

7. Read the sentence below from paragraph 15.

An X-ray machine mounted inside the device then emits X-rays as it rotates around the patient.

What is the tone of the sentence? How would the tone of the sentence change if the author had written the words *gadget*, *spews*, and *goes around* instead of the words *device*, *emits*, and *rotates*?

8. What is the author's point of view toward whether MRIs or CAT scans are better? How do you know? What conflicting point of view does the author acknowledge? How does the author respond to it?

9. Why does the author explain how doctors diagnosed internal issues over 100 years ago at the start of the article? Support your answer with evidence from the text.

10. Write a summary of the article for someone who has not read it. Do not include your own opinion or any information you may have known prior to your reading.

RI.8.9, SL.8.1.a, SL.8.1.c, SL.8.1.d

Compare and Contrast Texts

In this unit, you have read a science magazine article about near-Earth objects, a science journal publication about controlling epidemics, a persuasive essay about solar energy, and a magazine article about medical imaging. Complete the chart below with notes about how the authors expressed their points of view toward their subjects. Then use your notes to write a brief essay on a separate sheet of paper, comparing and contrasting how the authors expressed their points of view about these topics. Be prepared to discuss your ideas with the class.

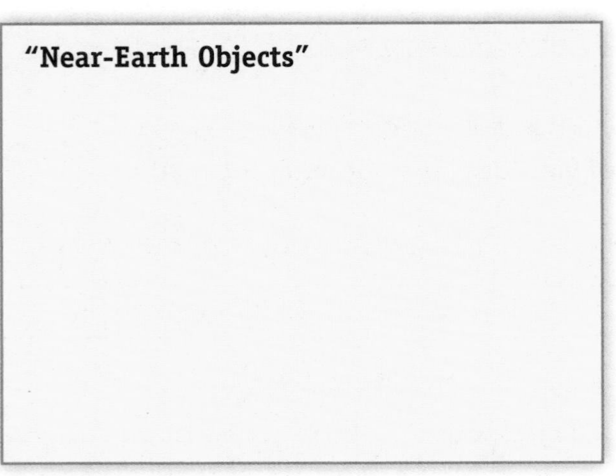

"Controlling Disease Outbreaks"

"The Power of Solar Energy"

"The Wonders of Medical Imaging"

Return to the Essential Question

How do authors use language and text structure to express their points of view?

In small groups or as a class, discuss the Essential Question. Think about what you have learned about understanding technical language, analyzing text structure, and determining an author's point of view and purpose. Use evidence from the four texts in this unit to answer the question.

L.8.4.c, L.8.4.d

Using Reference Materials

Guided Instruction If you are unsure of a word's pronunciation or its part of speech, or if you want to verify the meaning you have inferred from context, you can find the information you need in a reference source. **Reference materials** include **dictionaries, thesauruses**, and **glossaries**, and they exist in both print and digital formats. Read the example dictionary, glossary, and thesaurus entries below for the word *harness*.

Dictionary:

harness (har-niss) 1. *noun.* A piece of equipment made of leather straps that connects a draft or working animal to something heavy that it must pull, such as a cart or wagon. *We need to tighten the harness, or the horse may get loose.* 2. *verb.* To gain control of something in order to use it. *Let's harness our creativity and focus it on one idea.*

Glossary:

harness to bring under control in order to make effective use of

Thesaurus:

harness 1. (n) Synonyms: gear, equipment, trappings. 2. (v) Synonyms: curb, tame, govern, secure. Antonyms: disconnect, free, liberate, unlock.

Guided Practice Use the dictionary, glossary, and thesaurus entries above to complete the sentences below.

1. The word *harness* can be used as a noun or a ______________.
2. The letter "n" in the word *harness* is pronounced in the ______________ syllable.
3. The word *liberate* is a/an ______________ for the word *harness*.
4. The sentence "The harness was old, and the straps were fraying" uses the word *harness* as it relates to the ______________ definition given for the word.

Independent Practice Reread paragraph 20 of "The Wonders of Medical Imaging" on page 194. Use context clues to make a preliminary determination of the meaning of the words *molecular* and *radioactive*. Then, using a reference source, write the meanings of the words as well as their pronunciations and parts of speech.

____

____

RI.8.4, RI.8.5, RI.8.6, RI.8.10, L.8.4.c, L.8.4.d

Read the following magazine advertisement and magazine article that include technical language, particular text structures, and a point of view. Then answer the questions on pages 201 and 202.

The VSC 1:
A Smart Choice

1 Environmentalists often complain about the pollution created by cars, trucks, and SUVs. They advocate for stronger regulations for carbon dioxide emissions, and they see the auto industry as their adversary. But the automobile industry has recently come up with a viable solution to car pollution. It's the latest and best microcar on the market: the VSC 1. ("VSC" literally stands for "Very Small Car.")

2 The VSC 1 is about 8 feet long, weighs about 1,700 pounds, and seats just two people—much smaller and lighter than the average car, truck, or SUV. As a result, it requires far less fuel in order to run. In fact, while the average midsize car averages about 27 miles per gallon, the VSC 1 averages 50 miles per gallon of fuel. This translates into less oil drilling and less destruction of the environment.

3 The gasoline-fueled VSC 1 is a smart choice when it comes to carbon dioxide. Its emissions rating is just 87 g/km (grams of carbon dioxide per kilometer driven). Compare that to a typical SUV's rating of 150 g/km. As you can see, the VSC 1 emits nearly 50 percent less polluting carbon dioxide into our air than an SUV. But you can do even better: the all-electric version of the VSC 1 runs on fuel cells that emit no carbon dioxide at all!

4 The VSC 1 is a smart choice for the environment. But it's also a smart choice for your budget. A midsize car averages $30,000, and an SUV $40,000, but you can purchase a gas-fueled VSC 1 for as little as $12,500! If you're ready to be smart about the environment *and* your budget, then the VSC 1 is for you!

Microcars:
Not Smart and Not Safe

1 Advertisers often tout the low cost of microcars. They fail to mention that nonpolluting, all-electric microcars can cost as much as luxury midsize cars. And many other kinds of microcars require a special type of fuel that is more expensive than gasoline. The high costs of this fuel could reduce the financial advantage of owning a microcar.

2 But the biggest problem with the microcar is safety. Microcar manufacturers cite the cars' cagelike frame to counter any safety concerns. This type of frame is modeled after the roll cages that protect race-car drivers when they crash. But no frame can overcome the laws of physics. A tiny car will sustain great damage when hit with the force of a bigger, heavier car.

3 If you're still interested in a microcar, consider this: The bestselling version received only three stars in Europe's five-star crash rating system.

Circle the letter of the correct answer choice.

1A. What is the meaning of the word *force* as used in "Microcars: Not Smart and Not Safe"?

a. personal strength

b. ability to cause an object to undergo a change

c. ability to make someone do something

d. mechanical power

1B. What detail from the text supports the answer to Part A?

a. "roll cages"

b. "safety concerns"

c. "protect race-car drivers"

d. "sustain great damage"

2A. What is the topic of the fourth paragraph of "The VSC 1: A Smart Choice"?

a. SUVs are too expensive.

b. It is important to protect the environment.

c. The VSC 1 is budget-friendly.

d. The VSC 1 is becoming popular.

2B. Which sentence from the paragraph supports the answer to Part A?

a. the first sentence

b. the second sentence

c. the third sentence

d. the fourth sentence

3A. How does the author of "The VSC 1: A Smart Choice" develop the idea that the VSC 1 is a "smart choice when it comes to carbon dioxide"?

a. by providing specific data

b. by providing an expert opinion

c. by countering a viewpoint

d. by using an example

3B. What detail from the text supports the answer to Part A?

a. "emissions rating"

b. "rating of just 87 g/km"

c. "a popular SUV"

d. "per kilometer driven"

4A. In "Microcars: Not Smart and Not Safe," what is the author's point of view toward the frame used in microcars?

a. It makes microcars as safe as full-size cars.

b. It is a good safety feature.

c. It is more effective than a roll cage.

d. It still does not make a microcar as safe as a regular car.

4B. Which detail from the text supports the answer to Part A?

a. "no frame can overcome the laws of physics"

b. "to counter any safety concerns"

c. "sustain great damage"

d. "modeled after the roll cages that protect race-car drivers"

5A. The author of "Microcars: Not Smart and Not Safe" responds to the conflicting viewpoint that microcars are budget-friendly by discussing

a. fuel costs.

b. the laws of physics.

c. emissions ratings.

d. safety ratings.

5B. Which detail from the text supports the answer to Part A?

a. "150 g/km"

b. "$30,000"

c. "more expensive than gasoline"

d. "just three stars"

RI.8.4, RI.8.6, L.8.4.c, L.8.4.d

6A. How are the purposes of the two authors alike?

- **a.** They both want to warn readers about microcars.
- **b.** They both want to encourage readers to buy microcars.
- **c.** They both want to inform readers about microcars.
- **d.** They both want to inform readers about microcar safety.

6B. Which detail from the text supports the answer to Part A?

- **a.** "environmentalists often complain"
- **b.** "a viable solution to car pollution"
- **c.** "tout its low cost"
- **d.** "but the biggest problem"

7. What impact does the use of the phrase "laws of physics" have on the meaning and tone in the second paragraph of "Microcars: Not Smart and Not Safe"?

____

____

8. Why does the author of "Microcars: Not Smart and Not Safe" explain that the microcar frame is modeled after race-car roll cages? Cite evidence from the text.

____

____

____

9. How do the words *complain* and *stronger regulations* in paragraph 1 of "The VSC 1: A Smart Choice" help you understand the meaning of the word *adversary*? How does knowing the dictionary definition—"enemy; opponent"—of *adversary* help you understand how environmentalists feel about the auto industry?

____

____

____

10. Without including your own opinion, summarize "Microcars: Not Smart and Not Safe."

____

____

____

Introducing UNIT 8

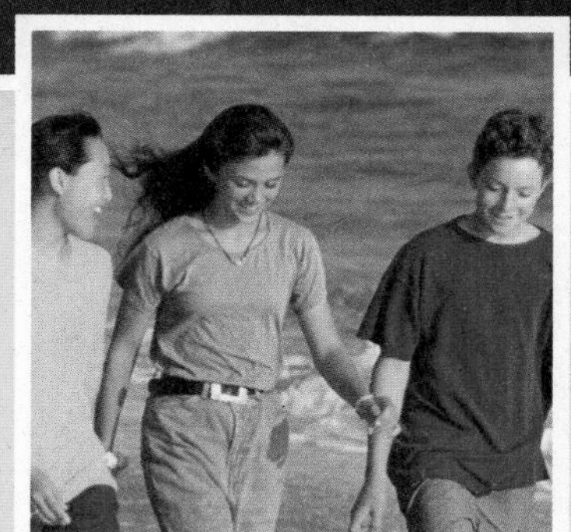

In this unit about scientific solutions, you will learn how to write a research report. In this type of writing, you first conduct research to answer a question. Then you organize your findings into a clear report that explains the results of your research to a reader. Writing a research report not only builds your knowledge about a topic, but also teaches you how to find reliable answers to your questions and how to put information together in a way that makes sense. These skills are useful in school and in life, such as when you have to decide how to vote on an issue or choose what computer to spend your money on.

When conducting research, gather evidence from multiple print and digital sources that are both credible and accurate. Then organize the information in your report by grouping related information, and develop your topic with facts and details. You must also accurately quote or properly paraphrase information you use from your sources, and cite the sources so that others can see where your information came from.

Progress Check Can I?

Before Unit 8		After Unit 8
☐	Conduct a short research project to answer a self-generated question.	☐
☐	Gather relevant information from multiple print and digital sources.	☐
☐	Quote or paraphrase information appropriately.	☐
☐	Develop and organize writing appropriate to the task, purpose, and audience.	☐
☐	Understand and use the conditional and subjunctive moods of a verb.	☐
☐	Use verb voice and mood correctly.	☐

HOME ✦ CONNECT...

In this unit, your child will learn to conduct research to answer a question and to present the findings of the research in a report. Your child will **group related information and develop the report topic with relevant facts and details**. Help your child with these skills by working together to identify how authors of other types of informational texts, such as newspaper and magazine articles, group information and develop their topics with facts and details.

You can assist your child with learning how to **conduct research** by discussing where and how to find information about a topic. Identify a question that you and your child might research together—for example, one prompted by a television show or news article. Then ask your child what kind of book or Internet source might contain the desired information. Check out books from your local library and look up Web sites for reliable media organizations and government agencies. Guide your child as he or she reviews the source to find relevant facts and details. Encourage your child to take notes on index cards or in a computer program and to group related information.

Activity: Explore with your child the unit theme "scientific solutions." Together, research and discuss what scientists consider to be the greatest scientific solutions of the past 100 years. You and your child might choose to create a time line that shows five or six of the innovations, or you might choose to write a biography of the scientist who came up with the solution.

IN THIS UNIT, YOUR CHILD WILL...

- Learn to conduct research and write a research report that introduces a topic, organizes information logically, and ends with a conclusion.
- Use relevant facts, details, and examples to develop the topic.
- Paraphrase and quote information from sources.
- Include transitions, such as *however* (to signal a difference) and *another* (to signal an addition).
- Choose precise language over vague or general terms.
- Form and use verbs in the conditional and subjunctive moods.
- Correct inappropriate shifts in verb voice and mood.

NOTE: All of these learning goals for your child are based on the Grade 8 Common Core State Standards for English Language Arts.

WAYS TO HELP YOUR CHILD

Help your child understand what it means to develop a topic with facts, details, and examples. When having a conversation with your child, ask what kind of fact, detail, or example might support or help explain a point he or she makes. If your child has difficulty responding, ask questions to guide your child to recognize the kind of information that would develop his or her point.

ONLINE

For more Home Connect activities, continue online at sadlierconnect.com

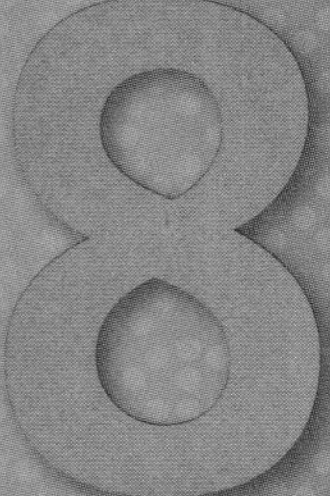

Research to Build and Present Knowledge: Write Research Reports

Essential Question:
How can writers use their research to inform readers about a topic?

W.8.2.a–e, W.8.7

CREATING AN ORGANIZATIONAL STRUCTURE

Logan used an outline like the one below to organize his research report.

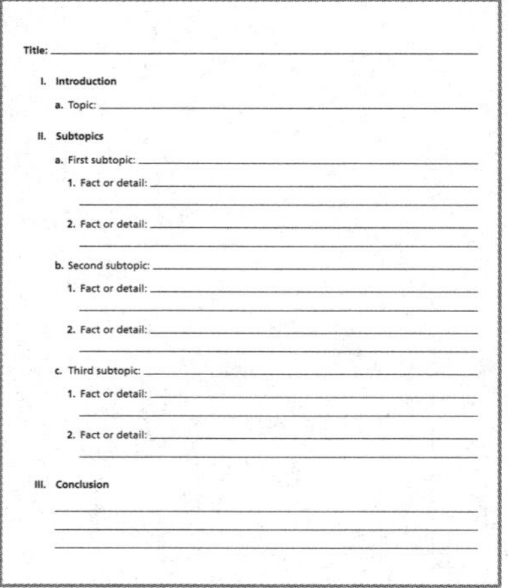

Title: ______

I. **Introduction**
   a. Topic: ______

II. **Subtopics**
   a. First subtopic: ______
      1. Fact or detail: ______
      2. Fact or detail: ______
   b. Second subtopic: ______
      1. Fact or detail: ______
      2. Fact or detail: ______
   c. Third subtopic: ______
      1. Fact or detail: ______
      2. Fact or detail: ______

III. **Conclusion**

______

TITLE

- Signals what the research report will be about
- Should interest the reader and give an idea of the writer's position on the topic

INTRODUCTION

- Introduces the topic and previews what is to come
- Establishes the formal tone of the report, using precise language and transitions that link ideas

ORGANIZATION

Subheadings group related information and establish an organizational structure.

Read a Student Model

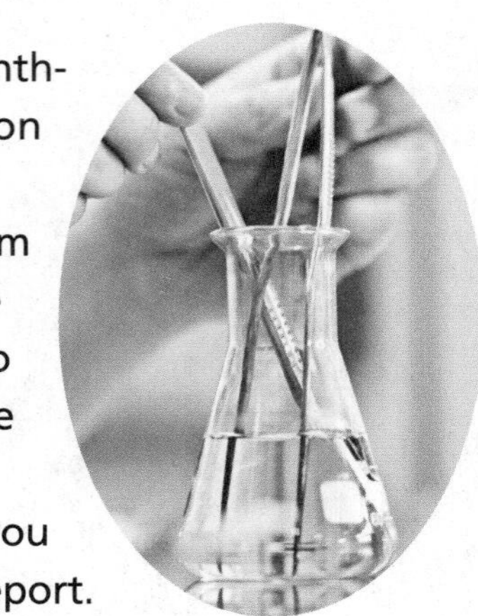

Logan is a student in Ms. Watson's eighth-grade Language Arts class. Ms. Watson gave Logan's class an assignment to write a research report about a problem that affects many people around the world and the scientific solution[s] to the problem. The report should include well-organized information from multiple sources. Think about a topic you might choose for your own research report.

Providing Water for Everyone

According to the United Nations, one out of every eight people worldwide does not have adequate access to water. In some countries, as much as half the population lacks access to clean drinking water. People who lack clean water are more likely to suffer and die from disease. Farmers without enough water to irrigate their crops suffer financially and often live in poverty. Fortunately, scientists have developed several strategies to help address the world's water crisis by increasing and maximizing the supply of safe water. These strategies include desalination, trickle irrigation, and distillation units.

Desalination

The oceans make up 97 percent of our water, but ocean water is not drinkable due to its high salt content. Human kidneys cannot process that much salt. A person drinking only ocean water might die in just a few days. The salt content of ocean water also kills plants, so salt water cannot be used to irrigate crops.

W.8.7, W.8.8, WHST.8.9

However, removing salt from ocean water is one effective method for increasing the world's supply of safe water. According to the American Water Works Association, there are two ways to desalinate ocean water. One way is to heat up the water and collect the steam. When the steam is cooled, it turns back into water—but without any salt. The other way is to run the water through a special filter that removes the salt. Desalination facilities are particularly useful for countries that border an ocean.

Trickle Irrigation

Currently, about 70 percent of the world's usable water is used to irrigate crops. The most common methods of irrigation—flood irrigation and overhead (or sprinkler) irrigation—waste as much as 50 percent of the water they use. With these methods, much of the water evaporates or is delivered to areas where it is not needed. Trickle irrigation, however, uses pipes that run along the crops and are "capable of delivering water precisely at the plant," says Michael A. Kizer, irrigation specialist. So water is not wasted; instead, it is maximized.

Distillation Units

People in less developed countries often live in areas where there is no plumbing. They use buckets to get water from wells, lakes, and rivers, but this water is often contaminated with disease-causing bacteria and toxins. However, a distillation unit can filter contaminated water to make it usable. One type of distillation unit is about as big as a dishwasher. It can provide clean water for one hundred people a day.

PARAPHRASING

Logan paraphrases information by putting it in his own words. He also gives credit to the source of the information.

Box the sentences that paraphrase information about how to desalinate ocean water. Circle the source of the information.

QUOTATIONS

Including a quotation from an expert gives credibility to the ideas in your research paper.

Underline the quotation and expert source Logan includes. Put an asterisk before the idea that the quotation supports.

RELEVANT INFORMATION

Make sure the information you gather from your sources is relevant—relating directly to your topic—and useful. Logan provides relevant information about the water problem in less developed countries.

Circle the relevant information about the problem with water from wells, lakes, and rivers.

W.8.2.f, W.8.6, W.8.7, W.8.8

CONCLUSION

Logan's conclusion supports and summarizes the ideas he presents in his report.

Underline the sentence that summarizes the topic of Logan's report.

The United Nations recently announced that the number of people lacking access to safe water was reduced by 50 percent between 1990 and 2010. However, we are still in the midst of a clean-water crisis. Approximately 2.5 billion people worldwide would benefit greatly from improved access to clean water. Furthermore, approximately 3,000 children die every day from diseases and complications due to unsanitary water or dehydration. We can hope that in the years ahead, solutions such as desalination, trickle irrigation, and distillation units—as well as future inventions—will continue to increase people's access to safe water.

LIST OF SOURCES

Use a variety of print and digital sources when gathering information. Be careful to use only accurate information from reliable, trustworthy sources. Try checking the information by looking at other Web sites or at print materials. Include a source list at the end of your research report so that readers can see that your information came from reliable sources. A source list also allows readers to find the sources of your information if they are interested in your topic.

Circle the sources that are books. Box the sources that are Internet sites.

Sources

American Water Works Association. 2011. Desalination of Seawater. Denver, CO: American Water Works Association. Print.

"Provide Access to Clean Water." National Academy of Engineering of the National Academies. N.p., n.d. Web. 15 Aug. 2013.

"World meets goal of boosting access to clean water but lags on better sanitation—UN." UN News Centre. United Nations, 6 Mar. 2012. Web. 15 Aug. 2013.

World Water Assessment Programme. 2006. Water: A Shared Responsibility: The United Nations World Water Development Report 2. Paris and New York: United Nations Educational, Scientific and Cultural Organization and Berghahn Books. Print.

W.8.6, W.8.7, W.8.8, W.8.9, WHST.8.9

Use index cards like the ones below to take notes for your research report about a problem and the scientific solution or solutions related to it. You should use both print and digital sources to find information. You will then use your notes to create your outline on page 210.

Problem: ______________________________

Source 1

Summarize or paraphrase information:

Source 2

Summarize or paraphrase information:

Source 3

Summarize or paraphrase information:

WRITE RESEARCH REPORTS

W.8.2.a–f, W.8.4, W.8.5, W.8.6, W.8.7, W.8.8, W.8.9, W.8.10, WHST.8.9

Use this outline to organize your research report for the Common Core Review on page 215. Then write your first draft on another sheet of paper. Develop your subtopics with relevant facts and quotations and write in a formal style, using precise, domain-specific vocabulary. Use transition words to create coherence.

Title: ______________________________

I. Introduction

a. Topic: ______________________________

II. Subtopics

a. First subtopic: ______________________________

1. Fact or detail: ______________________________

____

2. Fact or detail: ______________________________

____

b. Second subtopic: ______________________________

1. Fact or detail: ______________________________

____

2. Fact or detail: ______________________________

____

c. Third subtopic: ______________________________

1. Fact or detail: ______________________________

____

2. Fact or detail: ______________________________

____

III. Conclusion

____

____

____

L.8.1.c

Conditional and Subjunctive Moods

Guided Instruction A **verb** is a word that shows an action or a state of being. The **conditional mood** of a verb is used to express an action or a state of being that might happen or might exist in the future if something else happens. To express the conditional mood, use the words *might*, *could*, or *would* with another verb. The **subjunctive mood** of a verb is used to express a wish, a state of existence contrary to reality, or a hypothetical situation. The most commonly used form of the subjunctive is the verb *were*.

- **Conditional Mood**

  The table might break if you put that heavy box on it.

  If you practice more, you could shine as the soloist in the concert.

  If my grandparents moved out of state, I would be sad.

- **Subjunctive Mood**

  She wishes she were at the football game. (expresses a wish)

  If I were you, I would wear a jacket. (expresses a state contrary to reality)

  If you were to enter the race, you would probably win it. (expresses a hypothetical situation)

  Notice that the subjunctive mood often appears in a sentence that has another verb in the conditional mood.

Guided Practice Underline the verb in the conditional or subjunctive mood in each sentence. Then write which mood it is.

1. He might become upset if you use his phone without asking first. _______________
2. If she were to change schools, people would miss her. _______________
3. I would review all my notes before taking the test if I had more time. _______________

Independent Practice Write three original sentences, two using the conditional mood and one using the subjunctive mood of a verb.

1. ____
2. ____
3. ____

Verb Voice and Mood

Guided Instruction A **verb** can be used in the **active voice** or the **passive voice**. In the active voice, the verb shows the sentence's subject performing the action of the verb on the object.

Subject	Verb	Object
The soccer player	*kicked*	*the ball.*

In the passive voice, the verb shows the sentence's subject receiving the action of the verb; the action is performed by the sentence's object.

Subject	Verb	Object
The ball	*was kicked*	*by the soccer player.*

Generally, the active voice is the preferred voice, and writers should be careful not to shift unnecessarily from the active voice to the passive voice (and vice versa).

A verb can also be used in different **moods**. A mood expresses a state of being. You have learned about the **conditional** and **subjunctive** moods. Three additional moods are the **indicative**, the **imperative**, and the **interrogative**.

- The **indicative mood** expresses a state of fact.

  He is my brother. I am giving him my train set.

- The **imperative mood** expresses a state of command.

  Listen to your mother. Turn off the lights. Do it now!

- The **interrogative mood** expresses a state of questioning.

  Why are we walking this way? Do you know where we're going?

Use the correct form of the verb for the mood needed. Do not shift from one mood to another unnecessarily within a sentence. For example:

Are you going to the computer lab and send me that file.

This sentence shifts from the interrogative mood to the imperative mood and does not make sense to the reader. It should be rewritten as:

Are you going to the computer lab? Send me that file.

L.8.1.d

Guided Practice Rewrite each sentence below to correct the underlined inappropriate shift in verb voice or mood. The correct voice or mood is indicated after each incorrect sentence.

1. Put the dishes away, and then <u>you should</u> sweep the floor. (imperative)

   ____

2. If I <u>was</u> you, I would do my homework first. (subjunctive)

   ____

3. After Joe closed the door, <u>the light was shut off by him</u>. (active voice)

   ____

4. I <u>will go</u> to the store now if I had money. (conditional)

   ____

5. <u>Is</u> the sky blue. (indicative)

   ____

Independent Practice Write five sentences that contain an inappropriate shift in verb voice or mood. Then switch pages with a partner, and rewrite your partner's sentences to correct the inappropriate shift.

1. ______________________________
2. ______________________________
3. ______________________________
4. ______________________________
5. ______________________________

SL.8.1.a–d, SL.8.3, SL.8.4, SL.8.6

Discuss the Essential Question

How can writers use their research to inform readers about a topic?

Prepare for a class discussion about the Essential Question by responding to the questions below. Support your point of view with reasons and examples.

1. How did Logan organize information about his topic?

2. Which relevant information did Logan use to develop his topic?

3. What sources did Logan use? How did he make use of the sources?

Use your notes above as you discuss the Essential Question with your class or in small groups. Follow the discussion rules on the "Did I?" checklist (page 58). Use the organizer below to record your ideas and what you hear in the classroom.

Ideas I Agree or Disagree With		Questions I Asked
Agree		
Disagree		
New Ideas I Had During Discussion		**Questions I Answered**

W.8.2.a–b, W.8.7, W.8.8, L.8.1.d

Read this draft introductory paragraph from a student research report and answer the questions below.

(1) Air pollution from cars and coal-burning power plants is a problem that affects the health of people around the world. (2) Breathing polluted air can cause major respiratory problems for some people, including triggering asthma attacks in people who suffer from asthma. (3) Lung cancer and heart disease can even be caused by breathing polluted air. (4) Scientists have found some solutions for reducing air pollution and making our air healthier to breathe.

1. What is the topic of this research report?

a. triggers of asthma attacks

b. coal-burning power plants

c. solutions for reducing air pollution

d. lung cancer and heart disease

2. Based on this introduction, what is a subhead that you would expect to see in this research report?

a. Tropical Diseases

b. Reducing Pollution from Cars

c. The Benefits of Coal Power

d. Air Pollution Is Not a Problem

3. Which of the following is a source that might be credited in this research report?

a. *Plants Make the World Green*

b. *Exercises for a Healthier Heart*

c. *The Ten Most Famous Scientists*

d. *Our Air Pollution Crisis*

4. Which sentences provide information about how air pollution causes health problems?

a. 1 and 2

b. 2 and 3

c. 3 and 4

d. 1 and 4

5. Which of the following is the best way to revise sentence 3?

a. Heart disease and lung cancer can even be caused by breathing polluted air.

b. Breathing polluted air can even cause lung cancer and heart disease.

c. Heart disease and lung cancer are caused by breathing polluted air.

d. Breathing polluted air and lung cancer can even cause heart disease.

6. Which detail would best develop this topic?

a. the number of people affected by air pollution

b. the number of people with lung cancer

c. the number of people in the world

d. the number of people with heart disease

UNIT 8 COMMON CORE REVIEW

W.8.2.a–f, W.8.4, W.8.5, W.8.6, W.8.7, W.8.8, W.8.9, W.8.10, L.8.1.c, L.8.1.d

Read these next two paragraphs from the student research report and answer the questions below.

> (1) For decades, cars have been a major source of air pollution. (2) The engine in a conventional car burns gasoline to power the vehicle, and pollutants are created and released into the air through the car's tailpipe. (3) However, a recent scientific advancement—the electric car—is helping to reduce air pollution. (4) One kind of electric car "produces up to 60 percent fewer emissions than a conventional car," writes Susan Cosier of Audubon magazine.
>
> (5) In the United States, coal-burning power plants are a major source of air pollutants. (6) The pollutants are released through smokestacks. (7) Recently, some power plants have begun installing "scrubbers" in their smokestacks. (8) These scrubbers collect many pollutants. (9) One large plant has reduced its mercury emissions, which can cause heart problems, by 90 percent using scrubbers. (10) Imagine how much cleaner our air would be if all power plants used scrubbers.

7. Box the sentence that contains an inappropriate shift from active to passive voice.

8. Explain why the writer includes the source of the quotation in sentence 4.

____

9. Circle the sentence that expresses the conditional mood of a verb.

10. Write a concluding summary for this research report.

____

____

____

Assignment: On a separate piece of paper, provide a final draft of your research report. Use what you have learned about verb voice and moods, and watch out for inappropriate shifts in either. Think about how you and your classmates answered the Essential Question. Check your outline to be sure you organize your ideas well. Paraphrase and quote relevant source information properly, and use precise language and transitions.

Introducing UNIT 9

This unit returns to a focus on literature to help you integrate knowledge and ideas through literary analysis. In this section, you will read texts that focus on the theme of facing one's fears. The texts range from excerpts from classic American fiction and film script adaptations of those works to an original story about a contemporary quest. You'll have opportunities to analyze the ways centuries-old traditional themes, character types, and story events are given new life and vitality as they are incorporated into new texts or adaptations of existing texts.

The next time you visit a movie theater, note how many of the films are adaptations of a text: a bestseller, a classic novel, a young adult book, a play, or even a comic book. In this unit, as you read portions of film scripts based on classic works, you'll understand the many choices an author must make when adapting a story from one medium to another. You'll be able to appreciate film adaptations more when you can evaluate them in terms of how they stay faithful to, or depart from, their original text sources.

Progress Check Can I?

Before Unit 9		After Unit 9
☐	Analyze how adaptations of works compare to their original sources by evaluating the choices made by the adapters.	☐
☐	Analyze how modern texts draw on themes, character types, and events from traditional literary sources.	☐
☐	Interpret texts by making artistic and ethical connections to a variety of cultural, historical, and other influences.	☐
☐	Use the relationships between particular words to determine word meanings.	☐

HOME ✦ CONNECT...

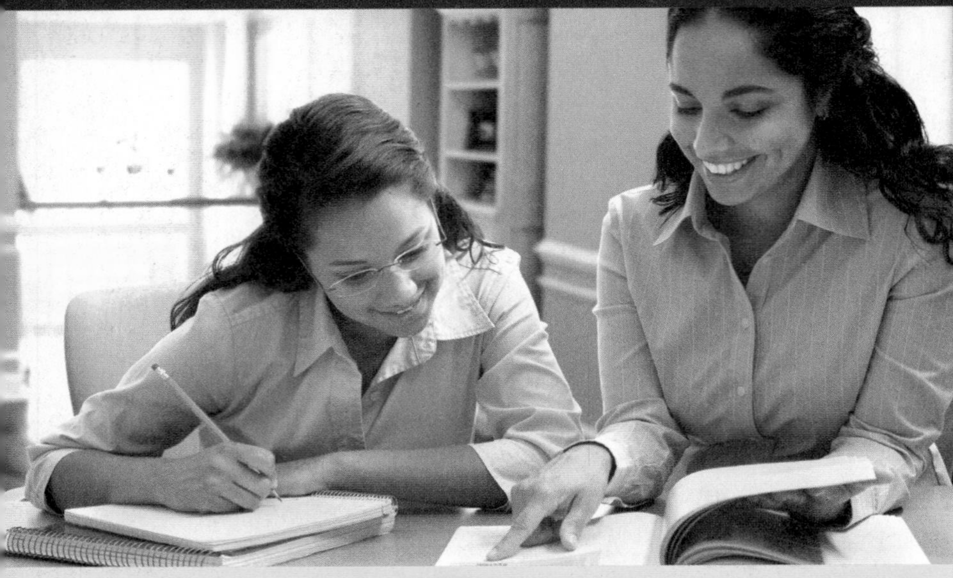

This unit begins by encouraging students to consider how to **analyze film adaptations of fiction** by comparing and contrasting film script adaptations to the essential elements of the original works—including the plot, setting, characters, and characters' feelings and actions. You can help your child prepare for this unit by watching a film version of a favorite work of fiction and discussing the similarities and differences between the two versions. Ask your child to consider the reasons the adapter might have had for making these changes.

Students will also **analyze sources of fiction**, evaluating how contemporary works draw on ancient, traditional story elements, making them seem fresh and new. Discuss myths, fairy tales, and other traditional stories your child is familiar with. Focus on recurring themes, story patterns, and character types: the wise elder, the beautiful princess, the hero on a dangerous quest, and so on. Discuss with your child how such age-old characters, plots, and themes take new forms in contemporary stories, films, comic books, games, and television shows.

Activity: Talk with your child about the unit theme, "facing your fears." Ask your child to make a list of his or her three worst fears. If your child is sensitive about this, then explore some commonly held fears instead, such as fear of heights, flying, or spiders. Work together to generate a list of possible strategies a person could use to combat those fears.

IN THIS UNIT, YOUR CHILD WILL...

- Read excerpts from classic American novels and their movie script versions, as well as a contemporary quest tale.
- Analyze how adaptations of literary texts differ from the original texts.
- Evaluate the choices creators of adaptations make.
- Learn how modern texts draw on age-old themes, story patterns, and character types.
- Make artistic and ethical connections between modern texts and other ideas and perspectives.
- Use word relationships to determine word meanings.
- Compare and contrast ideas on the theme of facing one's fears in several literary works.

NOTE: All of these learning goals for your child are based on the Grade 8 Common Core State Standards for English Language Arts.

WAYS TO HELP YOUR CHILD

Help your child practice analyzing common ideas, or archetypes, that appear across literary works. Work together to make a list of popular films. Talk about common themes, character types, and plot events in these films and decide which of them echo elements that your child has encountered in traditional and classic works of literature. Talk with your child about why these timeless elements might help to make a film popular.

ONLINE

For more Home Connect activities, continue online at sadlierconnect.com

UNIT 9

Reading Literature: Integration of Knowledge and Ideas

Essential Question:

How do authors use their interpretations of other works to create new art?

Guided Instruction

RL.8.7

WORDS TO KNOW

accumulate
contemplated
dexterously
exasperated
formidable
tumult

Literary texts often inspire films and plays. Some adaptations are faithful to their original texts, while others are very different. By **analyzing adaptations of literary texts**, you can determine how the adaptation relates to the original text source.

CITE EVIDENCE

A To determine how faithful an adaptation is to its source, identify major elements of the original text. Put an asterisk next to each character who is introduced on these two pages. How many characters are there? Which character is identified by name?

B A story's point of view may reveal a particular character's thoughts and feelings. Underline the evidence that tells whose thoughts are being revealed here; then underline sentences that tell what this character has realized about himself. How might a film version reveal this information?

The Red Badge of Courage

by Stephen Crane (excerpt)

(Genre: Novel)

This abridged chapter is an excerpt from the classic 1895 novel set during the American Civil War.

Chapter One

1 ...[Henry] perceived now that it did not greatly matter what kind of soldiers he was going to fight, so long as they fought, which fact no one disputed. There was a more serious problem. He lay in his bunk pondering upon it. He tried to mathematically prove to himself that he would not run from a battle. . . .

2 Previously he had never felt obliged to wrestle too seriously with this question. In his life he had taken certain things for granted, never challenging his belief in ultimate success, and bothering little about means and roads. But here he was confronted with a thing of moment. It had suddenly appeared to him that perhaps in a battle he might run. He was forced to admit that as far as war was concerned, he knew nothing of himself.

3 A little panic-fear grew in his mind. As his imagination went forward to a fight, he saw hideous possibilities. He **contemplated** the lurking menaces of the future, and failed in an effort to see himself standing stoutly in the midst of them. He recalled his visions of broken-bladed glory, but in the shadow of the impending **tumult** he suspected them to be impossible pictures.

4 He sprang from the bunk and began to pace nervously to and fro. "Good Lord, what's th' matter with me?" he said aloud.

5 He felt that in this crisis his laws of life were useless. Whatever he had learned of himself was here of no avail. He was an unknown quantity. He saw that he would again be obliged to experiment as he had in early youth. He must **accumulate** information of

RL.8.7

himself, and meanwhile he resolved to remain close upon his guard lest those qualities of which he knew nothing should everlastingly disgrace him. "Good Lord!" he repeated in dismay.

6 After a time the tall soldier slid **dexterously** through the hole. The loud private followed. They were wrangling.

7 "That's all right," said the tall soldier as he entered. He waved his hand expressively. "You can believe me or not, jest as you like. All you got to do is sit down and wait as quiet as you can. Then pretty soon you'll find out I was right."

8 His comrade grunted stubbornly. For a moment he seemed to be searching for a **formidable** reply. Finally he said: "Well, you don't know everything in the world, do you?"

9 "Didn't say I knew everything in the world," retorted the other sharply. He began to stow various articles snugly into his knapsack.

10 The youth, pausing in his nervous walk, looked down at the busy figure. "Going to be a battle, sure, is there, Jim?" he asked.

11 "Of course there is," replied the tall soldier. "Of course there is. You jest wait 'til to-morrow, and you'll see one of the biggest battles ever was. You jest wait."

12 "Thunder!" said the youth.

13 "Oh, you'll see fighting this time, my boy, what'll be regular out-and-out fighting," added the tall soldier, with the air of a man who is about to exhibit a battle for the benefit of his friends.

14 "Well," remarked the youth, "like as not this story'll turn out jest like them others did."

15 "Not much it won't," replied the tall soldier, **exasperated**. "Not much it won't. Didn't the cavalry all start this morning?" He glared about him. No one denied his statement. "The cavalry started this morning," he continued. "They say there ain't hardly any cavalry left in camp. They're going to Richmond, or some place, while we fight all the Johnnies. It's some dodge like that. . . ."

Guided Instruction

CITE EVIDENCE

C Authors do not always immediately identify when and where a story takes place. Instead, readers may have to use clues in the text to determine the setting and time period. Circle the paragraph on this page that offers the best clues to helping the reader figure out the time period of this story. How would you figure out the setting and time period of a film version?

D In both texts and films, you can learn about characters from their diction, or word choice. Box words or sentences that are examples of dialect—words and phrases used by people from a particular region or social class. What does the dialect tell you about these characters? What could a film reveal about them beyond what the text reveals?

E Double underline words and phrases on this page that describe how the characters act and speak. How would this information be conveyed in a film script?

Comprehension Check

Based on the excerpt so far, what would be the biggest challenge in adapting this novel to film?

Guided Instruction

RL.8.7

WORDS TO KNOW

altercation
epithet
impulsively
montage
scrimmage
tolerant

CITE EVIDENCE

A Both texts and films use dialogue to reveal character. Circle the questions that Henry asks Jim. What do these questions reveal about Henry? How important would it be to keep Henry's questions in a film adaptation?

B Because universal themes apply to basic human concerns, they may be explored in a variety of storylines. Underline a sentence that suggests this novel's theme. What does the theme have to say about life that might apply to characters and situations beyond the specific ones mentioned in the novel excerpt?

The Red Badge of Courage *continued*

16 The youth remained silent for a time. At last he spoke to the tall soldier. "Jim!"

17 "What?"

18 "How do you think the reg'ment 'll do?"

19 "Oh, they'll fight all right, I guess, after they once get into it," said the other with cold judgment. . . . "There's been heaps of fun poked at 'em because they're new, of course, and all that; but they'll fight all right, I guess."

20 "Think any of the boys 'll run?" persisted the youth.

21 "Oh, there may be a few of 'em run, but there's them kind in every regiment, 'specially when they first goes under fire," said the other in a **tolerant** way. "Of course it might happen that the hull kit-and-boodle might start and run, if some big fighting came first-off, and then again they might stay and fight like fun. But you can't bet on nothing. Of course they ain't never been under fire yet, and it ain't likely they'll lick the hull rebel army all-to-oncet the first time; but I think they'll fight better than some, if worse than others. . . .[M]ost of 'em 'll fight like sin after they oncet git shootin'," he added. . . .

22 "Oh, you think you know–" began the loud soldier with scorn.

23 The other turned savagely upon him. They had a rapid **altercation**, in which they fastened upon each other various strange **epithets**.

24 The youth at last interrupted them. "Did you ever think you might run yourself, Jim?" he asked. On concluding the sentence he laughed as if he had meant to aim a joke. The loud soldier also giggled.

25 The tall private waved his hand. "Well," said he profoundly, "I've thought it might get too hot for Jim Conklin in some of them **scrimmages**, and if a whole lot of boys started and run, why, I s'pose I'd start and run. . . . I'd run like the devil. But if everybody was a-standing and a-fighting, why, I'd stand and fight. Be jiminey, I would. I'll bet on it."

26 "Huh!" said the loud one.

27 The youth of this tale felt gratitude for these words of his comrade. He had feared that all of the untried men possessed great and correct confidence. He now was in a measure reassured.

RL.8.7

Red Badge

(Genre: Movie Script)

1 INTERIOR SHOT: SOLDIERS' DINING HALL ON THE SPACESHIP *GETTYSBURG.*

The year is 2216. The soldiers' dining hall is a large room on the giant battle spaceship Gettysburg. *A young man in his early 20s,* HENRY, *wearing his private's uniform, is pacing near the tables. No one else is present, suggesting that it's the equivalent of late night or early morning.*

HENRY (VOICEOVER)

I have a bad feeling about this. I can't stop thinking about what it's going to be like when the fighting starts. The Krynites are supposed to be unpredictable, and without mercy. And their ships may be faster than ours.

Henry looks around, thoughtfully, as music swells in the background.

HENRY (VOICEOVER)

5 Maybe I shouldn't have enlisted so **impulsively**. Maybe this was a big mistake.

Sad music plays over a brief montage: HENRY *at the recruiter's office, signing forms;* HENRY *putting on his uniform;* HENRY, *now in uniform, hugging a small child, a girl age 5, outside the ship's docking station. The* ***montage*** *ends with* HENRY *looking sadly at a holographic picture of the girl.*

HENRY (VOICEOVER)

What's wrong with me? .... Pull it together, man, you've got nothing to be afraid of.

Guided Instruction

CITE EVIDENCE

C A faithful adaptation will take place in the same setting described in the source material. However, some adaptations completely change the time and place of the original story. Double underline the elements of this film script excerpt that describe the setting of the film version.

D In film, a *voiceover* is offscreen narration or dialogue; it may reveal the thoughts of a character. Box a statement in one of Henry's voiceovers that is similar to something he says aloud in the novel. Are Henry's voiceovers true to the character as he was portrayed in the original novel?

E Place an asterisk by the section of the script adaptation that provides background to Henry's situation. If similar background had been in the novel excerpt, how would it have been presented? How would that have affected the text?

Comprehension Check

So far, what is the biggest change from the novel to the movie script? What elements are similar to the original? How might the changes affect the themes of the original story?

Guided Practice

RL.8.7

WORDS TO KNOW

diffidently
engaging
incursion
nonchalant
speculatively

CITE EVIDENCE

A Some films may "update" their source texts by changing the gender, ethnicity, or ages of characters. Circle the introduction of a character whose gender doesn't match the original text's character. Why might this change have been made?

B Box a description of how Henry tries to appear more confident than he feels. How is this like or unlike the way Henry is portrayed in the original novel? What might account for the differences?

C Place an asterisk next to dialogue that suggests the Sergeant trusts Henry. How is the dialogue between Henry and Jem in this section similar to and different from exchanges between Henry and Jim in the original text?

Red Badge *continued*

INTERIOR SHOT CONTINUED: SOLDIERS' DINING HALL ON THE SPACESHIP *GETTYSBURG*

Enter JEM, *the leader of* HENRY'S *squadron. She's in her late 20s, wearing an officer's uniform.*

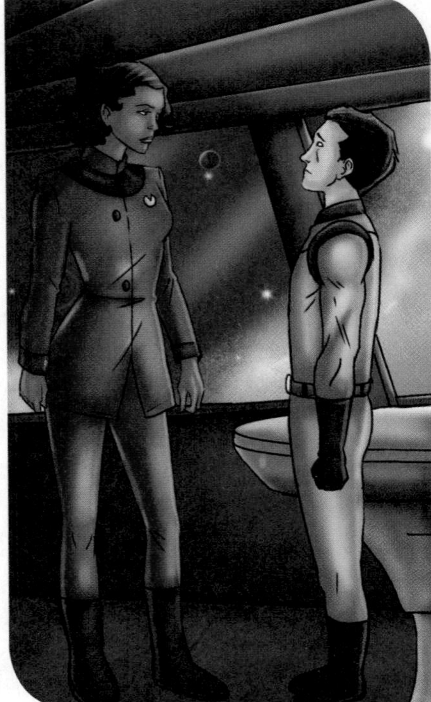

HENRY

(*a bit* **diffidently**)

Good evening, Sergeant.

JEM

Have you forgotten your salute, Private?

HENRY

(*standing at attention and saluting*)

JEM

(*chuckling*)

At ease, Private. I'm not one to stand on ceremony. You're up late, aren't you? Couldn't sleep? Pre-flight jitters?

HENRY

(*trying to look* **nonchalant**, *but he's obviously nervous*)

Just thinking about **engaging** the enemy, Sergeant. Do you know when we're moving out?

JEM

(*looks at him* **speculatively**)

I'm not sure I'm supposed to say, so keep this to yourself. We're pushing out tomorrow at about 500 hours.

HENRY

Think we'll see much action?

JEM

Likely. We'll be in the assault group with the other, low-level fliers. Wait a minute… this is your first flight out, isn't it?

HENRY

(a little flustered, but he catches himself)

It is. My first full day on ship, and this is my first trip out. But I'm telling myself that it should be an easy one—make an **incursion** into enemy territory, hit some targets, and come back to the *Gettysburg*. That's about it, right?

Comprehension Check

1. Which of the following is NOT a way that the movie script is different from the original?

a. changing a character from male to female

b. eliminating a male character

c. changing the main character's gender

d. changing the main character's age

2. *Red Badge* is primarily different from *The Red Badge of Courage* in that

a. it is historical fiction set in the past.

b. it is science fiction set in the future.

c. it has only male characters.

d. it has more characters.

3. What element do the film script and the excerpt from the original novel share?

a. descriptions of how men act and talk before a big battle

b. an explanation of how the main character ended up as a soldier

c. the main character's feelings of fear and uncertainty before his first battle

d. the main character's conflicts with a more experienced soldier

4. Both *Red Badge* and *The Red Badge of Courage* are about all of the following EXCEPT

a. military duty.

b. courage under fire.

c. romantic love.

d. life in wartime.

5. Using textual evidence, work with a partner to explain how faithful *Red Badge* is as an adaptation of *The Red Badge of Courage*.

____

____

____

____

____

____

Independent Practice

RL.8.7

WORDS TO KNOW

bolstered
cognizant
liability
recruit
vigilant

CITE EVIDENCE

A Circle the parts of the film script that discuss characters not present in the original. What reasons would a filmmaker have for adding new characters?

B Underline the most important question Henry asks Jem. How is the way Henry asks Jem this question different from the way Henry asks Jim a similar question in the original story?

C Place an asterisk by the action Jem takes that is different from the action taken by Jim in the original story. How does this change affect the film script adaptation?

Red Badge *continued*

JEM

Let's hope so. Just keep your cool and work with the team. But you should know we've got some hotheads in our squadron. Berman, for one. He doesn't know when to be afraid, and that can make him a **liability**.

HENRY

Am I the only first-timer in this crew?

JEM

No, Berman and Morales are the only returning fliers. You and the other six privates on our squadron are new **recruits**. So you have to be **vigilant** out there and look out for yourselves. Remember your training. You don't want somebody replacing you on the next round, right?

She smiles slightly, trying to lighten the young man's spirits, but HENRY *looks a bit alarmed.* JEM *is turning to walk away when* HENRY *interrupts her.*

HENRY

Sergeant, have you ever seen—I mean, do you ever worry that someone will lose their nerve? Just fly out of a fight?

JEM

You do what you have to do when the time comes. But everyone, if they're honest, will admit to sometimes just wanting to abandon their posts when things get bad.

HENRY

You . . . I mean, even you've felt that way? Like running out on a fight?

JEM

Even me. But I don't. I stay and fight with the rest of them. And you will, too.

HENRY *rubs his forehead and looks apprehensive, but he tries to keep his emotions to himself. In response,* JEM, **cognizant** *of the young man's uneasiness, hands him a red pin shaped like a square.*

JEM

Here, take this. For luck. I wore it on my uniform the first couple of times I went out, and I came back, didn't I?

HENRY

(*Bravely, clutching the red badge; the gift has* **bolstered** *his spirits, and he's grateful.*)

Thank you, Sergeant. Thank you very much.

HENRY (VOICEOVER)

That little red badge gave me a sense of reassurance that carried me through my first fight. And though I didn't know it then, the red badge would end up saving my life one day. . . .

Comprehension Check

MORE ONLINE sadlierconnect.com

1. What problem do both versions of Henry face?
   - **a.** They both regret the past.
   - **b.** They are both afraid of their first battle.
   - **c.** They are both missing their families.
   - **d.** They are both too eager to fight.

2. What do both Jem in the film version and Jim in the original story do for Henry?
   - **a.** tease him about his fears and worries
   - **b.** guarantee that he will be safe
   - **c.** give him a red badge for luck
   - **d.** provide reassurance

3. Which element from the original is NOT left out of the adaptation?
   - **a.** the details about how new soldiers are viewed
   - **b.** the altercation between two soldiers
   - **c.** Henry's sense of gratitude after being reassured
   - **d.** Henry trying to pretend that his question about running away is a joke

4. At the end of both versions, Henry feels
   - **a.** comforted.
   - **b.** discouraged.
   - **c.** nauseated.
   - **d.** frightened.

5. What can a reader gain by reading both an original text and its adaptation?

____

____

____

____

____

____

Guided Instruction

RL.8.9

WORDS TO KNOW
foreboding
imposing
meandered
ramshackle
reclusive

Modern fiction texts often draw on traditional story patterns that have been around for generations. **Analyzing sources of fiction** can help you better understand how authors can take familiar, age-old character types, themes, and story patterns and make them seem fresh and new again.

CITE EVIDENCE

A **Archetypes** are character types that have existed in different versions for centuries. The innocent young hero is one archetype; the wise figure or mentor who advises the hero is another. Circle the names of the characters who might fill the roles of hero and mentor.

B A scary-looking old house with a mysterious inhabitant is a familiar image in stories and films. Put a box around each adjective used to describe the mansion and the person who lives there. What kind of story do these descriptive words lead you to expect?

The Letter Quest

(Genre: Realistic Fiction)

Chapter One

1 Evan Littleton stood at the corner of the dead-end block, gazing up the lengthy, curving, wooded drive that **meandered** up to the **imposing** mansion far off in the trees. The mansion wasn't quite as impressive as you drew closer to it; though it was somewhat castle-like, it was actually a rather **ramshackle** structure, a bizarre mixture of antique architectural styles that didn't quite go together. The main part was constructed of dark red brick, though it was hard to see any of the outer surface, since the building was draped in a sprawl of dark green ivy. Most of the windows were shuttered, and the mansion itself looked sad at best, **foreboding** at worst. The sky always seemed cloudier around the mansion, though Evan knew that was impossible, especially since it was sunny at his house, only a block away.

2 In truth, in spite of all his ideas and memories about the mansion, Evan had only been up to it once, about a year ago. He hadn't wanted to get closer then, and he certainly didn't now, but at the time he'd had a very good reason for venturing out to the mansion. But, like all the other kids in the neighborhood, he was afraid of the old man who owned the house. The **reclusive** Mr. Wrigsby, according to local lore, never emerged from his home, and the longer he stayed hidden, the more strange and frightening everybody seemed to find him.

RL.8.9

3 Of course, Evan wouldn't be staring at the Wrigsby mansion now if it wasn't for Mrs. Smith. Mrs. Smith taught seventh- and eighth-grade English at Fairleigh Middle School, and this was Evan's second time in one of her classes. He liked Mrs. Smith very much; she was one of the kindest teachers in the whole school, and she handed back every assignment with notes of encouragement.

4 Mrs. Smith had seen Evan scribbling in his notebook whenever he got a chance, and when he had finally—after more than a year—worked up the courage to show her the adventure novel he was working on, her whole face had lit up. "Evan," she had told him, "you've such a fine imagination. I hope you'll keep going; you could become a professional writer someday." Since then, she'd been helping him work on his writing once a week, during homeroom.

5 Because he respected his teacher so much, when Mrs. Smith had pulled him aside after class the previous day and explained that she needed his help, Evan had agreed, even when he understood that she was asking him to do something that would be difficult for him.

6 As usual, Mrs. Smith had gotten right to the point. "Evan, I need your help in meeting an important challenge. You may or may not know about this, but all of the teachers here at Fairleigh are working to have the school recognized for its historic importance."

7 Evan knew a little something about the school's history and spoke up. "You mean because of Eleanor Bradford, the famous inventor? Some people think she taught science here!"

8 "Yes, Evan, and I'm one of the people who thinks she was a teacher here, but the records from that era seem to have disappeared, so there's no actual evidence. Our only hope is to find some of her personal correspondence that mentions the school and that would prove her historic presence here. We're hoping to get the school declared an historic landmark. I think you can help us meet that goal."

Comprehension Check

Based on the text so far, how did Evan end up at the Wrigsby mansion?

Guided Instruction

CITE EVIDENCE

C A common ancient story pattern is the quest. In a **quest**, the hero—who is usually an extraordinary individual—is given a difficult task to perform or a challenge to face. Underline the details on this page that suggest this is a quest story.

D A quest will often center on a necessary object or goal. Put an asterisk next to the paragraph that reveals this object or goal. What will Evan be asked to do?

E A story may have elements of more than one genre. A science fiction story, for example, might have elements of horror or romance. Double underline details in paragraph 8 that remind you of a mystery story. What is the mystery? How do these details draw the reader in?

Guided Instruction

RL.8.9

WORDS TO KNOW

articulate
impeded
interminably
proximity
scrupulous
simultaneously

CITE EVIDENCE

A A quest usually involves some kind of journey. Circle the paragraph that tells you Evan's quest will involve a journey.

B A quest must include a reason for the hero to continue on his or her journey, even when it is difficult. Put an asterisk next to the paragraph that explains why Evan must take on this quest. Will it be a strong enough reason for him?

C Most quests include an antagonist, or opposing character, who either creates the reason for the quest or hinders it. Underline the sentences that describe Evan's feelings about his antagonist, Mr. Wrigsby. What kind of character from traditional literature—such as folk or fairy tales—does Mr. Wrigsby seem to be like?

The Letter Quest *continued*

9 Mrs. Smith continued, "Did you know that Eleanor Bradford used to live nearby, at what is now the Wrigsby estate? Mr. Wrigsby is her grandson. I understand that you live in close **proximity** to Mr. Wrigsby, Evan—practically next door, in fact. I've written to him regarding this matter, but he has never responded. Would you pay him a visit and ask him if he has some of his grandmother's letters?"

10 Evan's stomach suddenly felt hollow, and his mouth went dry. "If you could convince Mr. Wrigsby to lend you any correspondence from his grandmother that would help our cause, it would be a tremendous boost to our campaign for Fairleigh's historic recognition," Mrs. Smith continued. "In fact, it's the *only* way we could gain such recognition." She had then explained that Evan was the best candidate for the job, since he was not only a neighbor but also **articulate** and polite. "And," she added with a wink, "if you let Mr. Wrigsby know you're the young man who did that good deed for him last year, I think he might be more inclined to listen to you." Evan, not wanting to admit that he was scared of both the mansion *and* its owner, had given Mrs. Smith his word that he would go call on Mr. Wrigsby.

11 Thinking about Mrs. Smith's words now gave Evan confidence. Why was he so nervous, anyway? He was thirteen, he was less than a block from home, and he had indeed been to this house before. True, he had not met the mysterious Mr. Wrigsby when he did his "good deed" last year; he had only spoken with the gardener, leaving a very "special delivery" with him. Maybe the gardener would be there this time, too, and Evan could talk to him instead and not have to deal with Mr. Wrigsby. But no matter what, Evan told himself, *I can do this.*

RL.8.9

12 Evan pulled open the iron gate that guarded the end of the driveway and forced himself to start walking up the long path, which stretched out **interminably** before him. At least the long walk would give him time to practice what to say. Maybe, by the time he reached the front door, he wouldn't be so worried about who would open the door on the other side. What was the worst that could happen, anyway?

13 As he walked along, Evan kept trying to focus. He imagined himself greeting Mr. Wrigsby confidently and winning his trust and respect. After all, his goal now—just as it had been the last time he'd been near the mansion—was simply to do the right thing. Evan was the kind of person to whom doing the right thing mattered. He got that trait from his parents, he supposed; maybe all kids whose mothers were judges and whose fathers were on the police force (or the other way around) tended to be **scrupulous** about doing what was right. But just having a desire to "do the right thing" was no guarantee it would be easy.

14 The wind picked up around him, and Evan crossed his arms over his chest for warmth. *This is silly,* he thought. *It's only April, and there's no reason for it to be cold.* He started to walk more quickly, only to find his progress **impeded**; tree branches bent down toward the ground here, and he had to duck under them, **simultaneously** watching his footing on the path.

15 He was unprepared for the series of shrieks and screeches that suddenly greeted him. Startled, he froze in his tracks, hardly daring to breathe, wondering if it was a wild animal or Mr. Wrigsby or . . . something else. The noise had hardly sounded human, but then it didn't sound like any animal he recognized, either. He heard the shrieks again, and his heart started to beat faster; they were coming from inside the mansion! If he hadn't given his word to Mrs. Smith, he wouldn't have been able to stay on the path, let alone continue his journey up to the front door.

16 Gathering his courage, and leaving himself no time to even think, Evan reached up and rapped the large bronze lion's head knocker on the door twice.

Comprehension Check

List the quest elements in the story so far. How can they help the reader evaluate this text?

Guided Instruction

CITE EVIDENCE

D Many literary works explore age-old themes such as the struggle between right action and wrong choices. Put an asterisk next to the paragraph that identifies an inner conflict Evan experiences. What is not "easy" for him? Why does he continue on his quest in spite of his feelings?

E In every quest story, the hero faces obstacles that make his quest challenging and tempt him to give up. Circle the paragraphs on this page that describe some of Evan's first obstacles on this adventure. What is the effect when Evan continues in spite of the obstacles he faces?

Guided Practice

RL.8.9

WORDS TO KNOW

blurted
futile
incrementally
interject
wizened

CITE EVIDENCE

A Underline details that reveal a change in Evan's feelings about his quest. Why are his feelings suddenly changing?

B Work with a partner to identify a potential obstacle that appears in this section. Put an asterisk next to the paragraph describing the problem. How is this obstacle different from the one that appears earlier in the story?

The Letter Quest *continued*

Chapter Two

17 For a few moments, everything was silent, and Evan felt silly for getting so worked up; maybe the sounds were coming from somewhere else nearby. After all that anxiety, perhaps the house was empty, and he had endured that tense walk up the long path to the mansion for nothing. He'd been so afraid, and had tried to be so courageous, only to have his efforts prove **futile**. He breathed in and out, steadily, and waited; he counted backward from one hundred, and, when he'd finished, decided that nobody was at home that day. Well, he'd given it his best shot; he shouldn't feel bad about it. Actually, he was relieved.

18 Just as he was turning to leave, though, placing one foot back on the path to return to his own house, he heard a creaking, squeaking sound. He turned his head and saw the front door of the Wrigsby estate slowly, **incrementally** opening outward a few inches. Evan spun around to face the door again, almost in spite of himself. He stood frozen as if hypnotized, watching with awe as the **wizened** head and upper body of a small, very elderly gentleman peered out, turtle-like, from behind the door's edge.

19 "Go away," the man said wearily, "I don't know if you're raising money for the school band, or a scholarship fund, or if you're here to apply for the position of dog-walker, but I don't want to deal with any of it." Evan tried to **interject** a denial, but the old man, who spoke much more quickly than he moved, talked over him: "You'll have to come back tomorrow, when the housekeeper's here. You can talk to her about whatever it is."

20 As slowly as it had opened, the door started to close. Without stopping to think, Evan stepped toward the door. A torrent of words rushed out. "Mr. Wrigsby, I'm very sorry to have disturbed you, but my name's Evan Littleton, and I'm here with a very important request from the teachers at Fairleigh Middle School."

21 The door stopped closing. Evan couldn't see Mr. Wrigsby's face, but he knew the man was at last listening to him. "Please, Mr. Wrigsby; I won't take up much of your time. I'm not here to ask you for a donation, and actually, I'm allergic to dogs, so I'd

never make a good dog-walker." Evan inhaled, thinking he might as well ask now, since it could be his only chance, and **blurted**, "I've come to ask if you can help us prove that your ancestor, Eleanor Bradford, once taught at Fairleigh. Can you help?"

Comprehension Check

1. Which of the following is NOT true of Evan and his quest?

a. He does not really understand the purpose of his quest.

b. He has to overcome his fear of Mr. Wrigsby.

c. He has to conquer his own anxiety as he walks toward the mansion.

d. He is willing to take on the quest because he likes and respects Mrs. Smith.

2. What makes Mr. Wrigsby the antagonist in this story?

a. People think he is sickly.

b. People are sorry for him.

c. People are afraid of him.

d. People think he's mean to animals.

3. Which of the following words BEST describes Evan's encounter with Mr. Wrigsby in this chapter?

a. frightening

b. hostile

c. reassuring

d. challenging

4. How does Evan react to the obstacle presented by Mr. Wrigsby?

a. He is defeated by it.

b. He tries to overcome it.

c. He freezes in indecision.

d. He decides to try again later.

5. Referring to the elements of a quest in this story, explain what is unusual or original about the story as an example of a quest narrative. For instance, you may compare it to quest narratives such as *The Lord of the Rings* or the *Harry Potter* novels.

____

____

____

____

____

____

Independent Practice

RL.8.9

WORDS TO KNOW

appraising
belated
grizzled
novelty
raucous
unnerved

CITE EVIDENCE

A Circle the paragraph on this page that shows Evan reflecting on one of the themes in this text: what he is frightened of. Make a personal connection to this passage.

B Put an asterisk by the paragraph that reveals whether the quest has succeeded or failed. Explain how the outcome of Evan's quest is like or unlike the outcome of quests in myths, folk tales, and fantasy stories.

The Letter Quest *continued*

22 Mr. Wrigsby now stuck his head fully out from behind the door and gave Evan an **appraising** look. He wrinkled his nose, pondering Evan's question as if it related to world peace, or some other crisis of great import. Then, to Evan's amazement and disbelief, the old man's **grizzled** face creaked open a little bit to reveal some teeth: he was smiling, and, Evan thought, maybe even chuckling. "No one's poked around here to ask me about any relations in years and years, so you've got the element of **novelty** on your side, son. Come in, but you have to promise not to tire me out."

23 Filled with a sense of victory and relief, Evan nodded and stepped over the threshold. Only then did he remember that he was supposed to be scared of Mr. Wrigsby and frightened of this house. Well, here he was, facing the formerly feared ogre while standing in the strange house that used to haunt his dreams.

24 As he followed Mr. Wrigsby, Evan relaxed. The house was brighter and cozier inside than he could have imagined, decorated in pleasant colors. Mr. Wrigsby invited him into the kitchen and made a pot of tea, which he served with lemon cookies. After that, it was surprisingly easy for Evan to bring up Eleanor Bradford and her letters; even more surprisingly, it was easy for Mr. Wrigsby to soften that grim face once more and say that he did have letters, and that he would be proud to collect them together and share them with the school. "Grams would have liked that," he told Evan, and then, with a chuckle, pointed out they'd finished the tea and eaten all the cookies. It was time for Evan to go.

25 They walked to the front door together. Suddenly, the same horrible shrieking sounds that had **unnerved** Evan on the walk up to the mansion started up again. He almost jumped, but he quickly realized that the noise was coming from a room off the entryway. There were several enormous cages there, each one occupied by a variety of colorful and exotic tropical birds.

26 "My feathered friends," Mr. Wrigsby explained. "They can be a bit **raucous**, can't they?" And he chuckled. "But you already knew that I was something of an 'animal person,' didn't you?"

27 Evan looked at him questioningly.

28 "Yes, I know all about you, Evan," Mr. Wrigsby continued. "In fact, it's the reason I let you in today. You see, even though I

never came out to meet you that day, I was watching you and my gardener through the window." He paused. "You were the neighborhood boy who found and returned my lost cat Blake last year. The boy who nobly refused a reward." He smiled again and reached out to shake Evan's hand. "I'll always be grateful to you for bringing Blake home to me. Consider the letters your **belated** reward. Come back tomorrow and you can have the whole lot."

Comprehension Check

MORE ONLINE **sadlierconnect.com**

1. Mr. Wrigsby describes Evan as "noble" because Evan

a. talked to him even though he was obviously afraid of him.

b. did what his teacher asked him to do.

c. refused a reward for bringing back Mr. Wrigsby's cat.

d. was polite and articulate.

2. Which of the following BEST describes the kind of hero Evan is?

a. self-doubting but lucky

b. shy and unwilling

c. nervous but determined

d. confident and assured

3. What happens to Evan by the end of the story?

a. He becomes more shy and withdrawn.

b. He becomes anxious and excitable.

c. He becomes sad and melancholy.

d. He becomes confident and brave.

4. When we finally learn what "good deed" Evan had done for Mr. Wrigsby previously, we understand

a. that Mr. Wrigsby has a good memory.

b. a key reason Mrs. Smith thought Evan was perfect for the task.

c. that Mrs. Smith knew Evan was a nice person.

d. that Evan is known for doing kind deeds for neighbors.

5. What is it about Evan that ultimately helps him succeed in his quest to get the letters? Use text evidence to support your answer.

Little Women

by Louisa May Alcott (excerpt)

(Genre: Novel)

This selection is an excerpt from Chapter 15 of the classic novel about the March family, set during the American Civil War.

1 "November is the most disagreeable month in the whole year," said Margaret, standing at the window one dull afternoon, looking out at the frost-bitten garden.

2 "That's the reason I was born in it," observed Jo pensively, quite unconscious of the blot on her nose.

3 "If something very pleasant should happen now, we should think it a delightful month," said Beth, who took a hopeful view of everything, even November.

4 "I dare say; but nothing pleasant ever does happen in this family," said Meg, who was out of sorts. "We go grubbing along day after day, without a bit of change, and very little fun. We might as well be in a treadmill."

5 "My patience, how blue we are!" cried Jo. "I don't much wonder, poor dear, for you see other girls having splendid times, while you grind, grind, year in and year out. Oh, don't I wish I could manage things for you as I do for my heroines! You're pretty enough and good enough already, so I'd have some rich relation leave you a fortune unexpectedly; then you'd dash out as an heiress, scorn every one who has slighted you, go abroad, and come home my Lady Something, in a blaze of splendor and elegance."

6 "People don't have fortunes left them in that style now-a-days; men have to work, and women to marry for money. It's a dreadfully unjust world," said Meg bitterly.

7 "Jo and I are going to make fortunes for you all; just wait ten years, and see if we don't," said Amy, who sat in a corner, making mud pies, as Hannah called her little clay models of birds, fruit, and faces.

8 "Can't wait, and I'm afraid I haven't much faith in ink and dirt, though I'm grateful for your good intentions."

9 Meg sighed, and turned to the frost-bitten garden again; Jo groaned, and leaned both elbows on the table in a despondent attitude, but Amy spatted away energetically; and Beth, who sat at the other window, said, smiling, "Two pleasant things are going to happen right away: Marmee is coming down the street, and Laurie is tramping through the garden as if he had something nice to tell."

10 In they both came, Mrs. March with her usual question, "Any letter from Father, girls?" and Laurie to say in his persuasive way, "Won't some of you come for a drive?... Come, Jo, you and Beth will go, won't you?"

RL.8.7, RL.8.9, RL.8.10

11 "Of course we will."

12 "Much obliged, but I'm busy;" and Meg whisked out her work-basket, for she had agreed with her mother that it was best, for her at least, not to drive often with the young gentleman.

13 "We three will be ready in a minute," cried Amy, running away to wash her hands.

14 "Can I do anything for you, Madam Mother?" asked Laurie, leaning over Mrs. March's chair, with the affectionate look and tone he always gave her.

15 "No, thank you, except call at the office, if you'll be so kind, dear. It's our day for a letter, and the postman hasn't been. Father is as regular as the sun, but there's some delay on the way, perhaps."

16 A sharp ring interrupted her, and a minute after Hannah came in with a letter. "It's one of them horrid telegraph things, mum," she said, handling it as if she was afraid it would explode and do some damage.

17 At the word "telegraph," Mrs. March snatched it, read the two lines it contained, and dropped back into her chair as white as if the little paper had sent a bullet to her heart. Laurie dashed downstairs for water, while Meg and Hannah supported her, and Jo read aloud, in a frightened voice,—

18 Mrs. March:
Your husband is very ill. Come at once.
S. HALE
Blank Hospital, Washington.

19 How still the room was as they listened breathlessly, how strangely the day darkened outside, and how suddenly the whole world seemed to change, as the girls gathered about their mother, feeling as if all the happiness and support of their lives was about to be taken from them.

20 Mrs. March was herself again directly, read the message over, and stretched out her arms to her daughters, saying, in a tone they never forgot, "I shall go at once, but it may be too late. Oh, children, children, help me to bear it!"

21 For several minutes there was nothing but the sound of sobbing in the room, mingled with broken words of comfort, tender assurances of help, and hopeful whispers that died away in tears. Poor Hannah was the first to recover, and with unconscious wisdom she set all the rest a good example; for, with her, work was the panacea for most afflictions.

22 "The Lord keep the dear man! I won't waste no time a cryin', but git your things ready right away, mum," she said, heartily, as she wiped her face on her apron, gave her mistress a warm shake of the hand with her own hard one, and went away, to work like three women in one.

23 "She's right; there's no time for tears now. Be calm, girls, and let me think."

24 They tried to be calm, poor things, as their mother sat up, looking pale, but steady, and put away her grief to think and plan for them.

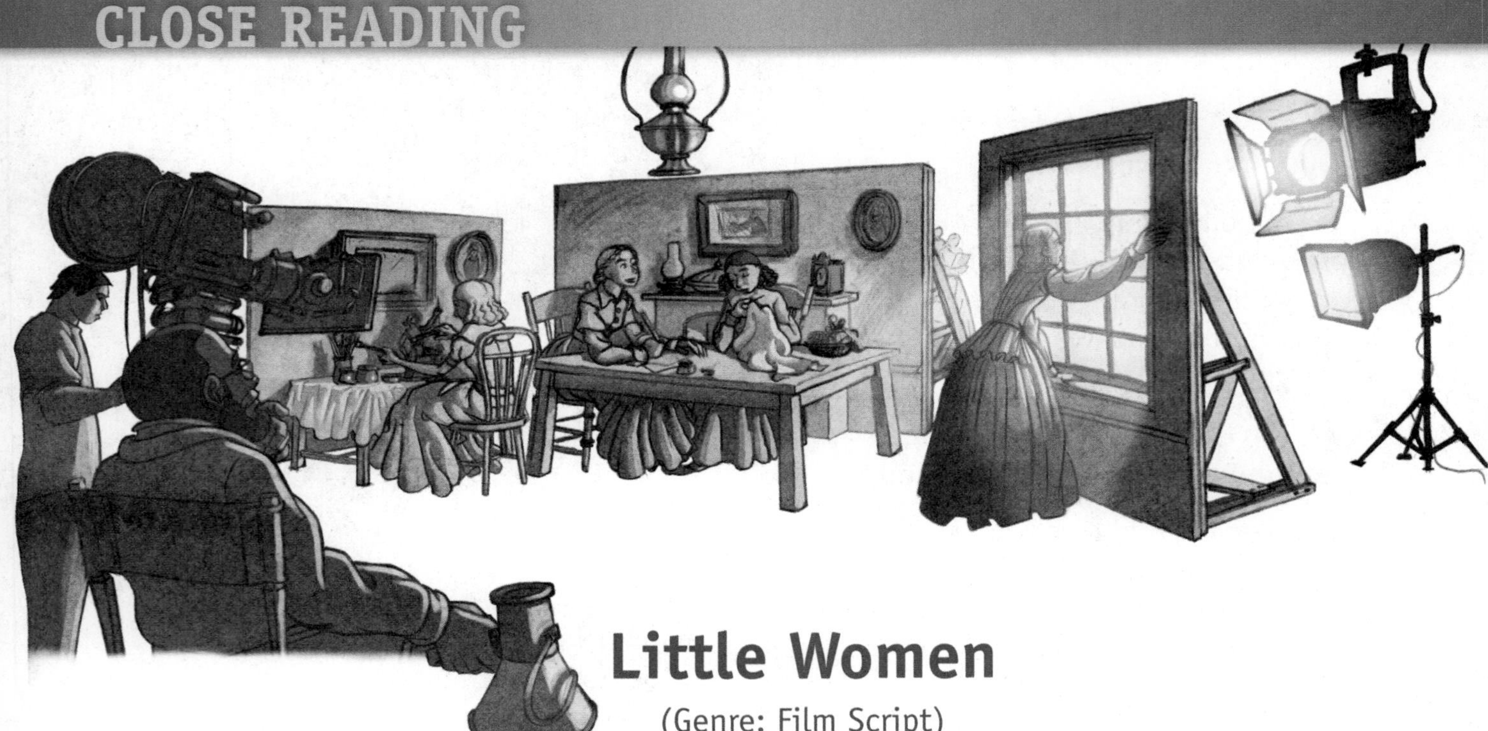

Little Women

(Genre: Film Script)

1 INTERIOR PARLOR, HOME OF THE MARCH FAMILY.–DAY.

It is a cold day in November and almost dinnertime. The home is dingy but cozy, with well-worn, mended furniture. The four March daughters, MEG, AMY, JO, *and* BETH, *are gathered in the parlor.* MEG, *who is 17, is seated by one window;* BETH, *who is 14, is seated by another.* JO, *16, is placed at their worn dining table, and* AMY, *13, is off to the side working on an art project.*

MEG

(*grumpily*)

I do hate Novembers. Nothing good can come of them.

JO

(*dreamily*)

Oh, cheer up, Meg. You're just blue because you work so hard and don't have enough fun. If you were a character in one of my novels, I'd arrange it all so you had a marvelous sweep of good luck. Imagine if you were to inherit a fabulous fortune! How fine that would be.

MEG

(*with a tone of despair*)

5 That isn't the way the world works, Jo.

AMY *is only half-listening; she is focused on making a clay sculpture.*

AMY

Why shouldn't we have all the beautiful things we want? Don't worry, Meg. Between Jo's writing and my art, our whole family will be rich some day.

BETH *walks over to the window beside* MEG *and pats her back consolingly.*

BETH

(*with a sweet smile*)

I'd rather have all of you than any fortune. And I think something good is happening. See? Here comes Marmee up the path; she's home in time for supper.

10 MRS. MARCH *enters. She is in her 40s and dressed carefully and cleanly, although her clothes are patched. She walks around and gives each of her daughters a kiss.*

MRS. MARCH

(her voice hopeful)

Has Father written?

MEG *shakes her head.* MRS. MARCH *looks wistful, but does not appear concerned.*

MRS. MARCH

Jo, would you be a dear and pop down to the post office? There should be a letter for us.

JO

Of course, Marmee. Meg, should you like to come?

MEG

No, I've some mending to do.

JO *is leaving the parlor when a bell rings. She goes to the door and comes back rapidly, carrying a folded envelope by the corners, as if she's afraid it will bite her.*

JO

It's one of those horrid, terrible telegraphs.

MRS. MARCH *grabs it to look it over and trembles. Meanwhile,* JO *grabs the telegraph back. The other three girls race to their mother's side. As* MEG, AMY, *and* BETH *look on with apprehension,* JO *begins reading it to the others.*

JO

"Mrs. March: Your husband is very ill. Come at once. S. HALE, Blank Hospital, Washington." Oh, Marmee!

They embrace, and everyone begins to cry. MRS. MARCH *is trying to console her daughters as well as herself.*

MRS. MARCH

There's no time for tears now. I must go, no matter how I find him. You all must be strong for me.

She reaches out and wipes the tears from BETH's *face.* JO *and* MEG *embrace consolingly, and* AMY *leans over to hug her mother around the neck. Their faces grow resolute.*

Comprehension Check

1A. Which of the following BEST describes the script version of *Little Women*?

- **a.** It is completely faithful.
- **b.** It is mostly faithful.
- **c.** It is partly faithful.
- **d.** It is hardly faithful.

1B. Which aspect of the script BEST supports the answer to Part A?

- **a.** All the characters and key events are included.
- **b.** Most of the characters and key events are included.
- **c.** The setting is slightly different.
- **d.** The setting is identical.

2A. What fear do the main characters face in both versions?

a. feeling unhappy in romantic love

b. being separated from one another

c. learning of a loved one's sickness

d. losing all of their wealth

2B. Which piece of text evidence best supports the answer to Part A?

a. "there's no time for tears now."

b. "I do hate Novembers."

c. "Your husband is very ill."

d. "Has Father written?"

3A. What action does Jo take in the script but not in the original version?

a. She receives the telegraph at the door.

b. She tries to cheer up Meg.

c. She reads the telegraph aloud.

d. She mentions the stories she writes.

3B. Which text evidence best supports the answer to Part A?

a. "'Oh, cheer up, Meg.'"

b. "'How fine that would be!'"

c. "Jo and Meg embrace . . ."

d. ". . . carrying a folded envelope"

4A. Which cultural value seems MOST emphasized in both versions?

a. the importance of class position

b. the significance of money

c. the importance of family

d. the limitations of gender roles

4B. Which evidence best supports the answer to Part A?

a. ". . . a marvelous sweep of good luck"

b. "The Lord keep the dear man!"

c. "I'd rather have all of you . . ."

d. "It's a dreadfully unjust world."

5A. Which of the following character types is in one version but not the other?

a. the dutiful daughter

b. the loving mother

c. the wise, faithful servant

d. the suspicious neighbor

5B. Which evidence best supports the answer to Part A?

a. "Poor Hannah was the first to recover . . ."

b. "Laurie dashed downstairs . . ."

c. ". . . Meg . . . supported her . . ."

d. ". . . Jo read aloud . . ."

6. Describe an element that is exactly the same in both the novel excerpt and the movie script of *Little Women*. Support your answer with text evidence.

7. Identify an element that is different in the film script from how it is in the original novel and explain why the adapter made this decision.

8. Explain how the March family responds when faced with their worst fear. What attitude toward the idea of "family" does this response suggest? You may refer to either excerpt. Be sure to use text evidence in your response.

9. Select two elements from the *Little Women* novel excerpt and explain why they would be essential parts of any adaptation. Be sure to use text evidence in your answer.

10. Analyze the March family's response to bad news and compare it to either your own response to bad news or to a response that you have read about or seen on television. You may use a separate sheet of paper if necessary.

RL.8.7, RL.9, SL.8.1.a, SL.8.1.c, SL.8.1.d

Compare and Contrast Texts

In this unit, you've read a short excerpt from the novel *The Red Badge of Courage* and a portion of a film script, *Red Badge*, based on the novel. You've also read a brief excerpt from the novel *Little Women* and a portion of a film script based on it. Use the chart provided below to organize your ideas about the similarities and differences between the two fiction works and their adaptations. Then, on a separate sheet of paper, write an essay explaining which adaptation you think is more effective, and why. Include your ideas about how the adaptation differs from the original and why the adapter may have made the changes he or she did. Be prepared to discuss your ideas with the class.

Elements of Original Version	Elements of Adaptation
Selection 1: *The Red Badge of Courage*	**Selection 1:** *Red Badge* film script
Selection 3: *Little Women* novel	**Selection 3:** *Little Women* film script

Return to the Essential Question

How do authors use their interpretations of other works to create new art?

In small groups or as a class, discuss the Essential Question. Think about what you have learned about analyzing adaptations of fiction and analyzing sources of fiction. Use evidence from the three texts in this unit to answer the question.

L.8.5.b

Word Relationships

Guided Instruction You can use what you know about one word to figure out the meaning of a related word. Do this by looking for **synonyms**, or words that have similar definitions. When you look at words with similar meanings that are used in the same sentence or in surrounding sentences, you can better understand the shades of meaning of each word.

First Word	Related Word	New Meaning
shrieks	screeches	Both nouns describe loud, harsh sounds; put together, they convey an almost frightening quality of unpleasant noise
slowly	incrementally	Both adverbs describe deliberate, plodding movements; put together, they give the impression of gradual progress

Examples

- From "The Letter Quest": "He turned his head and saw the front door of the Wrigsby estate slowly, **incrementally** opening outward a few inches."
- From "The Letter Quest": "He was unprepared for the series of shrieks and **screeches** that suddenly greeted him."

Guided Practice Fill in the blank with a word that best matches the word in bold (its word relationship partner).

1. My sister, who drives **cautiously**, ______________ moved our parents' car closer to the edge of the curb.

2. The ______________ from your golden retriever are some of the loudest **barks** I've ever heard.

3. The theater was completely ______________; every seat was **vacant**.

4. I have never seen such a **gigantic** sculpture. It is really ______________ .

Independent Practice Find two newspaper articles and read them to see what other pairs of related words you can find. Using a separate sheet of paper, make a list of at least three related word combinations. Write three practice sentences that each use at least one of your new words.

RL.8.7, RL.8.9, L.8.5.b

Read the following brief excerpt from a short story and a brief excerpt of a film adaptation of that story. Then answer the questions on pages 245–246.

The Legend of Sleepy Hollow

by Washington Irving (excerpt)

1 All the stories of ghosts and goblins that [Ichabod] had heard in the afternoon now came crowding upon his recollection. The night grew darker and darker; the stars seemed to sink deeper in the sky, and driving clouds occasionally hid them from his sight. He had never felt so lonely and dismal. He was, moreover, approaching the very place where many of the scenes of the ghost stories had been laid. In the center of the road stood an enormous tulip-tree, which towered like a giant above all the other trees of the neighborhood, and formed a kind of landmark. Its limbs were gnarled and fantastic....

2 As Ichabod approached this fearful tree, he began to whistle; he thought his whistle was answered; it was but a blast sweeping sharply through the dry branches. As he approached a little nearer, he thought he saw something white, hanging in the midst of the tree: he paused and ceased whistling but, on looking more narrowly, perceived that it was a place where the tree had been scathed by lightning, and the white wood laid bare. Suddenly he heard a groan—his teeth chattered, and his knees smote against the saddle: it was but the rubbing of one huge bough upon another, as they were swayed about by the breeze. He passed the tree in safety, but new perils lay before him.

Sleepy Hollow Legends

1 EXTERIOR: A DESERTED STREET IN PRESENT-DAY SLEEPY HOLLOW—NIGHT.

ICHABOD CRANE, *a young (mid-20s) Hispanic man, is walking cautiously down the main street of Sleepy Hollow. It's late at night and the town is deserted and desolate. No one gets in his way. As he keeps walking, his mind wanders.*

ICHABOD (VOICEOVER)

I'd never heard more tales of fearful creatures, spirits, and terrors, than the ones I'd been told over the past few days in Sleepy Hollow.

ICHABOD *sees a massive, colossal tree in the distance. As he gets closer, he reflects on the tree's importance.*

ICHABOD (VOICEOVER, CONTINUED)

5 So many people had told me about this tree and the danger it presented, that when I saw it I couldn't help feeling scared myself. A cold fear gripped me.

RL.8.7, RL.8.9, L.8.5.b

Circle the letter next to the best answer.

1A. In a filmed version of this selection, which of the following details would be MOST unfaithful to the original source?

a. images of ghosts and spirits

b. a horse neighing with fear

c. whispers and subtle sounds

d. a partner accompanying the hero

1B. Which detail from the text supports the answer to Part A?

a. ". . . his knees smote against the saddle . . ."

b. "He had never felt so lonely and dismal."

c. "Suddenly he heard a groan . . ."

d. "Its limbs were gnarled and fantastic."

2A. Which of the following BEST matches the meaning of the word *scathed* as used in "The Legend of Sleepy Hollow"?

a. abandoned

b. angered

c. soothed

d. scratched

2B. Which evidence from the text supports the answer to Part A?

a. ". . . rubbing of one huge bough . . ."

b. ". . . the white wood laid bare."

c. ". . . a blast sweeping sharply . . ."

d. ". . . swayed about by the breeze."

3A. Which of the following BEST describes the relationship of the movie script adaptation to the original source fiction?

a. The script is shorter and does not have any references to the supernatural.

b. The script has a completely different character and setting.

c. The script uses more modern language and directly reveals Crane's thoughts.

d. The script has more vivid sensory descriptions of the tree.

3B. Which evidence supports the answer to Part A?

a. "It's late at night and the town is deserted . . ."

b. ". . . a young (mid-20s) Hispanic man . . ."

c. "No one gets in his way."

d. ". . . I couldn't help feeling scared myself."

4A. Which of the following most closely matches the meaning of the word *colossal* in the script version?

a. gigantic

b. significant

c. yonder

d. elderly

4B. Which evidence from the text supports the answer to Part A?

a. *"closer"*

b. *"massive"*

c. *"importance"*

d. *"distance"*

5A. What fear does Ichabod face in this literary excerpt?

a. He is afraid of night.

b. He is afraid of ghosts.

c. He is afraid of trees.

d. He is afraid of nature.

5B. Which evidence from the text supports the answer to Part A?

a. ". . . the tree had been scathed by lightning . . ."

b. "The night grew darker and darker . . ."

c. ". . . approached this fearful tree . . ."

d. ". . . approached a little nearer . . ."

RL.8.7, RL.8.9

6A. In the story version of "The Legend of Sleepy Hollow," how does Ichabod deal with his fear?

- **a.** He gives himself over to it and feels better.
- **b.** He relies on his horse to keep himself grounded.
- **c.** He discounts the believability of ghost stories.
- **d.** He uses reason to talk himself out of fright.

6B. Which text evidence supports the answer to Part A?

- **a.** ". . . crowding upon his recollection."
- **b.** ". . . sink deeper in the sky . . ."
- **c.** ". . . on looking more narrowly . . ."
- **d.** ". . . he began to whistle . . ."

7. Describe one strategy you would employ when developing the film version of this script in order to keep the adaptation as faithful as possible.

____

____

____

8. Describe two choices you would make when adapting this scene from the original text of "The Legend of Sleepy Hollow" into a new movie script. This movie script should be recognizable as an adaptation of the original.

____

____

9. "The Legend of Sleepy Hollow" has some elements common to traditional tales, such as folk and fairy tales. With reference to either the original story or the movie script adaptation, explain how Ichabod's story could be considered an archetypal quest story. Use textual evidence in your answer.

____

____

____

____

____

____

10. What archetypal elements from a quest story are missing from these excerpts from Ichabod's adventure? Use text evidence to support your answer.

____

____

____

____

Introducing UNIT 10

In this unit about facing fears, you will learn how to write an argumentative essay. An argumentative essay is a form of writing in which the writer tries to convince the reader to agree with his or her opinion on a topic.

When you write your argumentative essay, introduce the topic clearly and establish your claim—your opinion or position on the topic. Develop your ideas with logical reasons and relevant evidence gathered from accurate and credible sources. You should also acknowledge opposing claims—the reasoning of those with opposing opinions on the topic—and explain why you disagree with them. Use language and sentence structures that create cohesion and show how your ideas are related. In addition, your argumentative essay must feature a strong conclusion that supports your claim and leaves your reader with a final thought or a call to action.

Progress Check Can I?

Before Unit 10		After Unit 10
☐	Write an argumentative essay to support a claim.	☐
☐	Introduce a claim and distinguish it from opposing claims.	☐
☐	Support the claim with logical reasons and relevant evidence.	☐
☐	Use reliable sources to identify reasons and evidence.	☐
☐	Include language that connects ideas and creates cohesion.	☐
☐	Establish and maintain a formal style.	☐
☐	Provide a conclusion that supports the claim presented.	☐
☐	Use the subjunctive or conditional mood to achieve effects.	☐
☐	Use punctuation to indicate a pause or break.	☐
☐	Spell words correctly.	☐

HOME ✦ CONNECT...

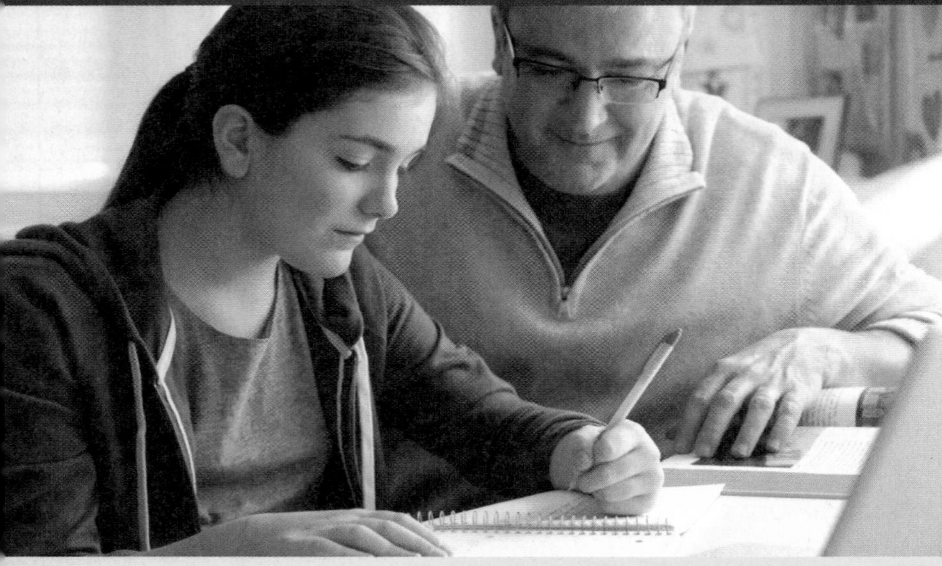

In this unit, your child will learn how to write an argumentative essay. This type of persuasive essay **states an opinion or position on a topic in the form of a claim**. Your child should be able to state a claim about a topic and then **support the claim with logical reasons and relevant evidence taken from accurate, credible, and reliable sources** such as reputable books, newspapers, and journals as well as government Web sites. An argumentative essay must include words, phrases, and clauses that make clear how the claim, reasons, and evidence relate to one another. It should end with a conclusion that restates the claim and leaves readers with a final thought or a call to action—something that the writer would like readers to think about or do in response to the essay.

Discuss a current topic with your child that can be examined from different sides, such as the minimum wage. Help your child develop an opinion on the topic as you research the issue together. Encourage him or her to articulate solid reasons for the opinion and support those reasons with facts or examples from reliable online or print sources.

Activity: Explore the theme "facing our fears" by working with your child to think of issues that relate to the idea of public safety, such as budgets for local fire departments or the roles of organizations that work for consumer safety. Help your child come up with a claim about public safety that he or she can convey in the form of a poster, comic strip, or other format that uses text and visuals.

IN THIS UNIT, YOUR CHILD WILL...

- Learn how to write an argumentative essay.
- Develop a claim to state an opinion or position on a topic.
- Support a claim with logical reasons and relevant evidence.
- Use reliable sources to identify supporting evidence for a claim.
- Use a variety of words, phrases, or clauses to connect ideas.
- Maintain a formal style.
- Write a strong conclusion.
- Use the conditional mood and the subjunctive mood in sentences.
- Use ellipses, dashes, and commas to indicate a pause or a break.
- Spell words correctly.

NOTE: All of these learning goals for your child are based on the Grade 8 Common Core State Standards for English Language Arts.

WAYS TO HELP YOUR CHILD

Have your child state an opinion on an issue that affects your community. Ask him or her to search for facts to support this opinion on the Internet or in print sources. Have your child make notes about any facts he or she identifies. Then have him or her consider how these notes could help a writer draft an argumentative essay about the topic.

ONLINE

For more Home Connect activities, continue online at sadlierconnect.com

Text Types and Purposes: Write Argumentative Essays

UNIT 10

Essential Question:
How can writers persuade readers effectively?

W.8.1.a, W.8.1.d, WHST.8.1.a, WHST.8.1.d

Read a Student Model

Julia is a student in Mrs. Maalouf's eighth-grade Language Arts class. Mrs. Maalouf gave the class an assignment to write an argumentative essay about the best way to confront a social problem. The essay must introduce a claim and support it with logical reasons and relevant evidence. Think about a topic that explores a social problem. Consider your opinion on the subject. Then write an argumentative essay to state your position and convince your readers to share it.

CREATING AN ORGANIZATIONAL STRUCTURE

Julia used a graphic organizer like the one below to organize her argumentative essay.

Title: ____

I. **Introduction**
  a. Topic of Essay: ____
  b. The Claim: ____
II. **Body Paragraphs**
  a. Main Idea: ____
    1. Reasons and Evidence: ____
  b. Main Idea: ____
    1. Reasons and Evidence: ____
  c. Main Idea: ____
    1. Reasons and Evidence: ____
  d. Counterclaims: ____
    1. Arguments Against Counterclaims: ____
    2. Reasons and Evidence: ____
III. **Conclusion**
  a. Restatement of Claim: ____
  b. Concluding Statement: ____

TITLE

- Gives readers a clue about the topic and the writer's opinion on it

INTRODUCTION

- Introduces the topic
- Establishes the writer's claim

FORMAL STYLE

- Includes academic language
- Avoids slang and contractions

The Problem of Plastic Bags and Bottles

On a California beach, volunteers pick up trash that has washed ashore. Two of the most common items they collect are disposable plastic water bottles and plastic bags from grocery stores. Across the United States, we throw away billions of these bottles and bags annually. This can have a huge impact on the environment. For this reason, a nationwide ban on plastic bags and bottles is essential to the planet's future.

There are many reasons to ban plastic bags and bottles. First, neither is biodegradable, or capable of decomposing over time. Organic garbage, such as food, will literally "rot away," but plastic will not. While many states require residents to recycle plastic bottles, many are still thrown away. Almost 90 percent of plastic bags are thrown away, too. Both items are deposited in landfills, where they will stay for years to come.

In fact, though, bags and bottles sitting in landfills is actually a best-case scenario, because many are not thrown away at all. Instead, plastic bags and bottles are frequently discarded on beaches, dropped in public parks, or left at campsites and other open areas where they pollute the environment. If we banned plastic bags and bottles, it would tremendously reduce the amount of litter cluttering our cities.

Also, many plastic bags and bottles are dropped into the sea, where they become a big problem for ocean wildlife. Fish and other sea creatures often mistake these items for food. When they eat plastic items, the plastic can kill them. For example, translucent plastic bags can resemble jellyfish in the water. Jellyfish are a staple in the diet of sea turtles, and the turtles often eat plastic bags in error. Also, Save Our Shores, a widely known environmental organization, reports finding a number of dead birds and fish entangled in plastic bags that likely strangled or suffocated the animals.

In addition, plastic is produced from petroleum. Disposable water bottles in particular are manufactured using a great deal of oil. Conserving oil reserves is therefore another reason to ban plastic bottles and bags. It is important to preserve this nonrenewable resource, because once we use it up it will be gone for good. According to the online newspaper Business Insider, if all plastic water bottles had been banned worldwide last year, it would have saved enough oil to run a million cars for one year! Therefore, it is wasteful to use petroleum to produce plastic bags and bottles.

W.8.1.b–c, W.8.9, WHST.8.1.b–c

REASONS AND EVIDENCE

Include logical reasons for your opinion. Support each reason with relevant evidence, such as facts and examples.

Underline a logical reason Julia includes in the first paragraph on this page.

SOURCES

Your sources for supporting evidence should be credible and accurate. Government agencies, educational institutions, news providers, and other large organizations are generally considered credible because their information can be confirmed in other places.

Put an asterisk before a credible source listed in this paragraph.

LANGUAGE THAT CONNECTS IDEAS

Include words, phrases, and clauses that clarify ideas and connect them to other ideas and information.

Box the clause that Julia includes to explain why it is important to preserve oil by banning plastic bottles.

W.8.1.a, W.8.1.e, W.8.9, WHST.8.1.a, WHST.8.1.e

COUNTERCLAIMS

Include opposing claims and explain why you disagree with them. Provide evidence to support your position.

Draw a box around two counterclaims in this paragraph.

CONCLUSION

This conclusion restates Julia's claim and includes a call to action—something that Julia would like her readers to do.

Underline Julia's call to action. Which reasons does Julia include in the conclusion to support her position?

Some people argue that banning plastic bags only increases the use of paper bags. Reportedly, the use of paper bags increased in San Francisco after the city banned plastic bags in 2007. However, paper bags are biodegradable and will break down over time. Paper bags can be recycled as well, which typically is not the case for plastic bags. Customers can also bring reusable bags to the supermarket to pack their groceries. In addition, water bottling companies and store owners argue that banning plastic bottles inconveniences and harms consumers. However, consumers can purchase a reusable bottle and fill that up with water instead of buying water in disposable bottles. In the long run, this would also be much less expensive for consumers.

According to the Environmental Protection Agency, the United States generates 32 million tons of plastic waste each year. If we banned plastic water bottles and plastic grocery bags, we would greatly reduce that number. Many American cities already have taken the step of banning plastic grocery bags, including Portland, Oregon, and Los Angeles, California. Concord, a town in Massachusetts, has banned the sale of plastic water bottles smaller than one liter. Tourist stations in Grand Canyon National Park also are prohibited from selling drinks in small disposable bottles. Plastic bags and bottles pollute the environment, harm wildlife, and deplete a valuable natural resource, so it is time for the entire nation to ban them. The needed action can happen one city at a time, so write or call your city council members and urge them to pass a local ban on plastic bags and water bottles.

W.8.1.a–e, W.8.4, W.8.5, W.8.6, W.8.7, W.8.8, W.8.9, W.8.10, WHST.8.1.a–e

Use this outline to organize your argumentative essay for the Common Core Review on page 259. The topic is the best way to confront a particular problem that affects society. State and support your argument clearly, using credible sources. Establish and maintain a formal tone and style, using precise words and phrases to connect your ideas. Write your first draft on a separate sheet of paper.

Title: ______________________________

I. Introduction

a. Topic of Essay: ______________________________

b. The Claim: ______________________________

II. Body Paragraphs

a. Main Idea: ______________________________

1. Reasons and Evidence: ______________________________

____

b. Main Idea: ______________________________

1. Reasons and Evidence: ______________________________

____

c. Main Idea: ______________________________

1. Reasons and Evidence: ______________________________

____

d. Counterclaims: ______________________________

1. Arguments Against Counterclaims: ______________________________

2. Reasons and Evidence: ______________________________

III. Conclusion

a. Restatement of Claim: ______________________________

b. Concluding Statement: ______________________________

____

Conditional and Subjunctive Moods

Guided Instruction You have already been introduced to the **conditional mood** and the **subjunctive mood**. In this unit, you will learn more about how writers use these moods.

■ Using the Conditional Mood

Writers use the **conditional mood** to express an action or a state of being that *might* happen or *might* exist in the future if something else happens. Sentences in the conditional mood usually include the word *if* along with the words *might, could, would,* or *should*.

If the paper company changed its policies, customers would benefit.

If Dad decides to come with us, we should change *the restaurant reservation.*

We might drive *to the park if it doesn't rain.*

You can also put the conditional into the past tense by adding *have*:

If I had bought a pizza, I would have shared *it with you.*

■ Using the Subjunctive Mood

Writers use the **subjunctive mood** to express something that is not true, such as a hypothetical situation, a possibility, or an action that has not happened yet.

If the waterpark were *closer, I could walk to it.*

If I were *to visit you, could we go see that new art museum?*

The subjunctive can also be used to express commands, demands, wishes, and requests. Sentences that express a command, demand, wish, or request often include the word *that*, as in these examples:

The king commands that *the entire court* be *present to hear his royal decree.*

Carol wished that *she* were *a famous movie star in Hollywood.*

I demand that *you* leave *my house this instant!*

I ask that *you* be *careful crossing the street.*

A final use of the subjunctive is to express the idea that something is necessary.

It is important that *everyone* be *present at the meeting.*

It's essential that *the chairman* hear *the committee's report.*

L.8.3.a

Guided Practice Rewrite each sentence. Change the underlined verb to the conditional mood or the subjunctive mood, as indicated, and make any other revisions necessary so that the resulting sentence is correct.

1. The car's engine died because you forgot to replace the oil.

   conditional mood: ______________________________

   ____

2. The president asked his whole staff to be present at the conference.

   subjunctive mood: ______________________________

   ____

3. Pablo took the class to become a better basketball player.

   conditional mood: ______________________________

   ____

4. It is necessary to buckle your seat belt.

   subjunctive mood: ______________________________

Independent Practice Follow the instructions below to create six original sentences in the conditional mood or the subjunctive mood.

1. conditional ______________________________

   ____

2. subjunctive: express a hypothetical situation ______________________________

   ____

3. subjunctive: express a command ______________________________

   ____

4. subjunctive: express a wish ______________________________

   ____

5. subjunctive: express a request ______________________________

   ____

6. subjunctive: express a necessity ______________________________

   ____

L.8.2.a

Punctuation for Pauses or Breaks

Guided Instruction There are three types of punctuation that can indicate a pause or break in a sentence.

- An **ellipsis** (. . .) appears when a speaker trails off in the middle of a sentence.

  "I wonder where I put that . . . ," Raj muttered to himself, lost in thought.

- A **dash** (—) shows a very sudden break in thought or speech.

  "I hate storms! They make me—" she stopped when a burst of lightning struck.

  A pair of dashes can also be used to set off part of a sentence that includes additional information.

  All four of his friends—Carlos, Max, Louise, and Anna—took the train to his house.

- A **comma** (,) can be used in pairs to set off part of a sentence that names or restates what has just come before.

  San Francisco, a city in California, has banned plastic grocery bags.

Guided Practice Rewrite the following sentences, adding an ellipsis, commas, or dashes to punctuate each one correctly.

1. We went to that new diner the one on Second Avenue last night.

   ____

2. My neighbors Mrs. Park and Mr. Lee organized the block party together.

   ____

3. "How do we think we should handle" Dana paused distractedly.

   ____

Independent Practice Write four sentences, each one using either an ellipsis, commas, a dash, or a pair of dashes to indicate a pause or a break. Be sure to use each type of punctuation at least once.

1. ______________________________
2. ______________________________
3. ______________________________
4. ______________________________

L.8.2.c

Correct Spelling

Guided Instruction There are many different spelling rules that can help writers spell words that follow a particular pattern. The following three spelling rules explain when to keep or drop a final silent *e* when adding a suffix to a word. Following these rules will make it easier for you to use correct spelling as you write.

- Keep the final silent *e* with a suffix that starts with a consonant.

  remorse + -ful = *remorseful* state + -ment = *statement*

  Here are two exceptions to the rule:

  awe + -ful = *awful* judge + -ment = *judgment*

- Keep the final silent *e* for words that end in a soft *c* or *g,* and with a suffix that starts with *a* or *o*.

  notice + -able = *noticeable* outrage + -ous = *outrageous*

- Drop the final silent *e* for all other words with a suffix that starts with *a* or *o*.

  dispose + -able = *disposable* fame + -ous = *famous*

Guided Practice In each sentence, circle any words that are misspelled.

1. It is advantagous to get the principal's endorsment before proceeding.
2. The morning was peacful until the construction crew began making that aweful noise!
3. In their statment, the activists explained plastic bags are not biodegradeable.

Independent Practice Rewrite each sentence, correcting any misspelled words.

1. The stain was noticable until John used the bleach from that advertisment.

   ____

2. It is inconceiveable that one could succeed in life without some encouragment.

   ____

3. Remember that recycleable items should not be thought of as disposeable.

   ____

4. She is resourcful; she can patch that inflateable mattress and sleep on it tonight.

   ____

SL.8.1.a–d, SL.8.3, SL.8.4, SL.8.6

Discuss the Essential Question

How can writers persuade readers effectively?

Prepare for a class discussion about the Essential Question by responding to the questions below. Support your point of view with reasons and examples.

1. Describe Julia's claim in her essay, "The Problem of Plastic Bags and Bottles."

___

___

2. What evidence does Julia include to support her claim?

___

___

___

___

3. What sources does Julia use for her supporting evidence?

___

___

___

Use your notes above to discuss the Essential Question with your class or in small groups. Follow the discussion rules on the *Did I?* checklist (page 58). Use the organizer below to record your ideas and what you hear in the discussion.

Ideas I Agree or Disagree With		Questions I Asked
Agree		
Disagree		
New Ideas I Had During Discussion		**Questions I Answered**

W.8.1.a–d, L.8.2.a, L.8.3.a

Read this draft introductory paragraph from a student argumentative essay and answer the questions below.

Promoting Recycled Paper Products

(1) In supermarkets, consumers often have the option of purchasing paper goods such as napkins and plates made from recycled paper. (2) Too many people do not embrace this option. (3) Instead, they purchase goods made from non-recycled paper. (4) Using products made from paper recovered from homes and offices is a smart consumer practice. (5) If more people bought such products, it would further protect the environment. (6) I strongly recommend that supermarkets and other stores stock only paper products made from recycled paper.

1. Which sentence states the writer's claim?

a. sentence 1
b. sentence 2
c. sentence 5
d. sentence 6

2. Which should be in sentence 1?

a. a dash, to set off information
b. two commas, to set off information
c. an ellipsis, to indicate a pause
d. a comma, to indicate a pause

3. Based on this introduction, which evidence would best fit in this essay?

a. facts about making products from recovered paper
b. personal profile of an owner of a paper manufacturing company
c. testimonial by a shopper in a well-known supermarket
d. information about recycled metal

4. Which of the following sentences would NOT contribute to a formal style?

a. The environmental cost of not using recycled goods could be devastating.
b. It's super important that people quit messing with the environment.
c. An astonishing variety of products can be manufactured from recycled paper.
d. Those who question recycling statistics should consult a government Web site.

5. Which word or phrase could go before sentence 6 to tie it to the previous ideas?

a. Instead,
b. Therefore,
c. By the way,
d. For instance,

6. Which sentence includes a verb in the conditional mood?

a. sentence 1
b. sentence 2
c. sentence 5
d. sentence 6

W.8.2.a–e, W.8.4, W.8.5, W.8.6, W.8.7, W.8.8, W.8.9, W.8.10, L.8.2.c, L.8.3.a

Read these next two paragraphs from the student essay and answer the questions below.

(1) Using recycled paper helps protect trees. (2) According to the Environmental Protection Agency, at least 37 percent of all paper goods are made of recycled paper. (3) The other 63 percent still comes from trees, plants, or wood scraps. (4) By stocking only recycled paper goods, stores could reduce the amount made from trees. (5) If every home in the United States replaced just one roll of regular paper towels with a recycled roll, it would save over half a million trees!

(6) Some will argue that asking stores to stock only recycled paper products limits shoppers' options. (7) But there is a variety of goods made from recycled paper, and there is no difference in quality between recycled and non-recycled paper. (8) Also, in my judgement, it is outragous to put consumers' preferences above the protection of the environment.

7. How does citing the Environmental Protection Agency support the writer's position?

____

8. Write the numbers of the sentences written in the conditional mood. _______________

9. Which words in sentence 8 are spelled incorrectly? How should they be spelled?

____

10. Write a brief call to action that could appear at the end of this argumentative essay.

____

____

Assignment: On a separate sheet of paper, provide a final draft of the argumentative essay you began on page 253. Use what you have learned about conditional and subjunctive moods, using punctuation for pauses or breaks, and spelling correctly. Think about how you and your classmates answered the Essential Question. Check your outline to be sure you included supporting reasons and evidence for your claim, using credible sources. Use precise words to connect your ideas. End with a conclusion that restates the claim presented in your essay.

Introducing UNIT 11

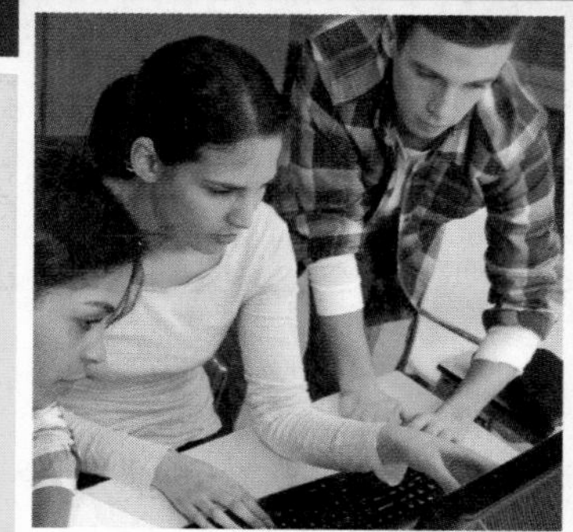

In this unit, you will examine how informational texts integrate knowledge and ideas. You'll consider how information is presented in different mediums—from print texts with images to Web sites that incorporate hyperlinks and videos—and evaluate the advantages and disadvantages of presenting information in each form. Next, you will consider the arguments made in informational texts, looking for sound reasoning and evaluating the strength of specific claims and their supporting evidence. Then you will read texts that approach the same topic from different perspectives, and you will identify any conflicting information or disagreement in those texts. You'll finish up with a reading selection that challenges you to integrate, or bring together, all of these skills.

This unit's texts unite around a common theme: important discoveries. As you complete your everyday actions and tasks, consider the technology you use. How were those technologies invented? How do they improve everyday life? Are there any drawbacks to using them, such as issues of health or safety? What ideas and inventions do you take for granted that are worth a closer look?

Before Unit 11 | **Progress Check** Can I? | After Unit 11

- [ ] Evaluate the advantages and disadvantages of different mediums, both print and digital, in presenting information. [ ]
- [ ] Identify the main argument and specific claims in a text. [ ]
- [ ] Evaluate the soundness of reasoning and relevance of evidence in a text. [ ]
- [ ] Assess two or more texts on the same topic and identify where their claims or interpretations of the topic conflict. [ ]
- [ ] Understand the difference between a word's denotation and its possible connotations. [ ]

HOME ◆ CONNECT...

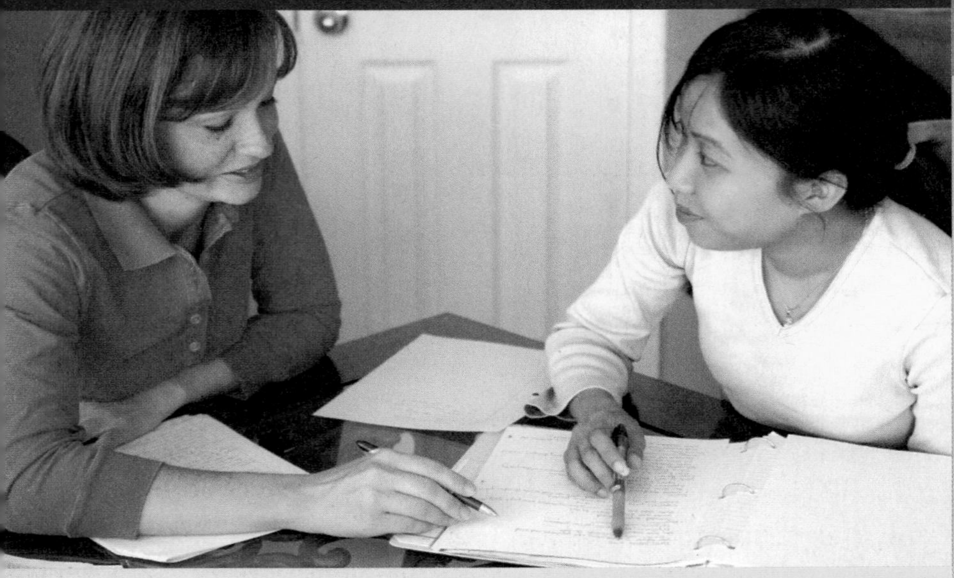

Your child will begin this unit by learning to **examine the characteristics of different mediums** in conveying information, from print texts to digital texts embedded with audio and visual support. Watch a TV news segment with your child. Discuss how the visual medium conveys information. Focus on the pros and cons of televised news over news presented digitally or in print.

Next, your child will **evaluate texts for arguments and claims as well as supporting evidence**. He or she will also learn to look out for unsound reasoning and irrelevant evidence. Help your child with this skill by working together to examine an argument in an article or political speech. Discuss whether the points made are well supported.

Finally, your child will learn how to **assess information on the same topic from two or more sources** and see how different sources present sometimes conflicting views. Help your child identify the variety of viewpoints on a subject of interest and determine which views are best supported and seem most valid.

Activity: Hold a "debate session" with your child. Let your child choose an issue and a specific side, pro or con, to support; you will support the opposite side. Each of you should prepare a claim and provide support and evidence in relation to it, trying to convince the other to agree with your point of view. During the debate, remember to test the validity of each other's claims.

IN THIS UNIT, YOUR CHILD WILL...

- Read four informational selections, including a Web article, a persuasive speech, an op-ed piece, and a science magazine article.
- Learn new academic and domain-specific vocabulary.
- Analyze the pros and cons of information presented in a digital media format.
- Assess the relevance and strength of a text's reasoning and evidence.
- Evaluate conflicting evidence across texts.
- Distinguish the basic meaning of a word and identify its positive or negative shades of meaning.
- Compare and contrast ideas on the theme of important discoveries across four selections.

NOTE: All of these learning goals for your child are based on the Grade 8 Common Core State Standards for English Language Arts.

WAYS TO HELP YOUR CHILD

Help your child practice assessing evidence and reasoning by building support for a claim together. Identify a subject that interests your child and help him or her write an opinion-based claim about it. Then work together to generate a list of facts, reasons, and other evidence that could support that claim in an argument or essay.

ONLINE

For more Home Connect activities, continue online at sadlierconnect.com

Reading Informational Text: Integration of Knowledge and Ideas

UNIT 11

Essential Question:
How can readers analyze texts written by different authors in different mediums?

Guided Instruction

RI.8.7, RST.8.7

WORDS TO KNOW

deteriorate
expiration
fermentation
medium
pasteurized
preservation
regulated

You can **evaluate the advantages and disadvantages** of using a particular medium to present information by considering the relative limitations and strengths of each medium, from print and video to digital text and audio.

CITE EVIDENCE

A Consider the **advantages and disadvantages of a medium** in order to evaluate its content. Text in any format can present information in depth and express complex, connected ideas. Underline the sentences that describe a process that occurs in a food that is not preserved.

B Box the sentence that explains why eating meat that has been sitting too long at an unsafe temperature is dangerous. Identify how the article goes on to provide further information on this topic. What advantage of online digital text does this feature show?

Types of Food Preservation: Pasteurization

(Genre: Web Article)

1 Suppose you are shopping for milk at the grocery store. Chances are that you will buy milk that has been **pasteurized**. In fact, you would have to go out of your way to find milk that is *not* pasteurized. In some states, you'd even find that it's illegal to sell unpasteurized milk. What is pasteurization, and why has it become such a widespread method of food **preservation** in this country? And why would milk that is *not* pasteurized be illegal?

The Basics of Food Preservation

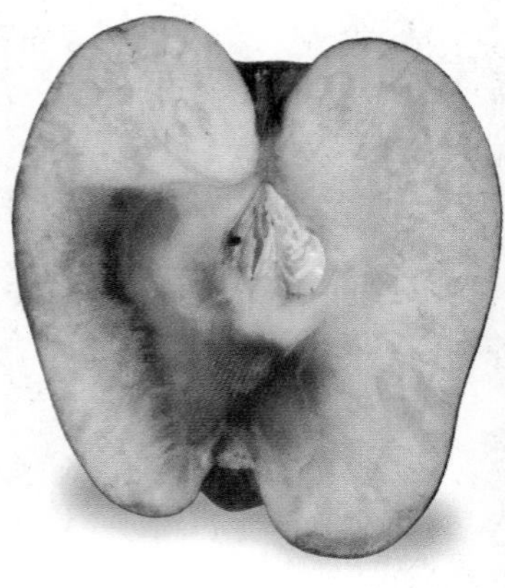

2 Let's start by thinking about why food must be preserved in the first place. If you have ever left apple slices out on a cutting board overnight, or forgotten to put leftover spaghetti and meatballs in the refrigerator, or started to drink from a carton of milk that is two weeks past its **expiration** date, then you have an idea of what can happen to food when it is not properly stored.

3 What happens to unpreserved food? Apple slices turn brown and eventually begin to shrivel up, losing their juiciness, their fresh bite, and their flavor. That's because oxygen in the air has interacted with enzymes in the fruit, causing the fruit to spoil. If you ate the browned apple slice, it would not taste good (but it probably would not make you sick). The spaghetti-and-meatball dinner, on the other hand, contains meat. Meat must be kept at 40 degrees Fahrenheit (40°F) or even lower before it is cooked. Cooked meat, if not refrigerated, should not stay less than 140°F for more than a few hours or it will start to spoil. Why?

4 Microorganisms quickly start to grow in temperatures above 40°F and below 140°F, and bacteria find meat an ideal growth **medium**. The various kinds of bacteria that can grow on poorly cooked meat, or on meat that has been sitting around too long in temperatures above 40°F, can make you mildly to seriously ill if you eat the spoiled food. Click here for a downloadable chart showing the ranges for food temperature safety.

RI.8.7, RST.8.7, RST.8.9

5 What about milk that is past its expiration date? Milk does not have a very long "shelf life," or time period during which it's safe to consume. Although properly stored pasteurized milk is safe to drink up to five days past its expiration date, it's recommended that milk be used as soon as possible after its container is opened. That's because the quality of its taste can be affected. Milk, like meat, is a perfect medium for bacteria. Bacteria that occur naturally in milk feed off the lactose, or sugar, in the milk and create a by-product called lactic acid. It's the lactic acid that turns milk sour, curdles it, and quickly makes it undrinkable. This outcome can occur even if the milk has been through the pasteurization process—a process **regulated** by the government to make sure your milk is safe to consume. (Click here to jump ahead to "The Pasteurization Process" in this article.)

Food Preservation: Types and Varieties

6 Over time, people developed different methods for preserving their food. By using tried-and-true preservation methods, food spoilage and possible foodborne illnesses are kept to a minimum. Dairy products and other proteins, such as meat and fish, must be kept cold through refrigeration. Fruits and vegetables must be kept cool or cold until they are eaten, and if they won't be eaten before they start to **deteriorate**, they must be preserved for future use in some way: freeze-dried, canned, frozen, pickled, or made into jams or jellies. You can get a better idea of what is involved in these various methods of food preservation by clicking here for a video demonstration.

7 Many other preservation methods exist for various types of foods: drying, vacuum-freezing, **fermentation**, or salting. Some preservation methods, such as canning, can keep some kinds of food edible for years. That is why many canned goods do not even have a printed expiration date. However, on most packaged foods there is usually a "best by" date warning the consumer when the food will start to lose its quality or flavor, or even become inedible or unsafe to consume. If you want to know how long it's safe to store various goods in your home, click here to download a handy chart showing food storage guidelines.

Comprehension Check

Based on the article so far, identify some benefits of presenting information about pasteurization in a Web article.

Guided Instruction

CITE EVIDENCE

C Online magazines may use hyperlinks to enable readers to navigate directly to specific information. Double underline the information on this page that would help you skip past material on other types of food preservation to get directly to more information on pasteurization on this Web site.

D Consider other mediums' advantages and disadvantages in terms of how they might present information. Circle the paragraph on this page that presents part of its information in a video format. What might this video teach that would be more difficult to convey through text alone?

E Scientific texts will often present information in two ways: 1) in the body of the text; 2) in a visual aid, such as a graph or chart. Put an asterisk next to the paragraph that embeds a visual aid that can be downloaded. What is the advantage of presenting the information in this way?

Guided Instruction

RI.8.7, RST.8.9

WORDS TO KNOW

beneficial
derived
manipulate
microbe
pathogen
sanitation

CITE EVIDENCE

A A great deal of information can be presented in a printed text; a reader can change his or her reading rate to get through the information faster or more slowly. An audio or video presentation, however, will take a certain amount of time to listen to or view. Place an asterisk next to the paragraph that contains a link to audiovisual information on Pasteur. Why does the Web article give you the option of watching the film?

B Online text can offer readers ways to go beyond the text to additional information or other features. Box each hyperlinked term on this page. Why are these terms hyperlinked? What kind of information would they be likely to lead you to?

Types of Food Preservation: Pasteurization *continued*

8 Let's go back to the case of milk. Most dairy products pose particular preservation and food safety problems because it is especially easy for them to spoil due to their naturally occurring yeast, molds, and bacteria.

Louis Pasteur and His Discovery

9 Until the invention of pasteurization techniques, people had no means to prevent milk and dairy products **derived** from milk from quickly spoiling.

10 Compared to other methods of food preparation, pasteurization is a relatively "recent"development. In the nineteenth century, a French chemist and microbiologist named Louis Pasteur (1822–1895) made discoveries that forever altered the fields of food preparation, medicine, and disease prevention. Considering how much Pasteur's various discoveries contributed to improving people's health and safety, it is difficult to single out one of his discoveries as the one that had the biggest effect. His contributions to germ theory—the idea that germs are the cause of disease—led to his discovery of the concept of vaccinations: injecting people with small amounts of a weakened virus in order to give them immunity to the living virus. He used this discovery to create vaccines for rabies and anthrax. Without Pasteur's work, many potentially fatal diseases would have had much more serious consequences for the world's population. If you'd like to learn more about Pasteur's contributions to medicine, click here for the 30-minute documentary film "Pasteur and Germ Theory."

The Pasteurization Process

11 Pasteur was keenly interested in the process of fermentation, or the chemical change of sugars to alcohol caused by **beneficial** microorganisms such as yeast. In fact, Pasteur's interest in fermentation is what led him to experiment with preserving food and drink. He started with alcoholic drinks, such as wine. He figured out that his achievements with heating wine to kill harmful bacteria could be applied to other types of food and drink preservation. Although Pasteur himself did not apply pasteurization principles to milk—that was the achievement of chemist Franz von Soxhlet in 1886—he paved the way for that innovation, which is why the process was named after him.

RI.8.7, RST.8.9

Guided Instruction

12 There are several different methods of pasteurization, but what is common to all of them is a carefully timed exposure to high (but not boiling) heat. To put milk through the process of pasteurization, people must **manipulate** the temperature of the liquid in very specific, exact ways, starting off by heating the milk to a particular temperature for a specific amount of time, then cooling it quickly. The increase and decrease of the milk's temperature is scientifically calculated to the exact minute. Specific information about the time, temperature, and other factors of the pasteurization process can be found on the Web site of the International Dairy Foods Association.

13 The United States Department of Agriculture (USDA), Food and Drug Administration (FDA), and other government organizations emphasize that professionals should handle the pasteurization process. The receptacles and containers through which the milk passes must be sterilized and clean, and people must follow sanitary practices and make sure that the cows themselves are disease-free. **Sanitation** is necessary, in fact, throughout the entire pasteurization process. To see exactly how important it is, watch a video of the entire milk pasteurization process here.

The Effects of Not Pasteurizing Milk

14 Pasteurization has a significant impact on how long milk may safely last. It changes how safe the milk is and how long it remains safe. Now consider what happens to a gallon of milk that does *not* undergo the pasteurization process.

15 What does "safe" milk mean? Raw or unpasteurized milk is full of microorganisms: bacteria, yeast, molds, and even disease-causing **microbes**. Among the harmful bacteria that can be found in raw milk are *E. coli* and *salmonella*. Over the centuries, milk has even been responsible for disease outbreaks, including epidemics of tuberculosis and diphtheria. Pasteurization successfully destroys such **pathogens**. Without the pasteurization process, harmful microbes would stay alive in the milk you drink. That's why pasteurized milk is considered "safe" milk.

Comprehension Check

How do the benefits and limitations of a Web article affect your comprehension of the text? Cite details from the passage.

CITE EVIDENCE

C Print and online media have many things in common, but online media has one obvious advantage: its hyperlinks can rapidly connect readers to additional information, important sources, and multimedia resources. Underline the sentences on this page in which hyperlinks appear. How would this information be conveyed in a print source?

D Different media convey information through different methods. Circle the paragraph that describes the need for sanitary practices in the pasteurization process. How is a multimedia resource incorporated here? What are the advantages of this approach, versus a print-only approach?

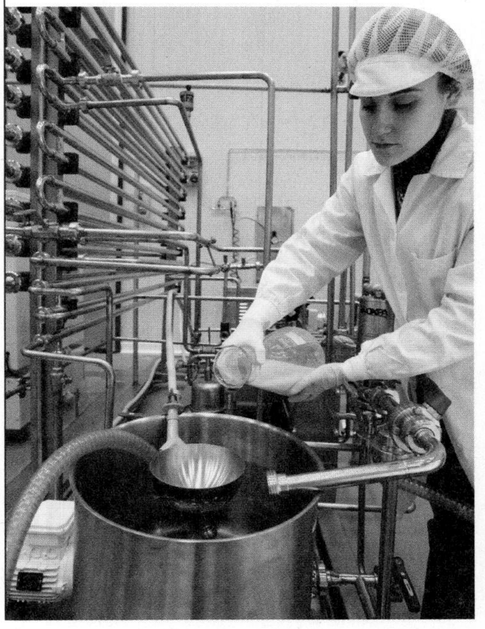

Guided Practice

RI.8.7, RST.8.9

WORDS TO KNOW
customary
devotee
hygiene
nutrient
probiotic

CITE EVIDENCE

A Working with a partner, underline the sentences that describe the beliefs of the members of the Slow Food USA movement. Why is the name of the organization hyperlinked? Where will the link take you if you click it?

B Double underline the sentences describing claims made about the benefits of raw-milk cheeses. What features of the digital online medium could the author have used to present this information even more effectively?

Types of Food Preservation: Pasteurization *continued*

16 Why is milk in particular so "dangerous"? First of all, cows themselves may carry diseases. Their udders and surrounding skin may be full of microbes, and the equipment used to milk them may not be completely sanitary. The people who handle the milk may not practice safe **hygiene**. There are many ways for milk to become exposed to a variety of harmful pathogens. That is why the USDA and other agencies recommend pasteurization, and it is also why it is illegal to sell packaged unpasteurized milk across state lines.

The Raw Milk Movement

17 There are some people, however, who think that pasteurization is not always a good thing, and who want the opportunity to purchase and consume raw milk and raw-milk products. Some states already allow retail or farm-to-consumer sales of raw milk, though other states outlaw it. (Click here for a map showing attitudes and legal stances toward the sale of raw milk and raw-milk products in all 50 states.) In recent years, some scientists, doctors, and popular figures in the world of health and nutrition have developed a renewed interest in the health properties of raw milk. They argue that the heat of pasteurization removes helpful, or **probiotic**, organisms (such as the ones that occur in yogurt) as well as essential **nutrients**, and that raw-milk products are nutritionally better for people. For example, Dr. Joseph Mercola and members of the Slow Food USA movement have come forward to suggest that non-pasteurized foods, such as raw milk cheeses, may in some cases have enormous health benefits for the human body.

18 Indeed, members of the Slow Food USA movement have focused their efforts on what they see as the healthful and delicious qualities of raw-milk cheeses. And they are not alone in their quest to bring back to the table certain types of raw-milk cheeses. In parts of the United States and Europe, many food **devotees** (you have probably heard them called "foodies") have resisted the process of pasteurization. They point to the fact that not all microorganisms are the same, and that many of the naturally occurring bacteria in milk and milk products actually result in beneficial changes to dairy products. They claim that pasteurization takes away the complex flavors and aromas of excellent handcrafted cheeses. They argue that pasteurization is unnecessary anyway, since the **customary** processes involved

in crafting and aging raw-milk cheeses make them perfectly safe to eat. Raw-milk cheese lovers are especially concerned about soft varieties of classic French cheeses such as Brie, Camembert, Sainte-Maure de Touraine, and Reblochon, and Italian cheeses like Pecorino di Farindola.

Comprehension Check

1. In referring to the processes involved in crafting raw-milk cheeses, this article

a. does not use a Web article's ability to present audiovisual support.

b. takes full advantage of a Web article's ability to present audiovisual support.

c. prepares readers to see videos relating to the topic.

d. hopes to convince readers to purchase raw-milk cheeses.

2. This online article's main advantage over a print magazine article is

a. its use of photographs to show some of the things discussed in the text.

b. its verbal descriptions of various processes.

c. its use of internal and external hyperlinks.

d. its use of strong supporting evidence.

3. So far, the article has used visual aids to support all of the following EXCEPT

a. the pasteurization process.

b. background on Pasteur's other accomplishments.

c. methods for preserving fruits and vegetables.

d. methods for crafting raw milk cheeses.

4. Which of the following would be most similar to this article in terms of its advantages and disadvantages in presenting information on pasteurization?

a. a video about pasteurization with an accompanying print guide

b. a class lecture about pasteurization

c. a print encyclopedia article on pasteurization

d. an audiobook about pasteurization

5. Explain how the author takes advantage of the Web article genre, a digital medium, to present information on the topic of pasteurization.

Independent Practice

RI.8.7, RST.8.7

WORDS TO KNOW

advocate
authentic
dilemma
enthusiast
immune system
pondering

CITE EVIDENCE

A Circle the paragraph that presents the opposing claim to claims about the benefits of raw milk. Where will the hyperlink in this paragraph take you? What is the purpose of the hyperlink?

B Box the link that references other views on the subject of pasteurization. What kind of medium is this link going to take the reader to? How else might an author present this information?

Types of Food Preservation: Pasteurization *continued*

19 The FDA regulations that govern the production of milk, cheese, and other dairy products in the United States are very strict. Yet often even stricter regulations have been put in place to guarantee the quality of European raw-milk cheeses. In Europe such cheeses are carefully aged and tended according to recipes and procedures that have been proven over time. Cheese lovers who long for the complex flavors of European raw-milk cheeses are highly motivated to fight against pasteurization regulations in the United States, since these rules make it difficult for small cheese producers to create unpasteurized cheeses equal in quality to those readily available in Europe.

Government Responses to the Raw Milk Movement

20 The FDA strongly disagrees with the claim that unpasteurized, or raw, milk may be better than pasteurized milk. In fact the FDA provides information to demonstrate that raw milk can threaten the health of children and adults, especially those with weakened **immune systems**. The FDA claims that raw milk is dangerous in comparison to pasteurized milk and can have serious consequences. To support this warning, the FDA relies upon research conducted by the Centers for Disease Control (CDC). The CDC also **advocates** against eating or drinking food that has raw milk in it.

21 People in other parts of the world share the views of the FDA and the CDC. For example, in Ontario, Canada, it is illegal to produce and sell non-pasteurized milk. (Read more about Canadian attitudes toward raw milk.)

22 What all this means is that the pasteurization process sets up an interesting **dilemma** for people who are both highly interested in eating **authentic** gourmet food and in preserving their own health. Should raw milk be permitted in certain circumstances, as raw-milk cheese **enthusiasts** say? Or should the findings of a scientist like Pasteur be relied upon, as the FDA says? These questions are complex ones. For some people there are no easy answers. For others who are **pondering** the raw milk and cheese question, the final word of the FDA is all they need to hear.

FDA Consumer Health Information
www.fda.gov/consumer

Raw Milk May Pose Health Risk

What's a building block in the food pyramid that's important for building and maintaining bone mass? It's milk.

Whether it's from cows, goats, sheep, or another mammal, milk and milk products are an important source of calcium throughout a person's life.

Most of the milk sold in the United States is pasteurized, a process during which the milk is heated to 161 degrees and kept there for 15 seconds. Pasteurization kills harmful bacteria—including salmonella, E. coli, and listeria—that can contaminate milk before it gets to your table. The Food and Drug Administration (FDA) and the Centers for Disease Control and Prevention (CDC) recommend pasteurization for all milk consumed by people in the United States.

Pasteurization Reduces Illness

Pasteurization of milk is an effective means of preventing outbreaks of foodborne illness, including tuberculosis, brucellosis, salmonellosis, scarlet fever,

Merci, Pasteur!

23 Consider the impact that Louis Pasteur and the process of pasteurization has had on your everyday life. Most likely, pasteurization affects you, your taste buds, and your health every time you eat a grilled cheese sandwich, drink a cup of hot chocolate, or pour a tall glass of cold milk. Every time you taste one of these treats, you benefit from discoveries made over one hundred and fifty years ago, and from decades of research conducted to keep you safe.

Comprehension Check

MORE ONLINE **sadlierconnect.com**

1. This online article has advantages over a print version because it includes

a. references to sources.

b. hyperlinks.

c. references to other Web sites.

d. visuals.

2. This online text offers all of the following benefits particular to its medium EXCEPT

a. video links.

b. hyperlinks.

c. audio-only content.

d. visual aids.

3. The last two pages of the article include support from

a. downloadable charts.

b. video clips.

c. hyperlinks.

d. audio sources.

4. This Web article could be strengthened by the inclusion of all of the following EXCEPT

a. a video of the process for making raw-milk cheeses.

b. a hyperlink to a veterinary clinic that specializes in cows and other livestock.

c. a chart showing statistics for foodborne diseases that come from dairy products.

d. interviews with FDA experts about the need for pasteurization.

5. Explain which medium (Web site article, print, video) you would choose to present the information discussed in this article. Include references to that medium's advantages and disadvantages.

____

____

____

____

Guided Instruction

RI.8.8, RST.8.8

WORDS TO KNOW

catastrophic
comprehensive
implicate
ingenuity
innovation
prosperous
tumultuous

By **evaluating the evidence and reasoning** used in a **persuasive text**, you can determine whether an author has adequately supported his or her argument and claims.

CITE EVIDENCE

A In a persuasive speech, the speaker may begin with a story or refer to events and situations that the audience knows about. Circle and identify the references President Obama cites in the opening of his speech. Why does he cite these examples?

B A **claim** is a position an author or speaker takes on an issue. To identify claims, analyze the logic of the language. Look for strong declarative statements with first-person pronouns (*we, I*) and verbs preceded by *should, can, cannot,* and *must*. Put an asterisk by the paragraph that presents the President's central claim.

Remarks by the President on America's Energy Security

by Barack Obama (abridged)

(Genre: Speech)

This speech by President Barack Obama was delivered at Georgetown University in Washington, D.C., on March 30, 2011.

1 . . . We meet here at a **tumultuous** time for the world. In a matter of months, we've seen regimes toppled. We've seen democracy take root in North Africa and in the Middle East. We've witnessed a terrible earthquake, a **catastrophic** tsunami, a nuclear emergency that has battered one of our strongest allies and closest friends in the world's third-largest economy. . . .

2 And as Americans, we're heartbroken by the lives that have been lost as a result of these events. We're deeply moved by the thirst for freedom in so many nations, and we're moved by the strength and the perseverance of the Japanese people. And it's natural, I think, to feel anxious about what all of this means for us.

3 And one big area of concern has been the cost and security of our energy. Obviously, the situation in the Middle East **implicates** our energy security. The situation in Japan leads us to ask questions about our energy sources. . . .

4 The United States of America cannot afford to bet our long-term prosperity, our long-term security on a resource that will eventually run out, and even before it runs out will get more and more expensive to extract from the ground. We can't afford it when the costs to our economy, our country, and our planet are so high. Not when your generation needs us to get this right. It's time to do what we can to secure our energy future.

5 And today, I want to announce a new goal, one that is reasonable, one that is achievable, and one that is necessary.

6 When I was elected to this office, America imported 11 million barrels of oil a day. By a little more than a decade from now, we will have cut that by one-third. That is something that we can achieve. . . .

RI.8.8, RST.8.8

Guided Instruction

7 . . . [O]ur best opportunities to enhance our energy security can be found in our own backyard—because we boast one critical, renewable resource that the rest of the world can't match: American ingenuity. American **ingenuity**, American know-how.

8 To make ourselves more secure, to control our energy future, we're going to have to harness all of that ingenuity. It's a task we won't be finished with by the end of my presidency, or even by the end of the next presidency. But if we continue the work that we've already begun over the last two years, we won't just spark new jobs, industries, and **innovations**—we will leave your generation and future generations with a country that is safer, that is healthier, and that's more **prosperous**.

9 So today, my administration is releasing a Blueprint for a Secure Energy Future that outlines a **comprehensive** national energy policy, one that we've been pursuing since the day I took office. And cutting our oil dependence by a third is part of that plan.

10 Here at Georgetown, I'd like to talk in broad strokes about how we can achieve these goals.

11 Now, meeting the goal of cutting our oil dependence depends largely on two things: first, finding and producing more oil at home; second, reducing our overall dependence on oil with cleaner alternative fuels and greater efficiency. . . .

12 . . . [T]he only way for America's energy supply to be truly secure is by permanently reducing our dependence on oil. We're going to have to find ways to boost our efficiency so we use less oil. We've got to discover and produce cleaner, renewable sources of energy that also produce less carbon pollution, which is threatening our climate. And we've got to do it quickly. . . .

Comprehension Check

What is President Obama's claim in this text so far? Use textual details to explain how that claim is supported.

CITE EVIDENCE

C In persuasive speeches, speakers often make emotional appeals, using words that inspire the audience to think or act in a certain way. Underline words on this page that make strong emotional appeals. What is Obama trying to make his audience feel? Considering that his audience is mostly made up of college students, use your knowledge of logic, language, and culture to decide if he has chosen the right words to appeal to their concerns.

D To find the points that a speaker wishes to highlight, look for words such as *only*, *most important*, or *essential* that place emphasis on one idea. Put a box around the paragraph that presents the President's strongest statement of his claim. What is he advocating as the best solution to the problem? Is he using facts, judgment, or speculation?

Remarks by the President on America's Energy Security *continued*

RI.8.8, RST.8.8

WORDS TO KNOW

capacity
incentive
incorporate
regulatory
sector
substantially

CITE EVIDENCE

A Specific data in the form of numbers or percentages are usually considered solid **evidence in an argument**. On this page, underline quantitative (numerical) support that the President provides. Is this support persuasive? What source would have information to verify the data he presents?

B An effective persuasive speaker acknowledges parts of an argument that many audience members are likely to disagree with. He or she may acknowledge the controversy and offer a possible solution. Put asterisks next to the paragraphs where Obama talks about a controversial energy source. What does he admit about this energy source? What reassurances does he offer his audience? Explain whether his reassurances are effective.

13 . . . Today, about two-fifths of our electricity comes from clean energy sources. But we can do better than that. I think that with the right **incentives** in place, we can double our use of clean energy. And that's why, in my State of the Union address back in January, I called for a new Clean Energy Standard for America: By 2035, 80 percent of our electricity needs to come from a wide range of clean energy sources—renewables like wind and solar, efficient natural gas. And, yes, we're going to have to examine how do we make clean coal and nuclear power work.

14 Now, in light of the ongoing events in Japan, I want to just take a minute to talk about nuclear power. Right now, America gets about one-fifth of our electricity from nuclear energy. And it's important to recognize that nuclear energy doesn't emit carbon dioxide in the atmosphere. So those of us who are concerned about climate change, we've got to recognize that nuclear power, if it's safe, can make a significant contribution to the climate change question.

15 And I'm determined to ensure that it's safe. So in light of what's happened in Japan, I've requested a comprehensive safety review by the Nuclear **Regulatory** Commission to make sure that all of our existing nuclear energy facilities are safe. And we're going to **incorporate** those conclusions and lessons from Japan in [the] design and the building of the next generation of plants. But we can't simply take it off the table.

16 My administration is leading global discussions towards a new international framework in which all countries who are operating nuclear plants are making sure that they're not spreading dangerous nuclear materials and technology.

RI.8.8, RST.8.8

17 But more broadly, a clean energy standard can expand the scope of clean energy investments, because what it does is it gives cutting-edge companies the certainty that they need to invest. Essentially what it does is it says to companies, you know what, you will have a customer if you're producing clean energy. Utilities, they need to buy a certain amount of clean energy in their overall portfolio, and that means that innovators are willing to make those big capital investments.

18 And we've got to start now because—think about this—in the 1980s, America was home to more than 80 percent of the world's wind **capacity**, 90 percent of the world's solar capacity. We were the leaders in wind. We were the leaders in solar. We owned the clean energy economy in the '80s. Guess what. Today, China has the most wind capacity. Germany has the most solar capacity. Both invest more in clean energy than we do, even though we are a larger economy and a **substantially** larger user of energy. We've fallen behind on what is going to be the key to our future.

19 Other countries are now exporting technology we pioneered and they're going after the jobs that come with it because they know that the countries that lead the 21st century clean energy economy will be the countries that lead the 21st century global economy.

20 I want America to be that nation. I want America to win the future.

21 So a clean energy standard will help drive private investment in innovation. But I want to make this point: Government funding will still be critical. Over the past two years, the historic investments my administration has made in clean and renewable energy research and technology have helped private **sector** companies grow and hire hundreds of thousands of new workers. . . .

Comprehension Check

Find supporting details in the text that strengthen the President's claim. According to the President, upon what two things does a clean energy standard depend, and why?

Guided Instruction

CITE EVIDENCE

C Pay special attention to the parts of an argument that detail causes and effects, or problems and solutions, since they rely on **correct and relevant evidence**. Box the paragraph in which Obama details the effects of clean energy standards. State the cause-and-effect relationship in your own words. What kind of evidence could Obama provide to strengthen his point?

D Ask yourself whether a speaker's evidence directly relates to his or her central claim and whether the evidence is adequate and appropriate. Circle the paragraph that provides support for Obama's claim about America's ability to participate in clean energy production. Is the evidence relevant and sufficient?

Guided Practice

RI.8.8, RST.8.8

WORDS TO KNOW

mired

shortchanging

shuttered

terminate

CITE EVIDENCE

A Working with a partner, place an asterisk next to the paragraphs that explain what Obama identifies as the dangerous consequences of not funding clean energy. What effect is Obama trying to achieve by pointing out these consequences? Analyze whether this strengthens or weakens his claim.

B Underline the claim Obama makes in response to the problems you identified in Cite Evidence A. How does he show his determination to support clean energy? Is he using facts, judgments, or speculation?

Remarks by the President on America's Energy Security *continued*

22 . . . I've toured factories that used to be **shuttered**, where they're now building advanced wind blades that are as long as 747s, and they're building the towers that support them. And I've seen the scientists that are searching for the next big breakthrough in energy. None of this would have happened without government support.

23 I understand we've got a tight fiscal situation, so it's fair to ask how do we pay for government's investment in energy. And as we debate our national priorities and our budget in Congress, we're going to have to make some tough choices. We're going to have to cut what we don't need to invest in what we do need.

24 Unfortunately, some folks want to cut critical investments in clean energy. They want to cut our research and development into new technologies. They're **shortchanging** the resources necessary even to promptly issue new permits for offshore drilling. These cuts would eliminate thousands of private sector jobs; it would **terminate** scientists and engineers; it would end fellowships for researchers, some who may be here at Georgetown, graduate students and other talent that we desperately need to get into this area in the 21st century. That doesn't make sense.

25 We're already paying a price for our inaction. Every time we fill up at the pump, every time we lose a job or a business to countries that are investing more than we do in clean energy, when it comes to our air, our water, and the climate change that threatens the planet that you will inherit—we're already paying a price. These are costs that we are already bearing. And if we do nothing, the price will only go up.

26 So at moments like these, sacrificing these investments in research and development, in supporting clean energy technologies, that would weaken our energy economy and make us more dependent on oil. That's not a game plan to win the future. That's a vision to keep us **mired** in the past. I will not accept that outcome for the United States of America. We are not going to do that.

Comprehension Check

1. Which of the following best describes the focus of this speech?

a. funding energy research and progress

b. improving clean energy usage

c. decreasing oil dependency in the U.S.

d. ensuring the safety of nuclear energy

2. In this section, the President makes assertive statements about all of the following EXCEPT

a. how the government will have to make difficult choices about what to invest in.

b. how the U.S. can learn from China's experiences with clean energy.

c. how his policies have increased American employment.

d. where he sees America in the years to come.

3. Which of of the following sample statistics would NOT be relevant support for the President's claims?

a. number of jobs created by clean energy programs

b. list of cost savings produced by wind energy

c. percentage of clean energy utilities companies need in their portfolios

d. number of people in other countries who drive large cars

4. Which of the following claims is supported by specific, factual evidence in the speech?

a. private funding for clean energy

b. government funding for clean energy

c. America's former clean energy strength

d. America's current clean energy strength

5. How does evaluating the support in this speech contribute to your analysis of President Obama's larger claim? Use text evidence to support your response.

Independent Practice

RI.8.8, RST.8.8

WORDS TO KNOW

cynical
skeptical
tempered
unbridled
unsettling

CITE EVIDENCE

A Circle the paragraph that presents a claim Obama makes about this generation's ability to respond to the clean energy problem. What evidence does he use to support his ideas about his audience?

B Underline the statement that implies the audience must solve the clean energy crisis. How does Obama get the audience involved with his final claim? How creative is Obama's argument?

Remarks by the President on America's Energy Security *continued*

27 Let me close by speaking directly to the students here—the next generation who are going to be writing the next great chapter in the American story. The issue of energy independence is one that America has been talking about since before your parents were your age, since before you were born. . . . Maybe some of you are feeling kind of **cynical** or **skeptical** about whether we're actually going to solve this problem. But everything I have seen and experienced with your generation convinces me otherwise.

28 I think that precisely because you are coming of age at a time of such rapid and sometimes **unsettling** change, born into a world with fewer walls, educated in an era of constant information, **tempered** by war and economic turmoil—because that's the world in which you're coming of age, I think you believe as deeply as any of our previous generations that America can change and it can change for the better.

29 We need that. We need you to dream big. We need you to summon that same spirit of **unbridled** optimism and that bold willingness to tackle tough challenges and see those challenges through that led previous generations to rise to greatness—to save a democracy, to touch the moon, to connect the world with our own science and our own imagination.

30 That's what America is capable of. That's what you have to push America to do, and it will be you that pushes it. That history of ours, of meeting challenges—that's your birthright. You understand that there's no problem out there that is not within our power to solve.

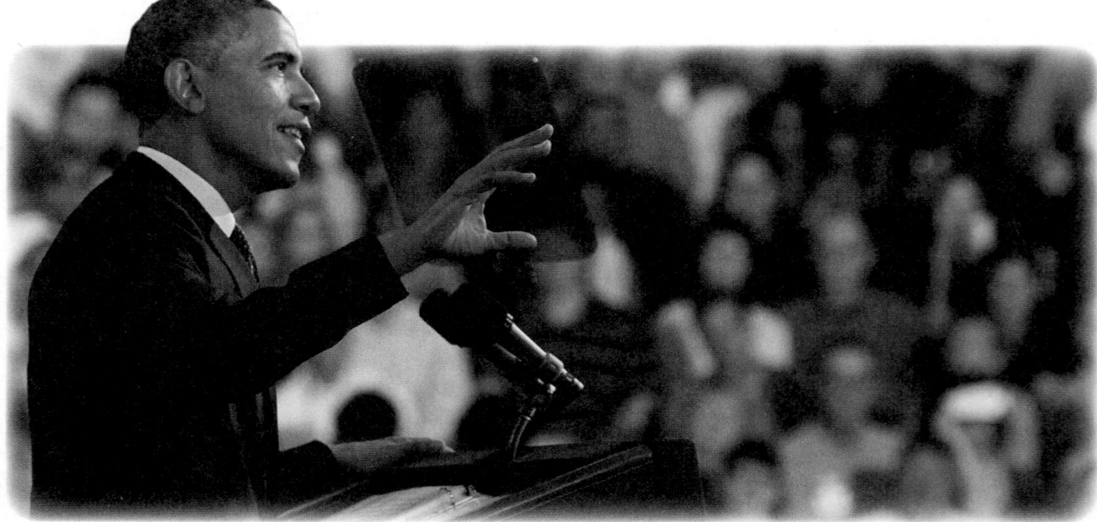

31 I don't want to leave this challenge for future presidents. I don't want to leave it for my children. I don't want to leave it for your children. So, yes, solving it will take time and it will take effort. It will require our brightest scientists, our most creative companies. It will require all of us—Democrats, Republicans, and everybody in between—to do our part. But with confidence in America and in ourselves and in one another, I know this is a challenge that we will solve. . . .

Comprehension Check

MORE ONLINE sadlierconnect.com

1. Based on what you have read, which of the following BEST summarizes the President's attitude toward his listeners?

a. He thinks they are uninformed.

b. He thinks they are too cynical.

c. He thinks they hold the solutions.

d. He does not think they have big dreams.

2. Which of the following text from the speech does NOT support the correct answer to question 1?

a. "cynical or skeptical"

b. "believe as deeply"

c. "your birthright"

d. "dream big"

3. Obama concedes, or admits, that solving the clean energy challenge will require

a. solutions from future generations.

b. time and effort.

c. raising taxes.

d. people from previous generations.

4. As part of his argument, Obama states that a solution to the clean energy problem is dependent on all of the following EXCEPT

a. financial support.

b. help from other nations.

c. scientific innovation.

d. bipartisan efforts.

5. Why might it be especially important to understand President Obama's claims in this final section? Support your answer with textual details.

Guided Instruction

RI.8.9, RH.8.7, RH.8.8, RH.8.9

WORDS TO KNOW

authorized
disclaimer
hybrid
inclusion
inherent
tsunami

You will often encounter opposing viewpoints or positions on the same topic in different texts. You must learn to identify where texts differ in their facts and interpretations in order to **analyze conflicting information**.

CITE EVIDENCE

A Op-ed pieces are opinion essays in the editorial sections of newspapers and magazines. They are written by commentators who express various viewpoints, often in response to other texts or other authors. Put an asterisk next to the sentence that identifies the ideas to which the author of this op-ed is responding.

B Look at the visual aids included with a source to determine points the author may wish to emphasize or illustrate. Circle the paragraph that refers to accompanying images in this text.

Op-Ed: President's Clean Energy Plan Must Be Refocused

by Staff Writer

(Genre: Opinion Piece)

APRIL 11, 2011.

1 **Disclaimer**: *The author of this editorial is responding to President Obama's recent "Remarks on America's Energy Security," delivered on March 30, 2011. Opinions expressed here are those of the author and do not necessarily represent, nor are they* **authorized** *to represent, the opinions of this newspaper or its publication group.*

2 The horrific images of the savage **tsunami** that devastated Japan exactly one month ago today have already started to fade from people's minds, and we have also started to lose focus on the **inherent** danger of nuclear power stations. These topics are quickly disappearing from our national discussions and media forums; it is as if people think such enormous issues can be simply wiped away, like a smudge off a window. Yet we cannot forget. We must honor the losses of the Japanese and aid them in their recovery. We must remember the dangers that nuclear power poses if it is not safely contained, and we must find a way to change our habits. There is no other option: We must stop using nuclear power.

3 We have only to look at a few images of the devastation and desolation caused by the tsunami and its aftereffects to be reminded of the depth and severity of this disaster. We must not forget what our friends in Japan have endured as a result of this disaster, or what they—and we—may still endure as a result. How can anyone, after seeing photographs and watching video coverage, forget the terrible power of those tremendous waves? Man-made structures, no matter how well-engineered or heavily reinforced they are, cannot stand up to the sheer force of such events. Just when we get overly confident and think we have ultimate power over nature, it rises up to remind us that

we are not the owners of this amazing planet, and we cannot control it. Earthquakes, volcanoes, tidal waves, hurricanes—all of these should remind us that nature is not controllable.

4 But we should also realize that the "natural" disaster that occurred in Japan last month is also an *un*-natural disaster. People built the Fukushima I Nuclear Power Plant in an area potentially subject to earthquakes and tsunamis. Any environmental harm that comes as a result of damage to the power plant is ultimately caused by human error—the error in this case being our overconfidence in our ability to construct facilities that can handle nuclear energy with 100% safety.

5 The tsunami has demolished the lives and livelihoods of so many people in Japan: it has taken their loved ones, their possessions, their homes, and their workplaces. This, too, we must remember, and in this, too, we must offer our support—moral, financial, or otherwise. And we must be clear: the consequences of this disaster are not limited to Japan. They may end up touching the lives of many more world citizens. At the very least, this tragedy should affect us in terms of how those of us who live outside Japan should think about handling and managing nuclear power sources.

6 The damage to the Fukushima I Nuclear Power Plant has already started to impact policy in the United States. Since the tsunami, President Obama and the U.S. government have focused attention on a **hybrid** clean energy program that still makes use of the power of nuclear energy. This plan has its strong points; it is aimed at lessening American reliance on foreign oil and reducing carbon dioxide emissions. But it has an enormous negative point that cannot be ignored: its **inclusion** of nuclear power in the clean energy portfolio.

CITE EVIDENCE

C Before comparing an author's opinion to the claims of others, identify the opinion the author is presenting. Underline the sentences that present the author's opinion about the disaster at the Fukushima I Nuclear Power Plant.

D In some cases, an author may make explicit comparisons between his or her own ideas and those expressed by other writers in other texts. Put an asterisk next to the paragraph that compares the author's opinions with President Obama's. With which of Obama's points does the author agree? What point does he or she strongly disagree with? Why is it important for a reader to identify and understand the ideas the author is expressing in this paragraph?

Comprehension Check

How does this author's opinion of nuclear power compare to the opinions of President Obama as described here and in the preceding selection?

Guided Instruction

RI.8.9, RH.8.8, RH.8.9

WORDS TO KNOW

countenance
emission
minimizing
platform
spearhead
underestimate

CITE EVIDENCE

A One author may comment on the "right and wrong" points of another author's approach to a topic. You can use such comments, as well as your own judgment, to evaluate both sides of the issue in more detail. Circle the paragraph that presents this author's commentary on what is correct and incorrect about Obama's energy claims.

B Identify a topic or subject that two texts have in common, and then look for the opinions or suggested actions proposed by each author. Examine and compare each opinion to make a more informed decision about the topic. Underline the sentences on this page that present this author's counterclaim about how to approach nuclear energy. How persuasive is this counterclaim?

Op Ed: **President's Clean Energy Plan Must Be Refocused** *continued*

7 The President is right to identify the development of clean energy programs as one of the country's highest priorities. But he needs to revise his **platform**. Perhaps he **underestimates** the urgency of the situation, or its nature. Whatever his reasons, he is wrong to include any reliance on nuclear power.

8 The United States should focus on truly clean energy: wind and solar power. That should be the bulk of this country's energy use and development going forward. We should minimize our reliance on oil, as the President says. But instead of regulating nuclear energy, as he recommends, we should stop using it altogether. The benefits are not worth the immense risks.

9 Let us look at what the President says about nuclear energy being a necessary part of the United States' energy resources. The President states that it is better to use nuclear power when we can in terms of **minimizing** our impact on climate change: "[I]t's important to recognize that nuclear energy doesn't emit carbon dioxide in the atmosphere. So those of us who are concerned about climate change, we've got to recognize that nuclear power, if it's safe, can make a significant contribution to the climate change question." The President also tells us that 20 percent of American energy usage—a significant amount—is based on nuclear energy. The biggest benefit of nuclear energy, though, it appears, is that it "doesn't emit carbon dioxide."

10 That all sounds pretty good. And it certainly is a good thing that 20 percent of American energy usage does not impact the climate in terms of carbon dioxide production. Yet the danger of carbon dioxide **emissions** starts to pale in comparison to the

hazards presented by radioactive materials. We have seen in Chernobyl and now in Japan the horrific problems that can result from damage to a nuclear power plant. We can continue working to make oil usage less damaging to the environment; we can continue working to decrease our reliance on oil, as the President stresses. But what can we do to remove radioactivity from the air, in the ocean, and in our bodies should it be released from a nuclear power plant?

11 Nothing.

12 Let's step back and look again at this remark in the President's speech: ". . . [W]e've got to recognize that nuclear power, if it's safe, can make a significant contribution to the climate change question." Look at these words: *if it's safe*. We should have learned by now that nothing "nuclear" is ever safe. It's not a matter of how well-regulated nuclear energy is, nor how well-engineered and protected the nuclear facilities are. Japan has shown us that. The negative possibilities and consequences of misuse or missteps in relation to nuclear power are far too severe. We cannot **countenance** the use of nuclear power, no matter how safe or regulated the government claims our nuclear power supplies are. We must find our energy solutions elsewhere.

13 The President states that he will **spearhead** a government revamping to ensure that what happened to Japan's nuclear power plant will never happen in the United States. He explains that eliminating potential danger from U.S. nuclear energy sources is extremely important: "I've requested a comprehensive safety review by the Nuclear Regulatory Commission to make sure that all of our existing nuclear energy facilities are safe." That is all very well, for now, but the nuclear energy damage has already been done. Future regulations cannot clean up past mistakes.

Comprehension Check

How does your analysis of the opinions expressed in the two selections help you to form your own opinion on nuclear energy? Explain how your opinion might change if you read only one author's opinion.

Guided Instruction

CITE EVIDENCE

C Two texts may disagree in matters of fact or interpretation. Look for evidence that is presented to support similar points so that you can analyze each author's interpretation of facts. Double underline the two sentences on page 282 that refer to energy usage percentages as described by President Obama. How is the author of this op-ed interpreting this information?

D If one author directly references the work or ideas of another, examine the statements carefully for bias and objectivity. Put an asterisk next to the paragraphs on these two pages that directly reference President Obama's language. Analyze whether the author of this op-ed gives Obama's opinions fair representation.

Guided Practice

RI.8.9, RH.8.8

WORDS TO KNOW

contingency
fundamental
groundwater
phenomenon
precaution

CITE EVIDENCE

A Circle the paragraph that introduces another example of problems with harnessing nuclear energy. Does the author cite facts, opinions, or logical judgments?

B Working with a partner, put an asterisk by each of the two paragraphs that identify the issues of government-regulated nuclear energy plants. Analyze how this information compares with the ideas proposed in President Obama's speech.

Op Ed: **President's Clean Energy Plan Must Be Refocused** *continued*

14 It would be one thing if the government could see into the future, identify every possible **contingency** that could lead to something going wrong at a nuclear power plant, and take steps now to prevent such mistakes from ever occurring. But no matter how much research people do or how many **precautions** the government takes, no one can fully anticipate the future.

15 During the nuclear energy plant disaster at Chernobyl in the Ukraine in 1986, people all around the world were given a wake-up call and a warning about the dangers of nuclear power: a reminder of how easy it is for that power, which may seem safe and regulated, to slip out of control. This was only twenty-five years ago. Suppose another nuclear power plant is damaged in twenty-five more years, and another is damaged twenty-five years after that. What will be the consequences to future generations of humans and animals on this planet?

16 Those of us in the United States might think, "Well, these nuclear power plant problems are terrible for the citizens of these other countries. But here in the U.S., the government is taking precautions to make sure those kinds of accidents don't happen on American soil." There are a few problems with this line of thinking.

17 First of all, what these historic events in Chernobyl and Japan have shown us is that accidents can happen, whether as a result of human error or a natural **phenomenon**. These accidents can expose unforeseen weaknesses in nuclear power plants and make previously "safe" locations completely unstable.

Chernobyl in the Ukraine

Fukushima I in Japan

18 Secondly, problems of radiation and nuclear waste are not limited to their immediate environments. Radiation gets into **groundwater**, lakes, rivers, and oceans. It contaminates life in the water, affecting the food web at a **fundamental** level. The consequences of radioactivity emerging from contained locations within factories and getting into the air, as in Chernobyl, or the water, as in the Japanese tsunami, have far-reaching effects on every living thing on the planet.

Comprehension Check

1. The claims presented in this article and in President Obama's speech agree that Americans should do all of the following EXCEPT

a. employ wind energy.

b. increase solar energy.

c. minimize oil energy.

d. regulate nuclear energy.

2. The op-ed author disagrees with Obama's opinion about nuclear energy because it

a. is exceptionally safe.

b. is potentially dangerous.

c. is substantially funded.

d. is perpetually popular.

3. In which of the following ways is the op-ed author's support of his or her claim most different from the way President Obama supports his claim?

a. The op-ed author focuses on Japan.

b. The op-ed author looks beyond Japan.

c. The op-ed author looks broadly at clean energy.

d. The op-ed author focuses on government spending.

4. This op-ed response to President Obama's speech is primarily supported by

a. opinions.

b. facts.

c. statistics.

d. quotations.

5. How does familiarity with the topics of President Obama's speech referred to in this article help you to analyze the issue and this author's presentation of it?

____

____

____

____

____

Independent Practice

RI.8.9, RH.8.7, RH.8.8

WORDS TO KNOW

curtailed
evaporation
exclusively
substantial
vanguard

CITE EVIDENCE

A Put an asterisk by the paragraph in this section that uses a visual aid to underscore an important point about the dangers of nuclear power spills.

B Circle the paragraph that presents the author's final position on the issue of clean energy. How does his or her opinion differ from President Obama's?

Op Ed: **President's Clean Energy Plan Must Be Refocused** *continued*

19 Think of the methods by which water passes through the atmosphere: **evaporation**, condensation, precipitation. In each of these stages, the water molecules can move through the air, travel around the world, and end up in entirely different locations. As these molecules pass through the world's air and water, they leave behind traces of radioactivity.

20 Recall that Japan is an island nation, that its disaster originated in water, and that the temporary solution for its damaged nuclear power plant was to soak the damaged nuclear cores in water. What happens to that water, eventually? It goes back out to sea and travels east, crossing oceans and slowly making its way to North American territories: Hawaii, Alaska, and the West Coast.

21 Consult your world map; Japan may be an island, but it is not isolated. The radioactive materials released in the tsunami will not be **curtailed** by Japanese borders or remain in Japanese waters. Such international boundaries make no difference to the ocean itself. Thus, what happens in Japan will eventually affect other parts of the world; no country exists in a vacuum. Our energy use affects other countries, just as their energy use affects us.

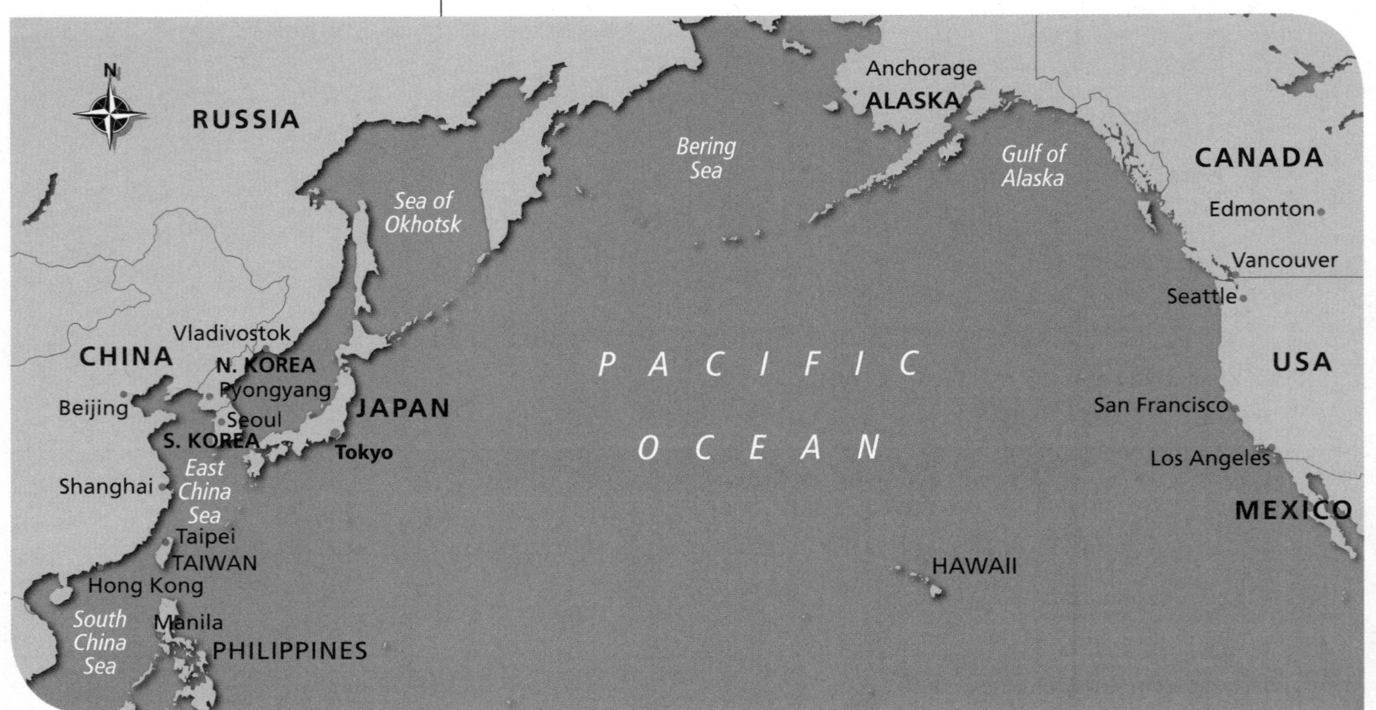

22 But change must begin at home, and since the President is calling for change in our approach to energy usage, we might as well make that change as positive, effective, and **substantial** as we can. As long as we are making changes to ensure that our energy use is responsible, safeguarded, and thoughtful, we should make those changes to their fullest extent.

23 We should move wholeheartedly into using lower-impact, environmentally safe sources of energy, such as wind and solar power. The government can and should fund and support this type of energy development and use **exclusively**, providing no place for nuclear energy. That way, our country can be in the **vanguard** of responsible behavior for nations around the world, leading the way by example.

Comprehension Check

MORE ONLINE **sadlierconnect.com**

1. This op-ed supports its claims using all of the following visual aids EXCEPT

a. photographs of Japan's tsunami.

b. photographs of Chernobyl.

c. a map of Japan to the West Coast.

d. a map of Chernobyl to the East Coast.

2. Ultimately, the op-ed author and Obama agree about which of the following types of energy in the clean energy plan?

a. nuclear energy and oil

b. wind and solar power

c. solar power and oil

d. nuclear energy and wind power

3. The author of this piece has doubts about all of the following EXCEPT

a. government regulation capability.

b. unpredictability of the natural world.

c. lack of a budget for wind/solar energy.

d. unforeseen future catastrophes.

4. Which of the following BEST describes this author's opinion about Obama's energy plan?

a. It is totally wrong.

b. It is mostly wrong.

c. It is partly right.

d. It is totally right.

5. Comparing this author's clean energy plan to President Obama's, explain which approach may be more realistic and which may be more idealistic.

RI.8.7, RI.8.8, RI.8.9, RI.8.10

Radio Waves:
From Then to Now
(Genre: Web Article)

How Radio Waves Were Discovered

1 The term *radio waves* might seem a little quaint today, especially if it only brings to mind the idea of how sounds are transmitted from an AM or FM analog radio station. But radio waves continue to play an important, even essential, role in twenty-first century communications and other fields.

2 How did radio waves come to play such an important role in contemporary life, and, what's more, how did people come to know about radio waves at all? What we know of radio waves today is due basically to the work of two men who lived and worked during the nineteenth century: one was from Scotland and one was from Germany. The former, James Clerk Maxwell, lived from 1831 to 1879; the latter, Heinrich Hertz, lived from 1857 to 1894.

3 By 1873, Maxwell had laid the groundwork and theoretical ideas for the study of what we recognize today as radio waves. He developed a set of equations, or mathematical formulas, that were essential to the field of electromagnetism. His interests created the perfect setting for the discovery of radio waves, since these waves are part of the larger family of electromagnetic waves.

4 Between 1885 and 1888, Hertz conducted experiments that built on Maxwell's ideas. Hertz took a radical approach: He adopted an examination technique that other scientists used to study waves of light, but, in a stroke of genius, he started applying it to the study of electromagnetic waves. Hertz extended Maxwell's ideas and figured out the existence, composition, and properties of a special type of electromagnetic wave, which is what we now know as the *radio wave*. Since 1889, other scientists and inventors have used Hertz's discovery to take full advantage of radio waves' unique properties and capabilities. (Read more about scientists who made important discoveries in electromagnetism.)

Physical Properties of Radio Waves

5 Radio waves, like other electromagnetic waves, can be measured according to several criteria, and we'll just look at a few of the most important here. First of all, a wave is measured in terms of its *period* or *cycle*: the segment in which the wave rises, falls, and returns to its starting point.

6 Next, a wave's size and shape can be measured through its *wavelength*. To find the wavelength, measure the distance from the

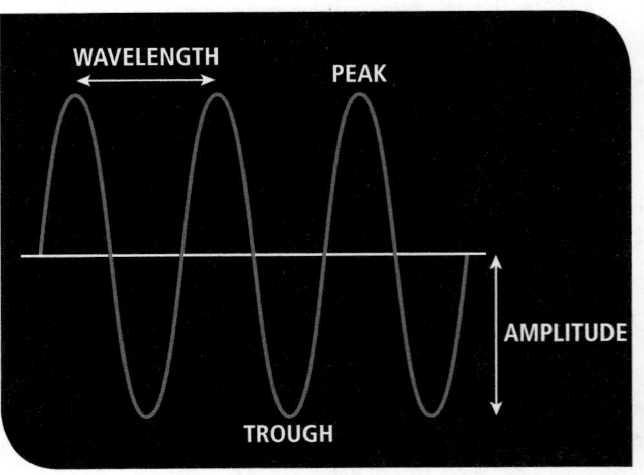

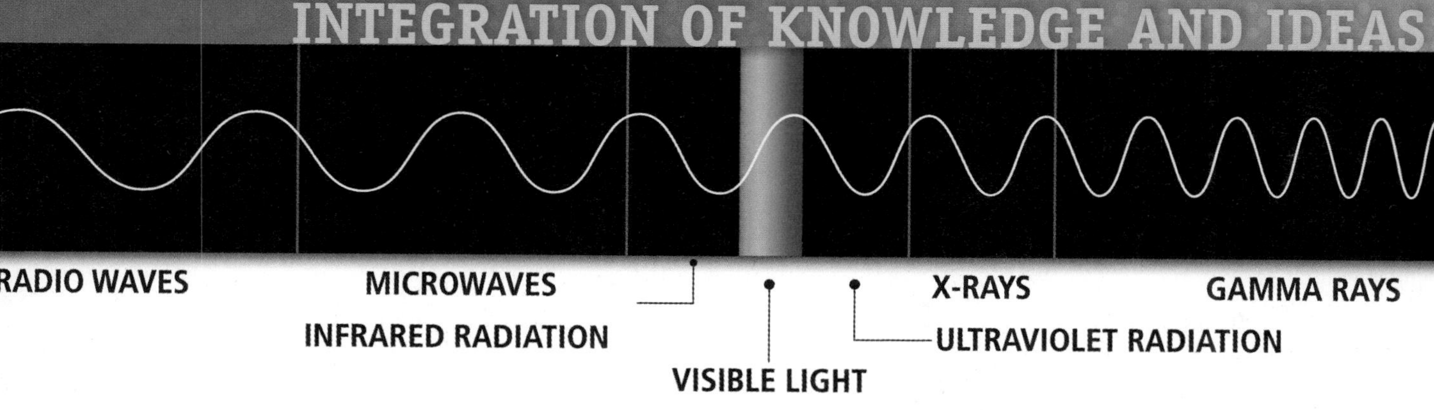

highest point in a wave—the crest—to the same point in the next wave. Click here to watch a video that demonstrates radio waves in action.

7 Finally, we can figure out how fast a wave moves by measuring its *frequency*. We can find the frequency by determining how many waves go by in a specific amount of time. Since we're discussing frequency, let's go back to Hertz for a moment; after all, his studies focused on the frequency of wavelengths. Most people measure radio-wave frequency by the length of one second, and this one-second period is referred to as a *Hertz*. Every time we see this measurement, we are reminded of the inventor who discovered these waves.

8 Radio waves lie on the electromagnetic spectrum, which includes the wavelengths of visible light: we know these as the rainbow colors of the spectrum that we can see. The spectrum also includes wavelengths that we cannot see but can measure. Radio waves are the longest wavelengths, with the lowest frequency; they occur at the "beginning" of the spectrum, and visible light is near the middle of the spectrum. The shortest wavelengths, with the highest frequencies—X-rays and gamma rays—are at the very "end" of the spectrum.

Real-Life Applications of Radio Waves

9 Since radio waves can move between sound and electromagnetic forms, they make up a fundamental part of many aspects of everyday life, from communications to the health industry. For instance, many of the delicate, important procedures that hospitals rely on use radio-wave technology: the MRI exam, for instance, depends on radio waves. Radio waves are also significant in the field of astronomy: astronomers can use radio waves to determine additional information about our world, the solar system, and beyond.

10 Finally, radio waves come in handy for all types of communication. Don't forget that radio waves convey music and information to huge audiences all around the world. Every time we talk on a cell phone or watch TV, we take advantage of radio waves. Last but not least, satellite technology, which bounces information from point to point all around the planet and even into outer space, does so through the use of radio waves. We probably could not do without any of these capabilities. These waves, and their part of the electromagnetic spectrum, are essential to our twenty-first century way of life.

Don't Touch That Dial

(Genre: Editorial)

1 Friends, as 1924 reaches its midpoint, there can be no denying that we live in a permissive age. Women's dresses and hairstyles have gotten shorter, the "flapper" has become fashionable, and the strains of jazz music fill our nightclubs. But there is one area in which we must be less permissive: in fact, in this area we cannot be too strict. And this area is that of the radio broadcast.

2 For almost two years now, the radio has been growing in popularity. It is easy to understand why, in 1922, a radio was installed in the White House. But soon almost twenty percent of American households will have a radio. Radios used to be for scientists, the military, and government officials only. People could not use radio broadcasts for personal purposes during wartime, for obvious reasons. Yet today, that is changing, and the change may not be for the nation's good. It has been only six years since World War I ended. We should not so soon forget our battles, or the losses that came with our victories. Radio technology could be used to save many lives in future battles. During times of war, radio can serve as an incredibly useful tool for communicating to those within its reach. Radio provides the government with an unparalleled tool for marshaling troops and readying civilians for whatever may come.

3 Today, however, more and more "amateurs" are trying their hands at radio transmittal. Some folks use their radio capabilities for frivolous purposes, and I believe they must be stopped. It might be tempting to fill the airwaves with the magical tunes of George Gershwin and Irving Berlin. Yet playing music is hardly a productive or realistic use of a complex technology that can support our society in essential ways.

4 One question we must address is that raised by the unknown capabilities of radio wave communication. How far does its reach extend? We now know that trans-Atlantic radio signals can be sent and received; can signals travel even farther, perhaps even to and from outer space itself? Scientists know that there are limits to how far we can transmit radio signals, since the Heaviside layer of gases around our planet prevents radio signals from leaving Earth. Yet what if radio-wave transmissions are being sent *to* us from another planet? Even now members of the Navy are being asked to listen for radio communications from the red planet Mars.

5 The possibility of receiving extraterrestrial communication (which, admittedly, may sound more like fiction than fact to some) must be an exception to the general rule of preserving the territory of radio reception and transmission for those who need it

most: members of our government and military, rather than average, everyday folks.

6 I implore you to consider the necessity of saving radio broadcasts for only important people and events. A radio should not be used for mere pleasure, and it should not be overused. The radio is not for fun or music; it is not for discussion or theater. It should be reserved for official broadcasts by our leaders, such as President Coolidge. Certainly, the radio may occasionally be used for educational purposes and public service programs, but never for mere entertainment.

7 Recall last December 6, when President Coolidge broadcast his "First Annual Message." As they did then, people should reserve their radios for such important transmissions. Suppose the President needed to reach all U.S. citizens suddenly, perhaps due to a national disaster?

8 It is imperative that the radio airwaves be open and free for our government's use. Remember, radio waves can provide the essential purpose of reaching many people rapidly. We have a responsibility to use radio waves for the greater good of the nation.

Comprehension Check

1A. Which of the following concepts in the Web article is presented using an advantage of the digital text medium that is not available in a print medium?

- **a.** information about James Clerk Maxwell
- **b.** information about the electromagnetic spectrum
- **c.** information about the Hertz measurement
- **d.** information about real-life applications of radio waves

1B. Which of the following textual details supports the answer to Part A?

- **a.** the electromagnetic spectrum diagram
- **b.** "Radio waves lie on the electromagnetic spectrum . . ."
- **c.** ". . . a wave's size and shape can be measured through its *wavelength*."
- **d.** "The former, James Clerk Maxwell, lived from 1831 to 1879 . . ."

2A. Which of the following is the central claim of "Don't Touch That Dial"?

- **a.** Radio broadcasts should be saved for official purposes only.
- **b.** Radio broadcasts should be used for both official purposes and pleasure.
- **c.** Radio broadcasts should occasionally be used for official purposes.
- **d.** Radio broadcasts should be used for educational purposes only.

2B. Which of the following textual details supports the answer to Part A?

- **a.** ". . . the radio may occasionally be used for educational purposes . . ."
- **b.** "It might be tempting to fill the airwaves with . . . magical tunes . . ."
- **c.** "It should be reserved for official broadcasts by our leaders . . ."
- **d.** "A radio should not be used for mere pleasure . . ."

3A. Which of the following BEST describes how the two selections differ in their treatment of the topic of radio waves?

a. Selection 1 describes radio-wave properties; Selection 2 is an opinion about the proper use of radio waves.

b. Selection 1 shows a diagram of radio waves; Selection 2 describes how radio waves work.

c. Selection 1 is mostly opinion; Selection 2 is mostly objective facts.

d. Selection 1 is written for scientists; Selection 2 is written for general readers.

3B. Which of the following supports the answer to Part A?

a. "Hertz . . . built on Maxwell's ideas"; ". . . we live in a permissive age."

b. "waves . . . can be measured according to several criteria"; "[Radio] should be reserved for official broadcasts . . ."

c. ". . . the study of electromagnetic waves"; "Radios used to be for scientists, the military . . ."

d. "Astronomers can use radio waves to . . ."; "How far does its reach extend?"

4A. Which resource would BEST support "Don't Touch That Dial" if it was posted on a Web site?

a. an animated diagram of radio waves

b. a hyperlink to articles on radio history

c. audio of President Coolidge's radio address

d. a video of a jazz concert

4B. Which of the following supports the answer to Part A?

a. "Some folks use their radio capabilities for frivolous purposes . . ."

b. "Suppose the President needed to reach all his citizens suddenly . . ."

c. ". . . the strains of jazz music fill our nightclubs."

d. ". . . the radio may occasionally be used or educational purposes . . ."

5A. Which textual evidence in "Don't Touch That Dial" is LEAST relevant to the author's claim?

a. the discussion of how radio waves can be used during wartime

b. the discussion of the Navy listening for radio waves from Mars

c. the discussion of how the President uses radio transmissions

d. the discussion of how radio waves should be used in future

5B. Which detail from the text supports the answer to Part A?

a. ". . . asked to listen for radio communications from the red planet Mars."

b. ". . . could be used to save many lives in future battles."

c. ". . . official broadcasts by our leaders . . ."

d. "We have a responsibility to use radio waves for the greater good . . ."

6. Describe how the diagram on page 289 contributes to your understanding of the ideas discussed in "Radio Waves: From Then to Now."

7. Describe the reasoning the author of the editorial "Don't Touch That Dial" uses to support his or her approach to the topic of the best use of radio waves. In what ways is the reasoning in this text limited, and why?

8. Describe one advantage and one disadvantage of the digital text medium as used in "Radio Waves: From Then to Now."

9. Suppose that "Radio Waves: From Then to Now" was presented as a print article. How would changing the medium from digital to print affect your interaction with the information?

10. Describe the primary way in which the online article and the print editorial differ in their ideas about the usefulness of radio waves.

Support a Claim

RI.8.9, SL.8.1.a, SL.8.1.c, SL.8.1.d, SL.8.3, SL.8.4

In this unit you've read a Web article about pasteurization, a persuasive speech and an op-ed on nuclear and clean energy, and an online science article on radio waves paired with an editorial on uses of radio waves. In the boxes of the chart, list the key claims made in each text. Then write a brief essay comparing and contrasting two selections, using the information in the chart to support the claim in the center. You may choose to compare two selections that have strong claims or compare a selection with a strong claim to one with a weak claim. Write on a separate sheet of paper. Be prepared to discuss your response.

"Types of Food Preservation: Pasteurization"

"Remarks by the President on America's Energy Security"

The strongest claims use sound reasoning, cite sufficient and relevant evidence, and acknowledge other points of view.

"Op-Ed: Presidents' Clean Energy Plan Must Be Refocused"

"Radio Waves: From Then to Now"

"Don't Touch That Dial"

Return to the Essential Question

How can readers analyze texts written by different authors in different mediums?

In small groups or as a class, discuss the Essential Question. Think about what you have learned about evaluating pros and cons in various mediums, assessing a claim's support and reasoning, and identifying opposing or conflicting claims about similar topics. Use evidence from the selections you've read to answer the question.

L.8.5c

Connotation and Denotation

Guided Instruction A word's **denotation** is its dictionary definition. Many words also have a **connotation**—a positive or negative shade of meaning that we associate with the word. For example, someone who is called *lazy* may show a constant tendency to avoid work; someone who is *lethargic,* a word with a similar denotative meaning, might only be temporarily inactive due to tiredness or illness.

Denotation	Connotative Words	Explanation
quickly (adverb implying an action taken with speed)	*rapidly* *swiftly*	*Rapidly* and *swiftly* indicate a speedy movement; they are both close in meaning to *quickly* and so share the same denotation.
	hurriedly *hastily*	*Hurriedly* and *hastily* negatively imply a rush, carelessness, or almost reckless speed.
	promptly	*Promptly* has a positive connotation, implying good timing.

Example:
From "Types of Food Preservation: Pasteurization":
"Fruits and vegetables, if not eaten **promptly**, must be kept cold as well."

Guided Practice Complete each sentence with a word from the chart that has the same denotation as *promptly* and an appropriate connotation.

1. With only fifteen minutes to complete his shopping, he moved efficiently and ____________________ through the supermarket.

2. Since the bell was about to ring any moment, I ____________________ completed the assignment questions, hoping for the best.

3. Knowing that being on time for his job interview mattered tremendously, Scott walked __________________ to the office.

4. When her neighbor asked for help, Maria volunteered ________________.

Independent Practice Use a dictionary to determine the denotation of an adjective or adverb you choose. Then make a list of at least four words with similar denotations but different connotations. On a separate sheet of paper, write a sentence using each word in an appropriate connotative context.

RI.8.7, RI.8.8, RI.8.9, L.8.5.c

Read the following scientific narrative and Web article that present information in different mediums, present support and reasoning for claims, and take different approaches to a similar topic. Then answer the questions on pages 297–298.

The Telephone at the Centennial

by Walter Kellogg Towers

1 The Philadelphia Centennial Exposition [1876]—America's first great exposition—opened within a month after the completion of the first telephone. . . .

2 [The judges] seemed to regard [the telephone] as a toy not worth their attention, and the public generally had displayed no interest in the device. . . . It was well past suppertime when [the judges] came to [Alexander Graham] Bell's table behind the stairs, and most of the judges were tired out and loudly announced their intention of quitting then and there.

3 At this critical moment, while they were fingering Bell's apparatus indifferently and preparing for their departure, a strange and fortunate thing occurred. Followed by a group of brilliantly attired courtiers, the Emperor of Brazil appeared. . . . Bell showed him how to place his ear to the receiver, and he then went to the transmitter which had been placed at the other end of the wire strung along the room. The Emperor waited expectantly; the judges watched curiously. Bell, at a distance, spoke into the transmitter. In utter wonderment the Emperor raised his head from the receiver. "My . . . ," he cried, "it talks!""

4 Skepticism and indifference were at an end among the judges, and they eagerly followed the example of the Emperor. . . .

5 [English scientist, Sir William] Thomson pronounced Bell's telephone "the most wonderful thing he had seen in America." The judges had forgotten that they were hungry and tired, and remained grouped about the telephone, talking and listening in turn until far into the evening. Bell's exhibit was . . . given the most prominent place that could be found. From that time forward it was the wonder of the Centennial.

—from *Masters of Space: Morse, Thompson, Bell, Marconi, Carty* (1917)

Museum Exhibit: **History of the Telephone**

1 In 1876, Alexander Graham Bell invented the "talking telegraph": the telephone, an innovation that forever changed the way people communicate. (Click here for a video reenactment of Bell's first public demonstration of the telephone at the 1876 Centennial Exposition.)

2 The museum is proud to announce the upcoming exhibit, *Telephones: From Then to Now.* The exhibit features over 170 actual telephones, from a reproduction of Bell's first telephone and early 1900s wall phones to the first mobile phones and the latest smartphones. (Click here for photos of some of the craziest phone designs of all time!) The exhibit will also feature interactive displays demonstrating the science behind how telephones, cordless phones, and cell phones work. (Click here to see a video of a middle-school class exploring the principle of variable resistance in a hands-on display.) The exhibit runs from September 8–January 10.

RI.8.7, RI.8.8, L.8.5.c

Circle the letter next to the best answer.

1A. Which of the following visuals would BEST support "The Telephone at the Centennial"?

a. a timeline of telephone history

b. a diagram showing the inner workings of Bell's telephone

c. a period illustration of Bell demonstrating his telephone at the Centennial

d. a period portrait of Alexander Graham Bell

1B. Which phrase in the text supports the answer to Part A?

a. "[It] opened within a month after the completion of the first telephone."

b. ". . . the public generally had displayed no interest in the device."

c. "The judges had forgotten that they were hungry and tired . . ."

d. "From that time forward it was the wonder of the Centennial."

2A. If you are trying to understand the impact of Bell's invention in 1876, an advantage the Web announcement has over the print article is that

a. it includes several hyperlinks.

b. it mentions a reproduction of Bell's first telephone.

c. it includes a video that shows the event described in the print article.

d. it is written in simpler, more contemporary language.

2B. Which of the following supports the answer to Part A?

a. "In 1876, Alexander Graham Bell invented . . . the telephone . . ."

b. "Click here for a video reenactment of Bell's first public demonstration . . ."

c. "The exhibit features over 170 actual telephones . . ."

d. "The exhibit will also feature interactive displays . . ."

3A. Which of the following is the closest denotative meaning of the word *innovation* as used in the museum exhibit announcement?

a. *process*

b. *equipment*

c. *trend*

d. *creation*

3B. Which of the following words from the text supports the answer to Part A?

a. *first*

b. *invented*

c. *demonstration*

d. *communicate*

4A. Which of the following is a claim expressed in "Museum Exhibit: History of the Telephone"?

a. Telephones matter because of the science that lies behind them.

b. Telephones are an amazing technology that had a profound effect on communications.

c. Telephones were originally thought of as "talking telegraphs."

d. Many examples of telephones will be on display.

4B. Which details from "Museum Exhibit: History of the Telephone" support the answer to Part A?

a. ". . . reproduction of Bell's first telephone . . ."

b. ". . . an innovation that forever changed the way people communicate."

c. "The museum is proud to announce the upcoming exhibit . . . "

d. "The exhibit features over 170 actual telephones . . ."

5A. In "Museum Exhibit: History of the Telephone," which reference is irrelevant to the claim of the telephone's technological importance?

a. the reenactment of Bell's first successful telephone demonstration in public

b. the link to photos of various phone designs

c. the link to a video of middle school students using a hands-on display

d. the mention of interactive displays

RI.8.7, RI.8.8, RI.8.9

5B. Which of the following textual details supports the answer to Part A?

a. "Click here for a video reenactment . . ."

b. ". . . changed the way people communicate."

c. ". . . the principle of variable resistance . . ."

d. ". . . craziest phone designs of all time . . ."

6A. One strong similarity between the information given in the two selections is that both

a. rely mostly on opinions, not facts.

b. acknowledge the telephone's importance.

c. focus on one historical event.

d. describe a mechanical process in detail.

6B. Which of the following textual details supports the answer to Part A?

a. "'the most wonderful thing he had seen in America'"; "an innovation that forever changed the way people communicate"

b. "they were fingering Bell's apparatus indifferently"; "a reproduction of Bell's first telephone"

c. "Bell showed him how to place his ear to the receiver"; "featuring over 170 actual telephones"

d. "In utter wonderment the Emperor raised his head"; "The principle of variable resistance"

7. Describe the disadvantages of presenting information about how telephones work in a printed text versus a digital text with hyperlinks.

____

____

____

8. If you were going to post "The Telephone at the Centennial" on the Web and take advantage of the digital medium, what features would you include?

____

____

____

9. Write a sample claim you could use to urge people to see the museum exhibit "Telephones: From Then to Now." Cite evidence from the announcement to convince people that the exhibit is worth seeing.

____

____

____

10. Both "The Telephone at the Centennial" and "Telephones: From Then to Now" make claims about the telephone. Explain how the texts disagree—or at least diverge—in their assessments of the importance of the telephone.

____

____

____

Writing Handbook

W.8.2, W.8.4, W.8.5, W.8.6, W.8.7, W.8.8, W.8.9.b, W.8.10

Over the course of this school year you will have an opportunity to express your ideas through several different kinds of writing: a fictional narrative, an informative/explanatory essay, an evidence-based essay, a research report, and an argumentative essay. This handbook will show you the steps of the writing process, guiding you from your initial ideas to a finished piece of writing. Once you know the steps of the process, you can use them for any type of writing.

STEP 1 Planning

In school, you will often have to write research reports. A research report conveys what a writer has learned about a particular topic. Let's suppose you decide to write a research report about animal intelligence and emotions. The planning stage is especially important when you are writing a research report. You might begin the writing process by asking yourself questions:

- **What** am I writing?

Start by asking questions about a topic that interests you. To answer the questions, research credible and reliable sources of information. Share what you learn in a logically organized and clearly written report. Support your ideas with facts and details from your research. Summarize, paraphrase, and directly quote your sources. Provide citations for your sources.

- **Why** am I writing? What is my **purpose**?

The main purpose for writing a research report is to provide one's readers with specific information about a particular topic. Another purpose is to develop your ability to formulate original questions about a topic and conduct research to answer them. The best research reports answer original and interesting questions with current and accurate information.

- **Who** is my audience?

Initially, your audience is your teacher and your classmates, but if you decide to publish your paper in print or online, your audience may expand to include anyone who wants to learn more about animal consciousness.

Planning and Research

- **Choose a topic that interests you.**

It is important to select a topic that is neither too broad, such as *the history of popular music*, nor too narrow, such as *When did Leonard Bernstein compose* West Side Story? Consider what you already know about the topic and then do some general reading. Scan online encyclopedia articles and nonfiction books. Use questions that come up as you read to develop a focus for your topic.

For fictional narrative writing, start by inventing an interesting character in a particular place who has a conflict to overcome.

- **Find supporting evidence.**

When writing any informational text, you must support your topic with evidence: examples, facts, definitions, and quotations. This evidence should come from reliable sources—writings by experts in a particular field, found in trustworthy books and periodicals, and on reliable Web sites.

If you are writing a fictional narrative, explore the central character's situation by using dialogue and descriptions of the people, places, and things involved in the story.

It helps to plan a piece of writing by making an outline. Here's an outline for a research report about animals' emotional intelligence. It shows the introduction, the subtopics, and the conclusion, and it cites the sources the writer consulted.

Can Animals Think?

I. **Introduction**

Topic: Although it was long thought that only humans, not animals, were capable of thinking and feeling, recent studies suggest that at least some animals are conscious beings.

II. **Body**

Subtopic 1: Do animals have consciousness?

Supporting Facts: People long thought that consciousness was a quality only humans possessed. But recent scientific experiments suggest that animals have consciousness, too.

Subtopic 2: Dogs can feel emotions.

Supporting Facts: A recent study of dog brains showed that their brains react to enjoyable thoughts just as human brains do.

Subtopic 3: Some animals can communicate their thoughts through language.

Supporting Facts: A parrot taught a variety of English words could communicate its perceptions.

III. **Conclusion** Recent scientific studies suggest that animals are conscious beings.

IV. **Sources:** National Geographic Online, New York Times, The Oxford Companion to Consciousness

If you are writing a narrative, instead of using subtopics, create a time line that shows the order of events in the story.

DIGITAL TIP

Consider using organizational software programs to help you structure your ideas in a way that works best for you. Type in your ideas and then view and organize them in multiple ways—through outlines, concept maps, and visual diagrams with icons.

PLANNING TOGETHER

Collaborate with a partner for feedback. Is the topic interesting? Is it too narrow or too broad? What other questions does your partner have? If possible, record your discussion and listen to it later as you prepare your outline.

STEP 1: Planning *(continued)* W.8.2.b, W.8.7, W.8.8, W.8.9.b

Researching Your Topic

Your next step involves finding good sources of information that are relevant and current. Strive for a balance of print and online sources, and make sure they are reliable, accurate, and credible.

- **Where to Look:** A knowledgeable reference librarian can guide you to reliable and credible print and online sources. Because experts and non-experts alike can post their ideas online, you cannot always trust what you read on the Web. Focus then on .com sources published by respected newspapers, magazines, or other trustworthy institutions. The reference database section of your library's Web site will guide you to other reliable sources, including government (.gov), university (.edu), and public organization (.org) Web sites. Read all your sources carefully, and avoid those that are biased or one-sided.

- **How to Search:** Formulate a specific, effective online search term. If you were researching animal emotions, the search term *animals* would be too broad to be useful. Key words such as *animal emotions intelligence research* would be more helpful. Carefully evaluate the sites your search term calls up. Some commercial Web sites pay search engine companies to put their links at the top of a search results page, so always skim each link's URL and summary to see if it is reliable and credible. If your search term does not call up useful links, see if your search engine provides you with alternative search terms, and click on one of the suggestions.

- **How to Judge:** A credible source is one written by an expert in a field of learning. Find credible sources in print and online: encyclopedias, newspapers and magazines, professional journals and newsletters, and books and Web sites. Do not assume that the information is accurate. Double-check by comparing and contrasting key facts in more than one source. Also, notice when a source was published. Use recently published sources to ensure that your information is up-to-date.

- **How to Take Notes:** Make photocopies of print sources and create pdfs of online sources. Highlight important information, including quotations you will want to use. Use these documents as the basis for your notes, which you can hand write on index cards or type up in files on a computer. Paraphrase and summarize the most relevant information from your sources. Be sure to cite the page number or URL of the source from which you got the information.

- **How to Cite Sources:** When you draft your report, you will need to write citations that tell your readers where you got specific information. In your notes, identify the title, author, and publication information for each source. You can use informal citations in your notes, such as: **Author. Title. Publisher. Date. Page number.** For online sources, identify the source as "Web," and include the URL and the date you accessed the information.

DIGITAL TIP

Use a reference management software program to help keep track of the sources you consult while researching for your report. Some programs automatically collect all the relevant details right from your Web browser. Others require you to fill in screens with publishing information.

W.8.2, W.8.4, W.8.5, W.8.6, W.8.7, W.8.8, W.8.9.b, W.8.10

STEP 2 Drafting

Use your outline to guide you as you write your first draft. Do not worry about issues of spelling and grammar at this stage. Use a computer if you want to be able to copy, cut, and paste text later when you revise. If you write by hand, leave room for revisions by skipping every other line. Here is a draft of a research report about whether animals possess consciousness.

Can Animals Think?

People long assumed that only humans experienced consciousness. Recent studies indicate that the workings of some animals' brains are similar to our own, and that animals can have emotional responses. Some can even use language.

Scientists wanted to find out if dogs really did feel such emotions. Recent technologies have enabled scientists to conduct humane experiments to determine the emotional capability of dogs. In the October 5, 2013 edition of the New York Times, professor Gregory Burns described an experiment in which he and his staff trained dogs to participate in brain scans. The scans revealed that a part of a dog's brain called the caudate nucleus responds to enjoyable experiences just as humans' brains do. The caudate nucleus "lit up" when the dogs reacted to owners' scents or promises of treats.

For more than thirty years, Harvard researcher Irene Pepperberg worked with an African gray parrot named Alex. Her goal was to teach Alex enough English so that he could tell her about his life. He learned a large enough vocabulary to describe things he saw—colors, shapes, numbers of objects, and so on. Alex clearly showed Pepperberg a level of thinking skills "generally ascribed only to higher mammals."

Other studies involving dolphins, primates, and crows have revealed similar findings: Animals have consciousness, and some of them can even tell us a little bit about what they think and feel.

W.8.2, W.8.4, W.8.5, W.8.9.b, W.8.10, L.8.1.b–d, L.8.3.a, L.8.4.c, L.8.4.d

STEP 3 Revising

The revising step is the opportunity for thinking about broad issues involving structure, voice, and language rather than the finer points of spelling and grammar. The items in the checklist below will help you evaluate your draft for revisions. If you are composing on a computer, read the draft on your screen and type in changes as you go. If you are writing by hand, mark up your draft by making notes between the lines and in the margins.

REVISING CHECKLIST

Ideas and Voice

- ☐ Have I clearly stated my purpose for writing?
- ☐ Have I included enough accurate and reliable information?
- ☐ Does my writer's voice sound direct, interesting, and well informed?
- ☐ Have I conveyed the information in an objective and balanced way?

Organization and Coherence

- ☐ Does the beginning introduce the topic clearly?
- ☐ Have I organized my ideas logically and chosen relevant supporting evidence, such as facts, concrete details, and quotations from experts?
- ☐ Have I used transitions to connect and clarify ideas and concepts?
- ☐ Does my conclusion follow from and support the information I presented?
- ☐ Have I varied my sentences for better style or to clarify meaning?
- ☐ Have I used verbs in the correct voice and mood and corrected inappropriate shifts?

Word Choice

- ☐ Have I correctly selected verbs to achieve a particular mood, or tone?
- ☐ Have I used specialized terms correctly and checked their definitions?
- ☐ Have I provided definitions for terms that readers might not know?
- ☐ Have I established and consistently used appropriately formal English?

REVISING TOGETHER

Email your draft or a recording of you reading it to someone you trust. After that person reads your draft, meet with him or her to work through the questions in the Revising Checklist together, taking notes as you go. Afterward, ask your partner for any additional comments about your draft. Use your notes and your partner's feedback to guide you as you make revisions.

W.8.2, W.8.4, W.8.5, W.8.9.b, W.8.10, L.8.1.c–d, L.8.3.a, L.8.4.c, L.8.4.d

Here is a draft with notes for revisions. To see the revised draft, turn to page 307.

My title needs to more accurately reflect my topic.

Can Animals Think ^and Feel?

I need to define the word *consciousness* in my introduction.

People long assumed that only humans experienced consciousness. ^Consciousness is defined as the ability to think and feel and be aware of oneself. Recent studies indicate that the workings of some animals' brains are similar to our own, and that animals can have emotional responses. Some can even use language.

I need to bring in a connection to real-life experiences.

^Many dog owners claim that they can tell when their pets are sad, jealous, or happy. Scientists wanted to find out if dogs really did feel emotions. Recent technologies have enabled scientists to conduct humane experiments to determine the emotional capability of dogs. In the October 5, 2013 edition of the New York Times, professor Gregory Burns described an experiment in which he and his staff trained dogs to participate in brain scans. The scans revealed that a part of a dog's brain called the caudate nucleus responds to enjoyable experiences just as humans' brains do. ^In humans, this part of the brain responds when we think of enjoyable things, such as friends and food. In the experiment, the caudate nucleus "lit up" in a dog as it reacted to owners' scents or promises of treats.

I need to make a more direct comparison between human brains and dog brains.

I need to make a clearer transition between the dog study and the parrot study.

^Another study used language to get a parrot to communicate its perceptions. For more than thirty years, Harvard researcher Irene Pepperberg worked with an African gray parrot named Alex. Her goal was to teach Alex enough English so that he could tell her about his life. He learned a large enough vocabulary to describe things he saw—colors, shapes, numbers of objects, and so on. Alex clearly showed Pepperberg a level of thinking skills "generally ascribed only to higher mammals."

My conclusion needs to bring back the topic to my readers' experiences.

Other studies involving dolphins, primates, and crows have revealed similar findings: Animals have consciousness, and some of them can even tell us a little bit about what they think and feel. ^So, the next time your dog wags his tail when he greets you, you can be sure that he really is happy to see you.

W.8.2, W.8.4, W.8.5, W.8.6, L.8.1.b, L.8.2.a–c, L.8.3.a, L.8.4.c, L.8.4.d

STEP 4 Editing

The editing step is your chance to review your writing at the sentence level to check for errors in grammar, mechanics, and punctuation. Read your revised draft carefully, and use the Editing Checklist below and the Proofreading Marks on page 307 to identify the errors in your draft. Always proofread and correct your own work before submitting it. Identifying your own mistakes can be difficult, though, so consider using the spelling and grammar checker on your computer and asking a partner to help you find errors.

EDITING CHECKLIST

Sentences

- ☐ Every sentence is a complete sentence, with both a noun and a verb.
- ☐ I have used sentence variety, writing a mix of simple, compound, and complex sentences.
- ☐ I have consistently used active voice and corrected any unnecessary passive voice.
- ☐ I have correctly used verbs in the conditional and subjunctive moods.
- ☐ I have not left out any words, and I have deleted any extra words.
- ☐ My sentences are written at an appropriate level for my audience.

Grammar and Usage

- ☐ The subject and verb of every sentence agree.
- ☐ All verbs are in the correct tense, and I have corrected any inappropriate shifts.
- ☐ All pronouns have clear antecedents, matching the nouns they replace.
- ☐ Verb tenses are used correctly and consistently.
- ☐ Linking words and phrases clearly show relationships between ideas.
- ☐ I have corrected inappropriate shifts in verb voice and mood.

Mechanics

- ☐ Each sentence begins with a capital letter and ends with the correct punctuation mark.
- ☐ Quotation marks and other punctuation marks are used correctly; no marks are missing.
- ☐ I have used the appropriate punctuation correctly to indicate a pause or break in a sentence or the omission of text.
- ☐ All publication titles and all proper nouns are capitalized correctly.
- ☐ All paragraphs are indented.

Spelling

- ☐ I have used a dictionary to check spellings and definitions of words I am unsure about.
- ☐ I have correctly used frequently confused words, such as homophones (*through/threw*; *where/wear*; *days/daze*).

PROOFREADING MARKS

Mark	Meaning	Mark	Meaning	Mark	Meaning
^	Add	⊙	Period	⬭	Spelling error
ℓ/	Take out	/	Small letter	¶	Indent
^,	Insert comma	≡	Capital letter	∾	Change order

W.8.2, W.8.4, W.8.5, W.8.6, L.8.1.b, L.8.1.d, L.8.2.a, L.8.2.c, L.8.3.a, L.8.4.c, L.8.4.d

Can Animals Think and Feel?

People long assumed that only humans experienced Consciousness. Consciousness is defined as the ability to think and feel and to be aware of oneself. Recent scientific studies indicate that the workings of some animals' brains are similar to our own, and that animals can have emotional responses. Some can even use language.

Many dog owners claim that that they can tell when their pets are sad, jealous, or happy. Scientists wanted to find out if dogs really did feel emotions. Recent technologies have enabled scientists to conduct humane experiments to determine the emotional capability of dogs. In the October 5, 2013 edition of the New York Times, professor Gregory Berns described an experiment in which he and his staff trained dogs to participate in brain scans. The scans revealed that a part of a dog's brain called the caudate nucleus responds to enjoyable expereinces just as humans' brains do. In humans, this part of the brain responds when we think about things we like, such as food and music. In the experiment, the caudate nucleus "lit up" when the dogs reacted to owners' scents or promises of treats

¶Another study used language to get a parrot to communicate its perceptions. For more than thirty years, Harvard researcher Irene Pepperberg worked with an african gray parrot named Alex. Her goal was to teach Alex enough English so that he could tell her about his life. He learned a large enough vocabulary to describe things he saw—colors, shapes, numbers of objects and so on. Alex clearly showed Pepperberg a level of thinking skills "generally ascribed only to higher mammals."

Other studies involving dolphins, primates, and crows have revealed similar findings: Animals have consciousness, and some of them can even tell us a little bit about what they think and feel. So, the next time your dog wags his tail when he greets you, you can be sure that he is really happy to see you.

STEP 4: Editing *(continued)*

Editing Tips

The editing step is your last chance to make sure your writing is correct and clear. These tips will help you make sure your writing is perfect before you hand it in.

- **Using Spelling and Grammar Checkers:** Like any tool, a spelling checker or a grammar checker is not foolproof. Use these tools to catch obvious mistakes, but be aware that they will not catch all your errors. Many spelling checkers do not correct the incorrect use of words that are often confused. For example, if you wrote: *Humans, unlike animals, do not always trust there instincts*, a spelling checker would probably not identify *there* as an error because although it is the wrong word, it is spelled correctly. A spelling checker also might not correct proper nouns that are not capitalized. Likewise, if you leave out a word or misplace a comma, the grammar checker might not highlight the error. So be sure to read your work carefully to double-check for errors even after you run the checkers.

- **Using Quotations:** Remember that direct quotations are a form of evidence you are using to support your ideas. That means you must tailor the quotation so that it neatly fits into the flow of your writing. This does not mean changing the original writer's words! But you can use ellipses to indicate parts of the quotation you are not using. You should seamlessly weave the quotation into your own writing while at the same time placing quotation marks around the words and identifying the source. You want to be clear about giving credit for ideas and words that are not your own; otherwise, you will be committing plagiarism.

- **Original:** Not all animals are ideal participants in experiments about animal consciousness. "Cats are far less cooperative and tolerant than dogs and birds when it comes to these studies."

- **Revised:** The animal consciousness studies are limited to certain species because, according to State University biologist Iris Plimpton, "cats are far less cooperative and tolerant than dogs and birds when it comes to these studies."

- **Citing Sources:** In a research report and other forms of informational and persuasive writing, you must provide a list of all the sources you used to support your ideas. A Works Cited or Bibliography page should appear at the end of your paper that uses the specific citation format recommended by your teacher. Here are some basic rules of citation, whatever the format.
    - List your resources alphabetically by author's last name, or by title if the source has no author.
    - Include all the relevant information—author's or authors' names, title, publication information, online address.
    - Indent all the lines after the first line of each citation.

Here are some citations from **Can Animals Feel and Think?**

Bayne, Tim, Axel Cleeremans, and Brian J. Skinner, eds. *The Oxford Companion to Consciousness*. Oxford Reference Online. Web. 2012.

Berns, Gregory. "Dogs Are People, Too. "*New York Times.* 6 Oct. 2013, NY. ed: SR5. Print.

Morrell, Virginia. "Minds of Their Own." *National Geographic*. National Geographic Online. 2008. Web. October 2013.

W.8.5, W.8.6

STEP 5 Producing, Publishing, and Presenting

If you plan to publish your work so that a wider audience can read it, you will want to take some extra steps before submitting it. The first consideration is how your finished product looks. Before you create a final copy, think about adding visuals and text features.

- Photographs and illustrations can draw readers' interest and add visual appeal to the page.
- Diagrams, graphs, charts, or maps can provide important information that is not easily explained in words.
- Headings and subheadings clarify the organizational structure of your ideas, which helps readers to understand and remember them better.

The last step in publishing is to create a clean and legible final copy for your readers. Print out a final copy or neatly rewrite a clean copy by hand.

Online Publishing and Digital Slide Presentations

Think about publishing your work online. If your school has a Web site for student writing, scan or upload the final copy of your work. Or you could apply to publish your work on a respected and trustworthy Web site. Ask your teacher for site recommendations. You could also create a blog with links for registered readers only to leave comments.

Another option is to turn your report into a digital slide presentation, which is a tool many professionals use when they give oral presentations. Use presentation software to create a set of slides that summarizes the key ideas and details in your report. Use visuals, such as bulleted lists, photographs, graphics, animation, and audio clips to enhance the information on your slides.

Here's an example of a slide from "Can Animals Think and Feel?"

This slide presents evidence the writer provided to support a key idea in the report: that dogs are animals that can feel enjoyment just as humans do.

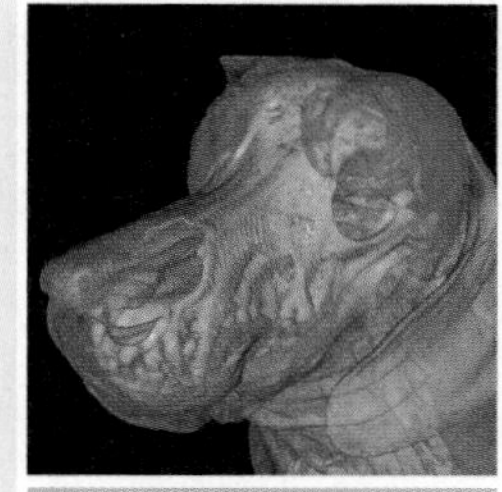

Animals Can Feel Emotion

- Dog brains contain an emotional center similar to humans'.
- It is called the caudate nucleus.
- Dog brain area "lights up" during brain scan when dog smells owners' scent or is promised food.
- Human brain area lights up when subjects think about enjoyable things such as food, music, or love.
- Dogs and humans feel enjoyment in similar ways.

STEP 5: Producing, Publishing, and Presenting *(continued)*

SL.8.1.a, SL.8.4, SL.8.5, SL.8.6

If you decide to share the information in your report by giving an oral presentation, you will need to think about your material in a new way. As you probably know from experience, you cannot just read your report aloud to an audience and expect people to pay attention and understand. You will need to translate your written words into an oral report by using an appropriate form of English and following these rules:

- Speak at an appropriately loud level and enunciate so that everyone can hear and understand your words.
- Use your introduction to tell listeners up front a few key points you want them to understand while listening to your report.
- Use your voice to keep the audience's attention by varying your pitch, rate, and volume.
- Make eye contact with your listeners and watch for audience feedback. If listeners appear confused or bored, change the pace at which you speak.
- When using visuals or audio, pause to allow your audience to respond to them. Clearly explain the connection between them and your topic.
- Ask listeners to hold their questions until the end of your presentation. Listen carefully and respectfully to the questions. Take time to think before you respond, and then answer politely. Elicit questions from several listeners rather than allowing one listener to take up all the question-and-answer time.

DIGITAL CONNECTION

Slide shows are not the only digital tools you can use during an oral presentation. Consider using software programs to create animation videos. Or, make a video of yourself giving the presentation. Enhance the presentation by using editing software and adding music and graphics. Then, post it online where your classmates can watch it on their own time.

Listening Tips

As you listen to a presentation, try to do the following:

- Pay attention to the presenter so you can focus on the words and ideas.
- Make connections between what you learn and what you already know.
- Take notes that include questions to ask or points to make later.
- Save your questions until the speaker requests them. Make your questions brief and direct. Listen carefully to the answers. If you want to pursue the question more deeply, make an appointment to talk with the speaker after the presentation so that others have time for their questions.

There are three parts to this performance task. Your teacher will provide you with copies of one or more reading selections that go with each part.

- "The Song of Wandering Aengus" Genre: Poem
- "Moon Party" Genre: Fantasy Fiction
- "In Search of the Ropen" Genre: Narrative Fiction
- "Deep Sea Creatures" Genre: Magazine Article
- "The Interesting World of Frogs" Genre: Magazine Article

Part 1: Literary Analysis

- ☐ Carefully read "The Song of Wandering Aengus" and "Moon Party" and take notes about important events, ideas, and details. Then answer Items 1–9 on pages 312–314.
- ☐ Read the writing prompt in Item 10 on page 314. Review "The Song of Wandering Aengus" and "Moon Party" with the prompt in mind. You will use both passages in this task.
- ☐ Write an essay on your own paper in response to the prompt.

Part 2: Narrative Writing

- ☐ Carefully read "In Search of the Ropen." As you read, take notes that help you understand the passage. Then answer Items 1–9 on pages 315–317.
- ☐ Read the writing prompt in Item 10 on page 317.
- ☐ Write a narrative on your own paper in response to the prompt.

Part 3: Research Simulation

- ☐ Carefully read "Deep Sea Creatures" and "The Interesting World of Frogs." Take notes about important ideas and details. Then answer Items 1–9 on pages 318–320.
- ☐ Read the writing prompt in Item 10 on page 320. Then review "Deep Sea Creatures" and "The Interesting World of Frogs."
- ☐ Write an essay on your own paper in response to the writing prompt.

Part 1 Literary Analysis

RL.8.1, RL.8.2, RL.8.3, RL.8.4, RL.8.6, RL.8.10, W.8.2, W.8.4, W.8.9, W.8.10, L.8.1, L.8.2, L.8.3, L.8.4.a, L.8.4.b

Read all parts of the question before responding. Circle the correct answer to Items 1–9. Use your own paper to respond to Item 10.

Item 1

Part A What words describe the progression of the events in the poem from the first stanza to the last?

- **a.** from playful to serious
- **b.** from tragic to joyful
- **c.** from realistic to fantastic
- **d.** from amusing to peaceful

Part B Which details from the poem support your answer to Part A?

- **a.** the fish turns into a girl who then disappears
- **b.** the sun and moon make gold and silver apples
- **c.** the narrator is young at the beginning of the poem and old at the end
- **d.** the narrator goes from catching a fish to chasing a magical girl

Item 2

Part A Which inference can you make about the narrator of "The Song of Wandering Aengus"?

- **a.** He was a young man when he first fell in love with the girl.
- **b.** He likes to eat apples and catch fish.
- **c.** He is a magician who cast a spell on the silver trout.
- **d.** He has died and is now a spirit.

Part B Which line from the poem supports your answer to Part A?

- **a.** "And cut and peeled a hazel wand"
- **b.** "And faded through the brightening air"
- **c.** "Though I am old with wandering"
- **d.** "I will find out where she has gone"

Item 3

Part A Which part of the description of the girl in the second stanza of "The Song of Wandering Aengus" is alluded to at the end of the poem?

- **a.** She is glimmering.
- **b.** She has apple blossoms in her hair.
- **c.** She knows Aengus's name.
- **d.** She fades away.

Part B What other previous image from the poem do the final lines bring to mind?

- **a.** the sweet taste of berries
- **b.** the silver trout caught by moonlight
- **c.** the vast lands through which Aengus wanders
- **d.** the warm kisses Aengus wishes for

Item 4

Part A In "Moon Party," how does the early description of Lyrica as special, beautiful, talented, and fun-loving contribute to the dramatic impact of the story?

a. Readers are surprised when Lyrica turns out to be the villain in the story.

b. Readers are surprised that Lyrica is not the *encantado* after all.

c. Readers are surprised that Lyrica is as old as she is.

d. Readers are surprised that Lyrica still wants to be the *encantado*.

Part B What event in the story supports the correct response to Part A?

a. Lyrica transforms from a dolphin into a woman.

b. Lyrica transforms from a woman into a dolphin.

c. The monkey succeeds at tricking Lyrica.

d. The Amazonians realize Lyrica plans to cause them harm.

Item 5

Part A Which word in this sentence from the story includes the same root found in *succeed*, a Latin root that means "go"?

"Lyrica's beautiful voice preceded her, and the Amazonians were equally struck by her physical beauty when she arrived in the circle of firelight."

a. preceded

b. equally

c. physical

d. circle

Part B Which words give a context clue that help you figure out the meaning of the answer to Part A?

a. "beautiful voice"

b. "struck by"

c. "when she arrived"

d. "of firelight"

Item 6

Part A What does the exchange in "Moon Party" between Lyrica and the old woman confirm about Lyrica's character?

a. Lyrica lacks confidence when she is around humans.

b. Lyrica is a lighthearted prankster who is misunderstood.

c. Lyrica's heroics include standing up to bullies.

d. Lyrica is cold-hearted and does not care if she causes harm to others.

Part B Which line from before this exchange hints at this fact about Lyrica?

a. "The other dolphins in the Encante were jealous of Lyrica."

b. "Lyrica was looking forward to using that voice to sing tonight!"

c. "'I pity you and your boring lives,' she thought to herself."

d. "As usual, they decided that she was some sort of goddess sent to them by the great moon god."

Item 7

Part A Which two words in this sentence from the story have roots (one Greek and one Latin) with the same meaning?

"Her human face morphed into the face of a dolphin, and then the transformation traveled down her body until once again she had a tail."

a. human, transformation
b. human, morphed
c. morphed, transformation
d. transformation, traveled

Part B Based on your knowledge of the roots and on context clues given in the sentence, what do the roots mean?

a. air
b. shape
c. life
d. touch

Item 8

Part A Which element of "Moon Party" is most important as it relates to the story's theme of being able to see the true nature of a person or creature?

a. the title
b. the descriptions of the settings
c. the explanation of the *encantado* legend
d. the characters

Part B Which words in the story signal a shift from building background to developing the theme?

a. "At last she began to see"
b. "First her tail became legs"
c. "But then an elderly woman"
d. "With only a few hours left"

Item 9

Part A Which analogy shows how "The Song of Wandering Aengus" and "Moon Party" tell a similar story?

a. wand : berry :: snout : harness
b. stars : flickering :: moon : glowing
c. glimmering : girl :: beautiful : woman
d. trout : girl :: dolphin : woman

Part B Which word from "Moon Party" best applies to the correct analogy in Part A?

a. celebrating
b. plotting
c. searching
d. shapeshifting

Item 10

Both the poem and the story tell about a shapeshifter. The poem describes a trout that turns into a girl, while the story is based on the Brazilian legend of the *encantado*, a dolphin who can change into a human and back.

Write an essay that analyzes the two shapeshifters and their impact on the humans that they interact with in the reading selections. Include information about the appearances and personalities of the two shapeshifters. Cite evidence from each text to support your analysis. Be sure to follow the conventions of standard English.

Part 2 Narrative Writing

RL.8.1, RL.8.2, RL.8.3, RL.8.4, RL.8.10, W.8.3, W.8.4, W.8.9, W.8.10, L.8.1, L.8.2, L.8.2.a, L.8.3, L.8.4.a, L.8.5.a, RH.8.6

Read all parts of the question before responding. Circle the correct answer to Items 1–9. Use your own paper to respond to Item 10.

Item 1

Part A What does *confounds* mean in this sentence from "In Search of the Ropen"?

"Our theory *confounds* the evidence saying that these flying dinosaurs died out some 65 million years ago, so plenty of people think we are nuts."

- **a.** begins with
- **b.** says the same as
- **c.** goes against
- **d.** is more original than

Part B Why did the writer use the word *nuts* in the sentence cited in Part A?

- **a.** She is unsure of the more scientific term to use.
- **b.** She chose a word with humorous connotations to dismiss people's foolish idea.
- **c.** She actually writes without much thought about her word choice.
- **d.** She is trying to represent herself as a well-rounded person rather than a pure scientist.

Item 2

Part A On what day does the turning point of the story described in these entries occur?

- **a.** Thursday
- **b.** Friday
- **c.** Saturday
- **d.** Sunday

Part B Which evidence from the story supports the correct answer to Part A?

- **a.** "The results are astounding."
- **b.** "I don't anticipate any luck in spotting a Ropen during the long night."
- **c.** "Still, it feels like progress to be moving toward the supposed feeding grounds."
- **d.** "Just as the cloud cover broke . . . we saw the Ropen lift off from the reef."

Item 3

Part A Which inference can you make based on information in the story?

- **a.** No one had previously interviewed natives of New Guinea about the Ropen.
- **b.** Not everyone on the expedition is a scientist.
- **c.** Before this expedition, there had been no credible pictures taken of a Ropen.
- **d.** Ropens will eat anything.

Part B Which sentence from the story supports your inference in Part A?

- **a.** "With the help of a native guide, we have had seven interviews with locals who have seen Ropens"
- **b.** "So now we are traveling to the northern coast of Umboi Island . . . where we think the Ropen feeds . . ."
- **c.** "One of the other scientists remembered an important fact from previous recorded interviews with natives."
- **d.** "As we return to the States, we will send the film to a government lab for analysis, hoping to quiet naysayers who will try to claim this is all a hoax."

Item 4

Part A What does the word *mollusk* refer to in this sentence from the story?

"The creature flew away, back to the center of the island, no doubt to feast on the huge *mollusk* it had managed to pry free from the reef."

- **a.** a seagoing vessel
- **b.** a sea creature
- **c.** an undersea rock
- **d.** a bed of coral

Part B Which words from the "Sunday" entry give context clues that help you figure out the meaning of *mollusk*?

- **a.** shell, feast
- **b.** giant, center
- **c.** island, pry
- **d.** claws, creature

Item 5

Part A Which sentence best expresses the theme of "In Search of the Ropen"?

- **a.** Science cannot often prove or disprove long-held beliefs.
- **b.** People can quickly turn rumors into beliefs.
- **c.** It's worthwhile to look for evidence of strange creatures in the world.
- **d.** Expeditions are excuses for taking exotic vacations.

Part B Which element of the story is most important in developing its theme?

- **a.** the title
- **b.** the unique setting
- **c.** the main character's problem
- **d.** the diary format

Item 6

Part A Which of the following is a valid inference about the scientist writing the journal entries?

- **a.** She is in charge of the expedition to find the Ropen.
- **b.** She doesn't hesitate to admit mistakes.
- **c.** She thought people were making up stories about the Ropen.
- **d.** She does not enjoy traveling.

Part B Which sentence from the story supports the correct answer to Part A?

- **a.** The prediction in my last entry was wrong!
- **b.** "The two days we have already spent in Papua New Guinea have been very fruitful."
- **c.** "This is not surprising, since pterosaurs are believed to be nocturnal."
- **d.** "Therefore, I don't anticipate any luck in spotting a Ropen during the long night."

Item 7

Part A The fourth paragraph of the Thursday entry features two sentences that use dashes. Which is NOT a correct use of this type of punctuation?

- **a.** to replace semicolons
- **b.** to indicate the interruption of a thought
- **c.** to set off an example
- **d.** to indicate that information is additional, not essential

Part B What is the best description of the information in dashes in this sentence?

"All five also estimated its size as the same—a 20-foot wingspan with a 10-foot tail—and stated that the animal has no feathers"

a. The information is interesting but doesn't help the reader understand the text.

b. The writer includes this information as scientific data.

c. The information provides answers to questions the reader might have.

d. The facts are unnecessary and unrelated to the story.

Item 8

Part A Based on this text, what do scientists known as *cryptozoologists* want to prove?

a. that humans and animals can get along

b. that wild animals can thrive in captivity

c. that animals believed to be extinct are still living

d. that dinosaurs were mythological creatures

Part B What sentence from the story supports the correct answer to Part A?

a. "In conducting the interviews, we carefully followed the rules our team established"

b. "This debunks the claims that what people really see in these sightings is a giant flying fox"

c. "One of the other scientists remembered an important fact from previous recorded interviews with natives."

d. ". . . we will send the film to a government lab for analysis, hoping to quiet naysayers who will try to claim this is all a hoax.

Item 9

Part A Which sentence from the story makes a comparison to help readers understand something?

a. "I think again about how all of the interviewees' descriptions match one another so perfectly."

b. "All of the people we interviewed saw the Ropen in flight, but one also saw it land and cling to a tree in the upright position."

c. "We think this bioluminescence helps the creature orient itself to the ground in the way landing lights on planes guide pilots."

d. "Some might say it sounds boring, but I am filled with a sense of excitement."

Part B Why is this type of comparison well suited for the author's purpose?

a. It helps the reader understand a difficult concept.

b. It works well to persuade readers of the existence of the Ropen.

c. It shows the author's imagination.

d. It describes something that cannot be appreciated with the senses.

Item 10

"In Search of the Ropen" begins with entries from the third day of the expedition to New Guinea. Write the entries for Days 1 and 2 (Tuesday and Wednesday). Base these entries on information from the existing story about what occurred on those days. Use your imagination and what you have learned from the story to add more relevant information. Think about how the early entries can develop the narrator's character and flesh out details about the setting. Be sure your entries fit into the overall mood, voice, and tone of the later entries.

Part 3 Research Simulation

RI.8.1, RI.8.2, RI.8.3, RI.8.4, RI.8.10, W.8.2, W.8.4, W.8.9, W.8.10, L.8.1, L.8.3, L.8.4.a, L.8.5.a

Read all parts of the question before responding. Circle the correct answer to Items 1–9. Use your own paper to respond to Item 10.

Item 1

Part A Which sentence best states the central idea of "Deep Sea Creatures"?

- **a.** Deep sea creatures do not have much to feed on in their environment.
- **b.** Deep sea creatures might seem strange, but they are very well adapted to their environment.
- **c.** The trench of Suruga Bay is a unique ocean environment.
- **d.** We will never discover all the creatures living in the ocean depths.

Part B Which detail from the text best supports this central idea?

- **a.** "A creepy fact is that giant spider crabs have been found feeding on the bodies of people who have drowned."
- **b.** "At a lesser depth in Suruga Bay—not more than 6000 feet—the strange gulper eel glides and resides."
- **c.** "This glowing body part is believed to attract other deep-sea dwellers so the gulper eel can eat them."
- **d.** "The Japanese consider the anglerfish to be a delicacy to dine on, comparing it to lobster in taste and texture."

Item 2

Part A What inference can you make about the deep sea creatures described in the text?

- **a.** They have long life spans.
- **b.** They do not thrive unless humans live nearby.
- **c.** They cannot survive life in shallow seas.
- **d.** They all have protective outer coverings.

Part B Which evidence from the text supports the correct inference in Part A?

- **a.** "We'll start with the giant spider crab, which is only found in Japanese waters."
- **b.** "Unfortunately, when a frilled shark is seen by human eyes, having come up into shallow waters, it does not usually survive long enough for scientists to make close observations of it . . ."
- **c.** "Chimaera broke away from their shark relatives some 400 million years ago and evolved into a unique species."
- **d.** "Rows of razor sharp teeth tilt inward in the anglerfish's mouth"

Item 3

Part A What type of adaptation have all the animals in "Deep Sea Creatures" made?

- **a.** size adaptations
- **b.** adaptations for finding food
- **c.** adaptations to cold temperatures
- **d.** speed adaptations

Part B Which sentence does NOT point to this type of adaptation?

- **a.** "Videos on the Internet claim to show a Megalodon . . . feeding on bait planted by scientists."
- **b.** "They use their long legs to rake up food."
- **c.** "This glowing part of its body is believed to attract other deep sea dwellers so the gulper eel can eat them."
- **d.** ". . . the chimaeras can use the changes in electrical fields to find and capture their prey."

Item 4

Part A What is the purpose of "The Interesting World of Frogs"?

a. to get readers interested in frogs

b. to entertain readers by providing unusual facts

c. to inform readers about the danger of frog extinction

d. to provide examples of new frog species and explain their importance

Part B Which sentence from the text supports the correct answer to Part A?

a. "You've probably learned plenty about extinction, the dying out of a species."

b. "The fact that so many new frog species are emerging is significant."

c. "Not surprisingly, the frog is bright green in color, which allows it to blend in with its environment."

d. "Far away, on the island of Borneo in Southeast Asia, a pea-sized frog was found living in a pitcher plant."

Item 5

Part A Which of the frogs in "The Interesting World of Frogs" brings to mind a traditional childhood story?

a. Pinocchio frog

b. vampire frog

c. crystal frog

d. flying frog

Part B Why does being able to connect the story to the frog help readers better understand the text?

a. The frog seems less bizarre when connected to a childhood memory.

b. The frog's actions are easier to visualize when connected to the story character's actions.

c. The frog's environment is similar to the story's setting, so readers can visualize it.

d. There is actually no connection between the frog and the story apart from a name.

Item 6

Part A Why did the author of "The Interesting World of Frogs" choose to use subheads to divide the descriptions of the frogs?

a. Each frog is unique, so transitions between descriptions would be difficult.

b. The author wants to show that all the frog species are related to one another.

c. This is the only way to show that the frogs are all equally important.

d. The frogs are so different that you can't write about them all in one paragraph.

Part B According to the text, how are the subheads linked together?

a. The frogs were all discovered in the same time and place.

b. The frogs are all from the same climate zones.

c. The frogs are the most interesting examples from a specific period.

d. The frogs are all colorful.

Item 7

Part A What does *burrow* mean in this sentence from "The Interesting World of Frogs"?

They *burrow* deep into the cracks between the boulders, where they can find a cool, moist environment.

- **a.** sink
- **b.** settle
- **c.** dig a passage
- **d.** escape from

Part B Which phrase in the sentence provides the best context clue to the meaning of the word?

- **a.** "deep into the cracks"
- **b.** "between the boulders"
- **c.** "where they can find"
- **d.** "a cool, moist environment"

Item 8

Part A What inference can you make about the frogs described in the text?

- **a.** They are all found in areas where malaria is a problem.
- **b.** The species will soon spread to other areas.
- **c.** All of them will soon face extinction.
- **d.** Their tadpole forms also often have unique features.

Part B Which sentence from the text supports the inference you made in Part A?

- **a.** "In fact, the scientific community probably classifies more new species every year than you have ever dreamed."
- **b.** "What sets it apart is that at the tadpole stage, these frogs have black fangs that stick out of the bottom jaw."
- **c.** "scientists have discovered two species of frogs distinguished by their small size"
- **d.** "they change their preferred dwelling place to the surface of the boulders."

Item 9

Part A Which two animals described in "Deep Sea Creatures" and "The Interesting World of Frogs" have the most in common?

- **a.** giant spider crab and vampire frog
- **b.** gulper eel and flying frog
- **c.** frilled shark and crystal frog
- **d.** anglerfish and Pinocchio frog

Part B What types of details given in the texts reveal the animals' similarities?

- **a.** size and unusual appendages
- **b.** ways of moving and eating
- **c.** teeth and body color
- **d.** diet and breeding habits

Item 10

"Deep Sea Creatures" introduces us to interesting animals under the sea, whereas "The Interesting World of Frogs" tells us about unique frog species that mostly live on land. Write an essay in which you compare the two sets of creatures and the special adaptations they have made to survive on land versus in the sea. Then give your opinion about which one species, among all of those discussed in the two texts, is most likely to survive the longest, and why. Remember to use textual evidence in the form of quotations, details, facts, and examples to support your ideas.

There are three parts to this performance task. Your teacher will provide you with copies of one or more reading selections that go with each part.

- Paired Selection: "Palspace Hero" Genre: Realistic Fiction
  and "Mini-Review" Genre: Television Review
- "The Pitch" Genre: Humorous Fiction
- "Paul Revere's Deposition" Genre: Historical Narrative
- "The Greatest" Genre: Magazine Article
- "Heroism and Head Injury" Genre: Web Article

Part 1: Literary Analysis

- ☐ Carefully read "Palspace Hero" and "Mini-Review," and take notes about important events, ideas, and details. Then answer Items 1–5 on pages 322–323.
- ☐ Carefully read "The Pitch" and take notes as you read. Then answer Items 6–9 on pages 323–324.
- ☐ Read the writing prompt in Item 10 on page 324. Then review "Palspace Hero" and "The Pitch" with the writing prompt in mind. You will use both passages in this task.
- ☐ Write an essay on your own paper in response to the prompt.

Part 2: Narrative Writing

- ☐ Carefully read "Paul Revere's Deposition." Take notes that will help you understand the passage. Then answer Items 1–9 on pages 325–327.
- ☐ Read the writing prompt for Item 10 on page 327.
- ☐ Write a narrative on your own paper in response to the prompt.

Part 3: Research Simulation

- ☐ Carefully read "The Greatest" and "Heroism and Head Injury." Take notes that will help you understand the passage. Then answer Items 1–9 on pages 328–330.
- ☐ Read the writing prompt in Item 10 on page 330. Then review "The Greatest" and "Heroism and Head Injury." Take notes that will help you respond to the prompt.
- ☐ Write an essay on your own paper in response to the prompt.

art 1 Literary Analysis

RL.8.1, RL.8.2, RL.8.3, RL.8.4, RL.8.6, RL.8.7, RL.8.9, RL.8.10; W.8.2, W.8.4, W.8.9, W.8.10, L.8.1, L.8.2, L.8.3, L.8.4.a, L.8.5.a, L.8.5.a–b

Read all parts of the question before responding. Circle the correct answer to Items 1–9. Use your own paper to respond to Item 10.

Item 1

Part A What is the meaning of this sentence from paragraph 1 of "Palspace Hero"?

"Quantity, not quality, was the name of the game"

a. From day to day, the value of something changes.
b. The value of a thing depends on how much of it there is.
c. An app called "Quantity" is popular among Vanessa's pals.
d. The excellence of a thing is more important than the amount.

Part B What information from the story supports your answer to Part A?

a. Vanessa uses an application on her smart phone as an alarm clock.
b. Vanessa carefully checks the identity of everyone who requests her friendship online.
c. Vanessa does not care who asks for her friendship online because she is unfeeling.
d. Vanessa's peers envy her when she has lots of Palspace "pals."

Item 2

Part A Select the phrase that best describes Vanessa from "Palspace Hero."

a. heroic and selfless
b. insecure and arrogant
c. well-meaning but misguided
d. unpopular and unlikable

Part B Select TWO pieces of evidence that support your response in Part A.

a. She uses a smartphone app for an alarm clock.
b. She has a large number of "pals" on Palspace.
c. She plans to use her social network to boost Marguerite's popularity.
d. She gives a digital "okay" to messages that her "pals" post online.
e. Her efforts to shift her "pals'" perception of Marguerite do not work.

Item 3

Part A Which of the following best states a theme from "Palspace Hero"?

a. It is important to help people even if they do not want help.
b. Helping animals is more important than helping people.
c. No good can come from social media.
d. Popularity can be overrated.

Part B Which quotation from the text supports your answer in part A?

a. "So Marguerite did know about the posts, Vanessa realized, her stomach churning."
b. "'Don't do me any favors . . . I don't need the kind of "pals" that you have.'"
c. "She was just grateful to be in demand and occasionally even the object of envy"
d. "her peers . . . constantly compared how many 'pals' everyone had."

Item 4

Part A What wish drives Vanessa's "Save Marguerite" campaign?

a. She does not want to play the hero.
b. She does not want to feel like a bully.
c. She wants to get even more "pals" on Palspace.
d. She wants to get to know Marguerite on a deep, personal level.

Part B What event motivated Vanessa's wish?

a. She was sick of her friends writing mean things about Marguerite.
b. She wants to try to get even more Palspace "pals."
c. Thoughtlessly she had voted "okay" on unkind posts about Marguerite.
d. She found out that Marguerite had been trying to "pal" her without success.

Item 5

Part A Based on the mini-review of *East Ridge High*, which statement accurately infers the reviewer's feelings about the print story "Palspace Hero"?

a. The story is somewhat preachy, but both characters are well developed.
b. The character of Vanessa is too simplistic, and the story is too preachy.
c. The character of Vanessa is better developed than the character of Marguerite.
d. The characters are so poorly drawn that the TV show had to start from scratch.

Part B From "Mini-Review," select TWO pieces of evidence about the print story that support your response to Part A.

a. The reviewer says that Palspace is a sponsor of the TV show.
b. The reviewer refers to Vanessa's "complexity in the print story."
c. The reviewer says that the movie is more preachy than the book.
d. "Palspace Hero" comes from a book called *East Ridge High*.
e. The reviewer says that Vanessa and Marguerite become allies.

Item 6

Part A In "The Pitch," what is the meaning of *pitch*, as used in the following passage?

"All right, Mr. Bunyan . . . You want our financial backing . . . , so make your pitch; set the scene for us."

a. the throwing of a baseball by a pitcher to a batter
b. the position of a single tone on a scale of sounds
c. a presentation designed to sell a product or idea
d. an up-and-down motion (of a boat, for example)

Part B Which word relationship in the passage above supports the answer to Part A?

a. the metaphorical relationship between "Mr. Bunyan" and "pitch"
b. the cause and effect between "you want our financial backing" and "pitch"
c. the grammatical relationship between "make" and "your pitch"
d. the synonymous relationship between "pitch" and "scene"

Part A What conflict occurs between the producer and Paul Bunyan in "The Pitch"?

a. Bunyan does not want to give artistic control to the producer.

b. The producer objects to Bunyan felling trees in the movie.

c. The producer does not want Bunyan to star in his own film.

d. Bunyan does not want to hire the Jersey Legend to co-star.

Part B Which evidence from the story best illustrates the answer to Part A?

a. Bunyan insists on doing his own stunts.

b. Bunyan clearly has an age-old grudge against the Jersey Legend.

c. Bunyan is a stocky figure with bushy eyebrows and ill-fitting clothes.

d. The producer says logging in the New York area won't seem heroic.

Item 8

Part A What characteristics does Bunyan have in common with many heroes of legend?

a. He is a skilled lumberjack.

b. He can straighten out winding roads.

c. He is unusually clever and resourceful.

d. He is strong and has a trusty companion.

Part B What information supports the answer to part A?

a. He wields a heavy axe with ease, and Babe is his sidekick.

b. He has well-thought out strategies for fighting modern crime.

c. He wants Thor and Perseus to appear in a movie with him.

d. He is more interested in lumber than in fighting crime.

Item 9

Part A In "The Pitch," which of the following does NOT reflect the main character's attempt to change with the times?

a. He sets his story in modern-day New York City.

b. He wants to bring his story, like other heroes' stories, to the big screen.

c. His story will be one of strength, courage, and ancient rivalry.

d. He has learned the technique of selling an idea to a Hollywood producer.

Part B Choose TWO pieces of evidence that support your answer to Part A.

a. He wears a designer jacket to the meeting.

b. He shows his strength by wielding an axe and cutting down trees.

c. He has wanted to confront the Jersey Legend for a hundred years.

d. He wears a lumberjack's flannel shirt and woolen cap.

e. He does not bring his sidekick Babe with him to the meeting.

Item 10

The main characters in "Palspace Hero" and "The Pitch" share a key requirement of heroism: the willingness to make a sacrifice or take on a challenge. Yet both characters encounter obstacles to their heroic urges.

Write an essay that analyzes how the authors of both "Palspace Hero" and "The Pitch" explore the question *Why is it so hard to be a hero?* To get started, think about the obstacle that causes problems for the "hero" in each story. Be sure to support your analysis with evidence from the text and to apply the conventions of standard English.

Part 2 Narrative Writing

RL.8.1, RL.8.2, RL.8.3, RL.8.4, RL.8.6, RL.8.10, W.8.3, W.8.4, W.8.10, L.8.1, L.8.2, L.8.3, L.8.4.a, L.8.5.c, RH.8.1, RH.8.2, RH.8.4, RH.8.5

Read all parts of the question before responding. Circle the correct answer to Items 1–9. Use your own paper to respond to Item 10.

Item 1

Part A What does the word *deposition* mean in the title and headnote of "Paul Revere's Deposition"?

- **a.** the removal of a monarch from power
- **b.** sworn testimony taken down in writing
- **c.** a depositing of a mold or other substance
- **d.** imprisonment, especially for political reasons

Part B Which words from the italic headnote at the beginning of the text provide clues to the meaning of *deposition*?

- **a.** *"these are the words"* and *"sworn legal"*
- **b.** *"under questioning by the British"*
- **c.** *"about his midnight ride"*
- **d.** *"Paul Revere"*

Item 2

Part A Why is Paul Revere going to Lexington?

- **a.** to arrest John Adams and John Hancock
- **b.** to prevent British soldiers from destroying an arms warehouse there
- **c.** to warn Adams and Hancock that British soldiers may be coming to arrest them
- **d.** to catch a ferry across the Charles River in order to get a horse to ride to Concord

Part B Which part of the text supports the correct response to Part A?

- **a.** paragraph 1
- **b.** paragraph 2
- **c.** paragraph 3
- **d.** paragraph 5

Item 3

Part A What happens to Paul Revere after his first encounter with British soldiers?

- **a.** He is stopped and questioned but then allowed to ride on.
- **b.** He gallops past them and is able to warn Adams and Hancock.
- **c.** He is stopped, but Revere tricks them into heading in the wrong direction.
- **d.** He and Prescott gallop away and jump a fence, leaving the soldiers behind.

Part B What information in the passage supports your response to Part A?

- **a.** "I saw two officers on horseback . . . I was near enough to see their holsters"
- **b.** "One of them started his horse towards me, the other up the road, as I supposed, to head me [off]"
- **c.** "He followed me about 300 yards, and finding he could not catch me, returned. I proceeded to Lexington . . ."
- **d.** "I to the right towards a wood at the bottom of the pasture, intending . . . to jump my horse and run afoot"

Item 4

Part A Why does Paul Revere ride on toward Concord with Dawes and Prescott?

- **a.** to lead the British away from Lexington, where Adams and Hancock are hiding
- **b.** to stay with Prescott, at his home
- **c.** to warn residents about a possible attack on the arms warehouse there
- **d.** to get some rest at an inn there after the long ride to Lexington

Part B What evidence in the text does NOT support the correct response in Part A?

a. Revere knows that the British may be planning to destroy the arms warehouse there.

b. Revere has new information about soldiers heading toward Concord.

c. Prescott and Dawes are already warning residents on the road to Concord.

d. Revere has been riding at a full gallop ever since he left Charlestown.

Item 5

Part A How does Revere respond when British officers tells him that they are looking for deserters?

a. He pretends to be a deserter from the British Army in hopes of becoming a spy.

b. He admits that he has already spread the alarm about the officers' true mission.

c. He pretends that he is just a tradesman on his way to Concord to do business.

d. He warns the officers that fifty or sixty militiamen are guarding the weapon storehouse.

Part B Which information from the passage supports your response in Part A?

a. "One of them. . . much of a gentleman, asked me where I came from"

b. "He asked what time I left. I told him, he seemed surprised"

c. "I told him . . . that I had alarmed the country"

d. "I would tell him the truth; I was not afraid."

Item 6

Part A What is the British officer's probable concern after talking to Revere?

a. Five hundred militia are ready to defend the weapons storehouse in Concord.

b. Fifty or sixty militiamen are currently guarding the warehouse in Concord.

c. People like Revere are being allowed to ride around the countryside.

d. The deserters he was looking for have been warned off by Revere.

Part B Which of the following suggests that Revere lied to the officer?

a. Since Revere lied about his name, he probably lied about other things.

b. Revere has shown himself to be a skilled horseman who can evade capture.

c. Revere scolds the officers, saying they have no right to stop and question him.

d. Revere has good reason to try to mislead the British officers.

Item 7

Part A Revere not only gives testimony in this document but presents a picture of himself. In this picture he is

a. smart and bold.

b. brave but self-serving.

c. friendly to the British.

d. exceedingly clever and handsome.

Part B What information from the passage supports your response in Part A?

a. Revere lies to the officer who detains him to save his own skin.

b. Hoping for good treatment from the officer, Revere tells him the truth.

c. Revere boldly evades the first officers and cleverly tries to discourage the second.

d. Revere knows Concord is at risk, but can't decide how best to warn people.

Item 8

Part A Why do the officers suddenly leave Revere alone when they get back to Lexington?

- **a.** Paul Revere trades his horse for his freedom.
- **b.** They seem to decide Revere is no longer the most important problem.
- **c.** After a brief pursuit, they give up on him when gets 300 yards ahead of them.
- **d.** He has convinced them that he is on their side by giving them valuable information.

Part B What text from the passage supports the answer to Part A?

- **a.** The sergeant assigned to guard Revere becomes too tired to do so.
- **b.** The officers have taken his horse and gone to investigate gunfire.
- **c.** He and Prescott split up, and the officers choose to pursue Prescott instead of Revere.
- **d.** Revere, Hancock, and Adams make a break for it, running two miles away from town.

Item 9

Part A Below are four claims about "Paul Revere's Deposition." Which claim is NOT supported by information from the text?

- **a.** Paul Revere took real risk in carrying out his mission.
- **b.** Paul Revere was not alone in carrying out his mission.
- **c.** Paul Revere alone acted heroically on his mission.
- **d.** Paul Revere's mission was an unqualified success.

Part B Which information from the list below supports your response in Part A?

- **a.** "I set off, it was then about 11 o'clock, the moon shone bright."
- **b.** "'if you attempt to run, or we are insulted, we will blow your brains out.'"
- **c.** "I had been there about half an hour when Mr. Dawes [on the same mission . . .] arrived from Boston."
- **d.** "They forced us in, and . . . Mr. Prescott said, 'Put on!' He took to the left, I to the right"

Item 10

You have read Paul Revere's version of the events of the night of April 18, 1775. Now imagine the story from the point of view of one of the British officers who capture Paul Revere. In your narrative,

- Include information about what the officer was doing before coming upon Paul Revere.
- Tell the story of capturing Paul Revere from the officer's point of view.
- Tell what the officer does after leaving Paul Revere.

Use narrative techniques, like dialogue and descriptive detail, to capture the mood and activities of that night. Guide your reader through the sequence of events with transitions. Finally, be sure to follow the rules of standard English.

Part 3 Research Simulation

RI.8.1, RI.8.2, RI.8.3, RI.8.4, RI.8.5, RI.8.6, RI.8.7, RI.8.8, RI.8.9, RI.8.10, W.8.2, W.8.4, W.8.7, W.8.8, W.8.9, W.8.10, L.8.4.b, L.8.5.a, RST.8.4, RST.8.6

Read all parts of the question before responding. Circle the correct answer to Items 1–9. Use your own paper to respond to Item 10.

Item 1

Part A What does *neurological* mean in the second paragraph of "The Greatest"?

a. relating to the nervous system
b. relating to the study of language
c. having to do with the cell nuclei
d. relating to the study of new diseases

Part B What Latin root best helps you understand the meaning of *neurological*?

a. *log,* meaning "word"
b. *ne,* meaning "new"
c. *nuc,* meaning "nut"
d. *neur,* meaning "nerve"

Item 2

Part A What is meant by saying that Ali's "capering got under Liston's skin and threw the champion off balance"?

a. Ali used an old boxer's trick of wiping an acid on his gloves to irritate Liston's skin.
b. Ali was so fast on his feet in the ring that he literally had Liston spinning around.
c. Ali's actions caused Liston so much stress that he broke out in hives.
d. Ali's pre-fight actions annoyed and unsettled the older boxer.

Part B Based on the language in the passage above, how would you describe the author's attitude?

a. admiring Ali's strategy
b. disapproving of Ali's behavior
c. sad about Ali's current health.
d. objective; he reports Ali's behavior as an unbiased observer

Item 3

Part A Which of the following best describes the author's point of view about the sport of boxing in "The Greatest"?

a. He is no longer a fan.
b. It played an important role in the lives of many young African American men.
c. It was beneficial for Ali, but most people should not consider it.
d. It should not be why Ali is remembered.

Part B Which information from the text supports your response in Part A?

a. The author points to Muhammad Ali's ability to avoid taking punches.
b. The author says Parkinson's has robbed Ali of "his famous speech, speed, and agility."
c. The author points to Ali's other accomplishments, such as his humanitarian work.
d. The author says many young African American men gained "accomplishment and respect" in the ring.

Item 4

Part A Which of the following best summarizes the author's message in "Heroism and Head Injury"?

a. Contact sports can teach valuable lessons about teamwork and tenacity.
b. Contact sports like boxing and football should be banned.
c. Contact sports may have their rewards, but the risk to amateurs is too high.
d. All players should be compensated for the injuries they receive in contact sports.

Part B What information from the text represents an acknowledgement of a conflicting viewpoint?

a. Research scientist John Hardy's view that boxing should be banned.

b. The view of NFL players like Scott Fujita about the benefits of football.

c. The study by Virginia Tech and Wake Forest University researchers.

d. The claim that safety measures adopted by the NFL have been slow to affect amateur play.

Item 5

Part A What does the word *sensors* mean in this passage from "Heroism and Head Injury"?

"7- and 8-year-old boys wore *sensors* that recorded the blows to the head sustained during football practices and games."

a. devices that measure physical stimuli like force, speed, or motion

b. vessels that dispense the fragrant smoke of a burning substance

c. people who review and remove objectionable material in texts

d. official reprimands by a governing body of one of its members

Part B Which phrase from the text supports the answer to Part A?

a. "7- and 8-year-old boys"

b. "that recorded"

c. "blows to the head"

d. "sustained during football practices"

Item 6

Part A Why does the author of "Heroism and Head Injury" include the information that 7- and 8-year old boys' head impacts included "eleven hits register[ing] 80 g's or more on the sensors"?

a. to show why so many football players' head impacts result in ER visits

b. to demonstrate the severity of head impacts that young players sustain

c. to prove that young players need to wear better helmets

d. to show that the vast majority of head impacts have no negative effects

Part B Which of the following is the best counterargument to the correct response to Part A above?

a. At a rate of about 1 in 300, severe head impacts do not occur very frequently.

b. Any head impact, no matter how small the force, is one too many.

c. People are too quick to use emergency services when a doctor's visit would be enough.

d. Players can avoid the negative effects of head impacts by wearing football helmets.

Item 7

Part A Why does the author of "The Greatest" cite the evidence that "even in the ring, Ali avoided being hit, and he said he didn't relish hurting his opponent"?

a. to show that Ali did not receive enough injuries to have brain damage

b. to show that Ali was not aggressive enough to be a true boxing champion

c. to resolve a contradiction between Ali the peace lover and Ali the boxer

d. to illustrate Ali's lightning-fast reflexes

Part B How does the author of "Heroism and Head Injury" use the same evidence in the article's sixth paragraph?

a. to illustrate Ali's lightning-fast reflexes

b. to show that professional boxers know how to avoid getting hurt

c. to explain why many people do not believe boxing caused Ali's Parkinson's disease

d. to make the point that over a long boxing career, brain damage is almost inevitable

Item 8

Part A Which of these claims from "The Greatest" contradicts a conclusion in "Heroism and Head Injury"?

a. Muhammad Ali has no regrets about his professional boxing career.

b. Being an accomplished athlete provides self-confidence and respect.

c. There are more important things in life than being a professional athlete.

d. Boxing did not necessarily cause Muhammad Ali's Parkinson's disease.

Part B What text from "The Greatest" supports the answer to Part A?

a. "Muhammad Ali is considered by many to be the greatest sports figure in history"

b. "He has lent his massive appeal to an annual celebrity Fight Night"

c. "the connection between Ali's boxing and Parkinson's is not certain"

d. "For Ali . . . the route to accomplishment and respect was found in the boxing ring."

Item 9

Part A Web articles like "Heroism and Head Injury" provide advantages that print magazine articles like "The Greatest" do not. Which of the following is NOT one of these advantages?

a. Readers can follow links to verify the sources of information in the article.

b. Readers can immediately find more information about related topics.

c. The author can easily add updated information or correct errors.

d. The author includes examples that vividly illustrate the subject matter.

Part B What information supports your response in Part A?

a. "The Greatest" does not provide any facts or details.

b. In "Heroism and Head Injury," Scott Fujita tells about begging to play football as a child.

c. "The Greatest" tells how Muhammad Ali surprised everyone by beating Sonny Liston in 1964.

d. "Heroism and Head Injury" provides links to endnotes where readers can verify information.

Item 10

You have read two texts that address, either directly or indirectly, the risks and benefits associated with sports like football and boxing. These texts are

- "The Greatest"
- "Heroism and Head Injury"

Consider the viewpoint each author expresses in discussing the risks and benefits of participating in these sports.

Write an essay that summarizes each author's viewpoint and analyzes the evidence the author uses to support that viewpoint. Then tell your view on the issue, and explain why you hold that view. Remember to use textual evidence to support your ideas.

A

abolished *(verb)* got rid of completely by law; banned

abridged *(verb)* reduced; made smaller or weaker

abundant *(adjective)* more than enough; plentiful

acclimate *(verb)* grow used to something; fit in

accumulate *(verb)* gather together; mount

accurate *(adjective)* correct; precise

accusation *(noun)* blame; a charge against someone

acolyte *(noun)* follower; apprentice

advocate *(noun)* one who stands up for or speaks for others or for a certain cause or idea; (verb) to speak out for a certain action, idea or philosophy; support

agitation *(noun)* shaking motion

altercation *(noun)* fight or argument

alternative *(adjective)* different from the usual

ameliorated *(verb)* improved; made better

amendment *(noun)* a formal addition or change to a document or contract; revision

ancestry *(noun)* heritage; people from whom a person is descended

anesthetic *(noun)* pain reliever; medicine that blocks pain or makes one sleep

anew *(adverb)* once again; starting all over again

animatedly *(adverb)* vigorously; with a lot of emotion or movement

apathetically *(adverb)* without caring or feeling

appraising *(adjective)* judging; evaluating the worth or qualities of something

apprehension *(noun)* anxiety or uneasiness; a sense of something bad about to happen

appropriate *(adjective)* suitable; fitting the situation

articulate *(adjective)* well-spoken

assemblage *(noun)* group working together for the same goal

attribute *(noun)* quality, trait, or characteristic

authentic *(adjective)* genuine; real

authorized *(verb)* given the power to say or do something; approved

avail *(noun)* use; help

avalanche *(noun)* a large, displaced mass of snow, ice, or rocks sliding down a mountainside

B

bacterium *(noun)* small organism that can cause disease in humans

begrudges *(verb)* resents

belated *(adjective)* given late or after the fact

beneficial *(adjective)* useful; helpful

biosphere *(noun)* Earth and the living things that inhabit it

blurted *(verb)* spoke suddenly

boardinghouse *(noun)* house where tenants rent rooms in which to live and may also receive meals and other services

boil *(noun)* swollen lump

bolstered *(verb)* built up or supported

bounteous *(adjective)* full of good things; plentiful

bristle *(verb)* stand up stiffly in defense or fear

burgeoning *(adjective)* starting to expand or grow

C

calamitous *(adjective)* terrible; disastrous

calamity *(noun)* terrible event; disaster

capacity *(noun)* ability to do something; capability

capsized *(verb)* tipped or spilled over

carcass *(noun)* dead body, especially of an animal

catastrophe *(noun)* disaster

catastrophic *(adjective)* disastrous

chaos *(noun)* disorder and wild confusion

clung *(verb)* held on tightly

cognizant *(adjective)* understanding; aware

collective bargaining *(noun)* negotiating with an employer as a group rather than as individual workers

commotion *(noun)* loud noise or argument

compatriot *(noun)* person who lives in the same country or belongs to the same group

compensation *(noun)* fair payment or reward

complicated *(adjective)* difficult to understand; with many different elements

composure *(noun)* calmness; control of one's emotions

comprehensive *(adjective)* covering many different ideas or goals; complete

conception *(noun)* idea; awareness

confide *(verb)* talk to, especially about secrets or problems

confirmation *(noun)* certainty of something

conflagration *(noun)* large fire

congregated *(verb)* gathered together in one place

consumption *(noun)* usage

contagion *(noun)* disease; something that can be passed from person to person, causing illness

contagious *(adjective)* spreading from person to person

contemplated *(verb)* thought deeply about something
contingency *(noun)* one of many possibilities that might occur
contract *(verb)* acquire a disease or condition
contraption *(noun)* machine, especially one that is strange or new
convulsion *(noun)* a violent shaking of the body
cordial *(adjective)* friendly and pleasant to be around
cost effective *(adjective)* worth the cost of doing
countenance *(verb)* accept
coveted *(verb)* wanted desperately to possess something belonging to another
cumulative *(adjective)* building up over time due to many small changes
curtailed *(verb)* stopped or cut short
customary *(adjective)* what is typically done; usual
cynical *(adjective)* suspicious of promises or ideals

D

dauntless *(adjective)* without fear; brave
definitive *(adjective)* clear and certain; obvious
derived *(verb)* coming from
designation *(noun)* name; classification
deteriorate *(verb)* go bad or break down
detriment *(noun)* something that causes difficulty or disadvantage
devotee *(noun)* follower; believer
dexterously *(adverb)* with great coordination and skill
diagnosis *(noun)* identification of a disease or condition
diameter *(noun)* distance across the middle of a round object
diffidently *(adverb)* in a shy and uncertain way
dilemma *(noun)* difficult decision among different choices
disclaimer *(noun)* statement explaining a lack of responsibility on the part of a publication or party
discord *(noun)* disagreement; conflict and strife
distracting *(adjective)* interruptive; taking attention away from something
distraught *(adjective)* very agitated or upset
distribution *(noun)* the handing out of something to a group in appropriate shares, or portions
domesticity *(noun)* home and family life
dramatically *(adjective)* in an intense or obvious way
dweller *(noun)* inhabitant; person who lives in a particular area
dynamism *(noun)* energy and vigor

E

efficiency *(noun)* ability to do something without wasting time or resources
elongated *(adjective)* stretched out; lengthened
emission *(noun)* substance coming out from something
emitted *(verb)* sent out
emulate *(verb)* try to be like someone else; copy
encapsulated *(verb)* describing the same ideas in a summarized form
encroaching *(verb)* coming onto the territory or property of another; trespassing
engaging *(verb)* meeting in battle
engraved *(verb)* carved into a solid object
ensuring *(verb)* making sure that something will happen; guaranteeing
enthusiast *(noun)* someone eager or enthusiastic about something
enticed *(verb)* attracted; tempted by something
entreated *(verb)* pleaded; begged
epidemic *(noun)* the spread of a disease through much of a population
epidemiological *(adjective)* having to do with the spread of disease in a population
epiphany *(noun)* sudden moment of clear understanding or inspiration
epithet *(noun)* nickname or insult
eradicating *(verb)* completely wiping out something
escalate *(verb)* grow into a bigger issue or conflict
espoused *(verb)* proclaimed
estimate *(verb)* make a educated, informed guess
evaporation *(noun)* process by which water is drawn up from bodies of water and turned into water vapor in the atmosphere
exasperated *(adjective)* annoyed; irritated
exclusively *(adverb)* for a certain purpose only
exemplary *(adjective)* serving as a good example to others; excellent
expiration *(noun)* when something runs out or is no longer good
exponentially *(adverb)* in a manner many times larger or more than
exquisite *(adjective)* extremely beautiful; perfect
extinguish *(verb)* put out or make go away; smother

F

faltered *(verb)* hesitated or felt doubt
fathom *(verb)* understand; conceive of

fermentation *(noun)* process in which something organic is chemically changed to alcohol
ferocity *(noun)* strong or violent emotion
feted *(verb)* celebrated and praised
fiscal *(adjective)* economic
floundered *(verb)* moved clumsily; staggered
flustered *(adjective)* upset and confused
foreboding *(adjective)* warning of or threatening danger
formidable *(adjective)* intimidating and powerful
fossil fuel *(noun)* fuel, such as oil and coal, that comes from the breakdown of ancient plants and animals
fostered *(verb)* brought about or caused
frailty *(adjective)* weakness; ability to be hurt or injured
friction *(noun)* action in which items rub together
fundamental *(adjective)* basic
futile *(adjective)* pointless; wasted

G

generated *(verb)* created
grizzled *(adjective)* gray-haired
groundwater *(noun)* underground water, such as in an aquifer
grueling *(adjective)* difficult and miserable

H

hapless *(adjective)* without luck
harmonious *(adjective)* agreeable; smoothly working together
homely *(adjective)* simple and natural
huddled *(verb)* gathered closely together in a group
hurled *(verb)* threw with great energy or violence
hybrid *(noun)* blend of two or more different things
hygiene *(noun)* practice of keeping clean

I

immensity *(noun)* huge size or difficulty
immobilized *(verb)* frozen in place; made unable to move
immune system *(noun)* the system of the body responsible for fighting disease
impeded *(verb)* got in the way of one's actions; hindered
implemented *(verb)* put into place
implicate *(verb)* show that something or someone is guilty or wrong
imposing *(adjective)* intimidating or frightening
impulsively *(adverb)* suddenly, without thinking it over
inability *(noun)* lack of capability to do something
incentive *(noun)* something that encourages someone to do something; reward
inclusion *(noun)* something or someone being a part
incorporate *(verb)* include
incrementally *(adverb)* in tiny steps; little by little
incursion *(noun)* attack; raid
industrial *(adjective)* having to do with factory work
infectious *(adjective)* able to spread to others
infinite *(adjective)* without end
ingenuity *(noun)* ability to come up with new ideas and solutions
inherent *(adjective)* existing as a natural part of something
initially *(adverb)* in the beginning; at first
innovation *(noun)* the development of new ideas
innovator *(noun)* person who comes up with new ideas
inscription *(noun)* words cut into a solid surface
insidious *(adjective)* evil in a way that is hard to notice
installed *(verb)* put in place
instinct *(noun)* inborn or natural knowledge
intangible *(adjective)* unable to be touched or explained
integrated *(verb)* became part of another group; joined
intensify *(verb)* become or make stronger
intent *(adjective)* focused on; intending to do something
interacted *(verb)* met and did things with
interchangeably *(adverb)* able to be switched out one for another
interject *(verb)* say something in the middle of another person's speaking; interrupt
interminably *(adverb)* seemingly without end
invidious *(adjective)* evil and dangerous
involuntary servitude *(noun)* state of being forced to work for another person or group, usually without pay or legal protections
isolated *(verb)* kept separated from others

J

jaundice *(noun)* yellowed skin caused by disease
judicial *(adjective)* of judges or courts; legal
justification *(noun)* reasons to support a decision or action; explanation

L

laurels *(noun)* symbols of honor, such as a medal or trophy

lauded *(verb)* praised; spoken well of

leisurely *(adjective)* comfortably and slowly

liability *(noun)* something that holds others back or causes difficulty

linear *(adjective)* in a straight line

logical *(adjective)* based in logic and evidence; reasonable

luminous *(adjective)* shining and attractive

luxurious *(adjective)* beautiful and plentiful

M

manipulate *(verb)* control and change

meandered *(verb)* wandered slowly; roamed

medium *(noun)* substance that supports or carries something else

microbe *(noun)* tiny organism

microorganism *(noun)* tiny organism; germ

minimizing *(verb)* describing or believing something to be smaller than it really is

minor *(adjective)* small and easily overlooked; unimportant

mired *(verb)* stuck

moat *(noun)* artificial body of water built around a castle or other building for protection

mobilized *(verb)* brought into action

monies *(noun)* funds; money

monitor *(verb)* watches closely to identify danger or problems

monotony *(noun)* sameness; state of no change or novelty

montage *(noun)* series of images

N

noble *(adjective)* morally good and pure; honorable

nonchalant *(adjective)* unconcerned and relaxed

novelty *(noun)* something that is new or different

nutrient *(noun)* beneficial substance in food

O

obligation *(noun)* duty that one must perform

obliged *(verb)* cooperated with; did as one was asked to do

omission *(noun)* state of being left out or excluded

oppressive *(adjective)* uncomfortable and smothering

overreacting *(verb)* making something into a bigger or more complicated issue than it really is

P

parasite *(noun)* living creature that lives in or feeds off of another creature

pasteurized *(verb)* heated in such a way as to destroy germs

pathogen *(noun)* organisms that cause disease or harm

peer *(verb)* look closely

periodical *(noun)* publication that comes out at regular intervals, such as a magazine

phenomenon *(noun)* natural event

photovoltaic *(adjective)* turning light into energy

platform *(noun)* statement of policy

plausibly *(adverb)* in a way that can be believed

poignant *(adjective)* sad; moving

pondering *(verb)* thinking something over carefully

precaution *(noun)* action taken in advance to avoid difficulty or trouble in the future

prematurely *(adverb)* in a manner that is earlier than expected

preservation *(noun)* making things last longer

probability *(noun)* chance; likelihood

probiotic *(noun)* bacterium that is beneficial to humans

prominence *(noun)* fame

proponent *(noun)* someone who works for or is in favor of a law, idea, or rule; supporter

prosperous *(adjective)* with increased wealth and success

province *(noun)* part of a larger area under the same rule

provision *(noun)* something given to others

proximity *(noun)* closeness; nearness

R

radiate *(verb)* emit in waves or rays

ramification *(noun)* effect; result

ramshackle *(adjective)* falling apart; badly constructed

ratified *(verb)* approved formally; confirmed

rationing *(verb)* limiting distribution of resources

raucous *(adjective)* wild and noisy

reclusive *(adjective)* avoiding others; solitary

recoiled *(verb)* turned away suddenly in fear or disgust

recruit *(noun)* someone newly joined

reflective *(adjective)* prone to thinking things over

regularity *(noun)* on a regular or common basis

regulate *(verb)* control, especially by rules or laws

regulated *(verb)* given rules to follow

regulation *(noun)* law or rule

regulatory *(adjective)* that which sets rules
repast *(noun)* meal
replicate *(verb)* copy; duplicate
reserves *(noun)* strength or resources held back to be used when needed
resonant *(adjective)* deep and booming or echoing
reverberate *(verb)* create a ripple effect; echo
rival *(adjective)* competitor

S

sanctioning *(noun)* formal acceptance of
sanitary *(adjective)* clean; free from germs
sanitation *(noun)* removal of germs and contaminants
scrimmage *(noun)* small battle
scrupulous *(adjective)* careful and exacting
sector *(noun)* part; section
secular *(adjective)* not part of religious life or belief
seismologist *(noun)* scientist who studies earthquakes
sentinel *(noun)* guard; one who watches for danger
shortchanging *(verb)* not giving something the money, resources, or attention it deserves
shuttered *(verb)* closed down
signifying *(verb)* showing or signaling
simultaneously *(adverb)* at the same time
skeptical *(adjective)* suspicious; untrusting
sluggard *(adjective)* lazy; slothful
solemn *(adjective)* serious or sad
spearhead *(verb)* lead
speculatively *(adverb)* in an evaluating manner
spherical *(adjective)* in the shape of a sphere; round
stark *(adjective)* strong and clear
stifling *(verb)* smothering or choking
stockpile *(noun)* stored supply
substantial *(adjective)* large or meaningful
substantially *(adverb)* in a noticeable way; significantly
subtle *(adjective)* small or hard to notice
suffrage *(noun)* the right to vote
surveillance *(noun)* watching for danger
symbol *(noun)* something that represents something else

T

tedious *(adjective)* boring
temperamental *(adjective)* having to do with personality or emotions; moody
temperate *(adjective)* milder and calmer
tempered *(verb)* shaped; affected
terminate *(verb)* end a position; fire
thermal *(adjective)* heating
thriving *(verb)* living or growing well; flourishing.
throng *(noun)* large group of people; crowd
till *(verb)* dig up soil in preparation for planting
tolerant *(adjective)* accepting of others
trajectory *(noun)* progression; path of development
tribulation *(noun)* difficulty; problem
trivial *(adjective)* not very important or serious
tsunami *(noun)* huge wave that washes onto land
tuition *(noun)* money paid to attend a school
tumult *(noun)* loud chaos
tumultuous *(adjective)* full of commotion and change
turbine *(noun)* engine with spinning blades; windmill
turmoil *(noun)* trouble and difficulty

U

unbridled *(adjective)* not held back or contained
underestimate *(verb)* think that something will be smaller or less than it really is
undeterred *(adjective)* unable to be stopped or put off
unfaltering *(adjective)* without stopping or hesitating
unionization *(noun)* collection of workers into organized groups that can negotiate with employers
unnerved *(verb)* frightened; made nervous
unsettling *(adjective)* causing discomfort or unease

V

vaccinated *(verb)* given a weakened or dead form of a disease-causing microorganism so that the body can develop an immunity to the disease
vanguard *(noun)* leading group
varsity *(adjective)* pertaining to the main team of a school
vastly *(adverb)* greatly
verify *(verb)* find out if something is true
vigilant *(adjective)* carefully watching out for danger

W

wafted *(verb)* moved gently by the wind
wistful *(adjective)* thoughtful in a sad or regretful way
wizened *(adjective)* wrinkled
woes *(noun)* problems; things that cause difficulties
workforce *(noun)* the workers in a particular industry or area

Y

yearning *(verb)* desire; longing
yore *(noun)* times in the distant past

INDEX